SHIPS OF THE PORT OF LONDON

first to eleventh centuries AD

SHIPS OF THE PORT OF LONDON

first to eleventh centuries AD

Peter Marsden

Drawings by Caroline Caldwell

ENGLISH HERITAGE

1994

ARCHAEOLOGICAL REPORT 3

Copyright © English Heritage 1994

First published 1994 by English Heritage, 23 Savile
Row, London W1X 1AB

Reprinted 2006

Printed and bound in Great Britain by 4edge Ltd, Hockley. www.4edge.co.uk

ISBN 13: 978-1-8570544-70-2
Product Code 51362
A catalogue record for this book is available from the
British Library

Edited by Kate Macdonald
Designed by Tracey Croft

Contents

List of figures 6

List of tables 8

Acknowledgments 9

Introduction 11

1 The port from the mid first to the mid third centuries
Historical context 15
Users of the port 16
Cargoes 19
Berthing 23
Warehousing 29

2 Blackfriars ship 1, 1962
Discovery 33
The ship 37
Reconstruction of the ship 55
Method of construction 76
Crew accommodation 80
Where was the ship built? 80
When was it built and used? 80
How was the ship used? 80
Stability and performance 88
The loss of the ship 91

3 The New Guy's House boat, 1958
Discovery 97
The boat 98
Reconstruction of the boat 101
Sequence of construction 102
Where and when was the boat built? 102
How was it used? 103
The loss of the boat 104

4 The port in the later third and fourth centuries
Historical context 105
Types of ships and boats in London 105
Cargoes 107
Berthing 108
Warehousing 108

5 The County Hall ship, 1910
Discovery 109
The ship 111
Reconstruction of the ship 119
Sequence of construction 124
Where and when was the ship built? 124
How was the ship used? 125
The loss of the ship 128

6 The port in the seventh to ninth centuries
Historical context 131
Users of the port 131
Cargoes 131

Berthing 131
Remains of ships and boats 133

7 The port in the tenth to eleventh centuries
Historical context 135
Users of the port 135
Cargoes 136
Berthing 138

8 Ships and boats of the tenth and eleventh centuries
Timbers from New Fresh Wharf, City of London, 1974 141
Planking from Billingsgate, City of London, 1982 ..153
Planks from Fennings Wharf, Southwark, 1984 154
Boat keel from Fennings Wharf, Southwark, 1984 .156
Wale from Fennings Wharf, Southwark, 1984 158
Possible oar or paddle, Hibernia Wharf, Southwark, 1979 159
Anchor, River Thames, Blackfriars, City of London, 1969 160

9 Conclusions
Shipbuilding traditions 163
Roman European merchant ships 174
Celtic shipbuilding 177
Development of berthing methods 177
Later port development 179

Appendix 1 The pottery dating evidence from Blackfriars ship 1 181
by Jo Groves, Museum of London

Appendix 2 Metallographic analysis of nails from Blackfriars ship 1 183
by Brian Gilmour, Royal Armouries

Appendix 3 Romano-Celtic ship caulking 189
by David F Cutler, Royal Botanic Gardens, Kew

Appendix 4 Analysis of resin 191
by John Evans, University of East London

Appendix 5 Theoretical stability and performance of Blackfriars ship 1 193
by Peter Marsden

Appendix 6 Dendrochronology of Roman and early medieval ships 201
by Ian Tyers, Museum of London

Appendix 7 Hair in caulking from Fennings Wharf boat fragments 211
by Michael L Ryder

Appendix 8 Headings for recording each fragment of ship 213

Appendix 9 Glossary of nautical terms 215

Summary 217

Bibliography 221

Index 225

List of illustrations

1 Map of Roman and Saxon settlement areas in London with ship find sites 11
2 Clinker rules 12
3 Types of iron nail fastening 13
4 Sites from Roman London, first to second centuries, on a map of the modern city 15
5 Roman cone-headed nail: New Fresh Wharf 16
6 Roman maritime objects from London 18
7 Roman boat hook 19
8 Trade routes to London, first to early second centuries 20
9 Trade routes to London, mid second to mid third centuries 21
10 Early Roman development of waterfronts in London Bridge area 25
11 Late first-century landing stage and quay, Pudding Lane 26
12 Late first-century timber quay and Roman timber drain, Pudding Lane 27
13 Section through late second-century quay, Custom House 28
14 Iron Roman docker's tools 29
15 Types of Roman timber quay construction 30
16 Room in late first-century warehouse, Pudding Lane 31
17 Second-century timber quay, Guy's Hospital 32
18 Location of Blackfriars ship 1 33
19 Site of wreck of Blackfriars ship 1 34
20 Coffer-dam holding bow of Blackfriars ship 1 ...35
21 Forward end of Blackfriars ship 1 36
22 Contemporary cartoon from the *Daily Mail* 37
23 Plan of ship as excavated ....foldout
24 Sections of plank fragments to show tree-ring patterns 38
25 Plan of forward half of Blackfriars ship 1 as excavated ....foldout
26 Plank from Blackfriars ship 1 with small peg 40
27 Blackfriars ship 1, port side looking forward 41
28 Excavating the mast-step frame from Blackfriars ship 1 42
29 Caulking in plank from Blackfriars ship 1 43
30 Floor-timbers 1 and 3, as recorded in 1963 43
31 Floor-timber 2, as recorded in 1963 44
32 Floor-timbers 4 and 5, as recorded in 1963 44
33 Floor-timbers 6 and 7, as recorded in 1963 45
34 Floor-timber 8 and stempost, as recorded in 1963 46
35 Side-frames 1–9, as recorded in 1963 47
36 Forward side of Blackfriars ship 1 48
37 Floor-timber 1 49
38 Floor-timbers 2–4 50
39 Reconstructed section across Blackfriars ship 1 .51

40 Collapsed port side of Blackfriars ship 1 52
41 Port ends of floor-timbers 3–5 52
42 Mast-step of Blackfriars ship 1 53
43 Mast-step in floor-timber 7..........................53
44 Mast-step and coin *in situ* 54
45 The coin of Domitian 55
46 Nails from Blackfriars ship 1 and the New Guy's House boat 56
47 Hooked nails from Blackfriars ship 1 57
48 Reconstruction of stages in fastening nails in Blackfriars ship 1 58
49 Section through alluvial deposits under Blackfriars ship 1, starboard side 59
50 Stern and sternpost, Blackfriars ship 1 60
51 Fragments of plank from stern of Blackfriars ship 1 61
52 Caulking in cone-headed nails from Blackfriars ship 1 61
53 Plan and long-section of Blackfriars ship 1, as recorded during excavation 62
54 Cross-section of Blackfriars ship 1, as recorded during excavation 62
55 Reconstructed bow elevation of Blackfriars ship 1 63
56 Profiles of Blackfriars ship 1 63
57 Knee timber from Blackfriars ship 1 64
58 Reconstruction of interior of Blackfriars ship 1 at the mast-step 65
59 Reconstructed side elevation of the stempost of Blackfriars ship 1 66
60 Alternative possible reconstructions of bow of Blackfriars ship 1 66
61 Ships on coins 67
62 Bruges boat mast-step 68
63 Mast heights for Blackfriars ship 1 69
64 Rig possibilities for Blackfriars ship 1 71
65 Low Ham villa mosaic 72
66 Broighter boat model 73
67 Bruges boat rudder 74
68 Newstead fort rudder 75
69 Reconstruction drawing of ship 77
70 Reconstructed stages in the building of Blackfriars ship 1 78
71 Finds from Blackfriars ship 1 81
72 Ragstone cargo from Blackfriars ship 1 *in situ* ... 82
73 Possible route of last journey of Blackfriars ship 1, with source of ragstone cargo 83
74 Map of Maidstone area 84
75 External face of Roman defensive wall of London 85
76 Recording Blackfrriars ship 1 in 1963 86
77 Map of outcrops of millstone grit in England and Belgium, with drawing of millstone of Blackfriars ship 1 87

78 *Teredo* borings in Blackfriars ship 1 88
79 Forces acting on a ship 89
80 Computer reconstruction of Blackfriars ship 1 90
81 Computer side elevation reconstruction of Blackfriars ship 1 91
82 Computer-drawn end elevation of Blackfriars ship 1 92
83 Computer reconstruction of waterlines of Blackfriars ship 1 92
84 Computer reconstruction of buttock lines of Blackfriars ship 1 93
85 Computer reconstruction of strakes from Blackfriars ship 1 93
86 Reconstructed stages in break-up of Blackfriars ship 1 94
87 Position of New Guy's House boat 97
88 Section of the New Guy's House boat 98
89 North end of New Guy's House boat 99
90 Frames from east side of north end of New Guy's House boat 100
91 Scarfed frame from New Guy's House boat 101
92 Inner planking from north end of New Guy's House boat 102
93 Construction of north end of New Guy's House boat 102
94 Reconstruction plan, cross-sections, and side elevations of New Guy's House boat 103
95 Gold medallion, third century AD 105
96 European trade routes to London, late third to fourth century 106
97 Excavation of the County Hall ship 110
98 County Hall ship boxed for transportation 111
99 County Hall ship being raised to street level ...112
100 County Hall ship in transit 113
101 County Hall ship on display 114
102 The Royal Family visit the County Hall ship ...115
103 Excavation of the County Hall ship 116
104 Approximate site of County Hall ship 117
105 County Hall ship as excavated, 1910–12 .foldout
106 Significant features of County Hall ship ..foldout
107 Constructional features of County Hall ship ...120
108 Cross-section of planks showing tree-rings from County hall ship 121
109 Recent drawing of fragment from County Hall ship 121
110 Frame with limber hole from County Hall ship ..122
111 Alternative framing patterns used in County Hall ship 122
112 Frame from County Hall ship 124
113 Reconstructed cross-sections of County Hall ship 125
114 Reconstructed plan of side elevation of Couty Hall ship 126
115 Reconstruction of structural elements of County Hall ship 127
116 Pulley block and belaying pin from County Hall ship 128
117 Possible state of river bed, AD300 129
118 European shipping routes to London, seventh to ninth centuries 132

119 Rivet from Maiden Lane, Strand 133
120 Seal of New Shoreham 136
121 European trade routes to London, tenth to eleventh centuries 137
122 Berthing sites in London, eleventh century 138
123 New Fresh Wharf beaching site and posts 139
124 New Fresh Wharf tree-ring sections of planks . 141
125 Plank fragment from New Fresh Wharf 142
126 Lap peg from New Fresh Wharf 143
127 Lap of plank from New Fresh Wharf 143
128 New Fresh Wharf fragments, 1–4 144
129 New Fresh Wharf fragments, 5–9 145
130 New Fresh Wharf fragments, 10–12 146
131 New Fresh Wharf fragments, 13–1 147
132 New Fresh Wharf fragments, 18–23 148
133 New Fresh Wharf fragments, 24–30 149
134 New Fresh Wharf fragments 150
135 Reconstruction of boat 1, from Danzig Ohra .. 151
136 Reconstruction of New Fresh Wharf timbers .. 152
137 Billingsgate planking 153
138 Fennings Wharf fragments 155
139 Fennings Wharf keel 157
140 Fennings Wharf wale 158
141 Oar blade, Hibernia Wharf 160
142 Viking type anchor, Blackfriars 161
143 Site of Viking type anchor 161
144 Radial and tangential log splitting 164
145 Distribution of Blackfriars-type ships 165
146 Distribution of plank-built Romano-Celtic-type vessels 166
147 Distribution of Mediterranean-type vessels 167
148 Distribution of clinker-built vessels and boat burials, fourth century BC to eighth century AD 169
149 Distribution of clinker-planked vessels and boat graves, ninth to thirteenth centuries AD 171
150 Distribution of pegged clinker vessels, ninth to eleventh centuries 172
151 Clinker plank fastenings, seventh to thirteenth centuries 173
152 Cross-sections of cog hulls and Blackfriars ship 1 176
153 Distribution of medieval ships with hooked nails holding clinker planks 178
154 Section of cone-headed nail 183
155 Wrought-iron structure of cone-headed nail ... 184
156 Hardness values of semi-cone-headed nail 184
157 Section of semi-cone-headed nail 185
158 Structure of semi-cone-headed nail 185
159 Structure of shank of semi-cone-headed nail .. 185
160 Corrosion products in nail shank 186
161 Hazel wood caulking 186
162 Contorted hazel caulking 189
163 Hazel wood shavings from edge of New Guy's House boat plank 189
164 Gas chromatograph of resin from caulking 191
165 Computer graph of righting moments 195
166 Height of transverse metacentres 196
167 Draught and Centre of Buoyancy 196
168 Volume distribution 197
169 One wave speed 198
170 Total wave resistance 198

171 Dendrochronology from Blackfriars ship 1 204
172 Dendrochronology from County Hall ship 205
173 Dendrochronology from New Fresh Wharf boats 206

174 Dendrochronology from Billingsgate boats 207
175 Dendrochronology fromFennings Wharf boats . 208

List of tables

1 Blackfriars ship 1: dimensions of the planks 39
2 Blackfriars ship 1: measurement of plank thickness (in mm) 39
3 Blackfriars ship 1: measured widths of side planking 40
4 Blackfriars ship 1: frame spacing 46
5 Blackfriars ship 1: maximum dimensions of recorded frames 48
6 Blackfriars ship 1: hooked nails per plank 56
7 Estimated mast height of Blackfriars ship 1 70
8 Fossils in a sample of the ragstone cargo in Blackfriars ship 1 83
9 Cargo loads found in some classical wrecks in the Mediterranean 90
10 Blackfriars ship 1: approximate dimensions of strakes 123
11 Frame spacing along keel of Blackfriars ship 1 ...123

12 Approximate dimensions of ships and boats at turn of bilge 127
13 Plank size relative to vessel size 152
14 Shipbuilding characteristics 154
15 Plank-built ships with mortice-and-tenon fastenings, Mediterranean tradition 168
16 Plank-built vessels of the Roman period found in central and northern Europe 175
17 Theoretical performance of Blackfriars ship 1 194
18 Total weight of Blackfriars ship 1 195
19 The deadweight coefficient of Blackfriars ship 1 . 197
20 Speed potential coefficients 199
21 Wood identifications 209
22 The hair types in eleventh-century caulking 211
23 Hair and wool fibre diameter measurements 211

Acknowledgements

Much of this published study of the early shipping of London is based upon a D Phil thesis in maritime archaeology for Oxford University, and of the various people who have responded to my requests for help and advice, the most important has been Sean McGrail, formerly Professor of Maritime Archaeology at Oxford University, whose guidance has been crucial. I am particularly indebted to him for introducing me to hydrodynamics and to the use of a computer to reconstruct and analyse the theoretical stability of ancient ships. My thanks are due also to John Goldman who guided me through the application of his computer program *Boatcad* to ancient ships, and also adapted the program for archaeological use. Both the Museum of London and English Heritage have been most generous in financing this research and its publication, beyond normal bounds. My debt to Caroline Caldwell, formerly of the Museum of London, is immense, for she made archive drawings of hundreds of surviving ship timbers, often working in damp and cold conditions. From these has she prepared most of the excellent drawings which illustrate this report. The Central Electricity Generating Board, now National Power, somewhat alleviated the spartan conditions, necessary for the preservation of the many waterlogged timbers, by generously setting aside a basement room in their headquarters building in London for our use.

Various specialists, some of them based outside the Museum of London, have made crucial contributions to this study. Ian Tyers, of the Environmental Department at the Museum of London, undertook the dendrochronological study of the ship timbers and the timber identifications with funding from English Heritage. John Evans of the University of East London identified the tar samples. Brian Gilmour from the Tower Armouries studied the construction of nails from Blackfriars ship 1. Peter Boyd identified the moss caulking from the New Fresh Wharf boat, Michael Ryder identified the hair caulking, and David Cutler of the Royal Botanic Gardens at Kew identified the caulking from the Blackfriars and New Guy's House vessels. Various other people have answered my many and varied queries, particularly Margaret Rule, who excavated the St Peter Port ship, Wieslaw Stepien of Lodz, Poland, Arne Emil Christensen of the University of Oslo, Norway, Ole Crumlin-Pedersen of the Institute of Maritime Archaeology at Roskilde, Denmark, and Olaf Hockmann of the Romisch-Germanisches Zentralmuseum in Mainz, Germany. Elizabeth Wright of Sheffield advised on the millstone trade during the Roman period, and David Kelly of Maidstone Museum, Kent, assisted in the study of Roman quarrying in west Kent. To these and to others, who are acknowledged in the text, I am profoundly grateful. Finally, my thanks are due to colleagues at the Museum of London who have helped with the administration of the project, in particular Francis Grew, Brian Hobley, Scott McCracken, and John Schofield. But particular thanks are due to Sean McGrail, Tony Dyson, and, at English Heritage, to Kate Macdonald, editor, who shouldered the burden of reading the text and, together with Frank Gardiner and Tracey Croft, who dealt with the many illustrations, advised on how the text could best be presented for publication. In spite of all of this mistakes and omissions are likely to occur, but as the final decision on the presentation is mine, so is responsibility for any errors.

Acknowledgements are due for permission to reproduce the following photographs: Fig 22, *The Daily Mail*, Fig 50, *The Times*, Fig 65, Somerset County Museum, and Fig 66, the National Museum of Ireland. The following authorities are also due these acknowledgements: Fig 6; the model warship prow is after RCHM 1928, and the writing tablet is after Wheeler 1946, Fig 10; these drawings are after Milne 1895, Fig 11; construction drawings are after Milne and Bateman 1983, Fig 13; the upper section is after Milne 1985, and the lower section is after Tatton-Brown 1974, Fig 15; the quay constructions are after Miller *et al* 1986, Figs 30–35 and 57 were recorded by the author, and Fig 135; the reconstruction is after Lienau 1934.

Introduction

The discovery of four small shipwrecks dating from the second, fifteenth, and seventeenth centuries in the River Thames at Blackfriars in London have provided very important evidence for understanding the ancient history of the port of London, and for reconstructing the history of ships and seafaring in Britain. The earliest wreck is at present the oldest known seagoing sailing ship yet discovered in northern Europe, and from its excavation it has been possible for the first time to assess how such vessels were used and behaved.

These wrecks are not the only early ships to have been found in the ancient port of London. Two other vessels, both Roman, were found abandoned on the outskirts of the port; one at the edge of the River Thames opposite Westminster, and the other in what was once a shallow creek in the Southwark marshes (Fig 1). Parts of many other vessels have been found broken up and reused along Saxon, medieval, and later waterfronts, and collectively they give us a detailed view of shipping in the port from each of the major periods of its history – Roman, Saxon, medieval, and recent. The subject of this volume is the shipping of the Roman and Saxon periods, and the later shipping, from the twelfth to the seventeenth centuries will be described in a subsequent report.

Understanding what these early ships were like is important, for since the port of London was founded by the Romans nearly 2000 years ago, its shipping has brought trade and wealth to generations of merchants, enabling London to become one of the leading financial centres in the world today. Until recently, nothing was known about the early waterfronts that formed the gateway through which so much of this wealth passed, because the earliest documentary records to throw light on the subject date from almost a thousand years after London was founded, and the first detailed pictorial representations are less than five hundred years old. Since 1972, however, a series of important archaeological excavations by the Museum of London has uncovered the remains of those Roman, Saxon, and medieval quays, docks, and warehouses, and much has been done, particularly by Gustav Milne and Trevor Brigham, to reconstruct the appearance of the waterfronts and explain their development.

Others have also been working to reconstruct the early history of the port: a team of environmental specialists at the Museum of London have been analysing the silts at the quaysides for microscopic diatoms holding evidence about the former salinity of the river, and have shown,

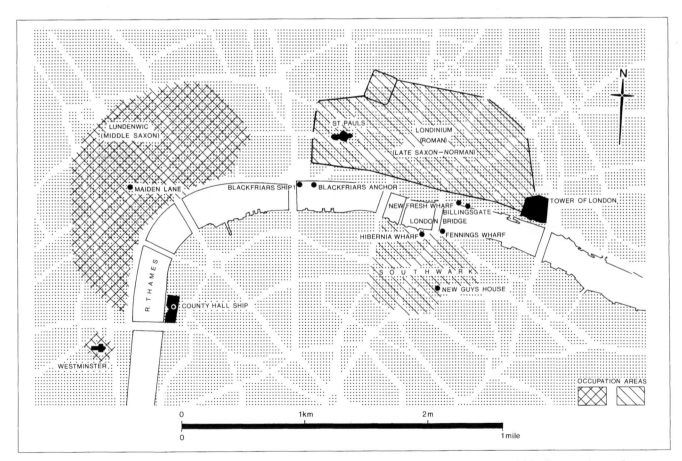

Fig 1 Map of London showing the settlement areas of the Romans (first to fourth centuries), middle Saxons (seventh to ninth centuries), and late Saxons (tenth to eleventh centuries). The sites of ship remains are also given.

amongst other things, that the river was tidal at London 2000 years ago. Ian Tyers, a tree-ring specialist, has managed to push back tree-ring dating in London to the period before the time of Christ, thereby helping to date many of the ships, and has shown whether or not they were built locally. Others have studied fish bones and plant remains, have identified seeds and pollen, and have even found traces of imported foodstuffs, such as olives. One of the most remarkable discoveries was made by Vanessa Straker in a charred store of grain burnt in the destruction of embryonic Londinium in AD 60–1. Although the grain could have come from many parts of the Roman Empire, including Britain, minute seeds of weeds were found that had also been growing in the field with the wheat when it was harvested. These grew only in the eastern Mediterranean, and showed that the grain was harvested around Palestine and northern Egypt. Why it was shipped to London is difficult to imagine.

Other specialists have studied the trade goods shipped to London throughout its long history, and by analysing the clays used in pottery have established where many of the imports were made. For the Roman period these include amphorae that were once filled with wines or olive oil from Italy, Greece, or Spain, and fine tablewares from Gaul and Germany. Once the sources are known it is not too difficult to reconstruct the most likely routes by which merchant ships carried them to London. The resulting picture of ancient London is of a vigorous port with trade links to many parts of Europe, and there are clear indications that the dynamism of ancient London was not unlike that of the modern City.

Although the ships are the primary subject of this book, it was clear from the outset that their remains do not make much sense outside their context, and it has been particularly important to link them to the evidence of waterfronts and cargoes. On this basis it is possible to envisage the types of vessels that were to be found in the port, to consider the cargoes that were carried, to reconstruct probable voyage routes, and to explore the most likely methods of berthing and warehousing. The chapters proceed chronologically, each major historical phase introduced by a very brief summary of the port of London in that period.

The study of the ships themselves has several objectives: to reconstruct their appearance, to determine when and where they were built, how they were built, how they were used, and when and how they were lost. That all these questions can be applied to the London ships and comparisons made with finds elsewhere owes much to the pioneering work of various international ship specialists, including Ole Crumlin-Pedersen in Denmark, Patrice Pomey in France, George Bass, Michael Katsev and Richard Steffy in the USA, and Eric McKee and Sean McGrail in Britain. They and others have set standards of research and clarity of synthesis and presentation that this volume seeks to follow.

Most of the fragments of ships and boats that have been found are small, but when substantial parts of the bottom, sides, and ends of an ancient ship are discovered, as in the case of Blackfriars ship 1, it is possible

to reconstruct what the vessel may have looked like and how its weight was distributed. The aim here is to enable the reconstruction to rely on the factual evidence of what was found, without becoming unduly hypothetical. Reconstructing a ship's appearance and construction is only part of the story, for when a vessel enters the water it comes to life in its natural environment, and in that state its theoretical behaviour can be predicted mathematically. Assessing how a ship will behave, its stability, speed, draught, and cargo loading, is a normal procedure used by naval architects when designing modern ships prior to the investment of large sums of money. Sean McGrail and John Coates are amongst the few who have applied these methods of analysis to ancient vessels, and although this work can be carried out slowly using a pocket calculator, there are now programs for use by naval architects with desk-top computers that will undertake the work far more quickly and easily. Where the evidence justifies such analyses, as in the case of Blackfriars ship 1, such a study is included here, but the value of the analysis is only as good as the accuracy of the reconstruction. With that proviso in mind, one of the results of this research is that for the first time it has been possible to quantify approximately the cargo load and behaviour of a seagoing Roman merchant ship in northern Europe.

Understanding ancient ships is hardly any more complex than any other specialist archaeological study, but it does require detailed interpretative recording of the parts of vessels when they are found. The excavators of various London sites have tackled the ship timbers in different ways according to the circumstances of the excavation, trying to understand the timbers in their

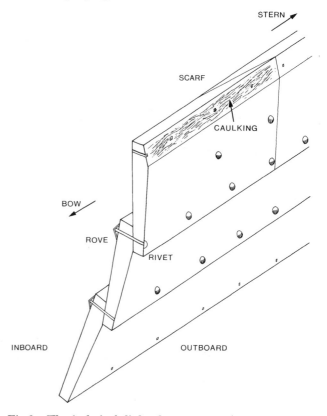

Fig 2   The 'rules' of clinker boat construction.

reused state, where appropriate, rather than as part of a ship. It was felt to be enough to record the remains in the ground, and sometimes to take a sample to give a view of the method of construction. Experience has shown that this view is wholly inadequate for the study of the timbers from ships. Instead, all the remains of any ship or boat need to be removed from an excavation and washed so that they can be recorded and sampled properly, despite the practical problems in saving, cleaning, and recording such remains, as the necessary space and facilities are not always readily available.

The timbers from Blackfriars ship 1 were recorded by the author in this way during 1963, and the original drawings have been reproduced here. However, the procedure adopted for the more recent finds has been to wash the fragments, mostly planks, and then to record their faces by tracing them carefully at 1:1 on film, and then reducing these photographically to 1:5, enabling publication drawings to be reproduced at 1:10. All fastenings, toolmarks, caulking, and the grain of the wood are shown on the tracings. After sectioning many of the tree-rings revealed in the timber were traced at 1:1 before dendrochronological analysis. These sections show how the timber was fashioned from the log. The construction details were also recorded on information sheets for each fragment (Appendix 8), and important features were photographed. Samples of wood, caulking, and fastenings were taken for detailed specialist analysis, with the result that there is now a very large archive for these ship remains at the Museum of London. It has not been practical to preserve all the pieces of timber, so a policy has been adopted by the Museum of keeping a representative selection of the best examples for permanent preservation.

Interpreting the original appearance of each ship timber during the recording process has been essential, and, as the post-Roman timbers were mostly planks from clinker-built vessels, it has been necessary to apply to them the rules of clinker plank construction (Fig 2). These are:

- (1) the upper strake or line of planks generally overlapped the lower outboard
- (2) the roves or diamond-shaped washers of rivets were placed inboard
- (3) planks scarfed endways to make a continuous strake were normally overlapped outboard towards the stern (Leather 1987, 86).

Although these rules of interpretation are probably correct in most cases, it is important to remember that they are not absolute. For example, a very rare sixteenth-century example of a 'reverse clinker construction' where the lower strakes overlap the upper outboard, contrary to rule (1) above, has been found in London. Repairs can also cause some scarf joints to face the bow, so that the interpretation of a plank with a single scarf cannot be as certain as that of several articulated planks with a number of scarfs all facing the same direction.

Nautical terminology is endemic to the description of ships, but its use can become a minor epidemic in a publication, to the extent that discussion is rendered unintelligible to most readers. In view of the fact that the meanings of some nautical terms can vary from place to place and from age to age (eg Falconer 1815; Sandahl 1951; McKee 1972, 26–30), it becomes clear that every effort should be made to reduce its use. Whether or not this ideal has been successfully adopted here is for the reader to decide. But this aim is complicated slightly by archaeologists who have developed a preference for certain international terms, and by the creation of new descriptive terms to replace existing obscure terminology. For example, the correct English term for the edge-joining plank construction of Greek and Roman ships is 'draw-tongued joint', but archaeological publications tend to use the term 'mortice-and-tenon joint' (eg Throckmorton 1987, 92–3), which is a more familar term, even though it was probably never used in this context by shipbuilders of any age. Similarly, in modern clinker shipbuilding, the plank edge where the strakes overlap each other is known as the 'land', but here the more descriptive term 'lap' has been used instead.

Studies of caulking methods, which make the joints between planks watertight, have demonstrated that in some vessels the caulking was placed in position before the last plank of the joint was assembled, and in others the caulking was inserted into the joint after the planking was in place. In recent years, to indicate these two processes the former has tended to be termed 'luting', and was applied particularly to Saxon, Viking, and medieval clinker-built vessels. The latter method was called 'caulking', and was applied to post-medieval carvel-built craft. However, the study of the Romano-Celtic vessels from Blackfriars, New Guy's House, and St Peter Port, Guernsey, has revealed a previously unknown caulking method whose process is not absolutely clear, so it would be impossible to follow the strict classification indicated by the terms 'luting' and 'caulking'. Since past English usage has been to term all wadding between plank joints 'caulking', it has been decided to use only this term throughout this report.

One of the interesting features of the remains of the wrecked London ships is the variety of fastenings used, necessitating a definition of each type of fastening to avoid confusion. In particular the terms 'rivet', 'turned

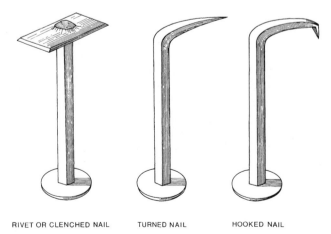

RIVET OR CLENCHED NAIL   TURNED NAIL   HOOKED NAIL

Fig 3 Types of iron nail fastening used in the early London ships.

nail', and 'hooked nail' (Fig 3) have been used, following the definitions published by McGrail (1987, 138–9). Consequently a glossary of technical terms with the meanings that are applied here has been provided, as Appendix 9.

1 The port from the mid first to the mid third centuries

Historical context

The port of Londinium is believed to have been created as a planned Roman city at about AD 50, several years after the Roman invasion of AD 43 (Merrifield 1983, 32–6). Its status during the first and second centuries is not known, but it has been suggested that initially it was a town controlled by Roman merchants from the Continent (Haverfield 1911, 169–70; Marsden 1980, 25–7). There was evidently a strong military presence in the area from the late first century, judging from the quantity of military objects that have been found (Merrifield 1983, 61–89), which suggests that it had become a seat of the provincial government. Londinium was not a British tribal centre, but its importance in the trading process was indicated by the classical writer Tacitus (*Annals* XIV, 33) who called it a famous centre of commerce teeming with merchants, *copia negotiatorum et commeatuum maxime celebre*. The embryonic city was destroyed in the Boudican uprising of AD 60–1, but during the next thirty years it was rebuilt and greatly enlarged (Fig 4), with a central forum, other public buildings and a pattern of streets built around the north end of the Roman London bridge crossing the River Thames (Marsden 1987, 15–67; Perring 1991, 16–21).

Much of London's wealth was no doubt derived from maritime trade, judging from the imported goods found there. The first and early second century deposits contain

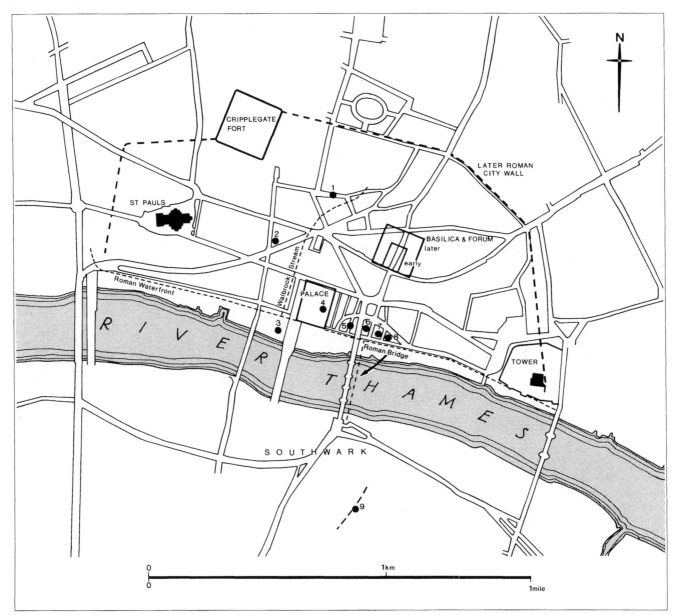

Fig 4   Some features of Roman London during the first and second centuries, with sites mentioned (numbered), on a map of the modern city.

huge quantities of imported pottery and other items from Gaul, Germany and the Mediterranean basin, representing cargoes which, together with waterfront berthing structures, suggest how the port might have been used. Although the late first century saw a boom in the development of other cities in the province of Britain, the sheer quantity and variety of goods in London suggests that it was the main port of entry and the provincial distribution centre for overseas trade (Tyers 1985, 41–2).

There is much less evidence of trade goods, domestic rubbish, and occupied buildings in London from the period c AD 140–180 compared with that of the early second century, suggesting that the population and maritime trade had become substantially reduced during that period, though building projects in Southwark and the City continued (Dennis and Schaaf 1975, 271; Sheldon 1978, 36). The reasons for this decline are not clear but may be due to the development of other British ports which were now taking trade away from London (Sheldon 1975; Marsden 1980, 107–17). The evidence for the trade and population of the city seems to increase in the late second and early third centuries but is still much less than that of the first and early second centuries (Rhodes 1986a, 91). By the early third century Roman London was encircled by a defensive wall (Fig 4) on its landward side (Merrifield 1983, 154–67), and monumental public buildings were constructed beside the waterfront in the Blackfriars area in the south-west corner of the city (Hill *et al* 1980). During the first half of the third century a substantial timber quayside was also constructed along the waterfront on either side of the bridge (Miller *et al* 1986, 62–8) and dumps of rubbish associated with it provide valuable information about maritime trade imports.

Users of the port

There is some evidence for the use of several types of ships and boats in the port of London between the first and the mid third centuries:

Local river vessels

The shape of the barges which carried goods up and down the river Thames is illustrated by the second-century vessel found near the south end of London Bridge at New Guy's House, Southwark (see Chapter 3), though the types of goods carried by them are not clear.

Smaller boats are possibly indicated by small dumps of mostly domestic rubbish of the period c AD 70–130 found more than 100m out from the Roman waterfront in the former bed of the River Thames on the Public Cleansing Depot site, Upper Thames Street (Fig 4, site 3). The pottery had been smoothed by the flow of the river, and the dumps were lenticular in section with the thickest part in the middle (*Excavation Register*, group nos 546, 552, 565). As they included a considerable amount of pottery which had been manufactured at Brockley Hill, Stanmore, 12 miles (19 km) north-west

of Roman London, it seems clear that the rubbish had been brought from the shore in small loads for disposal in the river.

Fishing boats

These were present on the Thames, judging from the quantity of fish bones and oyster shells that are generally found in Roman London. The bones of sprat, cod and Black Sea bream were found in deposits of c 70–125 AD at Billingsgate Buildings, Lower Thames Street (Wheeler 1980); eel, smelt, and fish of the carp family were found in deposits of similar date at 199 Borough High Street, Southwark (Locker 1988, 428), and bass was found at Billingsgate Buildings, Lower Thames Street, in a deposit dated AD 160–90 (Wheeler 1980).

Since sprat occurs nowadays in estuaries with a low salinity it is probable that this specimen was caught in the Thames estuary with a fine-mesh net. This is also indicated by the perishable nature of the fish which required them to be transported to London as quickly as possible, athough they could have been preserved by smoking or salting. The other fish could be caught by hook and line, perhaps with the type of hook found in the third-century quay dumps at New Fresh Wharf (Chapman 1986, no 14.19). The cod and bass were probably caught at the mouth of the Thames, but the Black Sea bream was fished beyond the estuary, perhaps in the Channel where it occurs today. Since these fish, and oysters, had to be carried a minimum of 40 miles (60 km) upstream to London, it is likely that they were kept alive in containers of sea water in the fishing boats, perhaps like that found in a Roman fishing boat in the Claudian harbour at Fiumicino, Italy (Scrinari 1979, fig 4). The enormous dumps of oyster shells around the late first-century landing stage for boats at Peninsular House, immediately downstream of the Roman London Bridge, indicates that this was where many of them were landed and sold (Bateman and Milne 1983, 212–4).

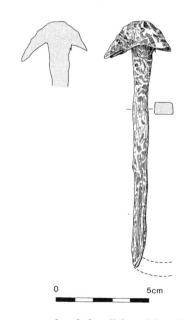

Fig 5   Roman cone-headed nail from New Fresh Wharf.

A number of small posts, noted in the first- to second-century river gravels on the Public Cleansing Depot site, over 30m from the contemporary Roman waterfront (Marsden, site archive report, Museum of London), were around 50mm in diameter, and were too small to be used for mooring ships. It is likely that they were parts of a fish weir, whose distance from the shore indicates that they were reached by boat.

Seagoing merchant ships

Although these are represented by trade goods imported from the Continent, the remains of a ship of this phase, Blackfriars ship 1, shows what at least one of these vessels was like. It had sunk about the middle of the second century AD, and the borings of mature *Teredo* in its hull timbers show that it had been in seawater for a long period (see Chapter 2).

Evidence that other Romano-Celtic vessels of Blackfriars ship 1 type visited the port of London is indicated by a distinctive broken hooked nail with a hollow cone head containing traces of an unidentified caulking (Fig 5). It was found in the dumped filling of a quay dated to AD 209–44 at New Fresh Wharf (unpublished nail from St Magnus House site, deposit III, 338). The form of the nail head shows that it had probably come from the side of a ship, with the break at a right-angled bend indicating that the hull was 0.107m thick. This is thinner than the side of Blackfriars ship 1, which was about 0.178m thick, thus suggesting a smaller vessel.

A wooden toggle (MoL acc no 90.297) of ash (*Fraxinus* sp) is possibly a fitting from a ship (Fig 6a) for it was found in a rubbish dump (ER 546) dating from the period AD 70–130 in the river gravels on the Public Cleansing Depot site, Upper Thames Street. Each end was a half-sphere 48mm in diameter, linked by a bar of wood about 13mm in diameter. It had been lathe-cut from a single piece of wood, the total length of the toggle being 77mm. It was later squashed to an oval shape, but the grooves left by the lathe show that it was originally circular in section. The central bar probably held a rope with a diameter of not more than 15mm, possibly from the rigging. Similar toggles have been found in several classical period shipwrecks in the Mediterranean basin, ten from the Kyrenia ship of the fourth century BC, so its nautical use is clear (Katzev 1985, 174; Pulak and Towsend 1987, 38–9). Similar toggles, containing rope-ends, have been found in Viking ships (Christensen 1979, Fig 11.5), but Roman toggles have also been found on land sites at London, Newstead, and Saalburg, and it has been suggested that they were used for fastening tent doors (Chapman 1977, 67–8, no 487). It seems likely, therefore, that they had a general use in fastening awnings both at sea and on land.

Warships

These were probably moored in the port of London, since the Roman governor of the province, representing the Emperor, is believed to have had his residence there (Marsden 1975). It is thought that his troops were quartered in the Cripplegate fort (Fig 4), built in the early second century AD (Grimes 1968, 15–40; Merrifield 1983, 77–83), and this could explain why part of a tile bearing a CL.BR stamp of the *Classis Britannica*, the British fleet (Fig 6c; MoL acc no 90.138)), was found in the second century filling of the defensive ditch of the fort, for the Governor's staff was drawn from a selection of the military units quartered in the province. Another tile fragment with a CL.BR stamp (Fig 6b) was found on the Winchester Palace site, Southwark, in a dump of tile over a hypocausted room with pottery of the late third to early fourth centuries, although the tile fabric itself is of late second to early third century date (information from Hedley Swain, Museum of London).

The type of warship perhaps seen in the port may be represented by a miniature bronze prow, inscribed (retrograde) in niello AMMILLA AVG FELIX (Fig 6d). This object, apparently commemorating a victory won by the warship *Ammilla*, was found in London before 1856 and is now in the British Museum. Haverfield regarded it as undateable within the Roman period, and thought that it had been imported into Britain (Read and Haverfield 1897). The ram resembles a dog's head, behind which are a palm branch and a circle, perhaps an *oculus*. The top of the stempost has the form of the head and bent neck of a goose or swan.

Shipbuilding

Building and repair yards must have been important in Roman London, as in any modern port, and may be indicated for London by the incomplete text on a wooden writing tablet (Fig 6e), probably of the first or second centuries AD, found in the Walbrook stream area at Lothbury (Fig 4, site 1), near the centre of Roman London. It refers to the sale of some objects from a shop *taberna*), to the building of a ship (*navem faciendam*), and to the making of a tiller for a rudder (*clavi faciendi*). The word *clavi* on this tablet has usually been interpreted as meaning rudder (Chapman 1974, 176), but Casson (1971, 390) has demonstrated that the term used in classical sources elsewhere normally means specifically the tiller of a quarter rudder (Wheeler 1946, 54–5).

Boat equipment

Examples of this are surprisingly rare in Roman London and are represented by the iron terminal of a boat-hook (Fig 7), found in the Walbrook stream valley (Merrifield 1965, fig 127). Another boat-hook found on the riverside at Smith's Wharf, London, before 1960, is said to have been found associated with first-century coins and samian ware, although it was not found in a formal archaeological excavation (Manning 1985, 75–6, pl 32, H49). Curiously, no iron fork-shaped terminals of set poles used for fending and propelling boats, particularly barges, by poling or punting, have been found in Roman deposits from London. They are common on the Rhine and around its mouth at that time (Ellmers 1972, 80, no

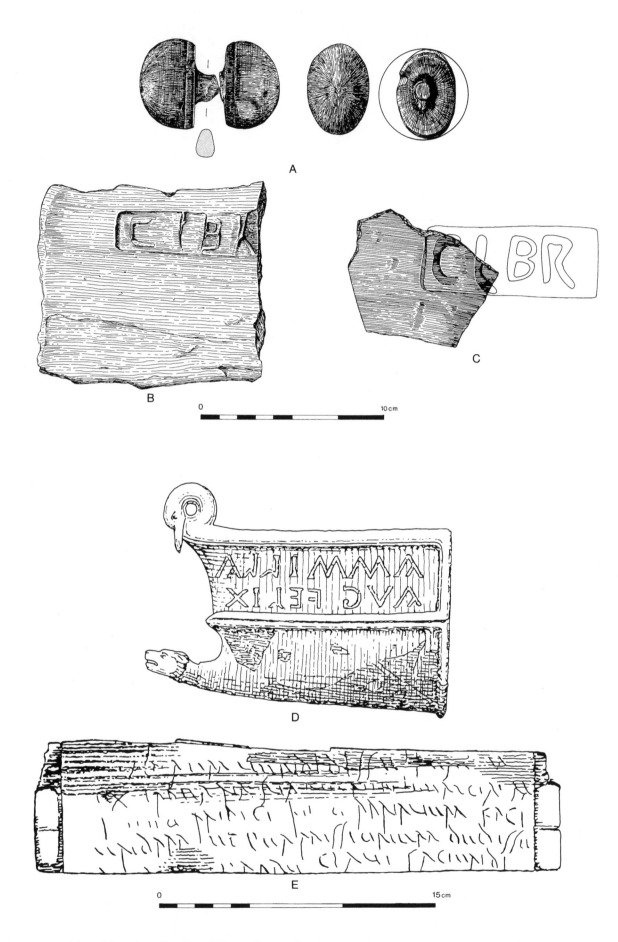

Fig 6   Roman maritime objects from London: (A) wooden toggle; (B) and (C) tiles with Classis Britannica stamps; (D) model warship prow; (E) writing tablet.

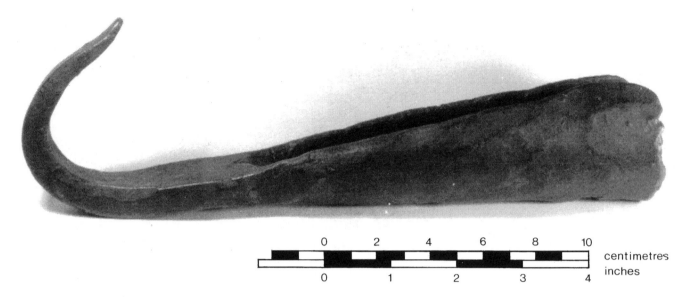

Fig 7   *Roman boat-hook, Bucklersbury House, London.*

59; De Boe 1978, 28; de Weerd 1988), and in the post–medieval period on the Thames at London (Wilson 1987, 48, 79). This absence seems significant, and suggests that during the Roman period barges were not usually punted or towed from the shore.

Cargoes

The common types of bulk cargoes shipped to London during this period and their handling method are suggested by the surviving examples of amphorae and barrels, showing their probable size, weight, and form. That there were other ways of packing for transportation, such as crates and sacks, there can be little doubt, but these have not survived. The sources of these trade goods enable important shipping routes to be reconstructed, and the environments of the voyages, whether rivers or the sea, suggest the types of ships used (Figs 8 and 9).

Imports into Roman London can be classified under two headings: bulk goods found in considerable quantities, such as some wines, olive oil, and building stone, and miscellaneous goods in smaller quantities, such as glass vessels and bronze statuary. The former are of particular interest since they could reflect whole cargoes from single sources. The latter, however, come from many sources suggesting mixed cargoes, perhaps brought along a number of routes which are now difficult to reconstruct.

The Mediterranean

Of the many imports from the Mediterranean in the first century AD, wine in Italian and Rhodian amphorae was particularly important, though the amphorae are found in fairly limited quantities suggesting that they arrived in Britain in mixed cargoes.

An unexpected early Roman import into London from the Mediterranean region, which could have constituted a single cargo, was a large quantity of grain found charred inside what was probably a shop burnt down in AD 60–1 (Straker 1987). Seeds of plants mixed with the grain indicate that the crop had been growing in the eastern Mediterranean. As Roman Britain may then have been an exporter of grain (Salway 1981, 618–20) it is difficult to understand why this consignment had been carried so far. It may reflect a bad harvest in Britain that year, or simply that British grain was not readily available. The grain deposit was up to a metre deep, but as no trace of containers was found it seems likely that it had been stored in sacks, such as those shown being offloaded from a ship depicted on a tombstone from Mainz, Germany (Ellmers 1978, 12).

After the middle of the second century the quantity of Mediterranean goods imported into London appears to have been much smaller (Marsden 1980, 110–17, 213, no 27), though they ranged from the high quality sculptures in Italian marble found in the temple of Mithras (Toynbee 1986), to wine in amphorae from the eastern Mediterranean and southern Gaul, and olive oil in amphorae from southern Spain and north Africa (Green 1986, 100–5).

Gaul

In the first and early second centuries samian ware manufactured in central and southern Gaul was a major import into London. At Regis House on the Roman waterfront, for example, the remains of over 600 decorated samian ware bowls and many plain vessels of similar pottery, were found from a fire at about AD 120, the so-called Hadrianic fire of London. It is thought that these were from a warehouse, and were due for transshipment to other parts of Britain (Tyers 1985, 41–2). On another site, samian ware from southern and central Gaul represented 27.2% (by weight) of all pottery found (Green 1980, 82). Since this had been manufactured at Les-Martres-de-Veyre, Lezoux, Montans, and La Graufesenque, it seems likely that it was shipped to Britain via

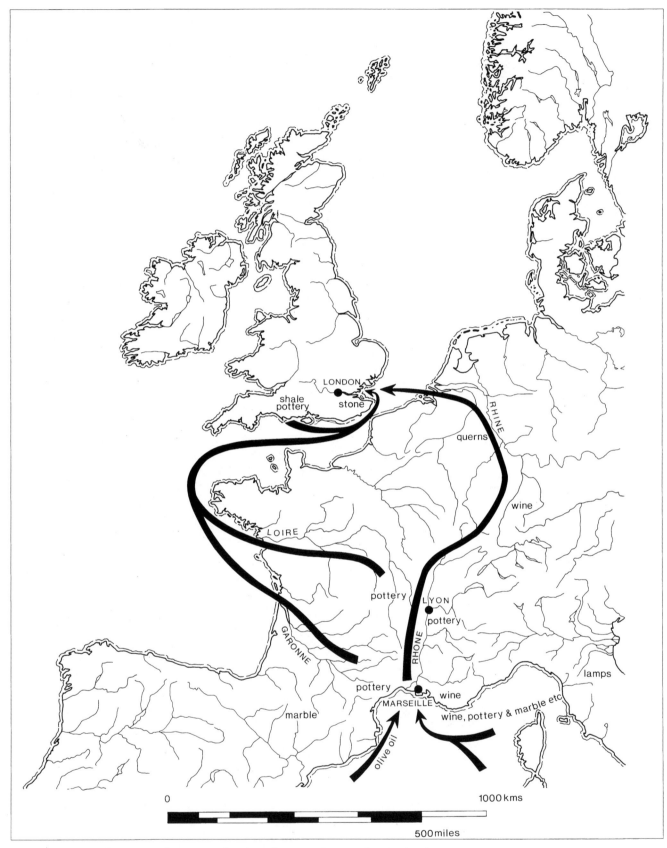

Fig 8   Suggested Roman trade routes to London, first to early second centuries AD.

the Loire and the Gironde, through the Bay of Biscay, and round into the English Channel to London. This was not the only tableware imported into London from Gaul, for fine colour-coated wares were brought from the Lyon region (Green 1978, 53), presumably on the Rhône–Rhine or Rhône–Loire routes.

The pottery may have been shipped in crates, and some of the woodwaste, found with broken barrels around the early Roman waterfront at Pudding Lane, may have been derived from broken packing cases (Bateman and Milne 1983, 217, no 23). The volume of a crate is suggested by one example found at Pompeii which

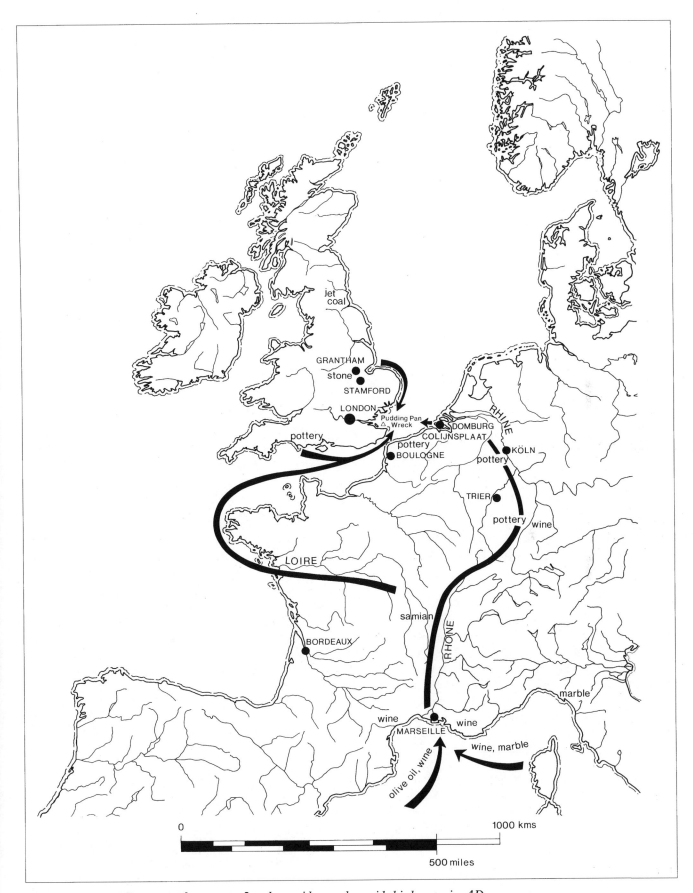

Fig 9   Suggested Roman trade routes to London, mid second to mid third centuries AD.

contained 90 samian bowls from south Gaul (54 bowls of form 37, 36 bowls of form 29), together with 37 Italian earthenware lamps (Atkinson 1914, 27).

Wine from southern Gaul, carried in flat-based Dressel 30 amphorae, was another substantial import into London. This, the second most common amphora type found in the city, is a particularly useful indicator of an important route by which they were carried to London since a distribution map of find spots in Europe shows a concentration along the rivers Rhône and Rhine (Peacock 1978). This would have meant 'double hauling' to carry the goods from one river to the other.

Subsequently the trade continued at a reduced level, though substantial deposits of later Roman rubbish containing an unusually high proportion of imported pottery (about 88%), was found in the early third-century timber quayside at New Fresh Wharf (Rhodes 1986a, 90). Of this 63% was samian, much of it unused, manufactured at Lezoux in central Gaul c AD 170–80. As this stock was apparently at least 40 years old when dumped it has been suggested that it consisted of debris from nearby warehouses in which cargoes had been stored (ibid). But this interpretation does not explain why the samian ware had remained undistributed for so long in a province where it was evidently in demand. It seems equally likely that it had been in long-term storage in Gaul before being exported, and that it was broken while in transit or being offloaded (Rhodes 1986b, 201). This was not the only waterfront site containing large dumps of later samian ware, as more was found at Swan Lane dating from the late second to early third centuries, and perhaps was also cargo breakages (DUA Site Catalogue 1986, 100; Rhodes 1986b, 201). These deposits indicate the continuing importance of the trade in this tableware, and as its centre of manufacture was not far from the river Loire it is likely that this river was used to ship it to the Atlantic, and thence through the Channel to London. The ship wrecked on Pudding Pan Sand in the Thames estuary, c AD 170–200 (Bird 1986, 140), is known to have been involved in this samian importation trade, probably to London, and, if its exact site could be located, it may give important information about the methods used to package and stow the cargo.

Spain

Olive oil from southern Spain, used for cooking and lighting, was in great demand in London since the globular amphorae (Dressel 20) in which it was carried is the most common type found there (Green 1980, 42, nos. 21–8). It is likely that it was shipped to London up the Rhône and then was carried overland to the rivers Rhine, Loire, or Seine, since this brought it through areas with an established market. Each empty Dressel 20 amphora weighed on average 28.42 kg and contained on average 62.83 litres of oil (Peacock and Williams 1986, 52). Since 1 litre of olive oil weighs 0.91 kg. (information from an edible oil merchant) the average weight of oil in one amphora would be 57.17 kg. The total weight of a single average amphora filled with oil would be 85.59 kg. As these amphorae were too heavy for a man to lift one of them, it is clear that some lifting mechanism was needed to load and unload ships.

Germany

Wine is believed to have been an important bulk cargo from Germany and was carried in barrels made from silver fir (*Abies alba*), a tree indigenous to the foothills of the Alps and Pyrenees (Hassall 1978, 45; Wilmott 1982, 47). As barrel-staves are often found on sites in London, such as at the first-century waterfront at Pudding Lane (Fig 4, site 7) (Bateman and Milne 1983, 217, no 23), it is clear that this wine trade was important in the first and second centuries. Fortunately a number of almost complete barrels of the first to second centuries have been found reused as well linings in London; from these it has been possible to calculate their weight when full. Two barrels were recorded in Queen Street (Fig 4, site 2; Wilmott 1982, 47–9), and another was found in Suffolk Lane (Fig 4, site 4), dating from the period AD 60–80 (Excavation Register 1034; Marsden 1975, 12).

The barrels in the two Queen Street wells (Wilmott 1982, 47, features 85 and 87) were incomplete, but seem to have been about the same size (1.22m high, 0.85m maximum internal diameter, and 0.68m across the ends). The internal height was about 1.17m and the mean diameter 0.18m. The volume of each was therefore π x r^2 x height (ie 3.14 x 0.181 x 1.17m = 0.966 m^3.). This represents 966 litres of wine weighing 966 kg since 1 kg of wine has about the same weight as water of equal volume. An empty barrel weighs about 200 kg, so that each full barrel weighed about 1.166 tonnes.

A larger barrel (MoL acc no 23893), originally probably weighing c 250kg (advice from Achersons Cooperage), was found in Suffolk Lane with a maximum diameter of 0.96m and was originally 1.83m high. Its average internal diameter was 0.86m and its internal height was about 1.77m. Its volume was therefore 3.14 x 0.185 x 1.77 = 1.028 m^3. This represents 1028 litres of wine, which would weigh about 1.028 tonnes. The weight of this full barrel was therefore about 1.278 tonnes.

Scenes on several Roman carved stone reliefs from Germany and the Netherlands depict barrels of wine being rolled on the ground, and being transported by barge down the Rhine (Ellmers 1978, 6–14), but what is not shown is how they were lifted into and out of the ships. Clearly, some lifting mechanism was necessary both in Germany and in London.

The continued use of the river Rhine in the third century (Rhodes 1986a, 91–2) to transport goods to London is demonstrated by finds from New Fresh Wharf, particularly by a large amount of east Gaulish samian, colour-coated pottery, hunt cup beakers, and mortaria, some of which were manufactured by Verecundus near Bonn.

Heavy bulk exports from Germany to London included millstones, believed to be of Mayen lava from the Niedermendig area, by the Rhine (King 1986, 94, 100–5), though individual millstones found in London have not been weighed.

Probably the most important source of information about the mechanism of maritime trade between Britain and the Continent are the groups of altars with dedications to the goddess Nehalennia which have been found at Domburg and near Colijnsplaat, Netherlands. These suggest that the mouth of the East Scheldt was a major point from which goods were shipped from the Rhineland to Britain in at least the late second century AD (Kooijmans *et al* 1971). The dedications had been set up at shrines probably by traders (*negotiatores*) who were shipping goods, such as the *negotiator cretarius Britannicianus* and the *cives Veliocassinius negotiator Britannicianus* (Fulford 1977, 57). From these and similar dedications by merchants engaged in trade with Britain that have been found at Cologne, Castell by Mainz (ibid), and Bordeaux (ibid, 59) it seems that shipping was carried out by individual shippers (*nautae*) and corporate groups of shippers (*societates*), and that there were agents (*actores navium*) representing the trading interests of the shippers on the larger vessels (Hassall 1978).

Britain

Apart from imports from the Continent, much of the domestic pottery used in Londinium during the first and early second centuries was manufactured locally (Green 1980, 76–7), and had evidently been carried overland to the city. However, the inclusion of Black burnished pottery, manufactured in Dorset and around Colchester, in rubbish of the period c AD 125–60 does suggest some seaborne trade around the south coast of England (ibid, 77). The quantity of pottery found in London suggests that it may not have been a major cargo at that time, and that it was mixed with other goods, such as Kimmeridge shale also from Dorset (Rhodes 1980, 132, no 687).

By the early third century the dumps of rubbish in the quay at New Fresh Wharf show that imports were reaching London from an increased number of places in Britain, primarily on the coast and beside navigable rivers, suggesting that local maritime trade was growing in importance. Most of these goods were ceramics from southern Britain and included domestic bowls, mortaria and slip-decorated beakers from the Colchester area, and bowls of BB2 ware probably from north Kent. Pottery made in south Devon (jars and tripod bowls of micaceous Black burnished ware) and Dorset (bowls, jars, dishes of BB1 ware) reflect more distant coastal trade along the Channel, as does pottery from the Pas de Calais – Picardy region of northern Gaul (Rhodes 1986a, 92). Other imports included hones of Kentish ragstone from north Kent and probably of Pennant grit from the Bristol region; and an armlet and bowl of Kimmeridge shale from Dorset. A few other items indicate minor trade links with northern Britain: jet pins from the Whitby area of Yorkshire; a small quantity of coal, probably from the Durham coalfield; and roofing slates probably from north Wales and Yorkshire (ibid; Rhodes 1986c, 245).

Architectural sculptured work in London, particularly of the third century, was mainly of carved Lincolnshire limestone, as is exemplified by a column of oolitic limestone, probably from the Grantham region, which was found in the early third century dumps at New Fresh Wharf (ibid, 244). The monumental arch, screen of gods, and two altars, all religious monuments whose stones were reused in the late Roman riverside defensive wall of London, are the best known examples of the use of such stone. They mostly date from the first half of the third century, and the stone is thought to have been quarried in the Barnack region, next to Stamford, and in the Weldon area, close to Corby (Dimes 1980). Since the suspected Roman quarry area is close to the rivers Welland and Nene, it seems likely that the stone blocks were taken downstream by barge to a deeper-water location for loading onto seagoing ships bound for London. The alternative means of transportation, by road, is unlikely in view of their considerable quantity, weight and size.

As the size of individual stone blocks is relevant to the volume of ships' cargoes and to their handling, it has been necessary to assess the weights of each of the 26 discovered blocks by calculating their volume from published measurements (Blagg 1980) on the basis that a cubic metre block of stone is equal to 2.4 tonnes (the approximate weight of Lincolnshire oolitic limestone: information from Steedly Construction Materials, Great Ponton Quarry, Lincolnshire.). Seventeen blocks each weighed between 0.242 and 0.722 tonnes; six blocks in the screen of gods each weighed between 0.122 and 0.636 tonnes; one altar weighed 0.756 tonnes; and two other blocks weighed 0.869 and 0.468 tonnes.

Other very common building materials were the clay roofing tiles and building bricks mostly manufactured in the London area (unpublished analysis of tiles from London, Museum of London archives). However, it is of particular interest that tile fragments in a variety of non-local fabrics were found in the early third century quay infill at New Fresh Wharf, and it has been suggested that some of these might have reached London as ballast in ships (Rhodes 1986a, 92; Betts 1986, 252). As there were more suitable and heavier forms of ballast than tile, such as gravel, it is difficult to account for the presence of these imported fragments.

The existence of estuarine shipping as early as the decade 50–60 AD is indicated by the very large quantity of Kentish ragstone and flint quarried from the chalk in the Medway valley, which was brought to London as building material (see Chapter 2). But the survival of such building materials, especially of such size, durability, and quantity indicates an importance probably now out of proportion to its original value relative to other goods.

Berthing

Was the Thames at London tidal?

The first problem facing seagoing ships reaching the Thames estuary was how they could sail upstream against the river current to reach Londinium. The second was how they could berth to offload their goods, both heavy and fragile. The discovery of planktonic and brackish water species of diatoms in the first century foreshore silt deposits in London has provided the answer, for it has shown unequivocally that the river there was estuarine, and therefore tidal, at that time (Bateman and Milne 1983, 209; Milne *et al*, 1983,

25–7). The ships could therefore be carried up to London on the tidal stream, probably taking several tides to reach their destination, while anchoring on the ebb tides.

Discovering the Roman tide levels in London relative to Ordnance Datum is essential to understanding the berthing arrangements, as these will give the depths of water available for ships at the quaysides. These levels are difficult to establish with precision, though careful research has limited the range of probabilities, and the matter has been complicated by the possibility that averaged tide levels in the area changed during the four centuries of Roman rule in Britain.

Low tide was evidently below OD in the first century AD since the top of Roman quarry pits dug into the foreshore on the Peninsular House and Miles Lane sites were at OD (Bateman and Milne 1983, 209; Milne 1985, 82). Moreover, during the second and third centuries complex timber waterfront constructions found on other sites were built on the river bed at 1m and 1.5m below OD, suggesting that low water may have then been at about that level (Tatton-Brown 1974, 124). A useful summary of the waterfront evidence has been published by Brigham (1990, 143–4) in which he accepts the conjectured high tide level of about 1.24m OD suggested by Milne (1985, 84), but Waddelove (1990, 256–8) casts doubt on this and points out that in the mid first century AD the settlement in Southwark lay below that level. Most recently, excavations in 1989–90 at Guy's Hospital, Southwark, have located a timber quay at the edge of a shallow creek in the marshes, and beside it was a contemporary land surface at 0.65–1.03m OD on which was found pottery of the early second century AD and the remains of a building (Fig 4, site 9). Tree–ring dating of the timbers from the quay also indicate a date in the late first to early second century (Site archive report, Museum of London). This quay was covered by silts containing later Roman pottery indicating that the marshes were subsequently periodically flooded, presumably at spring tides. It would seem, then, that during the latter half of the first and first half of the second centuries the ordinary tidal range was between about 1m below OD and 0.5m above OD, with this range being increased at spring tides from, say, 1.5m below OD to about 1m above OD.

Berthing, mid first century AD

The weight of the barrels of wine and some amphorae containing oil indicates that there was a fairly sophisticated system of berthing and warehousing established soon after the founding of the Roman city c AD 50, and that heavy loads could be lifted and transported from ship to shore. The Roman river bank has been carefully investigated on sites beside the earliest part of the Roman city, adjacent to modern London Bridge, at Peninsular House, Lower Thames Street, and at Miles Lane, Upper Thames Street, in the hope of finding the expected waterfront. But all that was found on the latter site, immediately upstream of the bridge, were several large quarry pits cut into the natural gravel and London clay

on the early Roman foreshore at OD (Fig 13a), and there were traces of posts along the river bank (Miller 1982, 144). On the former site, immediately downstream of the bridge, the natural river bank had been straightened and strengthened by a bank of gravel up to 0.8m high, its top lying at about 1.6m OD. A double line of piles had been driven into the crest of the bank to stabilise it. Further downstream on the site was found the corner of a post and plank revetment which survived to a height of c 1.8m OD. To the south of the embankment, in the Roman river foreshore, was found a further quarry pit cut down into the London clay from OD to about 0.6m below OD, and in its backfill were substantial pieces of a large barrel.

None of this reflects the expected trading waterfront of the 50s AD, and, instead of a quayside on the Peninsular House site, there was a sloping flint and chalk surface, like a hard, laid on the foreshore down to below 2m OD (Bateman and Milne 1983, 209), as if to make an access point for vehicles which could be pulled down to the edge of the water, and for ships to be beached for loading and unloading. This was situated on the site later probably occupied by the Roman bridge crossing the Thames, but before that it may have been the landing site of a ferry. The absence of a similar hard elsewhere suggests that it was also for more general maritime use and made use of the tides by allowing ships to beach and lift off again. This system of berthing recalls the beaching system found at the late Iron Age port at Hengistbury Head, Dorset (Cunliffe 1990) probably used by the Veneti whose Celtic ships had flatter bottoms than had Roman ships and were suited to tidal shallows, 'and when left aground by the tide had nothing to fear from reefs or pointed rocks' (Caesar III, 1). This type of beach waterfront, therefore, was particularly suited to the thick flat bottoms of Romano-Celtic ships like Blackfriars ship 1 (Chapter 2) and the broad New Guy's House barge (Chapter 3), than to the ships of Mediterranean type which often had projecting keels that were fastened to adjacent planking with mortice-and-tenon joints, and were probably suited to frequent grounding.

Berthing, late first to mid third centuries AD

A more classical Mediterranean arrangement of quays and jetties for berthing was built in London during the late first and early second centuries, and at about the same time the Roman bridge was constructed across the River Thames. This bridge is believed to have had timber–framed piers, one of which was c 7x5m and at least 2.2m high, and a dendrochronological study indicates that it was built between AD 78 and 118 (Milne 1985, 37).

Immediately downstream of the bridge was an open-work timber landing stage (Fig 10) parallel to the river bank, which dendrochronological evidence suggests was built between AD 69 and 91 (ibid). Although apparently built for loading and unloading ships, doubts have been expressed about the size of vessels that could be accommodated (Milne et al 1983, 29). It lay parallel to, and about 5m from, the contemporary river bank and was c

4.9m wide, and at least 35m long. Its south and west sides were built with horizontally laid baulks of squared oak, but the north or inshore side was more open and had vertical timbers at about 2m intervals. Other horizontal timbers tied the front and back together to form a box-like structure (Fig 11a). It is presumed that it had a timber deck and gangways linking it to the shore, but these had not survived. Also there was no trace of any mooring posts, and no evidence of cranes or other structures for offloading ships.

As the riverbed at the base of the landing stage lay at about OD there was probably no more than 0.8m of water at an average high tide to allow ships to berth there. This suggests that the landing stage was for small vessels with a shallow draught, such as oyster boats whose large dumps of shells from the estuary of the Thames were

found on the river bed both under and around the landing stage (Milne 1985, 92).

Probably contemporary with the landing stage, but just upstream of the Roman bridge, was a quay with a front wall also formed from large squared baulks of oak laid horizontally. This had been back-braced by further timbers, so that the whole area behind could be in-filled with debris (Miller 1982). It has been dated by dendro-chronology to between AD 45 and 79 (Milne 1985, 35 and 37) and is thought to belong to the latter end of the period, but possibly earlier than the Roman bridge. Before the end of the first century AD the landing stage was replaced by other lengths of similar quay which extended along at least 475m of the waterfront of Roman London, both upstream and downstream of the bridge. The main site at which this new quay has been studied

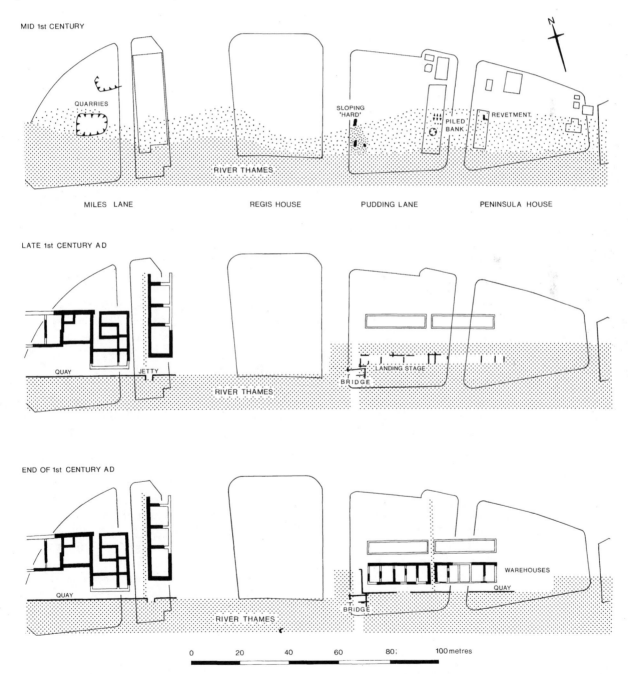

Fig 10 Early Roman development of waterfront sites at the north end of London Bridge.

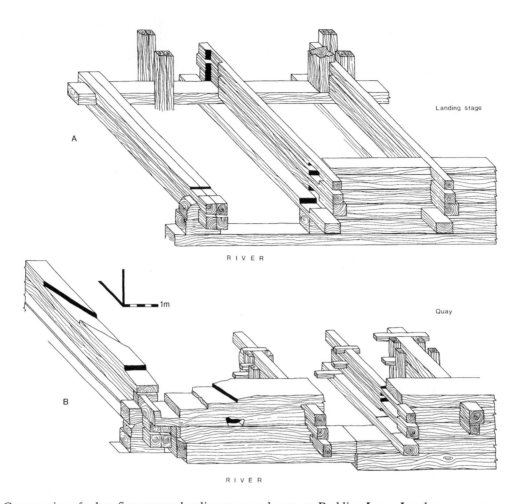

Fig 11   Construction of a late first century landing stage and quay at Pudding Lane, London.

is Pudding Lane (Milne 1985, 55–67) where it comprised at least five courses of superimposed horizontal squared oak beams forming a wall about 2m high (Fig 11b). It was back-braced with more horizontal beams at right angles to and parallel with the waterfront (Fig 12). The base of the quay on the river bed lay at about OD, and the top at about 2m OD. At the Miles Lane site the top of the quay wall was raised by adding two further courses of squared timber beams so that eventually the top lay at about 2.8m OD (Miller 1982). The area under the quay surface was filled with dumped debris containing pottery, three quarters of the sherds, by weight, being from amphorae (Tyers 1985, 41).

Since the depth of water beside the quay was probably no more than 0.8m (Fig 13a), it is unlikely that large heavily-laden ships could berth there, and this may explain why a jetty, about 3m wide, had been built out at least 5m into deeper water from the quay on the Miles Lane site, though the OD level of the river bed at the surviving far end of the jetty is unknown (Miller 1982, 147).

If larger sailing merchant ships did berth upstream of the bridge crossing the Thames, they would have had to pass under the bridge, perhaps through a drawbridge opening. Alternatively, cargoes could have been transshipped from merchant vessels moored downstream, into shallow-draught barges of the New Guy's House type, and these barges would carry the cargoes under the

bridge without difficulty to berth at a quayside upstream. Such an arrangement would be far from ideal, particularly if there was an insufficient depth of water at the quaysides for the larger ships. This may be the reason why in the early second century AD, judging from the date of rubbish in dumps in front of the late first century quay at Miles Lane and Pudding Lane (ibid; Bateman and Milne 1983, 218), the quay was replaced by a new waterfront further south out in the river bed. The rubbish was dumped in land reclamation between the two waterfronts, but as the early second century quay lies mostly under what is now Upper and Lower Thames Street it has not been excavated. The short period in which the late first century quay was in use makes it unlikely that its replacement was due to decay. It seems more likely that it was in response to a need for a deeper water berthing for larger ships. Moreover, it may be significant that it was at about this time that the Roman forum was rebuilt five times larger than its predecessor, presumably to accommodate an expected greatly increased volume of trade (Marsden 1987, 74–6; Brigham 1990a, 81). Part of a deeper water berth existed downstream by the early second century, near the south-east limits of the city, on the Custom House site. Here the lower part of a quay, built with horizontal oak beams with posts and planks in front, retained the river bank with its base at 1m or more below OD (Tatton-Brown 1974, 122), thereby giving a depth of water at high tide of at least 1.5m.

There was no evidence to suggest how ships were tied to the waterfronts. At classical ports in the Mediterranean, such as Portus at the mouth of the Tiber (Casson 1971, 368) and on the bank of the River Tiber in Rome (Shaw 1972, 107, fig 19), ships were tied by ropes to mooring stones, each pierced with a hole, set in the quaysides. As no mooring stones have been found in London, presumably because stone is not naturally found in the London area, it is likely that timber posts were used instead, though none has been definitely identified.

Once a ship had berthed cargoes had to be lifted out of the holds and lowered onto the quayside. Since some of the large packaged loads carried in ships were in excess of one tonne, it is clear that there must have been some lifting mechanism from the ship to the shore. However, no certain indication of cranes for unloading heavy goods has been noted, though an iron crane hook (Fig 14) has been found in the Walbrook valley (Merrifield 1965, pl 126). The heavy amphorae, barrels of wine, and blocks of stone carried as cargoes demonstrate the importance of lifting equipment for weights of more than one tonne on the late second and third century quaysides. The timber foundation of what might have been a crane was suggested for a quayside structure found at Billingsgate (Brigham 1990, 171–2), but in general the lack of preservation of the quay surfaces is no doubt the reason why traces of cranes have not otherwise been found (Ellmers

1981, 93–5). Classical sources show that in the Mediterranean area cranes and stevedores were an essential part of major ports (Casson 1971, 370). There are a number of possibilities, such as a mobile crane, shear-legs, the ship's spars or mast, or ropes fastened to a strong point and looped around the load so that it can be hauled by hand (a 'parbuckle', Kemp 1979, 629), but no clear evidence for any of these has been found. Even some common items, such as a full Dressel 20 amphora, were far greater than one man could carry so it is evident that the scenes depicted on Roman stone reliefs of men carrying amphorae over their shoulders (Casson 1971, pl 174) or bales of goods (Ellmers 1978, 12), are not always relevant to all such goods. Once lowered to the foreshore or to the quayside the heavy round barrels and amphorae could then be rolled up planks into carts, as may be depicted on a tombstone from Mainz (ibid). In spite of all this it is clear that fundamental questions about cargo handling on the waterfront of Roman London still need to be resolved.

At about the middle of the second century a new waterfront was constructed on the St Magnus House site upstream of the Roman bridge (Fig 15b). It is particularly interesting as it was contemporary with Blackfriars ship 1 and the New Guy's House barge, and was in use throughout much of the second century AD. It lay about 25m south of the late first century quay, and was built with closely spaced vertical posts clad with horizontal

Fig 12   Late first-century timber quay, with a later Roman timber drain, found in Pudding Lane, London.

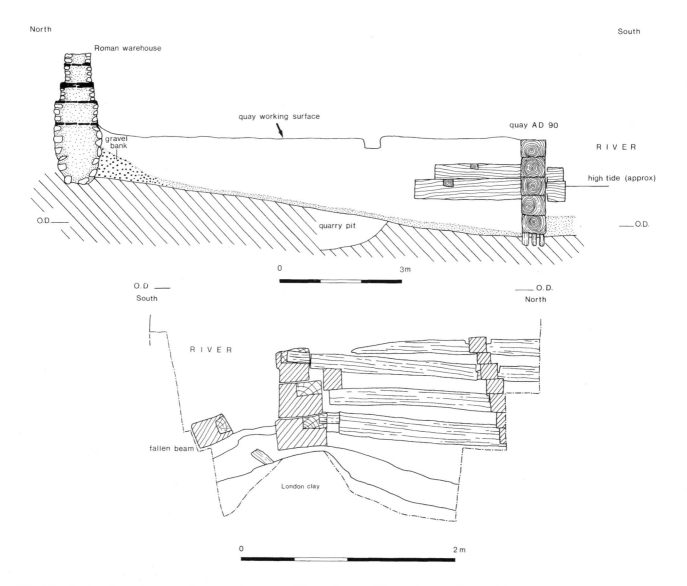

Fig 13   Section through a quay, late second century AD, at Custom House, Lower Thames Street.

planking whose base level indicated that the contemporary river bed was at 0.55m below OD (Miller *et al* 1986,
fig 53). This would give about a 1m depth of water at
high tides.

Subsequently, in the late second century, another
quay (Fig 15a) was built at Custom House downstream
from London bridge, close to the south-east corner of
the Roman city. This included massive horizontal oak
beams constructed to form a series of 'boxes' along the
waterfront, and immediately in front of it was a facing of
three rows of posts with planks between them. The river
bed at the base of the quay was at 1.5m below OD,
thereby giving a depth of water of a little over 2m at high
tide (Fig 13b). The deck of the quay had not survived,
but there were a number of upright posts that probably
helped to support it, and some of these were perhaps
used as bollards (Tatton-Brown 1974, 124–7).

A major new quay was constructed during the third
century along a considerable part of London's waterfront, perhaps as a single scheme, and a useful summary
of what is known about it and the later second-century
quay is given by Brigham (1990). The third-century quay

(Fig 15c) at New Fresh Wharf lay 8.25m south of the
second century revetment, and has been dated by dendrochronology to the period 209–44 AD. However, its
rubbish infill, which seems to be contemporary with its
construction, included samian ware dated AD 235–45,
suggesting that the quay may have been built in the latter
part of the time bracket (Miller *et al* 1986, 63–4). It was
traced for 45m east–west, but extended further, though
not as far downstream as the Custom House site. It
comprised at least four superimposed horizontal squared
oak beams, some up to 0.73m wide but most less than
0.4m, on a foundation of vertical oak piles. The quayfront was held upright by a series of squared tieback oak
beams, laid horizontally at a right angle to the quayfront,
which were anchored by upright timbers about 2–3m
inshore. Some of these upright timbers had sawn tops at
1–1.3m OD, suggesting that this was the original top
surface of the quay. Since there were many uprights, and
some appear not to have anchored the tieback timbers,
these may have formed the base of a building, possibly a
warehouse. Although the original surface of the quay had
been destroyed, it is unlikely to have been above the base

of the face of the adjacent later third-century riverside defensive wall at 1.6m OD (ibid, 68–9). It seems likely, therefore, that the Roman high tide level in that period may have been about the same as or a little lower than it was in the first century AD (c 0.5–1m OD), and as the river bed in front of the third century quay lay at 1m below OD there could have been about 1.5m of water there at high tide. This would allow sea-going vessels like Blackfriars ship 1 to reach the quayside at ordinary high water.

Calculation of the Roman low tide levels relative to the later waterfronts depends in part upon an estimation of the ease of access at that period to the river bed for construction work. The third century quay at New Fresh Wharf had a complex basal timber construction at about 1m below OD, a level that was presumably above low tide long enough to allow it to be built (ibid, 37), but at the Custom House site the base of the late second-century quay lay at about 1.5m below OD (Fig 13b), indicating that low tide may have reached this level (Tatton-Brown 1974, 148). Therefore the normal tidal range could have been from 1.0m below to 0.5m above OD, with more extreme levels at spring tides. The excavations at Guy's Hospital in 1990 have shown that high tide probably lay at about 0.5m OD by the middle of the second century, as a quayside there (Fig 17) had a gravel surface lying between 0.65m and 1.03m OD (Site archive report, Museum of London). The suggestion made by Brigham (1990, 144) that high tide then lay above this level, therefore, does not quite square with the evidence from Southwark and illustrates how difficult it

is to define ancient tide levels. Indeed, the matter is further complicated by the possibility that tide levels were themselves getting lower in the later Roman period (ibid, 145–8), and such a possibility would help to account for the lower base levels of the late second and third century quays.

Warehousing

Once the cargoes were offloaded from ships they needed to be placed in storage, and the excavations at Miles Lane and Pudding Lane uncovered late first-century buildings on the quayside which have been interpreted as warehouses (*horrea*). At Miles Lane, just upstream (west) of the Roman bridge, was one north–south building whose walls were constructed from Kentish ragstone and courses of bonding tiles (Fig 10). It was 9m wide, at least 36m long, and comprised a succession of rooms the largest of which lay at the south end fronting the quayside. This was set back c 7.5m from the quay, and apparently had an open south front facing the river, as if it was a shop or warehouse. Traces of other buildings lay immediately to the west, with frontages about 10m and 12m from the quay, but their plans were insufficiently complete to determine their functions (Miller 1982, 144).

At Pudding Lane, immediately downstream (east) of the Roman bridge, were two rectangular buildings facing the river and set back about 5m from the quay front (Fig 10). Both had walls of ragstone with courses of bonding tiles. One building was c 25m long and 6m wide, and was

Fig 14   Iron Roman docker's tools, from the Walbrook stream valley: a bale hook, a crane hook, and case-opener. Scale in inches.

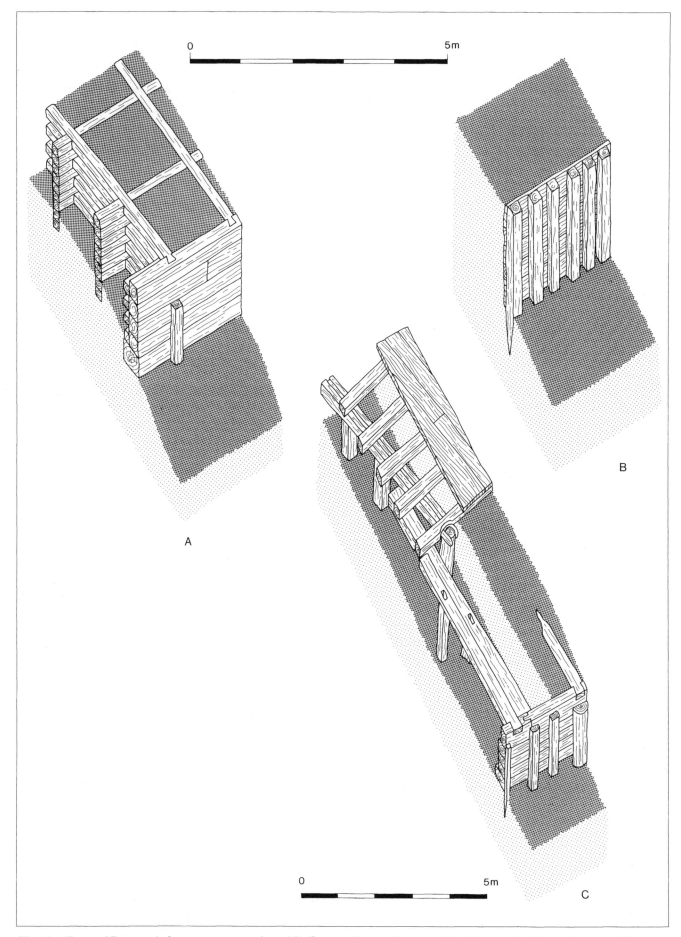

Fig 15   Types of Roman timber quay construction: (A) Custom House, London; (B) New Fresh Wharf, London; (C) Xanten, Germany.

divided into five open-fronted rooms, each *c* 4.3m wide, with timber floors at about 2m OD (Fig 16). A drain separated it from the second building which continued its line. This second building was also about 25m long, 6m wide, and it too probably had five open-fronted rooms with timber floors facing the river (Milne 1985, 73–5).

The buildings are thought to have been warehouses because they resembled buildings of that type in other parts of the Roman empire (ibid, 70), though the London buildings were small by comparison, perhaps indicating that cargo loads were generally smaller in the northern provinces compared with loads carried in the Mediterranean. The varying distance of frontages from the quayside in London suggests that the buildings had been planned piecemeal by various owners, rather than as a single waterfront scheme planned by a government authority, as, for example, occurred later at Leptis Magna (Bartoccini 1958). In this context it is worth noting that examples of equipment that might have been used in warehousing have been found in London. These include (Fig 14) an iron crane hook, an iron bale hook, and a case-opener (Merrifield 1965, pl 126).

An alternative form of possible storage building, found close to the river in Southwark, was of timber and measured 4.75m by at least 11m. It had a sunken timber floor at 0.10m OD and timber walls, and was entered down a ramp 2.20m wide from one corner and is thought to have been used for the cool storage of food and wine (Dillon 1989).

The variety of imported goods in the first half of the third century imply that warehouses were necessary for storage. However, the area immediately behind the second- and third-century quaysides is now beneath Lower Thames Street and has not been available for investigation. The late first-century warehouses at Pudding Lane, which then lay further inshore had been rebuilt after destruction by fire in the second century (Milne 1985, 29), on a plan that remained essentially the same as in the first century. This was a range of ten rectangular rooms, each measuring about 4.3m wide by 6m deep, with an entrance on the south side facing the river, behind a portico or verandah. The walls were of stone, but the floors varied from timber and mortar to brickearth (Bateman and Milne 1983, 222). Milne (1985, 30) has suggested that as they no longer lay on the waterfront they may not have served as warehouses but rather as shops. This need not have been so, for a study of Roman warehouse buildings at Ostia has shown that it was not always necessary for such buildings to be located on the waterfront (Meiggs 1960, 284).

Fig 16   A room in a late first century warehouse found in Pudding Lane, London. Note the burnt timber floor.

Fig 17   Second century timber quay found beside an inlet of the River Thames, Guy's Hospital, Southwark.

2 Blackfriars ship 1, 1962

A considerable amount of this ship of the second century AD has survived, making it possible to undertake a tentative reconstruction of the vessel in the light of modern knowledge, and an assessment of its stability and how it might have been used, in relation to its cargo and the contemporary waterfronts of Roman London. This vessel is important since it is the earliest known seagoing sailing ship yet found in northern Europe, and although of the Roman period it appears to belong to a native Celtic tradition of shipbuilding.

Discovery

The ship was discovered on 6 September, 1962 in the bed of the River Thames, during the construction of a new riverside wall at Blackfriars in the City of London. It lay between the Blackfriars road bridge and the railway bridges just to the east, and about 20m south of the then existing embankment wall (Fig 18). The new embankment wall now coincides with the forward half of the ship.

The ship was found during the clearance of obstructions for the construction of a gantry to serve a coffer-dam in which a length of the new riverside wall was to be constructed. A mechanical grab had pulled out pieces of curved and blackened oak frames studded with massive iron nails with cone-shaped heads. The author, then at the Guildhall Museum, was informed and visited the site at the next low tide. The timbers were identified as probably the frames of a carvel-built ship with flush-laid planking, and they were of sufficient interest to make an investigation of the site worthwhile.

During the spring tides of October 1962, a hole was gently dug at low water in the river bed by a mechanical grab under the supervision of the author. This was adjacent to the spot where the frame fragments had been found, and by digging during these extra-low tides that

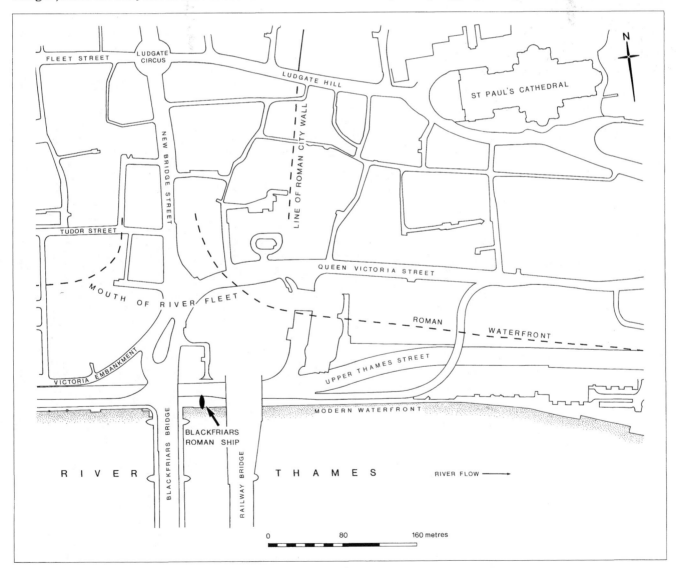

Fig 18 The location of Blackfriars ship 1.

33

occur only at monthly intervals it was possible to take advantage of the maximum period when the site was 'dry' – about two hours. Soon the ends of two frames with some planking still attached were revealed just under the surface of the present river bed (Fig 19). As this work was carried out without any funding, there was valuable help in equipment and labour from the contractor, and from volunteers who included actors and a playwright from the Mermaid Theatre, led by Bernard Miles. Also the London Fire Brigade generously carried out an 'exercise' by pumping muddy water from the hole. This first sondage clarified several points: it confirmed that a ship had indeed sunk there; it showed that it was carvel-built, and therefore was likely to date either from Roman times

or after *c* 1500; it demonstrated that it had sunk across the flow of the river and was aligned north–south; and it located its west side.

As the area inshore of the first sondage, just north of the gantry, was to be filled-in for road construction and would soon become permanently inaccessible, it was decided to carry out a second, larger, investigation there in November 1962. This time the main excavation was carried out by bulldozer and mechanical grab, the grab digging a sump hole to one side of the wreck. This occurred during further monthly low spring tides, with volunteer helpers including Patrick Minns who had assisted the author on the partial excavation of the Roman barge at Guy's Hospital (see Chapter 3). The

Fig 19   The site of the wreck of Blackfriars ship 1 at low tide, under the gantry between the two modern bridges.

Fig 20   The coffer-dam, at low tide, in which the forward half of Blackfriars ship 1 was excavated during 1963.

contractors, Cementation, were again extremely helpful and, with pumps hired by the Corporation of London, it was possible to hose mud and gravel from on top of the frames and planking into the sumphole. This action revealed the bottom of the ship and the lower end of what later proved to be its sternpost (Fig 50). Although rapidly recorded in relation to the gantry supports, this quick excavation established the position of the north end of the ship, but there was still no dating evidence.

Using the now known position of the ship's central axis it was possible to predict its position within the proposed coffer-dam, and to arrange for that area to be excavated and recorded *in situ*. The final excavation began when the coffer-dam was completed in July 1963 (Fig 20), but initially only three days were given, without any funding, though the contractor gave considerable help. A grab cleared the gravel overburden, and a hose pipe and valve fastened to the inner wall of the coffer-dam supplied a flow of water with which to 'excavate' the ship when the tide lay above that level (Fig 21). Although this caused initial problems of excess water in the wreck, this was eventually solved by opening up a series of drainage channels under the frames leading to a large sump hole outside the wreck.

As the excavation continued for three days, and at night under floodlights, it proved to be particularly exhausting, but soon the forward half of the ship came into view. The public too could see the ship from Blackfriars Bridge, and, as soon as its Roman date became certain the newspapers in nearby Fleet Street began pressing for its preservation (Fig 22). Following a visit by the Lord

Mayor of London, Sir Ralph Perring, the Corporation of London authorised the raising of the timbers so that they could be preserved. This was an important decision as it would enable them to be cleaned and recorded in detail.

The position of the main timbers of the vessel were recorded relative to each other on a plan and in long and cross sections (Fig 53), but filling-in the details would depend upon post-excavation recording. This was aided by comprehensive photographic coverage of the wreck.

The vessel was dismantled by cutting through the planks between the frames, and then underpinning each frame and sliding boards in place so that each ancient frame was boxed in modern timber. Ropes were passed underneath and the package was gently raised by crane out of the coffer-dam and onto a waiting lorry. These were then driven through the streets of the City to the Royal Exchange where the Guildhall Museum was temporarily housed, and one by one the boxed frames were lifted down by a team of labourers and lowered onto rollers formed by scaffold pipes. They were then rolled into the central courtyard of the Royal Exchange where they were covered by polythene.

Although the position of the timbers in the coffer-dam were clear it should be mentioned that there was some difficulty in relating exactly the position of parts of the ship from one excavation to the next because of the lack of precise surveying points on the river bed. The only constant features extant during the excavations were the gantry supports, large circular piles, but as these did not give exact surveying points the overall length of the ship should be considered as only approximate.

Fig 21   The forward end of Blackfriars ship 1, with the unfinished millstone and a section of alluvial deposits below the inward collapsed starboard side of the ship.

Recording the ship timbers

After being cleaned the timbers were recorded by the author, and the drawings are published here. First, an annotated plan of the top surface of each frame was drawn to a scale of 1:8. This was achieved by stretching a datum line and a tape measure down the middle of the frame, and offset measurements were taken to all features. All fastenings, the extent of the original surface, the grain of the oak, and the extent of the sapwood were carefully recorded while the timbers remained wet and undamaged by drying. Next a datum line was stretched along the after face of each frame and an elevation was similarly drawn, together with details of attached planking. Finally, a cross-profile of each frame was drawn with an estimate of how the frame had been cut from the log, and, to complete this record, Ralph Merrifield of the Guildhall Museum, photographed the timbers. It was then possible to place these detailed drawings in their correct relationship to each other, and so build up a plan and cross-sections of this part of the ship as it had existed *in situ*.

Recent study

In 1962 attempts to conserve the timbers by spraying them with polyethylene glycol failed. As they dried out, all the frames shrunk, split open and some fell apart as the wood became brittle, particularly as the Guildhall

Museum, and later the Museum of London, was obliged to move the timbers from store to store. Each time a timber was lifted pieces fell off. Nevertheless, 26 years later there were still many substantial pieces available for examination, and by that time advances in nautical archaeology had improved research objectives and techniques, and new facilities were available, such as tree-ring dating.

It is important to remember that when it was found, the type of construction of Blackfriars ship 1 was unknown, and that it was then a major step to suggest that it probably represented a Celtic method of shipbuilding current during the Roman period (Marsden 1967, 34–5). Subsequent archaeological discoveries in Europe have not only confirmed that conclusion, but have also demonstrated that the construction is part of a family of native shipbuilding techniques now termed Romano–Celtic. The 1967 publication, although adequate at the time, is no longer sufficient and it is now appropriate that a fully detailed study of the ship should be published, replacing the earlier report.

The remains of the ship

Representative examples of dried fragments are now stored in the Museum of London, but the majority of the surviving frames have been given to the Nautical Museums Trust and are displayed at the Shipwreck Heritage Centre, Hastings, at the Tower Pageant exhibition (on loan from the Trust) on Tower Hill, City, and at the Science Museum, London.

The after half of the ship is still largely unexcavated at Blackfriars, and lies on the north or inshore side of the new embankment wall under a roadway. Also, the extreme upper end of the stempost probably lies in the river bed just south of the embankment wall. Should future redevelopment make further excavation possible under the embankment roadway there is no doubt that much more information would be forthcoming from the ship, including a more precise construction date since many of the timbers include the latest tree-ring growth as sapwood.

The ship

A coding system has been used here for reference to individual timbers in the ship (Fig 23). The strakes have been numbered 1 to 9 from the central longitudinal seam outwards, each being prefixed with either P, for port side, or S, for starboard side. There were two types of frame: the floor-timbers which lay on the bottom of the vessel, and the side-frames which supported its sides. The floor-timbers are prefixed FT and are numbered 1 to 24 from the south end of the bow, the known spacing of many surviving frames making it possible to conjecture the number and position of those that were not uncovered during excavation. The side-frames are numbered from

1 to 11, also from the surviving south end, and are prefixed SF.

Which end was the bow?

Before describing the ship and reconstructing the stages in its building, it is important to establish which end was the bow and which the stern. The central portion of the vessel comprised the hold where the cargo lay, and at about one-third of the length of the vessel from the south end, at the south end of the hold, there was a large rectangular socket, measuring 0.35m by 0.25m, in floor-timber 7 on the centre-line of the ship. Since the ends of all but one of the floor-timbers from the middle of the ship to the south end were uncovered during excavation, and only floor-timber 7, containing the socket, was carefully shaped, it is clear that this timber was of greater significance than any other. This is therefore interpreted as being the mast-step or socket for the foot of the mast. In any single-masted vessel the mast is normally stepped amidships or forward of amidships, and as the mast of the Blackfriars ship was at about one-third of the length from the south end, that end was evidently the bow.

Confirmation of this was suggested by other features: firstly, the section across the bottom of the south end of the vessel had a V-profile to enable the ship to cut through the water, whereas at the north end the bottom of the ship was almost flat, with each side meeting the

'We found him in the bilges—says he demands to see Cleopatra!'

Fig 22   Cartoon from the Daily Mail (1963). Reproduced with permission.

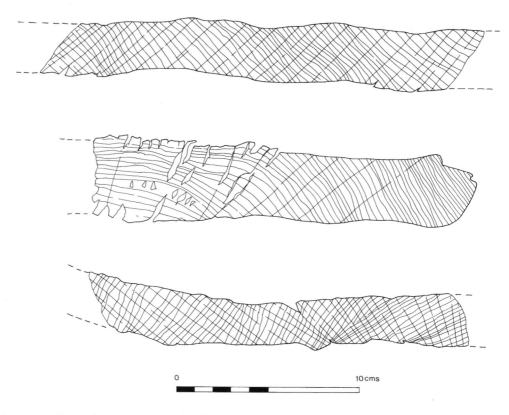

0   10 cms

Fig 24   Sections through plank fragments showing the tree-ring patterns.

bottom to form an angle or chine, more appropriate to the after end of a ship. And secondly, the south end of the ship was more massively constructed than the north end; the presumed stempost, for example, being 0.3m wide, and the supposed sternpost only 0.15m wide. It seems likely that the bow would be more heavily constructed than the stern, since it probably had to withstand greater stresses, particularly when taking the ground (ie beaching), as the flat bottom of the ship was clearly designed to sit on the sea or river bed at low water.

Materials used in the ship's construction

All the planks and frames were fashioned from oak (*Quercus* sp), but hazel wood shavings (*Corylus* sp, probably *C avellana*, a species which grows in south-east England; see Appendix 3), and pine resin were used as caulking materials between the planks (see Appendix 4). Hazel and birch (*Betula* sp) shavings, presumably including pine resin though samples from the stempost rabbets were not tested for this, were used as caulking between the planks and the stempost (identifications by C E Hubbard and David Cutler, Royal Botanic Gardens, Kew, and John Evans, University of East London). Trenails in the frames were of oak. The iron nails which fastened the planking to the frames had distinctive cone-shaped heads in which there was a 'caulking' of slivers of hazel wood with pine resin. Ordinary flat-headed iron nails with square shanks were used to fasten the ceiling planks to the frames inboard.

Construction of the ship

Planks

Although it is not now possible to find tool marks, the way in which the planks had been fashioned tangentially from the tree trunks suggests that they were sawn or hewn instead of split from the log (Fig 24). Some were of considerable size, particularly the thick keel-planks (P1 and S1) which were about 0.66m wide (see Table 1), and, judging from the tree-rings, were cut from trees more than a metre in diameter. The widest surviving part of plank P3 was 0.81m, and this had been cut from a tree also in excess of a metre in diameter. None of these planking measurements include an allowance for sapwood, as this had been removed by the shipwright.

Keel-planks

The Blackfriars ship did not have a keel in the usually accepted form. Instead it had two thick flat keel-planks (P1 and S1) each about 0.66m wide and 0.076m thick. These lay side by side with a central seam between them. It is likely that they extended from stempost to sternpost, a distance of about 11.3m, although they could not be traced along the whole length of the ship, as only the forward half of the vessel was completely excavated (Fig 23). They had been tangentially cut and placed with the side nearest the pith of the tree facing outboard. Their purpose was evidently to function as the main longitudinal strength members of the ship's bottom. The forward end of each keel-plank tapered in breadth towards the stempost, the tapering beginning beneath floor-timber 4, and ending immediately aft of floor-timber 2. Although

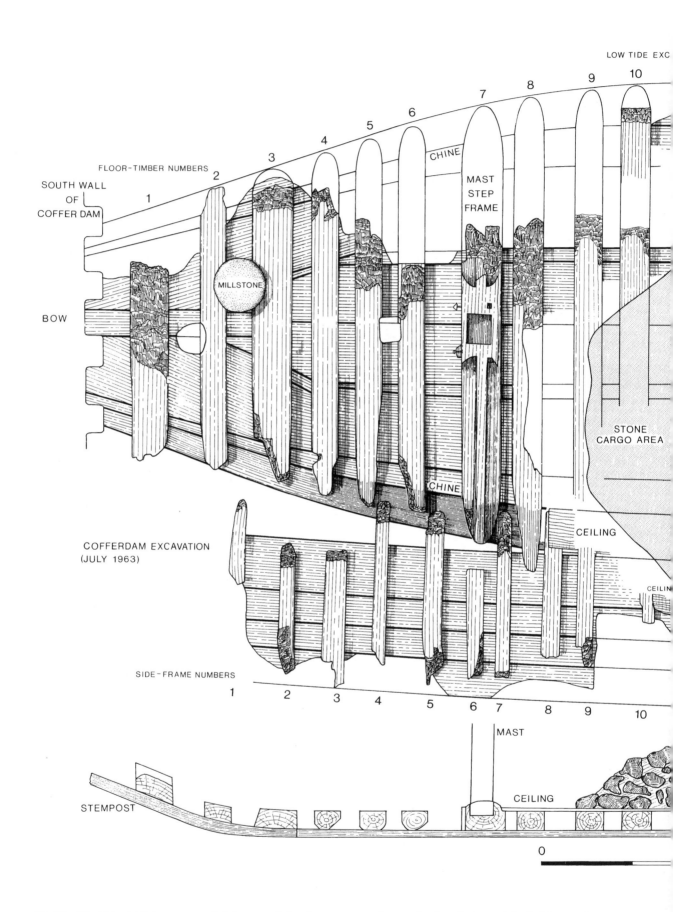

LOW TIDE EXC

10
9
8
7
6
5
4
3
2
1

FLOOR-TIMBER NUMBERS

SOUTH WALL
OF
COFFER DAM

BOW

MILLSTONE

CHINE

MAST
STEP
FRAME

CHINE

STONE
CARGO AREA

CEILING

COFFERDAM EXCAVATION
(JULY 1963)

CEILIN

SIDE-FRAME NUMBERS

1   2   3   4   5   6   7   8   9   10

MAST

STEMPOST

CEILING

0

Fig 23   Blackfriars ship 1 as excavated. It is assumed that the stern was at the same level as the forward half of the wreck.

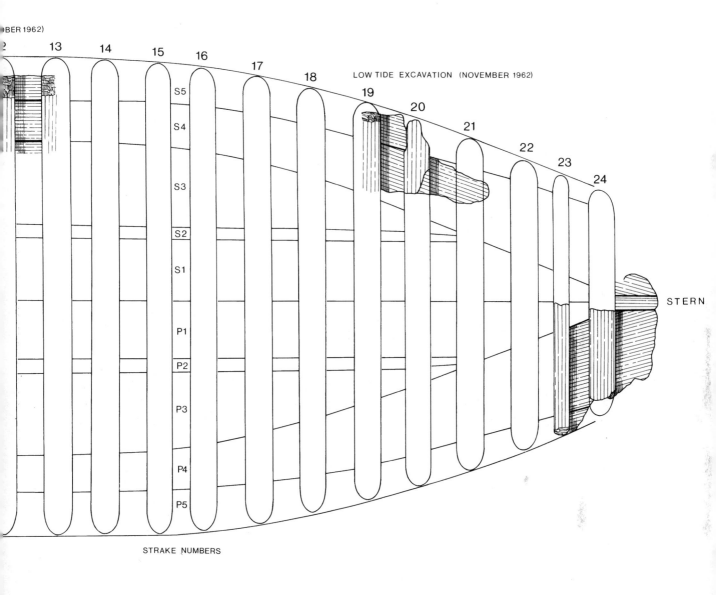

2   13   14   15   16   17   18

LOW TIDE EXCAVATION (NOVEMBER 1962)

19   20   21   22   23   24

S5
S4
S3
S2
S1
P1
P2
P3
P4
P5

STERN

STRAKE NUMBERS

'H WALL OF COFFERDAM

AGSTONE CARGO PROJECTED TO CENTRAL AXIS OF SHIP

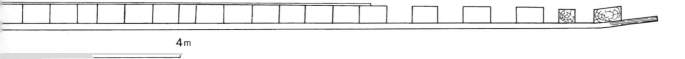

4 m

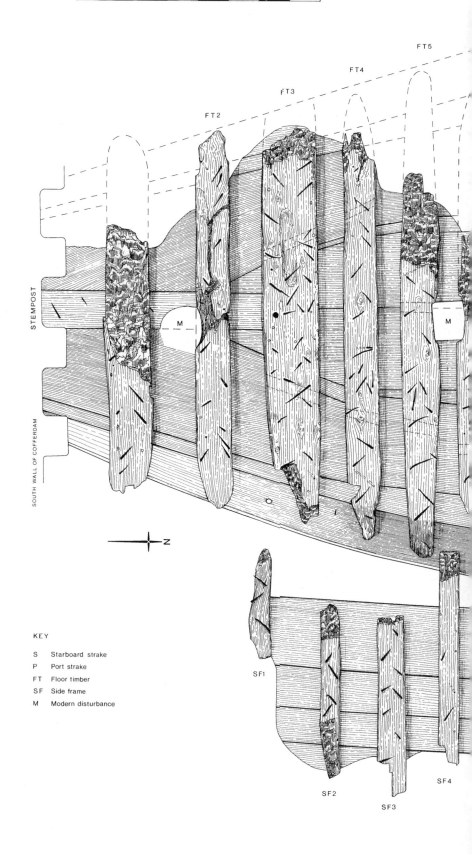

0   1   2m

FT5

FT4

FT3

FT2

STEMPOST

SOUTH WALL OF COFFERDAM

M

M

N

KEY

S   Starboard strake
P   Port strake
FT   Floor timber
SF   Side frame
M   Modern disturbance

SF1

SF2

SF3

SF4

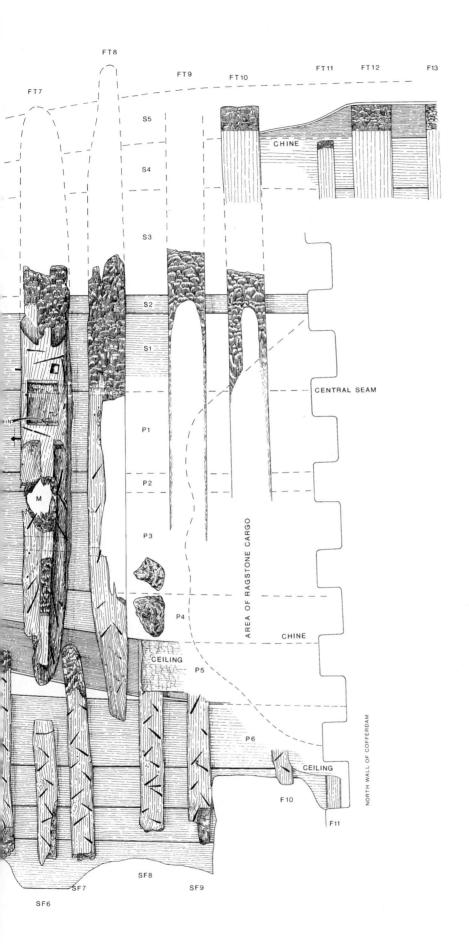

Fig 25   The forward half of Blackfriars ship 1 as excavated in the coffer-dam in 1963.

Table 1   Dimensions of the planks

plank	max width found (m)	thickness (mm)	estimated max width (m)
S5	–	c 51	–
S4	0.432	51	0.432
S3	–	25–38	–
S2	0.140	76	0.140
S1	0.635	71–84	0.635
P1	0.660	[?25]–76	0.660
P2	0.165	25–76	0.165
P3	0.813	31–51	0.864
P4	0.406	51–56	0.482
P5	0.546	c 51	0.559
P6	0.559	38–57	0.559
P7	0.330	51–63	0.330
P8	0.279	51–76	0.279
P9	0.406	c 51	0.406

the planks were only traced aft as far as floor-timber 11, it is presumed that they also tapered to the lower end of the sternpost in the same way, as in the third century Romano-Celtic ship found at St Peter Port (Rule 1990).

When found, keel-planks P1 and S1 were still attached to the underside of the frames by hooked iron nails, and it was not possible to investigate their hollow semi-cone-shaped nail heads *in situ* at the time. In the recently excavated St Peter Port ship fully cone-shaped nail heads held the keel-planks to the frames (ibid), their shape enabling them to contain a caulking of moss which would stop water seepage into the hull. These nail heads used in the Blackfriars and St Peter Port ships clearly needed protection when the vessel grounded, and the solution used in the St Peter Port ship was to recess their pointed cone-shaped heads in the thick keel-planks, but in the Blackfriars ship the nail heads were made thicker and only semi-cone-shaped, with sloping sides and flat tops. It was not possible to check fully whether or not some nail heads had been recessed in Blackfriars ship 1, but a re-examination of the nails still *in situ* in the dried frames revealed one nail under floor-timber 7 that was definitely not recessed in the keel-plank, and the im-

pression of wood grain from the planking preserved at the sides of other nails suggests the same conclusion. It thus seems that the builder of the Blackfriars ship had found an alternative solution to the protection of the nail heads by making them thicker and only semi-cone-shaped, so that they could still contain a caulking of hazel wood and pine resin.

Outer bottom planks

The outer bottom planks, strakes S3 and P3 and S4 and P4, were each about 0.03–0.05m thick (see Table 2). Strakes P3 and S3 began wide at the bow and narrowed towards the stern, and it seems that strakes P4 and S4 were wide at the stern, and narrowed towards the bow. On the starboard side strake S4 was traced as far aft as floor-timbers 20–1, at which point it became considerably wider. The position and size of its counterpart on the port side, strake P4, should have been comparable. In view of this, it seems reasonable to suggest that the wide strake found abutting the sternpost on the port side at floor-timbers 23–4 was probably a continuation of the strake P4. From the conjectured positions of the rest of the bottom strakes it would seem that strakes P3 and S3 must similarly narrow towards the stern.

A few small oak bungs circular in section, between 12 and 25mm in diameter, were noted in certain strakes (Fig 26). These seemed to fill drilled holes, so it is assumed that they either sealed aborted nail holes or represented fittings made at some temporary stage in the construction of the ship. As it was not possible to plot their positions and distribution during the excavation, their function cannot be resolved with certainty.

The difference in thickness between the keel-planks P1 and S1 and strakes P3 and S3 was about 25–5mm, and was bridged by the narrow strakes P2 and S2. Each of these was about 75mm thick where it adjoined the keel-planks, and thinned down to roughly 25–5mm where it abutted strakes P3 and S3. The narrow strake S2, on the starboard side, was traced as far aft as floor-timber 11. Its counterpart, strake P2 on the port side, was traced as far aft as floor-timber 8, but presumably both continued almost as far aft as the keel-planks.

Table 2   Measurement of plank thickness (in mm)

		bow							midships	
at frames	1	3	4	5	6	7	8		9
plank									
S5									
S4	–	51	–	–	–	–	–		–
S3	38	38	25	–	–	–	–		–
S2	–	76	76	–	–	–	–		–
S1	–	84	76	76	76	71	–		–
P1	–	76	76	76	76	71	–		–
P2	–	20	71	38–63	50–76	25–71	–		–
P3	–	44	38	31	51	–	–		–
P4	–	51	–	–	56	–	–		–
P5									
P6	–	51	51	–	38–50	38–57	63		51–57
P7	–	57	–	51	–	57–63	–		51–57
P8	–	51–76	51	71	–	63–70	51		–

The chine

The ends of floor-timbers 4 to 23, where uncovered, were angled upwards and outwards from the bottom, and the attachment of strakes P5 and S5 to these sloping ends marked the beginning of the sides of the ship. The lower edges of these side strakes, on either side of the bottom of the ship, met the outer edges of strakes P4 and S4 to form an internal chine angle of about 150 degrees at floor-timber 8 (Fig 27). There was no evidence that the chines had been protected from wear by the addition of any extra timbers.

The angle of each chine was determined by the angled ends of the floor-timbers. The chine or angle between the bottom and the sides of the ship became pronounced aft of about floor-timber 4, near the bow, and was found to extend fully formed as far aft as floor-timber 24, beyond which the relevant strakes had been destroyed.

Side planking

The collapsed port side consisted of four wide strakes, P6, P7, P8, and P9 (see Table 3), each about 50mm thick (Fig 40). These were fastened to the side-frames by hooked iron nails which were identical to those used in the floor-timbers, except that the hollow nail heads were fully cone-shaped (Fig 35).

Caulking between planks

The seams between the planks in the bottom of the ship were as much as 6–12mm wide, and contained a caulking of hazel shavings (*Corylus avellana*; see Appendix 3) which, although they did not appear to include any tar, did in fact contain traces of pine resin (Appendix 4). These shavings, which lay crosswise in each seam (Fig 29), and were not distorted as would have occurred had

Table 3 Measured widths of side planking

plank	width	position
P6	0.571m	Between SF 5 and SF 6
P7	0.311m	Between SF 1 and SF 2
P8	0.311m	Between SF 2 and SF 3
P9	0.387m	Between SF 6 and SF 7

they been driven into the seam, so it would appear that the caulking had been applied to a plank edge before the next plank was fastened in position. The fact that the pine resin was not visible indicates that the quantity was small, as would be appropriate to its use as an adhesive. It seems that the resin and the shavings had been applied in alternate layers to the edge of each plank, particularly as the edges of the planks forming the seams were simply cut straight and were not otherwise shaped to hold the caulking. The angle of the plank edges at the chines relative to the plank faces was not recorded, but it seems that the planks butted up to each other. It was not clear how high up the side of the ship caulking was used.

A wooden mallet (Fig 71b), roughly carved from the branch of a tree, was found between floor-timbers 5 and 6 in the bottom of the ship. It was of oak, and had some bark adhering to it. Since the hitting surface was not pitted, as would have occurred if it had been used with metal nails or even wooden pegs, it seems possible that it was used to apply the caulking.

Frames

All the side-frames, and floor-timbers 1 and 2 at the bow which required a strong curving form, were fashioned

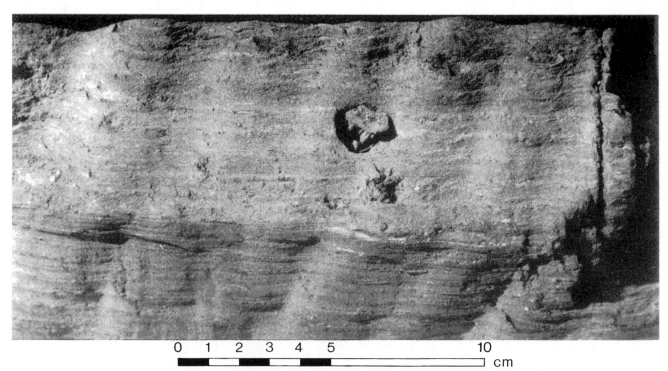

0 1 2 3 4 5   10 cm

Fig 26 Plank from Blackfriars ship 1 containing a small peg of uncertain purpose. Both ends of the peg are flush with the plank faces, so it served no purpose in the completed ship.

Fig 27   The port side of Blackfriars ship 1 looking forward, with the ends of floor-timbers 3–7 (right), and the lower ends of the side-frames (left). Note the chine between planks P4 and P5. Scale in feet.

Fig 28   Excavating the mast-step frame FT7 from Blackfriars ship 1. Scale in feet.

Fig 29   Edge of a bottom plank from Blackfriars ship 1, with the caulking in position, outboard face at bottom.

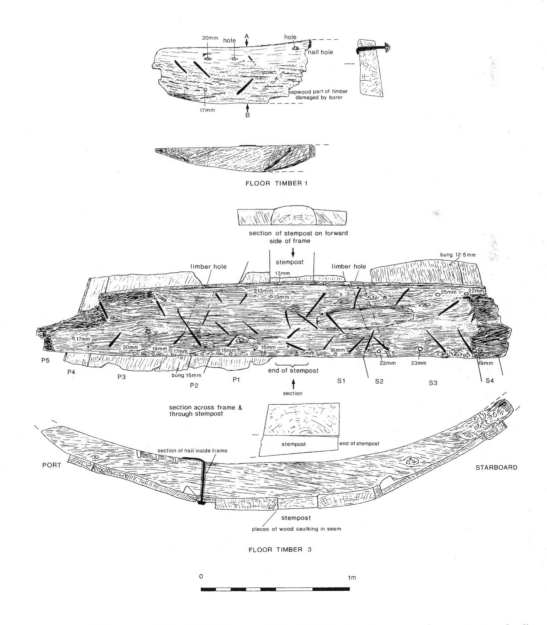

Fig 30   Floor-timbers 1 and 3 as recorded in 1963. The top of the individual section across the stempost and adjacent keel-planks as drawn is the outboard face. The stippling represents sapwood.

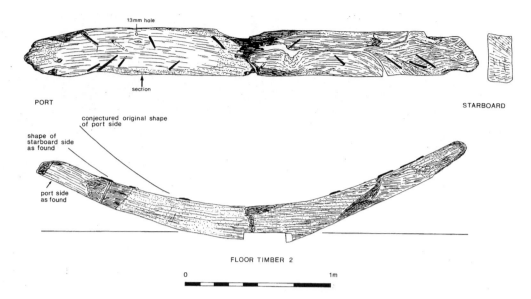

Fig 31   Floor-timber 2 as drawn in 1963. The stippling represents sapwood.

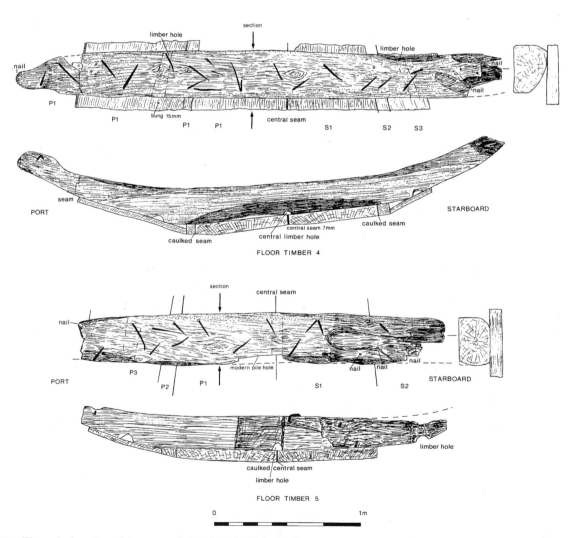

Fig 32   Floor-timbers 4 and 5 as recorded in 1963. The stippling represents sapwood.

from curved parts of trees (Fig 35). In contrast the main floor-timbers on the flat bottom of the ship tended to be shaped from substantial, relatively straight logs. The shipwright did not remove all the sapwood, although the bark had been stripped off, but he did place the rounded sides of the tree boles forming floor-timbers 3 and 4 on the underside next to the bottom planking, leaving the visible upper surface of the frames with a squared-off finish, even though this might weaken the support for the planking below (eg plank P1 below floor-timber 4). In one instance (floor-timber 8) part of a branch was included in forming the end of the frame (Fig 34).

Floor-timbers

The floor-timbers had generally been grouped in pairs in the main part of the ship (Fig 36) (see Table 4), and most of those that were uncovered were about 0.3m wide and 0.21m deep (see Table 5). Only floor-timbers 1 to 8 were available to be drawn in detail, since they alone were lifted (Figs 30–4). Of these, floor-timbers 3 to 8 were each found to contain semi-circular limber holes (about 50mm wide and 50mm high) in their undersides for the flow of bilge water. Floor-timber 3 had two limber holes, one on each side of the central axis of the ship, while floor-timbers 4 to 8 contained three, one on each side

some distance from the central seam and one actually over the central seam of the ship. As these holes occurred in the undersides of the floor-timbers they must have been cut before the frames were fastened to the planking.

Floor-timbers 1 and 2 overlay hooked nails which had fastened strakes P3 and S3 to the stempost (Figs 34 and 37). Floor-timber 2 was only 0.3m wide, and had been subject to some flattening after the ship sank (Fig 31). This was particularly noticeable on the port side when compared with the starboard side. The position of this timber has been carefully reassessed in view of its disturbance by a modern pile, for there is some doubt about its exact position relative to the adjacent frames.

Floor-timber 1 was wider than floor-timber 2, and tapered to a wedge-shaped end on the port side when seen from the after side. The broken starboard end was presumably of similar shape. It seems likely that the greater width of floor-timber 1 and its wedge shaped end(s) are due to its function as the first such timber in the bow.

Along the upper faces of floor-timbers 1 and 3 (Figs 37 and 38) were rows of empty vertical holes 19mm in diameter, extending through the thickness of the frames, but not into the strakes beneath (Fig 30). As two of these holes were exposed in the forward face of floor-timber 3,

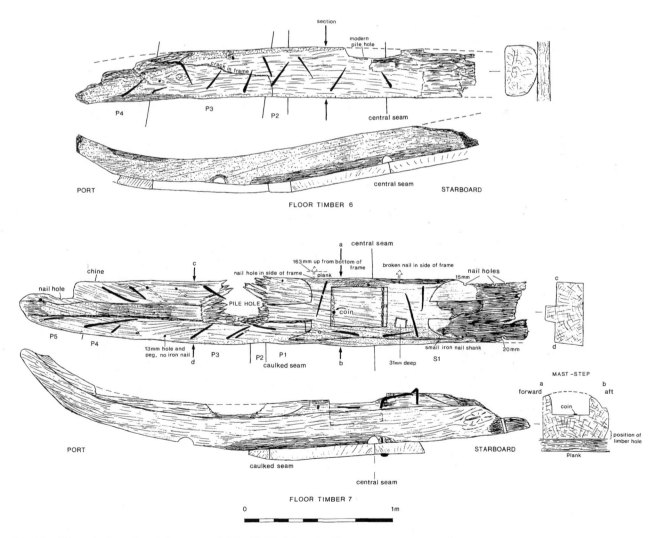

Fig 33 Floor-timbers 6 and 7 as recorded in 1963. The stippling represents sapwood.

Table 4 Frame spacing recorded in the ship

*	– FT1	0.559m	SF1	– SF2	0.406m
FT1	– FT2	0.343?	SF2	– SF3	0.317
FT2	– FT3	0.279?	SF3	– SF4	0.279
FT3	– FT4	0.216	SF4	– SF5	0.394
FT4	– FT5	0.178	SF5	– SF6	0.190
FT5	– FT6	0.190	SF6	– SF7	0.102
FT6	– FT7	0.381	SF7	– SF8	0.406
FT7	– FT8	0.114	SF8	– SF9	0.190
FT8	– FT9	0.356	SF9	– SF10	0.508
FT9	– FT10	0.216	SF10	– SF11	0.279
FT10	– FT11	0.317			
FT11	– FT12	0.152			
FT12	– FT13	0.292			
FT19	– FT20	0.267			
FT23	– FT24	0.229			

* denotes limit of excavation, and no frame found

presumably when that timber was finally shaped, it seems unlikely that they ever actually served any useful purpose in the ship. However, as they followed the frame edge not only in floor-timber 3 but also in the forward face of side-frame 8 (Fig 35) it seems likely that the holes were used as a guide to shaping the frames.

Side-frames

Although only the collapsed port side could be studied in detail (Fig 35), there is good reason to believe that the starboard side was similarly constructed and shaped, since it too had collapsed and its cross-section was photographed and partly drawn in 1963 (Figs 39 and 40). The port side-frames were 0.102–0.127m thick (moulding), and 0.152–0.241m in width (siding), and naturally curved timbers were chosen to match the required shape (see Table 5). One side-frame on the starboard side between floor-timbers 4 and 5 measured 0.216m wide (siding), and 0.101m thick (moulding).

In two instances, between floor-timbers 2 and 3 and between floor-timbers 3 and 4 (Fig 41), there were found traces of the iron nails which had originally held the lower ends of two of the side-frames to strake P5. They were not noted at the lower ends of other side-frames as there was insufficient time for such detailed study. This overlap of the outer ends of the floor-timbers and the lower ends of the side-frames, both being attached to strake 5, was very important when considering the building sequence, and in establishing the position of the side of the hull in relation to its bottom. It shows that the lower ends of the side-frames, where not broken, had not been attached to the ends of the floor-timbers, but had orig-

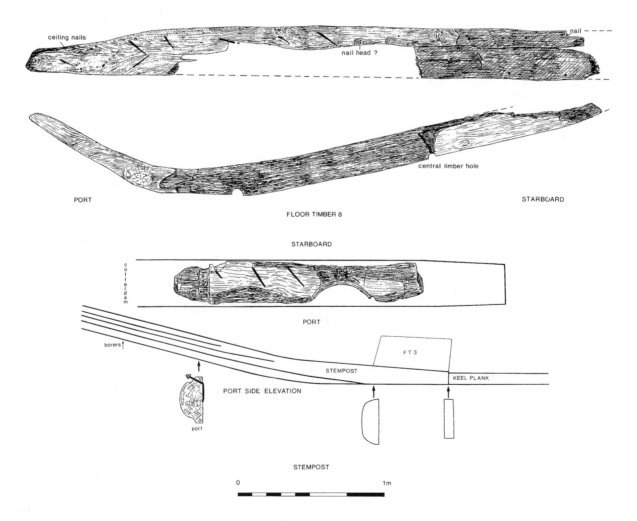

Fig 34 Floor-timber 8 and the stempost, as recorded in 1963. Stippling represents sapwood. Note that the whole outlined area of the stempost was found, but the drawn fragment was all that was saved for detailed recording.

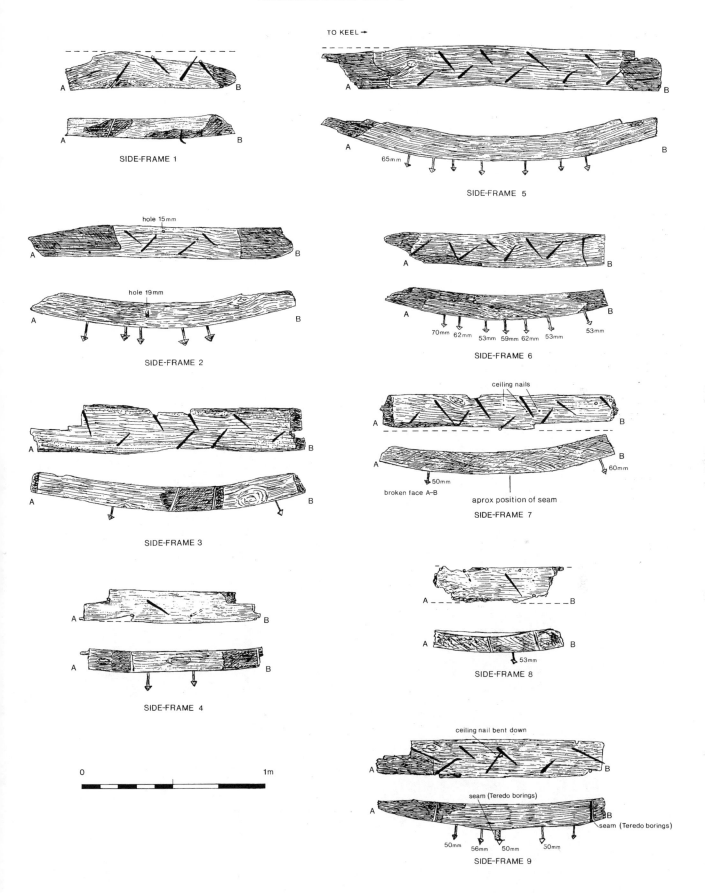

Fig 35   Side-frames 1–9 as recorded in 1963. Stippling represents sapwood. Note that these were only parts of the frames found and recorded on site.

inally been fastened to the lowest side strake P5, between the ends of floor-timbers. The result is that little of the inner surface of strake 5 was not covered by frames.

Strake 5 was the lowest plank of each side of the ship. It was a very important longitudinal strength member, and it is surprising that it was not thicker. As it formed

Table 5   Maximum dimensions of recorded frames

FT	width/ siding	thick/ moulding	port SF	width/ siding	thick/ moulding
1	0.356	0.216	1	0.190	0.102
2	0.305	0.216	2	0.152	0.127
3	0.457	0.229	3	0.241	0.114
4	0.305	0.203	4	0.165	0.102
5	0.317	0.203	5	0.216	0.127
6	0.330	0.216	6	0.178	0.121
7	0.444	0.330	7	0.190	0.114
8	0.317	0.203	8	0.184	0.102
9	0.320		9	0.190	0.114
10	0.330				
12	0.330	0.178			

one side of each chine there must have been considerable stress on the frame fastenings both in a seaway and when running aground. The builder presumably recognised this by overlapping there the ends of the floor timbers and the side frames. In addition the strake also supported the considerable weight of the side of the ship, and it is not surprising that, when the sides collapsed, they broke away from the bottom of the vessel at that point. However, this weakness was probably more apparent than real, for the collapse of the port side must have been a slow process. Side-frame 8 at least had remained attached to strake P5 next to the chine, as well as to the collapsed strakes P6–P9. The frame had been bent out-

wards and downwards, indicating that collapse was gradual and establishing exactly the location of the otherwise detached side relative to the bottom of the ship.

Mast-step floor-timber

Floor-timber 7 (Figs 28 and 30) was presumably fastened into position when the other floor-timbers were nailed to the lowest planking. Although this floor-timber was mostly 0.21m thick, the immediate surround to the mast-step was about 0.089m higher. Cut into its middle was a socket measuring 0.336m long (transverse to the ship's long axis), by 0.25m wide (along the ship's long axis), by 0.127m deep which is believed to have contained the foot of the mast (Fig 43). It is curious that the step lay 0.127m off the central seam of the ship, even though the raised middle part of the floor-timber and its limber hole were placed central to the long axis of the ship. The misplacement of the mast-step socket is so noticeable as to have been clearly deliberate, perhaps to correct a misplacement of the mast fittings at deck level. In this context it may be significant that the builder began to cut out the step in a slightly more central position, but that this was abandoned, thereby leaving a slight ledge on one side. If this interpretation is correct it suggests that the mast-step socket was cut in the frame after much of the hull had been built and when the shipbuilder was ready to step the mast.

On either side of the step, protruding horizontally from the forward face of the frame and about 0.15m above its bottom, were iron nails. One was broken, and

Fig 36   General view of the forward side of Blackfriars ship 1, showing the unfinished millstone in situ (left) and the mast-step (right).

Fig 37   Floor-timber 1 overlying the stempost and adjacent planks.

the other was complete with a cone-shaped head. Between the head of the nail and the face of the timber was a broken piece of oak board about 50mm thick. This seems originally to have continued across the front of the mast-step to the nail on the other side. Its purpose was evidently to strengthen the forward wall of the mast-step which was otherwise only 50mm thick. The restricted space in front of the floor-timber shows that these nails and the board must have been fastened before the frame itself was fastened into position, or before floor-timber 6 was fastened into position. Whichever was the case it indicates that the strengthening to the forward side of the mast-step socket was an original feature of the ship, and not a repair.

Running from the raised middle portion of the mast-step floor-timber 7 to the end of that frame, on the port side, was a median ridge rectangular in section, 0.10m wide and about 89mm higher than the general level of the top of the frame. On the starboard side was the beginning of a comparable ridge, but most of that side had been torn away in 1963 just before the archaeological excavation began. The purpose of these raised ridges is uncertain; the possibility that they held a bulkhead is unlikely due to the absence of nails, nail holes, or any other sign of fittings in the ridges. Consequently it is probable that their purpose was to add strength to the frame, acting as a girder, while minimising weight.

The coin in the mast-step

A worn bronze coin (*as*) of the emperor Domitian (Fig 45), minted in Rome in AD 88 or 89 (Mattingley and Sydenham 1926, Domitian 371), was found in a recess on the port side of the bottom of the mast-step socket (Fig 44). It lay reverse uppermost and originally would have touched the foot of the mast. This appears to have been significant, for the reverse of the coin had a representation of Fortuna, goddess of luck, holding a ship's rudder. The coin was considerably worn through having been in circulation, and it had presumably been chosen for its appropriate reverse type in the hope that it would bring good fortune to the ship. Since coins have not been found in the mast-steps of other Romano-Celtic ships from central and northern Europe, or in Scandinavian ships of the first millennium AD, it is likely that the luck coin ceremony was introduced from the Mediterranean. Coins have been found in classical shipwrecks, one of the earliest known examples being in the Chretienne 'A' wreck of the first half of the first century BC (Dumas 1964, 121, pl 52; Casson 1971, 232; Gassend *et al* 1984). It is interesting to note that the tradition of placing a coin in the construction of a ship still exists in certain countries, including Britain (Marsden 1965b).

Stanchions

On each side of the mast-step, and cut into the after side

Fig 38   Floor-timbers 2–4, with the millstone in situ. Floor-timber 2 (left) has been broken and displaced by a modern steel pile. Scale in feet.

of its raised surround, was a small socket about 76mm square and 31mm deep. They appear to be mortices into which were fitted tenons at the base of upright stanchions. These stanchions may have helped to support the deck construction around the mast, but as there was an extra side-frame (side-frame 6) on the port side of the ship, level with the mast-step timber which evidently strengthened the side at that point, it is just possible that they were supports for a bulkhead of transverse planks at the forward end of the hold. However, as there were no nails or nail holes in the sides of side-frames 5 and 6 which could have fastened the ends of the suggested bulkhead planking this interpretation is unlikely. Also, a

millstone lying on the floor-timbers forward of the mast-step frame was most likely lowered into the ship's hold and rolled over the frames to its final position, again suggesting that there was no bulkhead. It is more likely, therefore, that the stanchions supported the after sides of a mast-beam at deck level, whose port end was at least partly supported by side-frame 6 and whose starboard end was presumably partly supported by a comparable side-frame.

Fastenings

The massive hooked iron nails which attached the bottom planks to the floor-timbers varied in length but not in shape (Fig 46). The head of each was partly in the form of a hollow cone with sloping sides but was flattened on top (a semi-cone-headed nail) and about 30–50mm across. Although most of the nail shank was circular in section and 17mm in diameter, about 10mm of the length of the pointed end was square in section (Fig 47).

Before the nails were driven through the floor-timbers and side-frames, holes mostly about 19mm in diameter had first been drilled vertically through the frames, and an oak peg inserted in each (Fig 48.1). One such pegged hole, 13mm in diameter, in floor-timber 7 did not have a nail and illustrated this stage. These broad holes may have been of the minimum size which a narrow auger could drill across the grain and through a considerable thickness of oak without breaking. Normally 2–5 nails attached each plank to each frame (see Table 6), generally towards the fore and aft sides of the frames. After the pegs had been inserted it seems that a hole less than the diameter of each nail (17mm) was then drilled, from inside the ship, down the centre of each peg and then out through the external planking (Fig 48.2). It was only possible to position the hole in the frame and in the planking by drilling the hole from inside the ship. The iron nail was then driven in from outside the ship, so that the rim of its head was hard against the outer surface of the planking as if to make a reasonably watertight joint (Figs 48.3 and 48.4). The nails were remarkably functional, the hollow cone heads having been designed to contain a caulking of thin slivers of hazel wood (Fig 52), originally held in place with a small amount of pine resin, which made it watertight (Appendices 3 and 4). The shanks of the nails were circular in section to fit the holes drilled in the pegs in the floor-timber and, with the caulking-filled head, gave a tight fit and stopped seepage. About half the length of each nail shank was initially left projecting out of the upper surface of the floor-timber,

but of this only the point, which was square in section, had been bent at a right-angle to the shank (Fig 48.4). The rest of the upstanding shank was also bent through 90 degrees and hammered down against the upper surface of the floor-timber so that only the point of the nail was embedded in the wood (Fig 48.5). The purpose of this technique was to anchor the inner end of each nail so that it could not be pulled out. The general practice in the Blackfriars ship was to turn the nails towards the central longitudinal axis of the vessel, and also from the outer parts of the frames towards their centres. The purpose of this was probably to avoid splitting the floor-timbers.

The effort involved in manufacturing (see Appendix 2), driving, and turning these nails must have been considerable, for the longest nail noted (in floor-timber 3) was 0.736m from head to point. There were about 27–34 nails in each floor-timber (see Table 6) and it is estimated that there were about seven hundred nails to be fastened into the floor-timbers of the ship as a whole. When the ship was completed it is likely that about 1500 nails were used. Several examples of nails which were fastened to the floor-timbers and side-frames were weighed, and as a rough average each floor-timber nail weighed about 500g and each side-frame nail weighed about 340g. By multiplying these weights by the estimated total number of nails of each type it seems that the ship probably contained about 350kg of floor-timber nails of the semi-cone-shaped type, and about 272kg of side-frame nails with the cone heads – in all over half a tonne of nails. Although this is only a very rough estimate it does give some indication of the weight of these iron fastenings, and also of the considerable resources and effort put into the making and fastening of the nails.

As well as being nailed to the undersides of the floor-timbers, strakes P3 and S3 were fastened into rabbets on

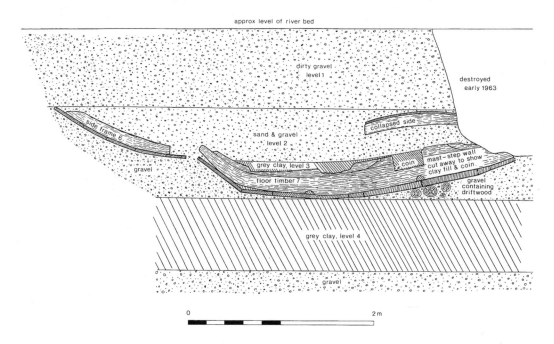

Fig 39 Reconstructed section across Blackfriars ship 1, showing the inward collapsed starboard side (right) and the outward collapsed port side (left).

Fig 40   The collapsed port side, looking aft. Note the stones of the cargo overlying the collapsed side.

either side of the stempost by cone-headed iron nails. These hooked nails had been driven through the strakes from outside the ship and through the sides of the stempost at an angle, and had been bent over the inner face of the stempost so that their points were embedded in the wood. Floor-timbers 1 and 2 overlaid these hooked

nails and had clearly been fastened in place after the strakes had been nailed to the stempost.

The method of fastening planks to the side-frames resembled that used in the floor-timbers, except that the hollow heads of the hooked nails were completely cone-shaped (Figs 47 and 48). In almost every instance the

Fig 41   The port ends of floor-timbers 3 (top right) to 5. The bottom of the collapsed side is top left. Note the broken end of a nail in the plank between floor-timbers 4 and 5. This originally held the lower end of a side-frame. Scale in feet.

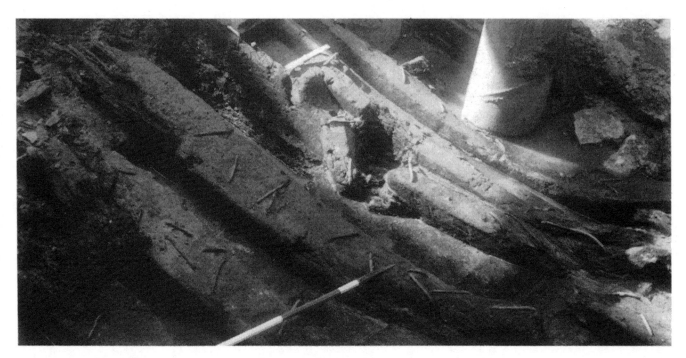

Fig 42　Blackfriars ship 1 looking aft, showing the mast-step. Scale in feet.

point of each nail had been bent downwards and towards the centre of the side-frame, presenting a herring-bone pattern on the inboard face of the frame. Surprisingly, the pointed heads of the cone-shaped nails used in the side-frames had little or no evidence of being hammered into the planking and the frames, as if the nail had offered little resistance when hammered into place. This was investigated by sectioning a nail (see Appendix 2), and suggests that each nail head had been covered by a wooden or metal block or 'dolly' that was recessed to the

Fig 43　The mast-step in floor-timber 7, looking aft. Note the mortice hole for a stanchion beside the step, and the votive coin in the step. Scale of one foot.

Fig 44   Close-up of the votive coin in situ in the mast-step, showing the reverse with Fortuna holding a rudder.

shape of the nail head so as to leave each head undamaged when being driven into place.

Stempost and sternpost

The lower end of the stempost was slotted into a recess cut into the forward end of the two thick keel-planks. At that point the stempost was rectangular in section and 0.266m wide and 76mm thick, so that its upper and lower faces were level with the upper and lower faces of the keel-planks. As the stempost curved upwards, the rectangular section rapidly developed a flat inboard surface and a rounded outboard surface, with a rabbet on each side into which the planking was fastened (Fig 34). The stempost had a maximum width of 0.3m and a thickness of 0.15m.

The lower end of the stempost was not attached to keel-planks P1 and S1, but was fastened to floor-timber 3 by four or five nails, all but one having been driven from outside the ship and bent over the upper surface of the frame. The exception had been driven from inside the ship leaving its cone-shaped head against the top of the frame. It is not known if it was bent under the stempost or was a spike whose point was wholly buried in that timber. Floor-timber 3 was much wider than any other

frame excavated, presumably because it covered the lower end of the stempost and held it in position.

The sternpost was not so well preserved, only a short length of its lower end being uncovered immediately aft of floor-timber 24 (Fig 50). At that point the sternpost was rectangular in section, like the lower end of the stempost, and was 0.15m. wide and 63mm thick. The start of its upward curve was noted under floor-timber 24, but a loose piece of planking found close to the stern suggested that higher up the planking was fastened into a rabbet in the sternpost (Fig 51).

Ceiling planking

The inner surface of the frames in the central part of the ship immediately aft of the mast was covered by a ceiling of planks 25mm thick, whose purpose was to line the hold and protect the hull from damage by the cargo. Although the weight of the cargo of building stone had broken those planks, there were traces of planking still in situ (Fig 72), and elsewhere there were small iron nails with square shanks in the upper surfaces of the floor-timbers and side-frames, and it is assumed that these had fastened the ceiling planks to the frames. Unfortunately the widths of the surviving ceiling planks could not be established because they had been so badly damaged by the overlying stone. It was noticeable that only a small number of nails had fastened the planks to the frames, as if to allow for the easy replacement of damaged planking. The inner curve of the hull indicates that the ceiling planks lay fore and aft.

The forward extent of the ceiling was evidently at the mast-step floor-timber (floor-timber 7), for this had a narrow ledge on its aft side in which was found a small broken nail of the same type and size as those which had apparently held the ceiling planks to the other floor-timbers. This ledge was level with the tops of the amidships floor-timbers, but below the median ridges and the mast-step surround in floor-timber 7. The ceiling

Figs 45a (obverse) and 45b (reverse)   Votive coin of Domitian from the mast-step.

planks therefore could not have extended forward of that ledge.

Small broken iron nails found on the port side-frames indicated that the ceiling planking had formerly extended up the inner sides of the hull from floor-timber 7 aft. One nail, in side-frame 9 (Fig 35), was not broken but had been bent down over one of the hooked iron nails, the distance between the flat head and the surface of the frame being 0.05m – presumably the thickness of the missing ceiling plank at that point.

Reconstruction of the ship

The aims of the reconstruction

As a considerable amount of the ship had survived to be excavated and recorded, an attempt to make a hypothetical reconstruction of the vessel is justified. A limited number of alternative reconstructions are possible but the aim has been to find a minimal solution with as little conjecture as possible. Moreover, as the ship was a working vehicle an essential aim is to assess how it might have functioned, looking particularly at its stability, sailing, steering, draught, cargo capacity, and weight, berthing and crew accommodation. The specific objectives of reconstruction, therefore, are to determine its hull shape and weight distribution which gave it stability, its construction which gave its hull strength and made it possible to establish how the vessel was assembled, and its methods of propulsion and steering which helped to control its performance.

Limitations of hull evidence

Certain minimal information about the features of any ship is essential before attempting the reconstruction of a whole vessel, and although exact details may not be known there should at least be some indication of length, form of the ends, midship beam, midship form, height of gunwale amidships, average hull density per square metre, and the distribution of weight. Such information can be either recovered from or postulated for Blackfriars ship 1.

Almost half of the bottom of the hull, including both ends, was excavated and recorded, making possible a reconstruction of the unexcavated lower parts of the hull. Substantial portions of both sides had also survived, in a collapsed state, to give a large amount of the hull shape in cross-section amidships, though the upper part of both ends, and the deck and gunwale were not found. As the quality of the evidence is so variable it is necessary to consider the reconstruction in stages: with the bottom, the sides, the bow and stern, the height of the deck and gunwale, and finally the superstructure, propulsion, and steering.

Reconstruction is not simply a process of 'filling in' the missing parts, for not only had the sides collapsed but also elements of the hull had suffered distortion. For example, the lower end of side-frame 8 (port) had remained attached to strake P5, while its upper end was

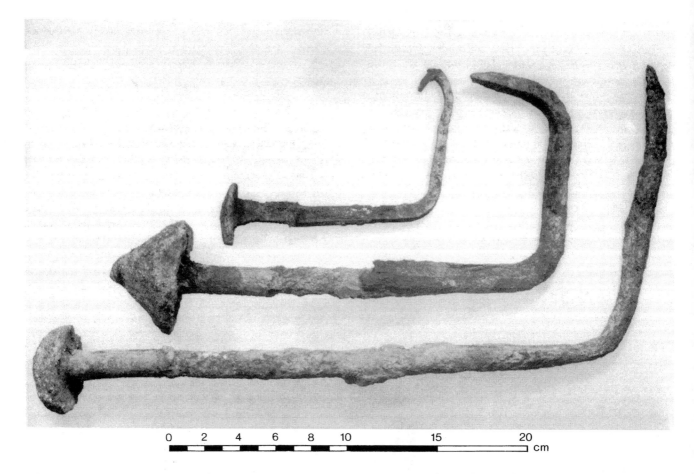

Fig 46 Nails that held the planks to the frames in the New Guy's House boat (top), Blackfriars ship 1 side planking (middle), and Blackfriars ship 1 bottom planking (bottom).

Table 6 Hooked nails per plank

frame plank	bow FT1	FT2	FT3	FT4	FT5	FT6	FT7	midships FT8
S4	0	2	1	(2)	(2)	(2)	(2)	(2)
S3	(8)	3	5	5	(4)	(4)	(4)	(4)
S2	–	(2)	2	1	2	(2)	2	(2)
S1	–	(4)	4	3	4	(3)	4	(3)
P1	–	(4)	5	6	3	2	4	(3)
P2	–	(2)	(2)	2	2	1	(2)	(2)
P3	(8)	5	6	4	4	7	8?	(5)
P4	0	3?	2?	1	(2)	2	4	4?
P5	1	(2)	(2)	(2)	(2)	(3)	2	5

Frame Plank	SF1	SF2	SF3	SF4	SF5	SF6	SF7	SF8	SF9
P6	3?	(3)	3+	4	4	2	6	5	3
P7	(3)	2	4	1	3	3	3	4	3
P8	(2)	2	1	3	2	2	1	(3)	(3)

( ) signifies an estimate

still attached to the collapsed strakes of that side. The frame had been bent outwards and downwards. The port side of the bow was also a little distorted by flattening compared with the starboard side (Figs 30 and 31)

which was less deeply buried, and is reflected in the shapes of floor-timbers 2 and 3.

Parameters for the reconstruction

There is a considerable degree of certainty about the main dimensions of the ship. Since the distance between the foot of the stem and sternposts is known (*c*11.3m), the overall hull length of the ship can be estimated fairly closely from the upward curves of the stem and stern-posts (*c*18.5m). Moreover, as the width and form of the bottom is also known at almost its greatest dimension, and the first strake of the sides (strake 5) was still in position to enable the collapsed side to be repositioned, it is possible to reconstruct the beam of the hull fairly accurately to about 6.12m.

How the reconstruction is achieved

Although Blackfriars ship 1 is of the Roman period its construction is very different from the Roman ships of the Mediterranean tradition. Consequently it is import-ant not to be influenced by the forms of Mediterranean ships when making a reconstruction. An attempted rec-onstruction was published in 1967 (Marsden 1967, 24–8) when there was no adequate means of testing its validity. It is now clear that this entailed reforming the discovered timbers of the bow beyond what was possible, and therefore the 1967 reconstruction is rejected.

The first objective in reconstructing the vessel is to establish the original shape and size of the discovered remains, from which the form of the missing parts can be conjectured on the relatively firm basis of what is known. This is initially achieved by drawing sections along and across the hull as found (Fig 53), and by identifying those parts that were damaged so that their original form may be restored as accurately as possible. The process of reconstruction here has been assisted by a computer program called Boatcad, used by modern boatbuilders for designing and undertaking theoretical stability tests on new boats. This enables the shape of discovered parts of ancient ships to be read into the program and allows for alternative reconstructions of the missing parts to be made easily. It is then possible to test the theoretical stability, and therefore the validity, of these alternatives on the assumption that the ship was originally stable.

Shape

Reconstructing the hull bottom

The most complete part of the surviving hull was its bottom up to strake 5. This included a large part of the forward half of the ship, with the lower part of the stempost, a portion of the starboard side amidships, two small areas of the sides of the bottom near the stern, and finally the lower end of the sternpost with its adjacent planking.

It was possible to link these pieces together and identify the strakes with a reasonable degree of confidence for

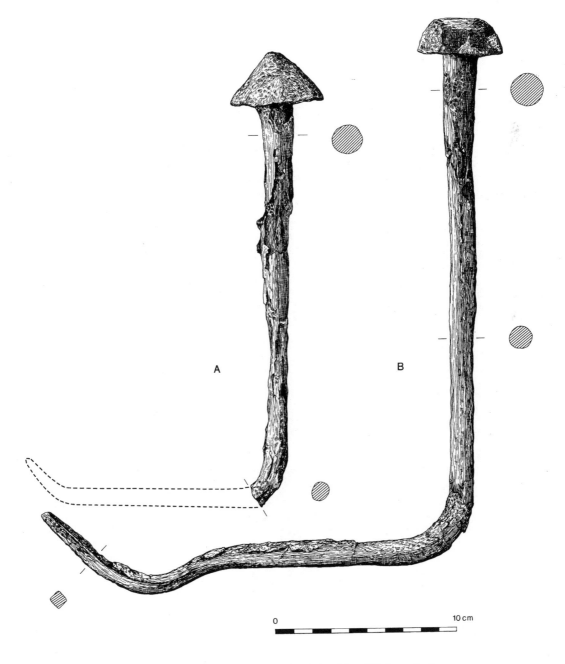

0   10 cm

Fig 47   Hooked nails from Blackfriars ship 1; (A) from the side of the ship; (B) from the bottom.

the following reasons: firstly, as the two thick central keel-planks P1 and S1 gave the ship longitudinal strength, they must, like the similar keel-planks in the St. Peter Port ship (Rule 1990), have extended from the foot of the stempost, which was discovered, to the foot of the sternpost, whose lower part (but not the extreme lower end) was also excavated (Fig 23). Secondly, as the remaining bottom planks were thinner, the narrow linking plank 2, c76mm thick on the edge next to the keel-plank and c50mm thick on the other edge next to the remaining bottom planks, is presumed to have run along much of the length of the keel-planks. Thirdly, the chine or varying angle between strakes 4 and 5 was noted in all excavated portions of the sides of the ship's bottom, extending from floor-timber 5 aft to floor-timber 24. This chine is particularly important in making it possible to identify these strakes and link together different recorded sections of the ship. These indicate that strake 4 was very narrow at the bow and broad at the stern, giving the plank a distinctive curving shape. This was the converse of strake 3, which was apparently broad at the bow and narrowed towards the stern. The shape of strakes 3 and 4, on each side of the ship, broad at one end and narrow at the other, would have been particularly suited to the conversion of a large single tree with a natural taper from the butt to the crown, and would explain why no scarf joints were seen in the planking, though scarfs could have been overlaid by frames.

The first step was to use the records of the vessel *in situ* and the drawings of the timbers that had been raised, to draw detailed long- and cross-sections of the ship as it was found in the coffer-dam. The drawings made of the ship *in situ* when excavated in 1963 included a longitudinal profile of the vessel as exposed in the coffer-dam, and also a cross profile at floor-timber 7 (Figs 53 and 54). These showed the relationship of timbers to each other, and once the stempost and frames had been raised it was possible to reconstruct the shape of the vessel as found, but lying horizontally instead of heeled over. On this basis a central longitudinal profile of the entire ship was drawn (Fig 23), based on the assumption that the keel-planks were horizontal throughout the length of the ship, as indeed they were between floor-timbers 3 and 8.

Since, for stability reasons, the shape of the port and starboard sides must have been similar, it was only necessary to reconstruct the shape of the side that was best preserved, in this case the port side, but using the remains of the other side as a check against error. The cross-sections were drawn at the after faces of floor-timbers 2–8, and a cross-profile at floor-timber 23. A further cross-section was reconstructed at about the forward face of floor-timber 1, with the angle of the planks, of known width, being based upon the rabbet angle that was found in the stempost (Figs 55 and 56).

The resulting picture of the vessel as found shows the hull bottom with small irregularities. These were caused by erosion of the plank edges, particularly the top of P5 between the ends of floor-timbers 3–5 where it was exposed to the flow of the river after the forward end of the ship had been washed away, by the lack of some precise measurements taken on site due to the necessary speed of archaeological work in the rescue conditions, and by the difficulty of reconstructing the exact transverse inclination of some cross-sections. It was not possible in the time available to record any plank edge bevels at the chine.

There are several clues to what the lower hull of the port side was like originally. Although the port half of floor-timbers 2 and 3 show clear evidence of having been flattened because the port side was more deeply buried than the starboard side, that distortion can be corrected

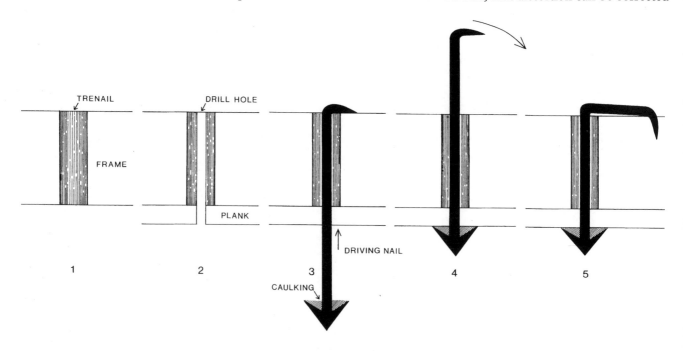

Fig 48   Reconstruction of the stages in fastening the hooked nails in Blackfriars ship 1. Not to scale.

Fig 49   Section through alluvial deposits under the collapsed starboard side, showing grey silt below ground. The ingress of gravel presumably represents when the sides began collapsing. Scale in feet.

by comparing the shape of the port side with that of the starboard side, which was probably closer to the original. The angle of the port side and its planks can be adjusted to fit (Fig 55).

However, when plotted on side and forward end elevations of the ship it was noted that the run of the plank seams between floor-timbers 4 and 8 were insufficient to allow the planks to meet the stempost. In fact it seems that the bow had been a little flattened relative to the rest of the ship. It was therefore necessary to deepen these profiles slightly to accord with the rest of the ship. Although this was necessary to make sense of the remains of the ship, it was considered that as much as possible of the shape of the timbers as found should be retained, and that 'correcting' any possible distortion should only be carried out when absolutely necessary.

The next step was to remove certain irregularities by identifying the broken plank edges from photographs and drawings and filling them in. The three guides were the existing undamaged seams of planks still lying edge-to-edge which enable missing portions to be calculated, the knowledge that when building the ship the shipwright would have ensured that the seams between planks would run in curving lines towards the ends, as would a modern shipbuilder, and that the shipbuilder would also shape the underwater hull so as to offer as little longitudinal resistance to the water as was compatible with the use of the vessel. The process of smoothing out a hull is called 'fairing', and in this study it was done by making

minimum alterations to the discovered intact plank widths, while allowing for eroded plank edges.

Reconstructing the hull sides

The collapsed port side up to strake 9 was then reconstructed in relation to the bottom. The actual fore-and-aft position of that side relative to the bottom was established by side-frame 8 which still remained attached both to strake P5 and to the collapsed side. This was done by comparing the outboard vertical curvature of side-frames 1–9 to establish whether or not they varied. There was found to be no significant variation (Fig 35). Since the lower ends of the side-frames overlapped the outer ends of the floor-timbers over strake 5, this strake was therefore attached to both, and as the outer ends of the floor-timbers had formed the angle at which strake 5 lay relative to the bottom, this gave the angle at which the side had to be reconstructed onto the bottom.

The profile of the ship as reconstructed at this stage at floor-timbers 7 and 8 shows a vessel with flared sides (Fig 56), but it is not clear how much of this flaring is due to a flattening of the hull sides. As floor-timbers 2 and 3 show that their port sides had been a little flattened (Fig 55), it seemed likely that there had been a similar amount of distortion on the same side near the middle of the ship at floor-timbers 7 and 8. By allowing for this flattening the angle of strake 5 at floor-timbers 7 and 8 was adjusted slightly to become more upright, and when the collapsed side was reconstructed on the bottom it was found that the flaring of the sides was removed.

The position of the hold

The hold lay amidships and was originally lined with ceiling planks which had been mostly destroyed, but small nails on the inboard faces of the frames which had fastened the ceiling indicated the original extent of the forward part of the hold. These show that the sides of the hold were so lined probably up to the deck level, suggesting that it was sometimes intended to fill the hold with cargo.

The forward end of the hold was situated on a ledge on the after face of floor-timber 7, and this was positioned about 2.3m forward of the central longitudinal point of the ship as reconstructed, and about 3.3m forward of the central point of the keel between the lower ends of the stem and stern posts.

The after extent of the hold was not established, but for reasons of stability it is presumed that the cargo was placed centrally to give the ship an even keel. On the basis of the length of the ship as reconstructed with unequal shapes at the ends the hold would be 4.6m long, but on the basis of the length of keel between stempost and sternpost the hold would be 6.68m long. As it is not possible to judge which hold length is correct the capacity calculations are based upon the average between the two lengths, about 5.7m, and show that the after end of the hold lay at about floor-timber 18. On this basis the hold would have occupied about 30% of the total hull length.

Fig 50   The stern, with the lower end of the sternpost, looking forward. Scale in feet.

Fig 51   Loose pieces of plank found at the stern. Note the nail and ?caulking indicating that it was probably fastened to a rabbet in the sternpost. Scale in feet.

Reconstructing the deck and gunwale

The reconstruction of the hold position is an important indicator of the extent of the deck, and although there are great uncertainties about the deck and gunwale heights and the form of the upper ends of the ship, the range of possibilities is limited. It is necessary to examine each of these in turn.

Strake 9 survived to a higher point than any other, and, when added to the reconstructed ship's bottom, it showed that the sides near amidships must have extended originally at least to 2.16m from the bottom of the hull, (ie more than 1.84m above the ceiling planks lining the bottom of the hold). With sides of this height the Blackfriars vessel must have had a deck of some form

rather than have been a fully 'open boat'. Allowing for the deck beams and planks, the minimum height of such a deck must have been about 2.15m above the hull bottom. Moreover, it is likely, for reasons of safety, that the sides continued above the deck as bulwarks, so it is suggested here that the gunwale, the uppermost longitudinal strengthening timber of the side, could have been about 0.7m above the deck. This level is based upon 0.68m in the Laurons ship (Gassend *et al* 1984), and 0.7m in the County Hall ship (p 129) in both of which the distance between the deck and the top of the gunwale were found. This would make the minimum height of the side of the Blackfriars ship amidships about 2.85m above the bottom.

A deck at this level could explain why the upper part of the collapsed port and starboard sides were broken at about 2.15m because, as the sides must have been joined by deck-supporting cross beams, these beams could have pulled the sides down in the same direction when they collapsed and caused the upper part of the sides to break off at the point of attachment (Fig 86).

Moreover a deck at about 1.84m above the ceiling of the hold would be at a convenient height to allow the crew to pass light-weight items, such as stores and equipment, by hand from the hold up to the deck. This height is also suggested by the County Hall ship, a vessel of roughly similar size to Blackfriars ship 1, whose deck was found to be about 1.3m above the top of the lowest frames (see Chapter 3), and by the Laurons wreck, southern France, of the second century AD, whose deck height was about 1.5m above its ceiling (Gassend *et al* 1984). The reason for this preferred height is indicated by the study of one hundred male adult skeletons from the Roman cemetery at Trentholme Drive, York, which showed that the average height of a man was then about 1.7m (Royal Commission on Historical Monuments 1962, 110). If the deck had been much above that level it would have been necessary for everything but the

Fig 52   The underside of two cone-headed nail heads (left, 45mm diameter, right, 35mm diameter) showing the caulking of split hazel twigs wound around the nail shank. Analysis of a sample of caulking showed that it included traces of pine resin.

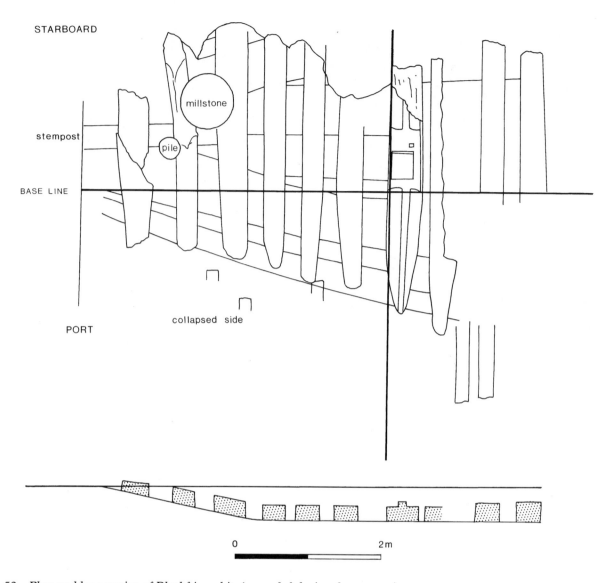

Fig 53   Plan and long-section of Blackfriars ship 1 recorded during the excavation.

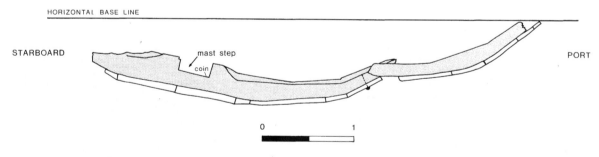

Fig 54   Cross-section of the ship recorded during the excavation.

heaviest items to be carried from the hold by the crew by means of ladders or to be lowered by rope and tackle, perhaps using the yard or shearlegs. Moreover, if the deck had been much higher the weight of the additional superstructure would have increased the draught and decreased the stability of the vessel.

Although none of the deck was found, its extent is in part indicated by the stone cargo and the conjectured extent of the hold amidships, for the weight and shape of the stones were such that they must have been lowered into the hold by some form of crane, rather than been dropped in by chute which would have risked damaging the ceiling

(p 83). This indicates that the deck had a large opening giving access for loading and unloading to various parts of the hold. However, convenience demands that fore and aft walkways probably extended along the edges by the sides of the ship, as occurred in the Laurons ship (Gassend et al 1984). The Laurons ship was about 16.2m long and 5.10m wide amidship, and its hold lay in the centre of the vessel, below a hatch 5.75m long and 3.2m wide, leaving a deck walkway 0.7m wide between the hatch and the side of the ship.

In classical times there were several methods of holding cross-beams to the sides of a ship, by slots in a beam

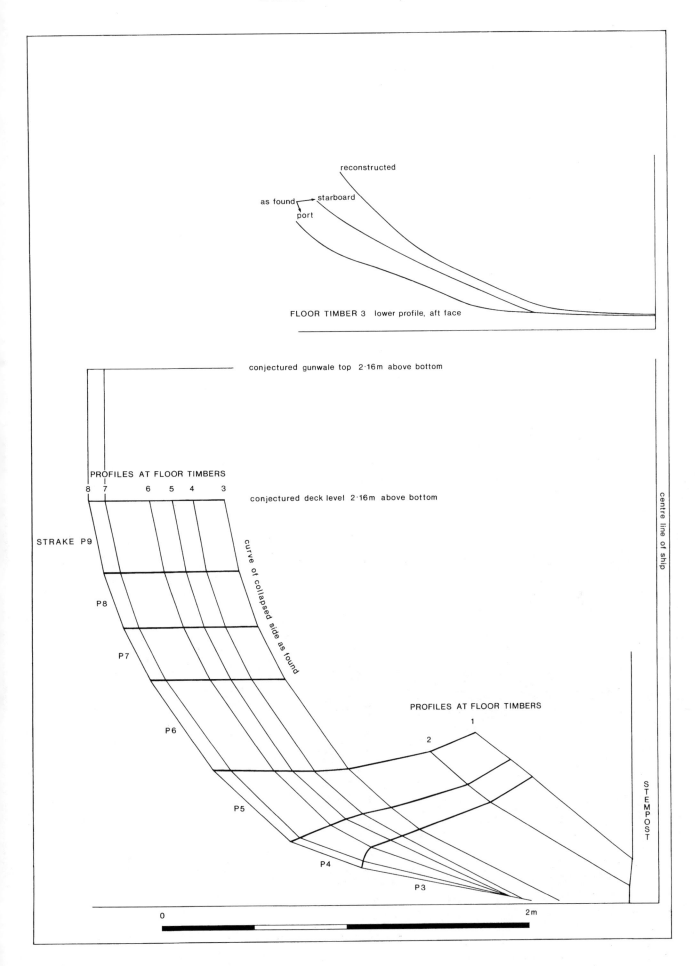

reconstructed

as found → starboard

port

FLOOR TIMBER 3   lower profile, aft face

conjectured gunwale top 2·16m above bottom

PROFILES AT FLOOR TIMBERS

8   7   6   5   4   3   conjectured deck level 2·16m above bottom

STRAKE P9

curve of collapsed side as found

P8

P7

PROFILES AT FLOOR TIMBERS

1

P6   2

P5

P4

P3

centre line of ship

STEMPOST

0   2m

Fig 55   Reconstructed bow elevation of the ship.

shelf, by slots in a wale, and by beam ends projecting out through the sides of a ship (Casson 1971, 210; Throckmorton 1987, 95; Gassend *et al* 1987). But these were all used in Mediterranean ships, and there is no evidence to suggest which method was used in Romano-Celtic

ships. Knees were used for this task in the medieval period and there is possible evidence that they were similarly used in Blackfriars ship 1.

This loose knee-shaped timber 0.114m square (Fig 57), found in the debris of the collapsed forward part of

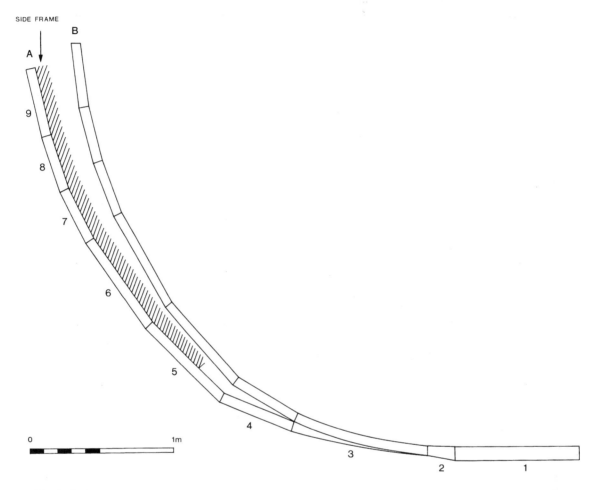

Fig 56   (A) Port side profile of the ship from the shape of the frames as found. (B) Adjusted profile of the ship to allow for a little flattening of the hull.

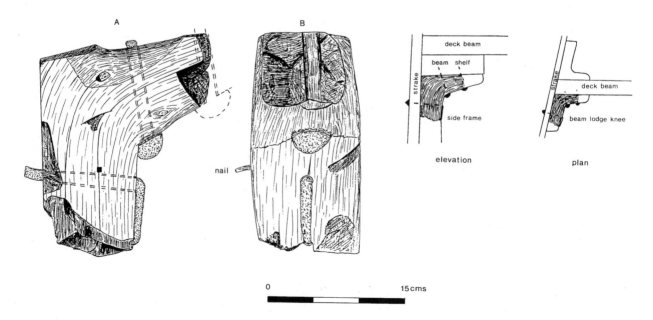

Fig 57   A knee-timber found loose in the wreck, with two possible alternative reconstructions of its use.

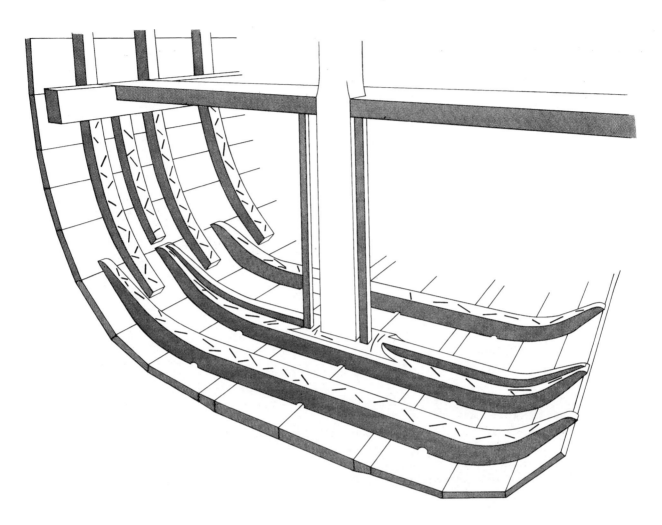

Fig 58   Reconstruction of the interior of Blackfriars ship 1 at the mast-step. The 'ceiling' planking (the boards in the hold that covered the frames) have been omitted, but they lay in the foreground up to the mast frame.

the vessel, could have been one of the supports for a system of deck beams, shelves or stringers, upon which a decking was laid. It had two adjacent flat surfaces forming an angle of 97°, as if it had been attached to two other flat timber surfaces. A nail, with its head and part of its shank broken off, had been driven through a trenail in the knee and bent against one face as if it had been fastened to the hull planking. In the other angle there was another broken nail with a cone-shaped head which had also been driven through a trenail in the timber, and about 0.05m from it was the hole left by another which had a similar cone-shaped head, as was shown by the mark left by its rim in the surface of the wood. It is possible that this timber was the upper end of a side-frame terminating in a knee to support a deck beam, though it is rather small compared with the discovered side-frames. It seems more likely, therefore, that this was perhaps a hanging knee or a lodging knee.

Further evidence of deck structure is suggested by two mortice holes cut in the mast-step frame beside the aft side of the mast. These presumably held tenons at the base of stanchions that supported a transverse mast-beam (Fig 58). This is also indicated by the extra side-frame 8, in line with the mast-step frame, which is best explained as part of the support for the end of the

mast beam. The main purpose of a mast-beam would be to help transfer the propulsive force of the sail and other stresses from the mast to the hull (McGrail 1987, 224). The position of the stanchions and this side-frame suggests that the mast was set into a recess cut in the after face of the mast-beam, as in the mast-beam of Zwammerdam ship 4 (de Weerd 1988, 149, 152).

Reconstructing the bow

A reconstruction of the ship published in 1967 (Marsden 1967, 24–5) envisaged that the bow had been considerably flattened by vertical pressure after the ship had sunk, and that the stempost was originally sharply curved upwards in longitudinal section, with a deep internal V-section across the bow. However, this deep V-section is much deeper than the angle of the rabbets in the stempost, and it is impossible to form that bow shape on the computer reconstruction from the remains without distorting the planks beyond the bounds of what is possible with wood. It is clear, therefore, that the 1967 reconstruction must be rejected.

The top surface of the stempost was found gently sloping upwards over a distance of 2.34m, its lowest edge rising at an angle of about 15 degrees to horizontal over a distance of 1.25m (Fig 59). As the adjacent planks had

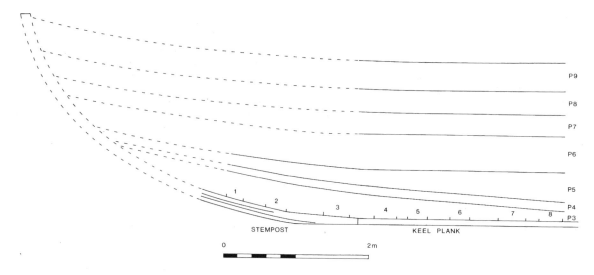

Fig 59   Reconstructed side elevation of the ship, forward.

remained attached to it throughout its length, it is unlikely that the bow had moved far from its original position relative to the bottom planking and the sides. Moreover, the angle of 40° to horizontal at which the strakes joined the stempost below floor-timber 1 is given by the shape of the rabbet in each side, and these too suggest little bow deformation. That some flattening of the bow might have occurred is suggested by the form of floor-timber 2 whose starboard side was not as much flattened as the port side. But had there been any substantial deformation of the stem by flattening, the planks would have become separated from the stem as occurred, for example, in wrecks at Kalmar, Sweden, (Akerlund 1951, plates 4c and 21b) at Skuldelev, Denmark (Olsen and Crumlin-Pedersen 1967, 96–7), and at Red Bay, Labrador (Grenier 1988, 71).

It is necessary, therefore, to determine the minimum reconstruction of the upper part of the bow to establish its most likely original shape, and two alternative solutions are suggested. The first is that the stempost curved a little more steeply upwards beyond the point at which it was found (Fig 60a), the height of the deck, as deduced above, placing limits on how far it was practical to extend a conventional bow in this reconstruction. The second is that the stempost was the base of a protruding forefoot or ram-like bow which supported an upright stem to which the upper planks were fastened (Fig 60b). This latter solution presents a problem of shipbuilding technique, for it is unclear how the upper part of the hull could be constructed and supported over the forefoot where no fittings for a vertical stempost were found. This problem cannot be resolved on the existing evidence. The theory that the forefoot was a feature of pre-Roman Celtic ships, as represented on Iron Age coins of Cunobelin (Fig 61b) found at Colchester and Canterbury (Muckleroy *et al* 1978; McGrail 1987, 234, 236; McGrail 1990, 43), raises the possibility that the Blackfriars ship was so equipped. Other Gaulish coins (Johnstone 1980, 88; Allen 1971) and a Roman bronze ship model from Blessey, near the source of the River Seine, France (Johnstone 1980, 88, 159), also show

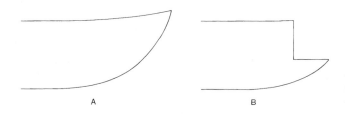

Fig 60   Alternative possible reconstructions of the bow.

vessels with a kind of forefoot (Fig 61a: McGrail 1990, 42), and it has been suggested by Johnstone (1980, 88) that the ships of the Veneti might have been called *ponto*, and were the same type of vessel as was depicted with a forefoot on a Roman mosaic from Tunisia. However, it is rather stretching the evidence to link Celtic ships of northern Europe with classical ships of north Africa in this way. A protruding forefoot was not always fitted in Celtic ships since another bronze ship representation from Blessey, France, and a gold model of a sailing boat from Broighter, Ireland, both of which are thought to be of Celtic workmanship, have no forefoot (Johnstone 1980, 128, 159) and several late Iron Age coins from north-western Gaul possibly depict ships without a projecting forefoot (Allen 1971). Therefore, the pre-Roman illustrations in northern Europe do indicate that native ships with a potruding forefoot and native ships with rounded bows were operating in the early first century AD, so, on that evidence, both forms of bow in the Blackfriars ship are possible.

Although it is impossible to decide with certainty between the alternative reconstructions of the bow offered here, and as there is no evidence that the Blackfriars ship had a forefoot, and the stempost was found gently curving upwards, the reconstruction with the long tapering curved bow is favoured as the solution which best fits the evidence.

Fig 61 (A) Drawing of a ship on a gold coin of the Atrebates, first century BC (after McGrail 1990, 42); (B) ship depicted on a bronze coin of Cunobelin, from Canterbury, AD 20–43; (C) possible ships on Gaulish coins (from Allen 1971).

Reconstructing the stern (Fig 50)

The lower part of the sternpost was found immediately aft of floor-timber 24, and as this was considerably wider than floor-timber 23, it seems likely that its purpose was to hold the lower end of the sternpost (Fig 23), just as the extra-wide floor-timber 3 held the lower end of the stempost. This means that the keel-planks were about 11.3m long between the lower ends of the stem and stern posts. The form of the stern seems to have differed from that of the bow, for the hard chine or angle between planks P4 and P5 was at an inclination of *c* 147° between floor-timbers 23 and 24, close to the lower end of the sternpost. This was in contrast to the bow, level with the lower end of the stempost, where the chine had ceased to exist. This suggests that the strakes were carried round almost horizontally to the sternpost, for there was little room in which to curve the planks upwards aft of floor-timber 24, at which point the lower end of the sternpost was beginning to rise upwards. On this basis the stern has been reconstructed with little plank sheer (ie an upward curve to the sternpost), and with a slightly shorter shape than the bow.

Propulsion

Mast size

The mast of the Blackfriars ship had not survived, and although evidence for the size of masts in ancient ships is very limited, it is possible to make an estimate in the present case. This is based upon the size of the mast-step, upon the height of the surviving mast of the Bruges boat, and upon several traditional rules for calculating mast heights since there is a relationship between effective mast height and sail size to the hull shape and size for various types of rig.

The mast-step socket of Blackfriars ship 1 was rectangular, measuring in plan 0.336m by 0.254m, indicating that the mast was either rectangular at the base, or square with one side held in place by a chock to ease its withdrawal. Assuming that it was circular in section above deck level, as was usual for masts of early times (eg as in the Bruges boat), it is unlikely to have been more than 0.254m in diameter, for had its foot been tapered this should have been shown in the shape of the mast-step socket. This is a little larger than the mast-step of the almost contemporary Bruges boat (Marsden 1976a, 32–7) which in its dried state measured 0.2m by 0.145m (Fig 62). As the former measurement was along the grain, where there would be minimal shrinkage, and the latter was across the grain, where shrinkage would be considerable, it seems likely that the diameter of the Bruges mast was close to 0.2m. This is confirmed by the discovery of the mast itself (Fig 62), whose maximum diameter was roughly recorded in 1903 as about 0.16m (ibid, 26). This is important, for it helps to determine the height of the Blackfriars mast to the extent that as both vessels are of the same tradition, and as there is close agreement between the surviving features found in both the Blackfriars and Bruges vessels, it is reasonable to expect that there was similar agreement in other respects, such as the length of the mast in proportion to the relative size of the two vessels.

A drawing of the Bruges mast was published in 1903, but only short fragments of the mast now survive (Fig 62). The drawing shows that the mast was at least 9.3m in length, with its surviving lower end tapered almost to a point, as if it had suffered considerable decay. The mast-step of the Bruges boat (Fig 62) was set in a frame almost identical to that of the Blackfriars ship, showing that it too had a flat bottom between chines, and that the sides rose up from this at an angle. The distance between the chines at the mast-step station in the Bruges boat was only 1.4m, but in the Blackfriars ship it was 3.92m, so the former vessel was evidently narrower. However, as the Bruges and Blackfriars vessels were of similar construction it is possible to relate proportionally the Bruges mast height to the Blackfriars ship to find the height of the latter's mast. This is done by calculating the proportion of a square sail, represented by the mast height (squared), relative to the volume of the vessel, represented by the beam (cubed). In the Bruges boat the mast height (9.3m) squared (86.49) is divided by the roughly estimated beam (4.7m) cubed (103.8) to give a proportion of 1:0.833. This proportion is then applied to the Blackfriars ship whose beam was about 6m. The Blackfriars mast height = 6^3 x 0.833 = 179.928 x 0.833 = sq root of 149.8 = 12.2m.

There are a number of formulae for determining mast height relative to the size of the hull and to the diameter of the mast, of which McGrail (1987, 226) gives three: a traditional Vestland Norwegian rule (a) that says that the height of a mast from the heel to the halyard hole near the top should equal the girth of the boat at that station. In the case of Blackfriars ship 1 the girth at the mast-step as reconstructed would be 9.8m, which is very close to

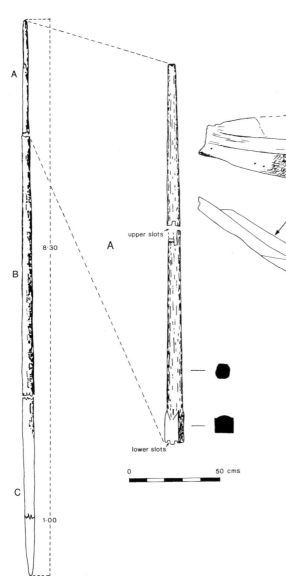

Fig 62   (Above) the mast-step frame of the Bruges boat; (far left) drawing of the mast of the Bruges boat published in 1903; (near left) drawing of the top of the mast published in 1976.

Falconer (1815, 265) says (e) that the length of a mast 'to the rigging-stop or hounds, [should be] three-fourths the whole length' [of the ship]. This means that the Blackfriars ship, estimated to be 18.5m long, would have a mast 13.9m high to the top of the shrouds. The mast itself would be a little higher, perhaps rising to about 14.5m. Falconer (ibid) also gives (f) the proportion of mast diameter to height as 'one-fourth of an inch to every foot in length'. This is a proportion of 1:48.

Sutherland (1711, 109) says (g) that 'The length of this ship's main-mast being considered, the next thing required is to make her diameter in the biggest place suitable to it, or the stress it will bear'. For every yard in length of a main-mast for a small ship the mast diameter should be 4/5 or 3/4 of an inch. This too is a proportion of 1:48. In both (f) and (g), as the base diameter of the Blackfriars mast, judging from the mast-step, was 0.254m, this would give a mast height of 12.1m.

Both the Vestland and Deane rules are for ships using the same northern seas in which the Blackfriars ship sailed, and it may be significant that a mast height based upon the average for the two rules, 12.6m, is very close to the suggested height of the Blackfriars mast based upon the Bruges mast (12.2m). Since these are all much below the height given by the Italian rules it seems that the latter should be discounted in this context. There could be special circumstances to account for the much greater mast heights according to Italian rules which may refer to very large ships only, rather as Deane, Falconer and Sutherland gave separate sets of rules for vessels with a large beam.

Although there are differences between the heights given by the Vestland, Falconer, Deane, and Sutherland rules, they are remarkably consistent within a range of 3.7m. and give a very approximate indication of what a

the estimate based upon the Bruges boat, particularly if a further metre is added for the mast height above the halyard hole, thereby making the total estimated mast height 10.8m. The second and third formulae are Italian from the fifteenth century, and so are for ships used in the Mediterranean basin. According to the second formula (b), the mast should be four times the ship's breadth, which in the case of the Blackfriars ship was about 6m, and would give a mast 24m high. According to the third (c), the mast should be 1.6 times the keel length, which in the Blackfriars ship was about 11.3m, thereby giving a mast 18.2m high.

Sir Anthony Deane (1670, 82) gives another formula (d) for determining the height of a mast for a ship with a beam of less than 8.23m: add together the keel length plus beam length plus half beam length (using a measurement in feet): divide the total by 5 to give a 'quotient' in yards: add to this the difference between the beam length and 27 in yards, and the total will be the mast height. In the case of the Blackfriars ship this gives 37.3ft plus 20ft plus 10ft equals 67.3ft, which divided by 5 gives a 13.46 yards quotient. Since the beam is 2.3 yards less than 27 add this to the quotient. This gives a mast height of 15.76 yards (14.4m).

shipwright would expect for a ship of the size of the Blackfriars vessel (Fig 63). These rules are no doubt based upon long experience in defining the most practical height of mast for a ship of given size used in northern seas. By taking the average of these calculations based upon these rules and the Bruges mast (but disregarding the Italian rules), it seems likely that the mast of the Blackfriars ship was about 12.7m. high.

Mast construction

Although there is no evidence to suggest whether or not the mast was carved from a single piece of timber, like

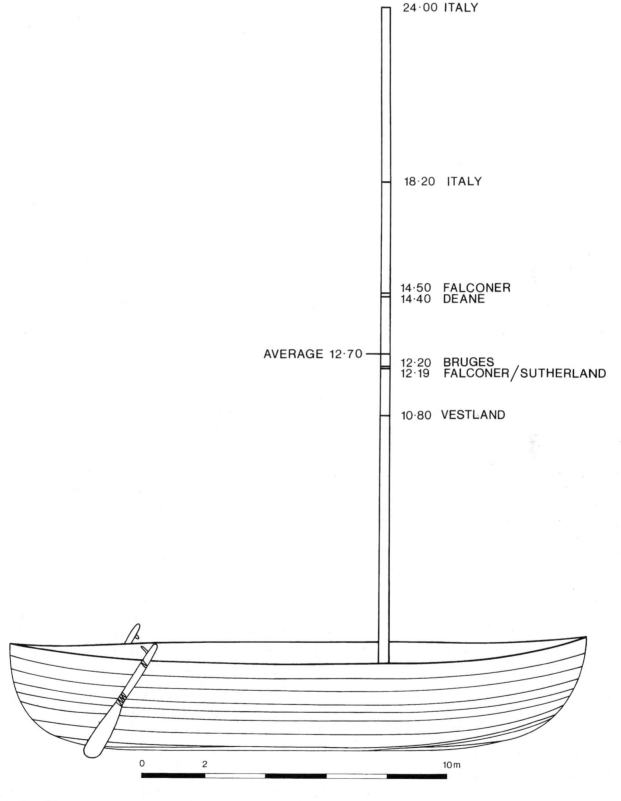

Fig 63   Possible mast heights for Blackfriars ship 1 based on various 'rules'.

that in the Bruges boat, or was of composite construction (Casson 1971, 231–2), its diameter of 0.254m was well within the range of available timber at that time, and it is most likely that it was a single piece. Its weight, however, has an important bearing on the stability of the ship, and, based upon the estimates given above, would have been in excess of three tonnes. This figure is calculated on the basis that the top of the mast was about 10.54m above deck level as reconstructed. With a lower diameter of 0.254m. tapering upwards, it is estimated that the mast had an average diameter of 0.18m. Its volume, therefore, would be $\pi \times r^2 \times$ height (3.14 x 0.09 x 10.54m = 2.98 cubic metres). By multiplying this by 800 (the specific density of oak being 800 kg/square metres; McGrail 1987, 20) the weight of 2384kg. is obtained. To this should be added the weight of the yard, sail, and rigging. The yard, for the purpose of these calculations, is estimated to equal the height of the mast above the gunwale, ie 10m., and with a notional average diameter of 0.06m its volume would be 3.14 x 0.03 x 10 = 0.94 cubic metres Multiplying this by 800 will give its weight as 752kg. The weight of the sail and ropes would depend upon the material and its thickness used, and cannot be calculated without further information. Nevertheless, this is sufficient for calculating the combined hypothetical weight of the mast and yard, which in this case is very roughly 3.6 tonnes.

Some circumstantial evidence for the construction of the mast is suggested by the location of the wreck upstream of the Roman bridge crossing the River Thames. As the ship had *Teredo* borings in its timbers, showing that it had sailed at sea, and carried a cargo derived from downstream, it must have passed under the bridge (Fig 4), one of whose timber piers (Fig 10) has probably been identified (Milne 1985, 44–54). Since the deck of the bridge is estimated to have been at *c*5–6m above the contemporary river level at low tide, the Blackfriars ship could not have passed beneath with its mast still standing. There are two possible solutions, that either the mast could be lowered, or that there was a drawbridge opening in the bridge to allow larger vessels to pass through.

The practical consequences of lowering the mast are important to consider, particularly if the ship had a crew of three, as is indicated by the evidence of food utensils found in the St. Peter Port ship, which was of similar size and construction (Rule 1993, 81). The combined weight of the mast, yard, and sail, over three tonnes, would be no easy load for this small crew to take down and put up, particularly if manoeuvering the ship under a restricted opening in the bridge, so it seems most likely that the mast of the Blackfriars ship could not be lowered. However, it is known that small sailing craft in the Mediterranean in classical times could lower their masts (Casson 1971, fig 191), so in principle there is no objection to the idea of the mast of the Blackfriars ship being lowered downstream of the bridge to enable the vessel to be towed upstream. But, in view of the fact that the County Hall ship, believed to have been another substantial sailing vessel (see Chapter 5), was also found upstream of the Roman bridge, it may well be that there was some simple arrangement, like a drawbridge, which allowed seagoing ships with tall fixed masts to pass through. It is significant that when the thirteenth-century stone London Bridge was built it was found necessary to include a drawbridge to give taller ships access upstream (Home 1931, 32). It seems most likely, therefore, that the mast of the Blackfriars ship could not be lowered.

Sail type

The mast-step of Blackfriars ship 1 was situated about one-third of the length of the vessel from its bow, and well forward of the widest part of the hull. It has been suggested that the ship was propelled by a single square sail (Marsden 1967, 28), but McGrail (1987, 225–7, 234) has highlighted the steering problems that could be created if a ship attempted to sail to windward using a square sail on a mast in that position (Fig 64b). The ideal position for the sail propelling the vessel, and hence the Centre of Effort, is almost amidships close to the Centre of Lateral Resistance of the underwater body of the hull (McGrail 1987, 220). It might seem, therefore, that an alternative rig, particularly a spritsail, on the after side of the mast nearer the midship position, would be more appropriate as its Centre of Effort would be aft of the mast (Fig 64a). Although sprit and lateen sails are occasionally shown on Roman iconography in the Mediterranean region (Casson 1971, 243–5), an overwhelming number of classical representations of ships show 'square' sails (ie of square or rectangular shape; Gillmer 1979) which make it clear that the 'square' sail was most commonly used on the larger ships throughout the Mediterranean region.

In contrast, representations of sails on ships of the Roman period in central and northern Europe are exceptionally rare, though reliefs from Bad Kreuznach and Junkerath, Germany, show vessels with rectangular sails, possibly with a high aspect ratio (ie taller than they are wide), stretched by horizontal battens (Ellmers 1978, 3; Casson 1971, fig 195). Outside the Rhineland there are very few northern European representations of Roman ships and boats, and probably the only example with sails from Britain is on a mosaic of the fourth century AD, with poorly executed scenes from the *Aeneid*, found in the Low Ham villa, Somerset, and now in the Somerset County Museum, Taunton (Fig 65). This shows three warships with square and diamond-shaped sails which

Table 7   Estimated mast height of the Blackfriars ship

Based upon the Vestland rule (a)	10.8m
Based on Sutherland (g)	12.1m
Based upon Falconer (f)	12.1m
Based upon the Bruges mast (d)	12.2m
Based upon the Deane rule	14.4m
Based upon Falconer (e)	c 14.5m
Based upon the Italian rule (c)	18.20m
Based upon the Italian rule (b)	24.00m

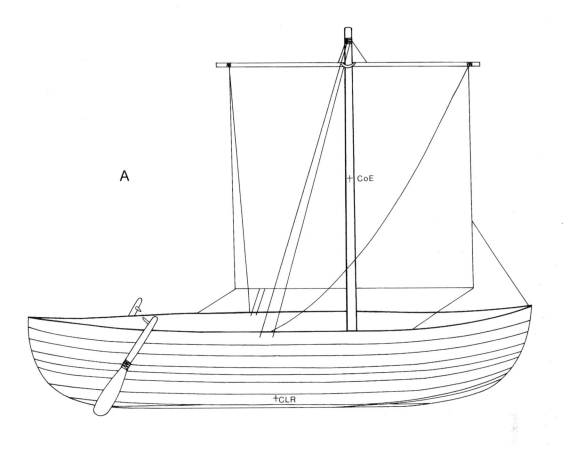

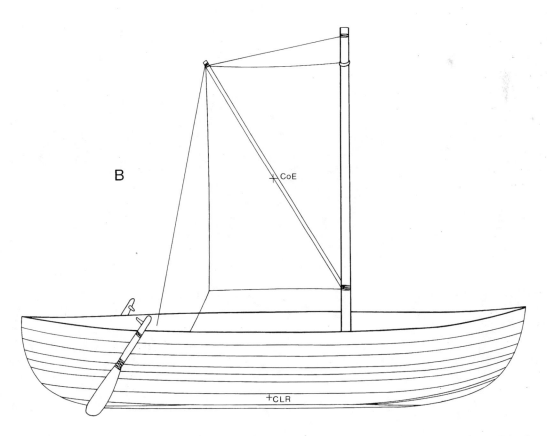

Fig 64 Alternative possible types of rig for Blackfriars ship 1. COE is the Centre of Effort, ie the centre of the forces of propulsion on the sail, and CLR is the Centre of Lateral Resistance of the hull.

Toynbee (1964, 241–6, pl LVIII) considers to have been copied from mosaic designs imported into Britain from abroad. If this is correct the ships need not represent types to be seen in Britain. Indeed the ships are crudely drawn and out of proportion both to the crews and to the structural features, and it seems that the mosaicist was not concerned with accuracy. It is therefore unlikely that the diamond shaped sails actually represent real sails, for such a type is not otherwise known in ancient times. The only other known indications of sails from the British Isles are an immediately pre-Roman native Celtic representation on a coin of Cunobelin (Fig 61b; McGrail 1987, 236), and a gold boat model from Broighter, Ireland (Fig 66; ibid, 187), which suggest square sails.

Several alternative interpretations, other than a square sail in the forward position in the Blackfriars ship, need to be considered. The mast may have been used for towing, though the prolonged use of the vessel in the sea, enabling the *Teredo* 'ship-worm' to grow to maturity, makes this an unlikely option. Moreover, the presence of known riverside marshes, creeks and tributaries of the River Thames, such as the Southwark and Bermondsey marshes which were flooded periodically during the Roman period (Sheldon 1978, 21) and river tributaries such as the Lea and Darenth, indicate that towpaths are unlikely to have existed for any considerable length on the lower reaches of the Thames where the Blackfriars ship sailed. This interpretation is therefore unlikely. A second mast and sail might have been stepped further aft

in the unexcavated area amidships, to act as a balance by moving the Centre of Effort of the sails nearer the Centre of Lateral Resistance of the hull. This may seem possible at first sight, for Roman ships in the Mediterranean are known to have had two masts at times (Casson 1971, 239–43). However, in those vessels the forward mast, the *artemon*, raked at such an angle that there was considerable horizontal pressure on its foot which in turn suggests that its step would be located in a longitudinal keelson (ibid, 208) rather than in a transverse frame as in the Blackfriars ship. Not only was the mast-step of the Blackfriars ship unlike this, but also the shape of the step socket and its location in a transverse frame shows that the mast in the Blackfriars ship was more or less vertical. This interpretation is therefore unlikely to apply.

The projecting forefoot cautiously suggested above (Fig 60b) might have provided a solution if it had lengthened the underwater body of the hull forward, and given the mast a more central position in the waterline length, closer to the Centre of Lateral Resistance. However, there is no reason to believe that the underwater body of this ship could have been lengthened, for this would have meant changing the existing form of strakes P3 and S3 and their attachment to the stempost. This solution, therefore, would not solve the problem. Alternatively, the ship could have had a fore-and-aft sail, such as a spritsail, which, because much of it would be situated on the after side of the mast, would have brought the Centre of Effort nearer amidships (Fig 64b). Although

Fig 65 Low Ham villa mosaic, with ships in a scene from the Aeneid.

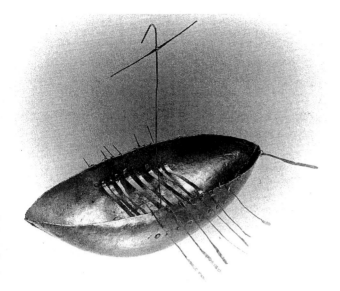

Fig 66   Small gold model boat, first century BC, Broighter.

these types of rig are not generally known in northern Europe until after the fifteenth century it has been suspected from mast positions that some of the Romano-Celtic barges on the Rhine had a form of fore-and-aft rig (de Weerd 1988, 143–5). In spite of the fact that there is no pictorial evidence for this type of sail in northern Europe during the Roman period, this remains a possible explanation.

Since none of these is wholly adequate it seems most likely that the ship carried a square sail, and that the master attempted to plan his voyage so that he had a following wind – in this way he would minimise the steering problem. This view is also suggested by the fact that this sail was by far the most commonly represented type in Europe until the sixteenth century. Waiting for days, even weeks, for suitable winds was a normal practice for sailing ships leaving northern European ports in recent centuries, and it must have been so during the Roman period.

However, McGrail (1987, 227) has pointed out the curious fact that in various other excavated vessels the mast has been found placed well forward of amidships. In seagoing ships, apart from Blackfriars ship 1 where the mast was situated about 36% of the reconstructed length from the bow, McGrail lists two Danish and six Dutch medieval cogs in which the masts lay between 24% and 34% of the length from the bow. Admittedly, there are other vessels, such as the Viking ships of Oseberg, Gokstad, and Skuldelev, where the masts were more centrally placed, and the fourteenth century cogs of Bremen and Vejby where they were at about 43%. But it is difficult to accept that so many ships could have had rigs other than the square sail when there is no other evidence, such as in contemporary representations (eg Fliedner 1969, 39–62), for such sails in northern Europe before the fifteenth century.

Why, then, were some masts set well forward? One likely explanation is that, as the middle of the ship contained the hold for the cargo, it was necessary to use the yard as a crane for lifting heavy and bulky goods, for many of the minor waterfronts and tidal shores that the Blackfriars ship probably frequented in northern Europe may not have had cranes. In order to swing the load outboard the mast would need to be situated forward or aft of the hold. It is possible, therefore, that to the master of the Blackfriars ship, the ability to transfer goods to and from the hold was more important than the ideal sailing quality, and that he was satisfied by his ship sailing best with a following wind.

The practical sailing consequences of this mast position are demonstrated by the Kyrenia ship of the fourth century BC whose mast, like that in the Blackfriars ship, was set at about 33% from the bow, at the forward end of the amidships hold. Although there is no certain evidence for the type of rig on this particular ship, the square sail is thought to be the only type known at that time (Casson 1971, 244). When a full-sized reconstruction of this vessel was built with a square sail, it was found to be both stable and to sail well, and even while close-hauled 50° to 60° off the wind was still able to make over 2 knots. Indeed, the ship is reported as being able to reach 12 knots with a following wind, but often averaged almost 6 knots over long distances (Katzev 1989, 8–10). However, there was probably a 'couple' set up in the ship between the forces acting at the Centre of Effort in the sail and the Centre of Lateral Resistance in the hull which would tend to turn the vessel away from the wind whenever it was sailing with a wind from the beam. This in turn would put considerable pressure on the rudders as they kept the ship on course, and may have been responsible for the breaking of a rudder while sailing close-hauled in strong winds (ibid, 8, 10). In view of this the publication of much more detailed information about the performance of the Kyrenia II reconstruction would be particularly valuable.

The similarity of the mast position in Kyrenia II to that in Blackfriars ship 1, together with the fact that in the reconstruction the length to beam ratio of 3:1 was roughly that of the Blackfriars ship, might be thought to show that in practice there were no insuperable problems in sailing the Blackfriars ship. However, the similarities between the two ships are limited, for the underwater body of the Kyrenia vessel was entirely different from that of the Blackfriars ship. It had a pronounced V-shaped bottom around the keel which would have not only have resisted leeway or sideways drift when the wind was off the beam, but also would have assisted the steering. In contrast the Blackfriars ship had a flat bottom, and, apart from its hard chines, had little to resist leeway. In practice, therefore, the Blackfriars ship was probably only really effective with a following wind.

The discussion above enables a solution to be suggested which meets all of the evidence but places operational limits on the ship, particularly when sailing with a beam wind. To what extent these limits could be overcome by tacking, for example, would depend upon the skill of the master, but the only way of establishing a solution is by building and sailing a full-size reconstruction of the ship. The Blackfriars ship could have had a square sail, and since the mast is likely to have been in the region of 12.7m high from the step, on the assump-

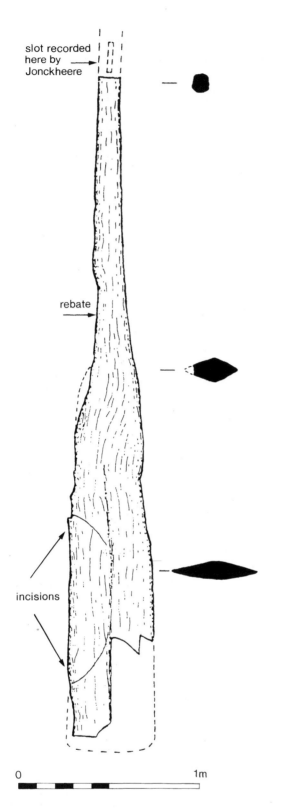

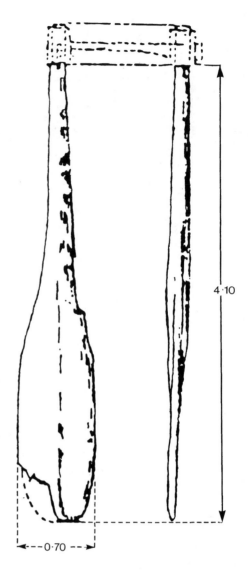

Fig 67   The rudder from the Bruges boat: (right) published in 1903; (left) redrawn and published in 1976.

tion that the gunwale was at 2.86m the approximate length of the yard would have been about 10m. This would give a sail about 8 x 8m square, or about 64 square metres in area.

A clue to the use of the sail are the rows of limber holes in the bottom of the ship, for these occur in the frames both above the centre line over the keel-planks, and nearer the sides of the bottom. As they allowed the bilge water to flow to a point near the centre of the ship where it could be pumped out, the side limber holes could best function when the ship was heeled at an angle of about 12 degrees. It is unlikely that the side limber holes functioned with the ship upright, for this would have occurred only when the bilge water had been allowed to accumulate to a depth of more than 0.2m. In a flat-bottomed ship this may have been an unacceptable volume of 'free surface' for it would have modified the centre of gravity and would have had an adverse effect on stability (Simpson 1979, 141). It seems, then, that the ship was sometimes expected to sail with a side wind that would keep the vessel heeled up to this angle. Such a heel suggests operating in beam winds. This matter was examined on the Boatcad computer program which confirmed that it would be difficult to heel the ship any further while sailing (p 90).

Steering

No evidence for the method of steering the Blackfriars ship was found. But, as the Bruges boat was of similar construction to the Blackfriars ship in features that could be compared, it is reasonable to suppose that both vessels were similar in other respects, such as the mast and rudder. The rudder of the Bruges boat is at the National Scheepvaartmuseum in Antwerp, and when originally recorded for the 1903 publication it was 4.1m long, and its blade 0.7m wide (Marsden 1976a, 28–9). Its top had broken off, but it did preserve part of the rectangular slot for the tiller (Fig 67). This showed that the tiller had projected at right angles to the rudder blade, as did the tiller in a boat's quarter rudder found in the first-century Roman fort at Newstead, Scotland (Fig 68). The Newstead rudder, 1.65m long and with a blade 0.14m wide, should be mentioned in this context since it is at present the only Roman rudder yet found in Britain (Curle 1911, pl LXIX, no 5).

A major question is whether or not the Bruges rudder was a quarter rudder originally attached to the side of the ship near the stern (McGrail 1987, 244–51), or a steering oar fastened near the sternpost (McGrail 1987, 241–4). An important clue is that it differed from the steering oars used on the Rhine boats and barges during the Roman period, for these had a tiller hanging down on the same plane as the rudder blade (Ellmers 1978, 4,6,10,11; de Weerd 1988, 162–80). This alone would suggest that the Bruges rudder was a quarter rudder.

Equally important was a recess 0.8m long in the shaft just above the blade and about 2m up from the present bottom. This may have been for a sleeve, perhaps of leather, to hold the rudder to the side of the ship, and since it is different from the short pivot recesses in the Roman steering oar from Lake Neuchatel (McGrail 1987, 243), this too would indicate that it was a quarter rudder. This interpretation is supported by the fact that steering oars, in the more recent past, were used in river craft rather than in seagoing vessels in northern Europe, whereas the Blackfriars ship was a seagoing vessel. A sleeve on the Bruges rudder would explain why there was no hole to fasten it to the hull, as is found, for example, in medieval quarter rudders (Christensen 1985, 152–5).

The identification of this as a quarter rudder enables an estimation to be made of the deck height at the stern of the Bruges boat. As there are no clear illustrations of Roman vessels with quarter rudders in northern Europe it is necessary to use medieval illustrations to discover the most likely angle from the vertical at which such rudders were most effective. McGrail (1987, 250) has shown that there is a considerable range of angle from 24° to 45° aft of the vertical, but that 30 degrees would be fairly average. Since the tiller height was 4m above the bottom of the rudder it would seem that, allowing for a man's height, the deck was at c 2m above the bottom – about the same height as has been suggested for the Blackfriars ship. Although the Bruges boat was narrower, it may have been of similar height, so that the rudder in the Blackfriars ship need not have been very much different in size.

McGrail (1987, 248) has suggested that there may be a correlation between the displacement volume of a ship (represented by length x breadth x depth) and the blade area of its rudder. The blade area of the Bruges rudder has been calculated to have been about 1.15 square metres and the hull volume of the Blackfriars ship some

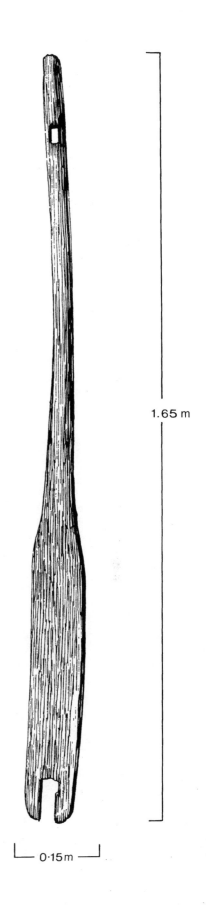

1.65 m

0·15m

Fig 68   Side rudder from the Roman fort at Newstead (after Curle 1911).

323.8 cubic metres. By dividing the cubic root of 323.6 (ie 6.86) by the square root of 1.15 (ie 1.07) the figure 6.41 is obtained. This is about the same size as the side rudders of the following vessels: Nydam 2 (6.49), Oseberg (6.41), and Gokstad 1 (6.31), but is smaller than the Gokstad 3 rudder (4.56). It is much larger than the Tune rudder (8.41), and suggests that the rudder size would have been effective on the Blackfriars ship.

It is not known if Celtic ships generally had only one rudder, as in the later Scandinavian and medieval ships, or a pair as in Classical ships. The little Celtic gold model boat from Broighter, Ireland, dates from about the first century BC (Fig 66) and seems to have had two quarter rudders, though it has been suggested (ibid, 244) that these might have been steering oars. Only one exists now, though there is a hole on the opposite quarter of the boat, probably for the attachment of another.

The only suggestion of the number of rudders possessed by the Blackfriars ship is the fact that her underwater body shape and her keel had only limited resistance to leeway. In order to overcome this problem it seems most likely that it had two quarter rudders, one on each side. Leeway is a common problem associated with flat-bottomed vessels, such as the Thames Barge and certain Dutch craft, and a measure of the problem is indicated by the solution developed in more recent times, which has been to use leeboards in addition to a rudder (Carr 1989, 104; Kemp 1979, 473).

Although it is not possible to determine how effective rudders of Bruges type would be without building and sailing a full-sized reconstruction, it is possible to suggest how they were used. As quarter rudders were always slanted at an angle on the side of any ship it seems likely that the recess for the sleeve lay on the forward side for it is only in this position that it would be possible to cradle the Bruges rudder. The rudder blade apparently had an equal area both fore and aft of its turning axis, though in its present shrunken state exact measurements are not certain. The blade is now 0.5m wide and 0.1m thick, but as it was recorded as being 0.7m wide when found there has evidently been a shrinkage of 28.6% in the radial plane of the wood. The thickness of the rudder, also probably radial, would, on a similar shrinkage ratio, originally have been 0.14m. The rudder then had sharp leading and trailing edges, and was thickest at the centre, with a flattened diamond shape in section. How this form of rudder blade would have behaved in the water is not known, particularly as modern rudders have sharp leading and trailing edges and an aerofoil shape to minimise turbulence and medieval quarter rudders usually had sharp leading edges and blunt trailing edges (ibid, 250). However, the presence of a stern cabin on the deck, as suggested by the Guernsey ship (Rule 1993, 128) might have made the use of quarter rudders rather difficult.

Conclusions

It must be stressed that the evidence given here has been used to create a minimal reconstruction of the ship, and that other more elaborate reconstructions involving additional hypotheses are possible. This particular reconstruction suggests that the vessel was originally about 18.5m long, with a beam of about 6.12m, and a gunwale height amidships of about 2.86m (Fig 69). There was a deck, most likely at about 2.16m. Both ends were sharp, and the single fixed mast probably carried a square sail just forward of the hold. In the deck amidships was a large hatchway to allow heavy goods to be lowered into the hold, perhaps using the yard as a crane jib. At the stern were probably two quarter rudders; and the main living quarters were probably located at the stern, where northern weather conditions would make a deck cabin desirable for the crew particularly when steering.

Method of construction

Reconstructing the building sequence of the ship as a whole depends upon being able to understand the stages in which its components were fastened together. Although it is not always clear whether the frames or the planks were set up in position first, it had been thought that after the keel-planks were laid down on the stocks the floor-timbers were then nailed to them. Thereafter, the rest of the bottom planking was fastened to the floor-timbers together with the first strake of each side (P5, S5) so that the side frames and then the side planking could be erected. It was thought that the seams in the ship were subsequently caulked (Marsden 1976, 52). However, recent, more detailed analyses of the nails, the planking and the caulking, using scientific equipment that was not available to archaeology when the vessel was excavated, shows that the picture was rather more complex, though with the exception of the caulking this original reconstruction still seems to be valid.

Preparing the timbers

The planks of the Blackfriars ship were tangentially cut from heartwood logs, presumably by using very large saws, such as is depicted in a Roman tomb relief from Gaul (Meiggs 1982, fig 14d; Rival 1991, 141). This shows two men sawing a large log raised upon a trestle, the saw having a long blade with a handle at each end, held by one man below the log and one man above. There is also some evidence that Roman military sawmills existed in Germany (Meiggs 1982, 186). In contrast the floor-timbers of the ship were hewn from substantial whole logs, and the side-frames were cut from smaller timbers grown to the appropriate shape. A knee (Fig 57), perhaps for the decking, was fashioned from a whole log and a branch.

Constructing the ship

It is clear that construction must have started with laying down the two keel-planks, P1 and S1. They had been tangentially cut and shaped, and were presumably laid on some form of stocks with the side nearest the pith facing outboard, and with sufficient access below for driving the nails. As the nails were up to 0.74m long, and it was necessary to have space below to swing the hammer that drove them into position, it is also clear that the stocks must have held the keel-planks at least 1.3m above the ground or perhaps over a construction pit. Moreover, as the finished vessel is estimated to have weighed up to 29 tonnes (Appendix 5), the stocks must have been very substantial, with some arrangement so that the completed vessel could be launched easily.

A study of the caulking between the planks shows that its mixture of hazel shavings and warmed pine resin had probably been applied to the edge of each plank before the next plank was placed in position (Appendices 3 and 4). In the case of the keel-planks this should mean that once they had been brought together edge-to-edge they were held together. Initially, this may have been by wooden battens nailed to each plank until it was possible to fasten some floor-timbers in position (Fig 70.1). In-

deed, temporary battens may have been used generally to hold the bottom planks while they were cradled on the stocks until all of the floor-timbers could be positioned (Fig 70.2). This would not only account for peg-filled holes in the planks, but also would seem to be similar to a practice in constructing carvel-built ships' bottoms in Roman, medieval and later times in Europe north of the Alps (Hoving 1991, 78; Litwin 1991, 116, 120; Moortel 1991, 42–3; Oosting 1991, 73).

In the time available during the 1963 excavation it was not possible to locate the positions of the small holes filled with oak pegs that were subsequently found in some saved planking fragments (Fig 26), but there were a sufficient number of holes to indicate that they may represent a system of temporary fastenings used during the building process. Exactly how these temporary fittings might have been used is suggested by the peg-filled

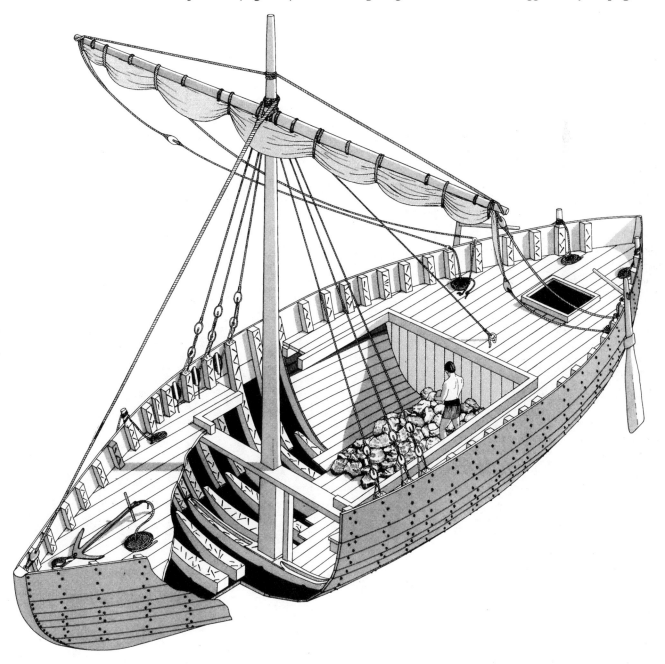

Fig 69   Cut-away reconstruction of Blackfriars ship 1, to show construction.

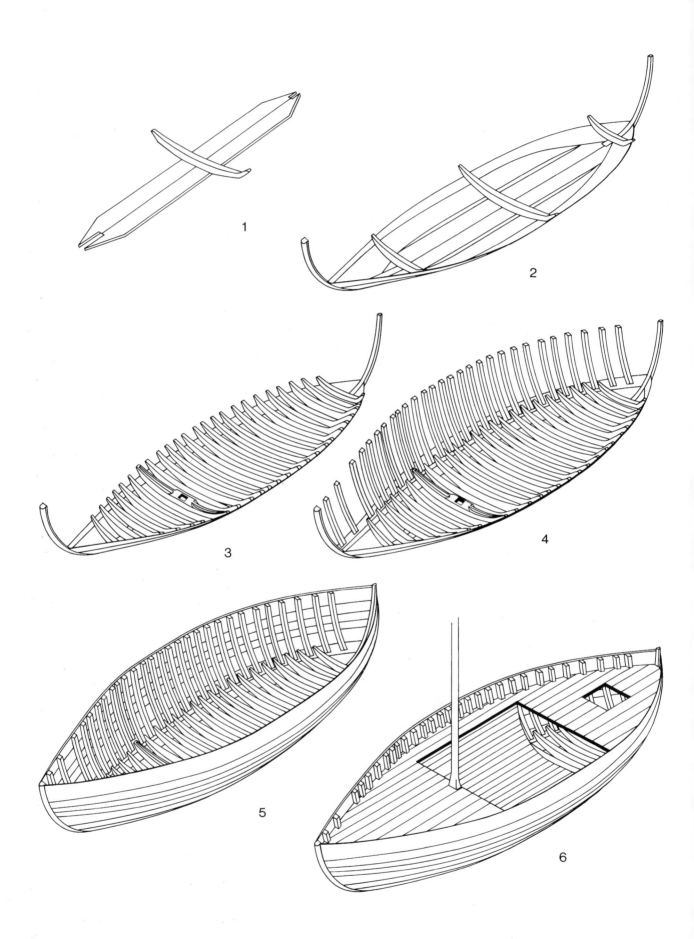

Fig 70   Reconstructed stages in building Blackfriars ship 1.

holes found in the Romano-Celtic barge from Bevaix, Switzerland (Arnold 1978, 33–4) which seems to show that battens crossed the seams between adjacent planks, rather as has been recorded on some relatively modern vessels (Hasslof, 1977, 74, fig 8.2). The peg holes in the Blackfriars ship, however, were round in section as if they had been drilled, rather than square as would be expected for a normal nail; it is clear, therefore, that in any future excavation these holes require detailed study so as to be more certain of their purpose.

The frames of the Blackfriars ship were fashioned from logs, apparently with rows of drilled holes as guides to the frame shapes. The floor-timbers, excluding 1 and 2, had limber holes cut on their undersides before they were fastened to the planks, and it is likely that nail holes, used to fasten them to the planks, were also drilled in the frames at that stage. This is suggested by the fact that the peg that filled each hole, and was itself drilled out for the nail (Fig 48), did not extend into the outer planking. Drilling through the frames at that stage would ensure the minimum amount of drilling required to fasten the planks to the frames once they were in position. All that was then needed when the frame was in position was to extend the drilled holes in the frames through the planks so that the iron nails could be inserted.

It is possible that after the keel-planks had been laid, a midship floor-timber (eg no 13) was set up in position to establish the transverse shape of the hull bottom at its greatest width. There is no evidence for this, but there is an indication that the broad floor-timbers 3 and 24 were fastened near the ends of the vessel at an early stage, for they were needed to hold the lower ends of the stem and sternposts before the ends of strakes P3 and S3 and P4 and S4 could be attached (Fig 70.1). The upper ends of the endposts were themselves presumably held temporarily by further structures. Once floor-timbers 1 and 2, attached over the nail fastenings for strakes 3 and 4 (the outer planking of the bottom) in the stempost, had been fixed then they would help to support those bottom strakes at the bow. Some, at least, of the floor-timbers must have been positioned on the keel-planks at this stage, otherwise there would be no nails driven.

The iron nails that held the planks and frames together throughout the ship were carefully prepared before being driven through the planks and frames from outboard, and before they were hooked by turning them through 180 degrees back into the inboard face of the frames (Fig 48). In each hollow nail head was a caulking of slivers of hazel wood wound around the shank together with some warm pine resin, which would give a watertight seal between the head and the outboard face of the hull once the nail was fastened in place. A study of the heads themselves (Appendix 2) suggests a likely reason for such an elaborate procedure. As there was very little distortion of the structure of the iron head, which would otherwise be expected had it been subject to violent hammering, it is probable that the head was protected by a 'dolly' while the shank was driven in. Moreover, the lack of distortion also suggests that the drilled hole in the plank and frame was only slightly narrower than the long nail shank since the frame evidently offered little resistance as the nail was hammered in. As this fit might have allowed water to seep into the hull and cause rot, it was probably a matter for concern to the shipwright who solved the problem by caulking the nail heads.

All of the floor-timbers must have been attached once the bottom planking was in position for these frames were needed to hold strakes P5 and S5 (Fig 70.3), the lowest plank of each side. The ends of the floor-timbers, therefore, not only fixed the angle of the sides relative to the bottom, but also allowed strakes P5 and S5 to support the lower ends of the side-frames which in turn held the side planking (Fig 70.4). After the bottoms of the side-frames were fastened to strakes P5 and S5, usually by two hooked nails, it is likely that the upper ends were temporarily fastened by longitudinal and transverse timbers to make them more stable while attaching the side planking. The side planks from P6 and S6 to P9 and S9 were then attached to the frames by hooked nails in the same way as was used in the floor-timbers (Fig 70.5). The holes in the side-frames had also probably been drilled before the frames were erected in position, since in these the drilled trenails did not extend into the side planking, and it would have been more difficult to drill the holes after the frames were erected.

The ceiling planking of the hold was fastened by a few iron nails to the inboard face of frames, as if the shipwright intended to make it easy to replace damaged ceiling planks from time to time, or to inspect the bilges. This occurred at a late stage in the construction process, and subsequent stages involved the completion of the decking and other upper works (Fig 70.6), indicated by the extra side-frame 6 and the mortice holes in the frame beside the mast-step. The mast itself was stepped, probably during a ceremony in which a coin was placed in a recess in the step just before the mast was lowered into position. The rigging and the rudders were installed last.

Wooden ships have been classified as either 'skeleton'- or 'shell'-built; the former having been constructed of planks that were attached to frames, and the latter built of planks into which frames were added to strengthen the hull (Greenhill 1976, 60–88). Blackfriars ship 1, on this basis, was essentially 'skeleton'-built at the sides, but the bottom could have been in part 'shell-built'. However, the evidence suggests that the shipwright considered that it was the frames that held the hull together and so it should be classified as primarily 'skeleton'-built.

The characteristic features of its construction are defined as follows:

- flush laid planking
- hooked iron nails with cone-shaped heads containing a caulking
- 'keel-planks'
- massive floor-timbers
- side-frames not attached to the floor-timbers
- a mast-step in a transverse floor-timber with median ridges
- caulking, both between the planks and in the nail heads, of applied hazel shavings in warmed pine resin

Crew accomodation

The size of the crew will have depended partly depend upon whether or not the ship was used on long sea voyages. The fact that mature *Teredo* borings existed in the hull of the Blackfriars ship shows that it was kept in salt water for considerable periods. Since these periods may represent voyages it is likely that the crew lived on board and had been able to cook meals there. The accommodation may have been in a deck cabin at the stern, as was often depicted in Roman mosaics, paintings, and sculpture in the Mediterranean area (Casson 1971, figs 140–5). The reason is that, as in more recent times, this was close to the position where steering and propulsion were controlled. But, as there are no certain representations of the Blackfriars type of ship in northern Europe, the accommodation arrangements are unknown from iconography. A careful study of the forward half of the ship for traces of rubbish or possessions of the crew revealed very little: just two fragments of a single pottery bowl on the bottom planking between two floor-timbers (Fig 71A), a wooden mallet (Fig 71B), and a piece of leather decorated with a fish (Fig 71C), the nautical design and the site context suggesting that this was part of an object used on board. Moreover, there was no trace of tiles, as are sometimes found in Mediterranean wrecks and are believed to be from the hearth and galley roof (Casson 1973, 178). It is concluded, therefore, that any living accommodation was at the stern. This is consistent with the evidence from the similar ship found at St. Peter Port, Guernsey, where traces of occupation, including part of a hearth, were found collapsed in the bottom at the stern (Rule 1993, 128). The finds from the St Peter Port ship are particularly interesting for they suggest that there was a crew of three (Rule 1990, 50, 55). This may have applied to the Blackfriars ship too since both the St Peter Port and Blackfriars ships were of similar size: the St Peter Port ship being *c* 14.05m long between the foot of the stem and sternposts compared with 11.3m in the Blackfriars ship. But the St Peter Port ship was narrower, the maximum length of its floor-timbers, and therefore its bottom, being 4m compared with 4.7m in the Blackfriars ship.

Where was the ship built?

Eleven samples of planking from Blackfriars ship 1 were studied by Ian Tyers, Environmental Department, Museum of London, for dendrochronological analysis, and from these it was possible to reconstruct a chronology for the ship's timbers covering 167 years. This matches well with many other London tree-ring chronologies demonstrating that the ship was probably built from trees growing in or near south-east England (see Appendix 6).

When was it built and used?

The date of construction of the Blackfriars ship should lie between AD 79, the year the coin of Domitian from the mast-step was minted, and *c* AD 150, the date of the pottery around the sunken wreck, or between AD 90 and *c* AD 150 if allowance is made for wear on the coin. However, the tree-ring study of eleven planks provides a likely felling range for the timbers of AD 130 –175 (see Appendix 6). It should be noted that since the floor-timbers originally retained much of their sapwood when excavated it is likely that a more precise date should be possible from future excavation.

No repairs were noted, except possibly near the forward end of plank P1, and there was no trace of wood decay or rot anywhere in the hull. Even the mast-step socket, which could have become rotten due to water seepage down the mast, was unaffected. It would seem, therefore, that the ship was not old when it sank. Although *Teredo* had infested the planking, *Limnoria* infestation had only just begun. On this basis it is unlikely that the ship was more than twenty years old when lost, and it may have been considerably less. The construction, use, and sinking of the Blackfriars ship, therefore, could all probably have occurred about the middle of the second century AD.

How was the ship used?

There are two main groups of evidence suggesting how the ship was used: firstly, the cargo of ragstone and the millstone, and the *Teredo* borings in the hull. Secondly, the ship's form and construction allow a theoretical assessment to be made of its performance and stability under a variety of conditions.

The ragstone cargo

The most obvious evidence for the use of the ship was its cargo of building stone that was presumably being transported to London from a landing place close to a quarry. The stone, piled up to one metre thick, was situated aft of the mast-step, where it was surrounded by grey clay (Fig 39, layer 3) and lay between the floor-timbers where it had broken through the ceiling planks (Fig 72). The grey clay lay over the lowest part of the hull and appeared to be a silt which had settled in the sunken hull before the sides collapsed.

Samples of the stone were submitted to the Geological Survey and Museum, where F Dimes and R Casey identified them as ragstone, probably from the Hythe Beds of Kent. The Hythe Beds 'rag', is a Cretaceous blue-grey sandy limestone of the Lower Greensand that outcrops in a fairly narrow band from the Sevenoaks area through Maidstone to Hythe and Folkestone (Fig 73). One sample of ragstone was identifiable by its fossils (Table 8) as having definitely originated in the Hythe Beds division of the Lower Greensand. The sample containing the fossils cannot be localised in Kent precisely, but its characters cannot be matched exactly outside west Kent. The fossils show that the neighbourhood of Maidstone is a likely source, particularly as this location is also suggested by the River Medway, which is the only navigible river flowing through the region where ragstone outcrops.

The last voyage of the Blackfriars ship was apparently down the winding River Medway from the Maidstone area (Fig 74), past the Roman town of Rochester (*Durobrivae*), and into the Thames estuary. As the voyage up the Thames was against both the prevailing south-westerly wind and the river current the ship must have used flood tides to reach Londinium.

That the stone was cargo and not ballast is indicated by the fact that this was the building stone that was extensively used in Roman London, and that an analysis of the force needed to right the ship when heeled (see Appendix 5) shows that no ballast was required. An

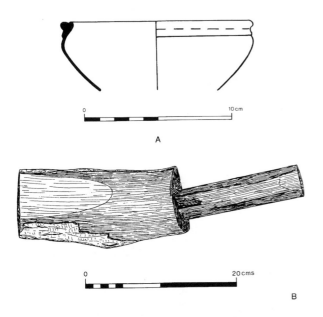

A

B

estimate of the quantity of stone carried in the ship depends upon the extent of the hold in which it lay and upon the volume of cargo found. For stability reasons it is probable that the hold was central to the ship, and that the ceiling extended aft to about floor-timber 18, giving a hold nearly 6m long. Since the depth of the stone appears to have been about 1m in the forward part of the hold it seems that the ship was carrying very roughly 26 tonnes of stone.

Apart from the fossil and river evidence indicating a quarry site in the Maidstone area, there are medieval records to show that in later times London acquired its ragstone exclusively from that region (Hewitt 1932, 391–2; Worssam 1963, 28–45).

It is difficult to suggest the precise source of the stone cargo as no Roman quarries have been found in the locality, presumably because they were enlarged in later times and Roman features were destroyed. It has been suggested that an apparently isolated Roman bathhouse at Brishing in the ragstone quarrying area of Boughton Monchelsea (Fig 74) might have been associated with quarrying (Taylor 1932). However, this is some distance from the River Medway, and it was probably as essential in Roman times as recently to avoid any unnecessary handling and transportation of stone from the quarries to the river. A more likely spot is Allington, a mile (*c* 1.5km) north of Maidstone, where the stone outcrops on the west bank of the Medway. Quarrying there has been taking place for centuries, and it may be significant that traces of Roman buildings have been found there (ibid). In support of the Allington site is the fact that it now lies

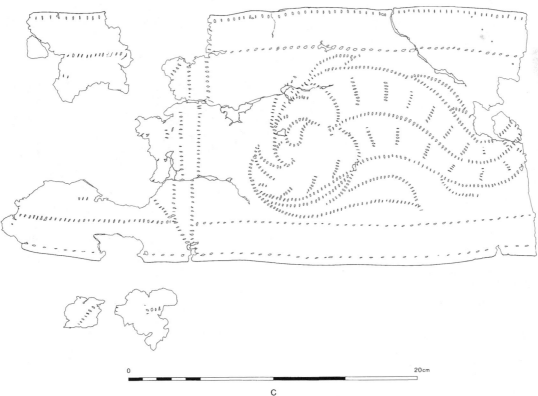

C

Fig 71 Objects found in Blackfriars ship 1: (A) fragments of a bowl; (B) a wooden mallet; (C) piece of leather pierced with a fish decoration

downstream of the natural tide limit of the River Med-way, and that in Roman times, when the sea level was lower (Devoy 1980), it is likely that ships could reach there on flood tides since the tidal range at Allington is now from 0.2m to 3.6m OD (Information from the Emergency Planning Officer, Southern Water Authority) and compares well with the tidal range for central London which was accessible to Roman shipping.

The method of extracting stone from the quarries and loading it into the barges in recent times may not have been very different from Roman practice. Recently, after being broken out of the quarry face by explosives and crow bar, the pieces were reduced to convenient sizes by sledgehammer for handling and grading for quality. It was then transported to the River Medway, often by rail, for loading into barges (Carr 1951, 290–3).

Many of the lumps of stone found in Blackfriars ship 1 were large and of irregular shape, and samples weighed: 2.7, 9.5, 10.9, 11.3, 14.0, 14.9, 16.3, 24.0, 27.0, 31.0kg (ie up to 60–70 lbs). It is likely, therefore, that they were lowered into the hold in containers, for had they been dropped onto the ceiling planking, only 25mm thick, particularly where it was not supported beneath by a frame, considerable damage could have resulted. In recent times ragstone has been loaded into Thames–Medway barges by means of chutes (ibid, pl 67), whose rusting remains could still be seen beside the Medway at Allington during the 1960s. But the individual lumps of stone were usually smaller in size than those

in the Blackfriars ship, and the ceiling planks in recent wooden barges were about 0.07m thick, and therefore were more able to withstand the impact (the late H Shrubsall, a Thames barge builder, pers comm).

During the Roman period the stone was carried far away from the quarry sites for use in public works (Fig 73), particularly the temple of Claudius at Colchester, the *pharos* or lighthouse at Dover, the defensive walls at Reculver, Richborough, and Rochester, as well as in many public buildings in London (Williams 1971, 172). Significantly, these distant locations could all be supplied by sea, and cone-headed nails of Blackfriars ship type, found at Richborough (Cunliffe 1968, pl LVII, no 284) suggest that Romano-Celtic ships visited that port. The reason for the transportation of stone to London and to other settlements was no doubt because of the absence of local building stone, and therein may lie an important clue to the organisation behind the voyage of the Blackfriars ship.

Enormous quantities of ragstone were brought to London during the Roman period, starting soon after the invasion of AD 43, for the stone was used in the foundations of walls pre-dating the Boudican destruction of AD 60–1 (Philp 1977, 15; Marsden 1987, 20). During the late first – early second centuries AD, a period of great expansion in London, ragstone was extensively used in public buildings such as the basilica and forum (Marsden 1987), public baths (Marsden 1976b), an amphitheatre (*Britannia* 1988, 462), a palatial residence believed to be

Fig 72   The cargo of Kentish ragstone in the hold of Blackfriars ship 1. The size of this load had been reduced by the site contractor in 1963 before it was photographed. Scale in feet.

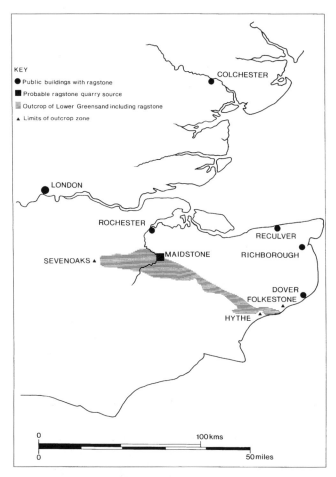

Fig 73   The last voyage of Blackfriars ship 1 is shown by the source of the ragstone cargo, near Maidstone in Kent.

for the governor (Marsden 1975), and a large military fort (Grimes 1968, 15–40). Some of these structures were constructed by the provincial government, and the stamps, believed to be of the Roman *procurator*, on tiles used in the walls of the palace and the basilica (Marsden 1975, 70–72; Merrifield 1983, 87–89) indicate the probable involvement of the Roman provincial administration there too.

The greatest single demand for the stone, however, must have been for the defensive city wall of London, built in the early third century AD (Fig 75). A rough indication of the size of the task of quarrying the stone and transporting it to London to build the defences can be made using data from Blackfriars ship 1. It is estimated that the ship may have carried about 20 cubic metres of stone weighing 26 tonnes, based upon the fact that one cubic metre of the loose stone weighs 1.3 tonnes (Information from ARC ragstone quarry manager, Allington, Kent). Since the defensive wall of Roman London had a ragstone volume estimated at about 35,000 cubic metres (Marsden 1980, 126–7), it would have required 1750 voyages by a ship the size of Blackfriars ship 1 to bring about 45,000 tonnes of the stone to London, a distance of some 112 km (70 miles) each way, for the landward defences alone. Although this gives only a very rough idea of the quantity of stone involved for this single public structure, it is indicative of the scale of manpower and shipping resources at the command of the Roman authorities. Since ragstone was being quar-

ried in the Maidstone area in huge quantities from the mid first to the third centuries for public buildings in south-east England, many constructed by the provincial adminstration, it seems likely that the quarry area was part of an 'imperial estate' owned by the Emperor, for this would guarantee output of the quarries over a long period on this scale. If this interpretation is correct the control of the output, men and transportation of stone would be in the hands of a *procurator*. There must have been a large workforce in the quarries, and it seems likely that the Roman sites in and around Maidstone (Fig 74) represent their settlements. The future investigation of sites there other than villas would be particularly interesting, especially if there was a substantial decline in the local non-villa settlements around Maidstone in the fourth century, when it seems that the demand, at least for public buildings in London, ceased.

Ragstone was not the only building material being shipped down the Medway to London, for the foundations of some first-century buildings and the Roman city wall required flint nodules that had been quarried from the chalk. Moreover, the chalk itself, at least in some structures in London, was converted into lime for the mortar (Evans 1980, 117). The Upper Chalk, in which the flints occur, outcrops lower down the Medway valley around Rochester, and it is likely that there were further quarries there. The proximity of the chalk outcrop area to the ragstone quarries suggests that this too was part of the postulated imperial estate. This could explain the function of the large early Roman villa excavated at Eccles, close to the River Medway and between Maidstone and Rochester, for it could have been the official residence of the *procurator* who administered production (Percival 1976, 94). Although the difficulties in identifying imperial estates should not be underestimated (ibid, 131–3), it is worth noting that part of the Weald south of the Maidstone area was involved in iron working for the Roman navy, the *Classis Britannica*. It is believed that this too was part of an imperial estate administered by the imperial *procurator*, possibly operating through local *procuratores*, who would in turn delegate the running of the individual works to a *villicus* or bailiff (Brodribb and Cleere 1988, 240). The stone quarrying, therefore, should be seen as part of an imperial exploitation of natural resources in south-east England, and ships of the Blackfriars type were part of its transportation system. But whether or not this ship was in private ownership and under contract for the voyage cannot be known.

Table 8   Fossils in a sample of the ragstone cargo of Blackfriars ship 1

Bivalvia	*Exogyra latissima* (Lamarck), *Plicatula placunea* (Lamarck), *Linotrigonia (Oistotrigonia) ornata* (d'Orbigny), *Anomia laevigata* (J de C Sowerby);
Annelida	*Serpula* sp;
Porifera	Spicules of undetermined genus and species

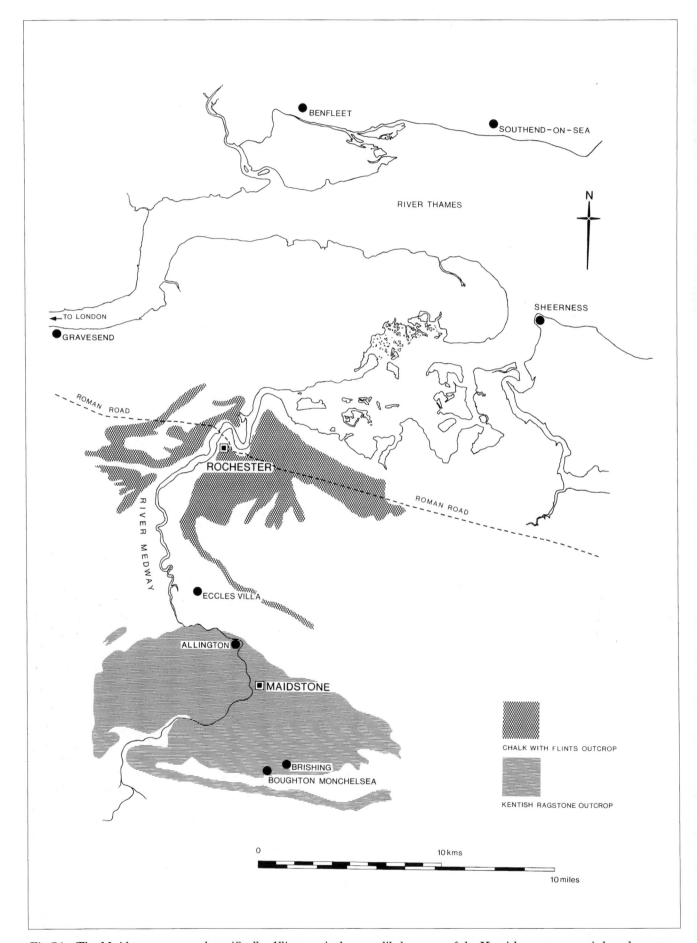

CHALK WITH FLINTS OUTCROP

KENTISH RAGSTONE OUTCROP

Fig 74   The Maidstone area, and specifically Allington, is the most likely source of the Kentish ragstone carried as the cargo in Blackfriars ship 1.

The millstone

A previous voyage is suggested by a large unfinished millstone found lying convex side uppermost, on top of floor-timbers 2 and 3 in the bow of the ship (Fig 76). It was a 'blank' awaiting finishing, for it had no hole in the centre and no grooves to spread the grain evenly when in use. A fragment of the stone was sent to the Geological Museum where F Dimes reported that it is Millstone Grit (Fig 77), similar but not identical to specimens in the Geological Museum from the Pennine region of Yorkshire. However, there is no certainty that the stone was quarried in England, for Millstone Grit also occurs in the Namur region of Belgium, around the Meuse valley where it is known geologically as the Namurian series of rocks (information from the Geological Survey), and where there is evidence for the ancient manufacture of millstones (Jottrand 1895). As the millstone in the ship was heavy and unfinished it seems likely that it was collected near the place of manufacture, which would favour Belgium rather than high in the Pennines since the former had a major river, the Meuse, flowing close to the quarries. The location of the millstone within the ship shows that it was not being used in the vessel, though it had been put aside on its own forward of the hold, as if it was intended that it should not be damaged by or mixed with any cargo.

A recent study of the Roman millstones and querns from the maritime port of London (King 1986) shows that of the 32 examples found, excluding the millstone from the Blackfriars ship, only 3 (9.4%) were of Millstone Grit. As the remaining 29 (90.6%) were of lava probably imported from the Rhine, this strengthens the view that the millstone was more likely brought from Belgium than from the Pennines. The main sources of millstones and querns found in London contrast with those found at the inland city of Verulamium (St. Albans) where it seems that British products were more important. Of the 33 Roman querns and millstones found at Verulamium at least 24% were believed to be from a variety of British quarries: 6 (18%) were of Puddingstone, 1 (3%) was of Old Red Sandstone, and 1 (3%) was of Greensand. However, 10 (30%) were of Millstone Grit, presumably from the Pennines or Belgium, and 15 (46%) were of imported lava probably from the Rhineland.

Fig 75   The external face of the Roman defensive wall of London, built of Kentish ragstone: early third century AD.

Infestation by marine borers

Samples of planking from the ship containing mollusc borings were examined by N Tebble and R Ingle of the Department of Zoology at the British Museum (Natural History). In one sample the holes had been bored by the ship-worm *Teredo* (Fig 78), but the exact species could not be determined. Another showed slight signs of attack by *Limnoria*, represented only by two or three charac-teristic holes amid the numerous *Teredo* channels. It seemed that in this single sample *Limnoria* had just begun its attack. *Teredo* only attack the underwater parts of a vessel, and as infestation was found in the stempost and in side-frames 7 and 9 at the seam between planks P6 and P7 the waterline of the ship must sometimes have been at least 1.22m above the underside of the keel.

Both *Limnoria* and *Teredo* are marine wood-boring creatures (Forest Products Research Laboratory 1950),

Fig 76   Recording Blackfriars ship 1 in the coffer-dam during 1963. The bow is at the top. Scale in feet.

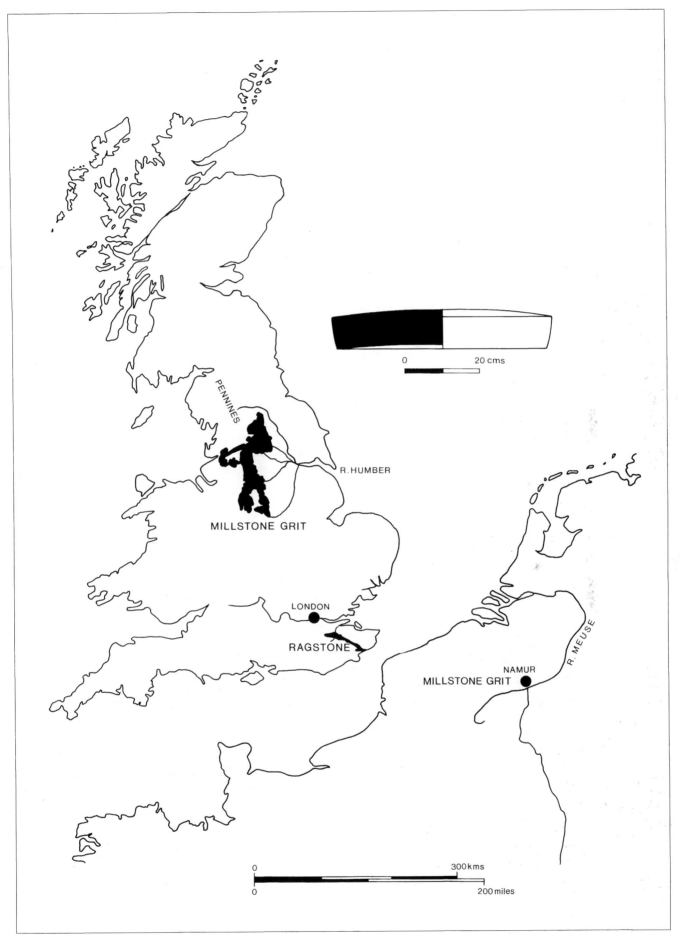

Fig 77   Outcrops of Millstone Grit in England and Belgium, and a drawing of the unfinished millstone found in Blackfriars ship 1.

and the former cannot live for long in water with a salinity of less than 16 to 20 parts per 1000, while the latter requires a salinity of at least 5 to 9 parts per 1000. *Teredo* is therefore found further up rivers than *Limnoria*. The average salinity of sea water is 35 parts per 1000, while the present salinity of the River Thames at London Bridge is about 3 to 4 parts per 1000 at high tide, and is negligible (about 0.04 parts per 1000) at low water (Information from the Port of London Authority). The infestation of timber by these creatures could not occur in the conditions now prevailing at London Bridge. There is much evidence to show, moreover, that during the Roman period the sea level in relation to the land in south-east England was considerably lower than at present (Devoy 1980), so that both the tidal limit and the minimum salinity required for the existence of these marine wood-borers would have occurred further downstream than at present. However, there is evidence that the tides, and therefore a little salinity, did reach London in the first century AD (Milne 1985, 81–4). Waterfront structures in Roman London have no *Teredo* borings, so clearly there was and still is an insufficient salinity for them to live. The infestation therefore occurred during the working life of the vessel while at sea or in a tidal estuary. The borings, although somewhat eroded, were mature and show that the ship had spent much of its time in seawater, for otherwise the freshwater of rivers would have killed the *Teredo* in about fourteen days.

Since the Blackfriars ship was sunk while transporting building stone from the Maidstone area to London, it should not necessarily be regarded as having been in-volved in trade when lost for it could have been on government service. Moreover, as much of this route lay in rivers where there was a low salinity, the mature *Teredo* infestation of some of its timbers must have occurred while engaged in previous voyages, perhaps while carrying goods from the Continent to Britain. The mill-stone, possibly from Belgium, may be a clue to this, and if its source has been correctly identified, would indicate how this ship moved from one commissioned job to another – sometimes perhaps involved in market trading, and at other times in the distribution of goods (Peacock and Williams 1986, 55–66).

Stability and performance

A sufficient amount of the ship has survived for a theoretical assessment of its stability and performance to be made. But to do this it is essential to define two of the key attributes of the vessel when afloat, its shape, and its total weight distribution. It is important to remember that a floating ship is subject to two opposing forces (Fig 79), gravity which tries to sink the vessel, and buoyancy which tries to force it up out of the water, and it is its balance in that state that is significant – particularly when this is disturbed by wind and waves which could cause it to capsize. The inherent stability of a ship is measured by the distance between the Centre of Gravity of the ship and the height of the transverse Metacentre (ie the Metacentric height, see Fig 79 and Appendix 5).

The behaviour of a floating hull is predicted by hydrodynamic rules that have been established over a long

Fig 78   Eroded Teredo borings in the planking of Blackfriars ship 1.

period of time by naval architects and scientists who have tested the design and behaviour of numerous ships. Such theoretical analyses are important nowadays since, before investing large sums of money in building a new ship, it is essential to know that when launched it will be stable and will do the job for which it was built. Since the rules of hydrodynamics apply equally to ancient ships as to modern vessels, it is necessary to consider how much information is needed to complete the reconstruction of a ship for which a stability study will be valid. The following at least should be known: the approximate overall length, the form of the ends, the midship shape and beam measurements, the height of the gunwale amidships, the height of the deck and position and size of the hold. Although it is not necessary to know how the ship was built it is essential to know where the weight was distributed about the vessel so as to calculate the stability and weight of the ship as a whole, and also (for the particular analytical method used in this study) the density/weight of an average square metre of the hull.

A method of assessing the stability and performance of a ship is described by McGrail (1987, 20–2, 192–203), but the task is made easier by using a computer program designed for the purpose. Several such programs exist, the one used here being called Boatcad. Although the method used is peculiar to the Boatcad program it does use established rules for assessing stability and performance (Rawson and Tupper 1983). Assessment begins with the input of the reconstructed hull shape using the offset measurements taken from the reconstruction drawings, whereupon the computer is asked to make the calculations. The parameters for the reconstruction of the Blackfriars ship, already discussed, are summarised below:

- overall length – 18.5m
- beam – 6.12m
- lowest height of gunwale – 2.86m
- deck height – 2.16m
- weight of hull and deck 25.23 tonnes (calculated by Boatcad)
- weight of superstructure – 4.5 tonnes
- length of keel –11.3m

Since the stability and performance calculations are given in Appendix 5, it is only necessary to give the main conclusions here. The calculations show that in the loaded condition the ship as reconstructed would have been difficult to capsize, for the Metacentric height (GMt), a measure of the righting moment, ranged from 0.77 to 1.1m. They also show that the working draught with a full hold was probably between 1m and 1.5m, just below the point of maximum stability. It seems that the ship could carry a cargo with a maximum weight of about 50 tonnes. Moreover, under normal circumstances it would not expect to travel at more than about 7 knots, though a maximum speed of 9 – 10 knots is theoretically possible under ideal conditions with a strong following wind.

Bearing in mind the volume of the hold and the weight and size of the different types of cargo, it is estimated that the ship could have carried a full hold comprising 12 large barrels of wine, each weighing 1.278 tonnes, of types that have been found reused in Roman wells in London; or 18.36 tonnes of grain; or 28 cubic metres of loose ragstone which would weigh 36.4 tonnes. The estimated 26 tonnes of ragstone found in the ship only partly filled the hold, and there was room for up to a further 24 tonnes of cargo. These weights explain why the heavy floor-timbers and thick keel-planks were not only necessary to strengthen the hull bottom to withstand grounding, but also to support high density cargoes, such as stone. Although these assessments are based upon a reconstruction of the ship, enough of the vessel had survived, particularly in its transverse section, to show that they are unlikely to be substantially different from actuality. Thus they are the first indication of the size, capacity, and performance of a seagoing merchant ship of the Roman period in northern Europe. To what extent the size of Blackfriars ship 1 was typical of shipping in the northern provinces is not yet clear. However, it is possible to place this cargo load into perspective by comparing it with the loads of some cargoes found in Greek and Roman wrecks in the Mediterranean (see Table 9). It is clear from this that the load carried by the Blackfriars ship was small.

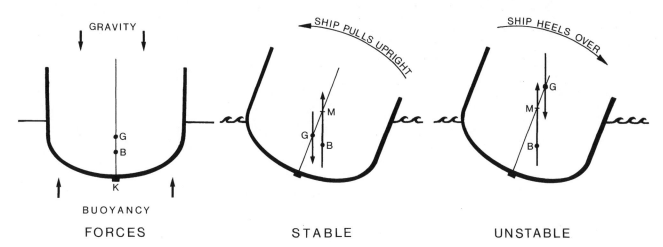

Fig 79   The forces acting on a ship, seen in cross-section. (B) is the Centre of Buoyancy; (G) is the Centre of Gravity; (M) is the Metacentre. For stability (G) must lie below (M).

Table 9   Cargo loads found in some classical wrecks in the Mediterranean

wreck	date	cargo type	approx cargo weight
Torre Sgarrata, Italy	second century AD	stone	170 tonnes
Marzamemi 1, Sicily	third century AD	stone	172–200 tonnes
St Tropez, France	second century AD	stone	200+ tonnes
Mahdia, Tunisia	first century BC	stone	230–50 tonnes
Isola delle Correnti, Sicily		stone	350+ tonnes
Madrague de Giens, France	first century BC	amphorae (6500)	325 tonnes
Albenga, Italy	first century BC	amphorae (11000–13500)	500–600 tonnes

(Gianfrotta and Pomey 1981, 282–4)

If the discovered parts of the waterfront of Roman London are representative of the best of the berthing facilities provided by the ports of the northern provinces during the Roman period, then it seems likely that the depth of water at the quayside at high tide of between 0.5 and 1.5m probably indicates that Blackfriars ship 1 was one of the larger seagoing merchant ships of that region. This interpretation is supported by a review of the weight of the heaviest single items that were shipped around northern Europe at that time, for these rarely, if ever, exceeded 1.25 tonnes. Much more study is needed of the volume and weight of shipped goods found on land sites, but already these suggest that Roman merchant shipping in the Mediterranean could carry much greater loads than was carried by shipping in the northern provinces.

Having made a detailed study of the Blackfriars ship and assessed its theoretical performance, it remains to complete this reconstruction by 'fairing the lines'. This means producing a set of drawings in which the slight irregularities caused by distortions, erosion, incomplete evidence, and other uncertainties, are largely removed. The discovered lines of the seams between the hull planks indicate that the shipwright intended that they should be evenly curved as is the traditional practice in shipbuilding. Consequently, it is necessary to remove these irregularities by finding a median line for each seam. Had the planks been recovered from the site and then drawn it would have been possible to make scale models of each, and by bending these to determine the original hull form. Unfortunately this was not possible and so it is necessary to rely upon the site plan and the recorded widths of planks shown in section at various stations, the dimensions of which are not always known exactly. It is possible to plot these out on the Boatcad program to give the best fit of all that was found, and from this to compile a total reconstruction of the ship. Boatcad can produce the following drawings to illustrate its reconstructed shape:

- a plan of the ship (Fig 80)
- a side elevation (Fig 81
- end elevations (ie a 'body plan', Fig 82)
- waterlines (Fig 83)
- buttock lines (Fig 84)
- strake diagrams (the shape of each strake when laid flat, Fig 85)

Views of the ship can also be made on Boatcad to show the hull form from various angles, and these are then used as the basis for drawings which suggest what the vessel might have looked like (Fig 69).

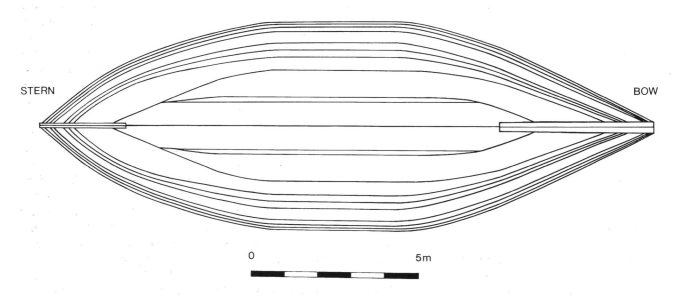

STERN   BOW

0   5m

Fig 80   Computer plan of a reconstruction of Blackfriars ship 1.

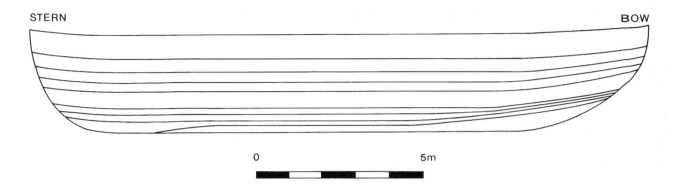

STERN

BOW

0   5m

Fig 81   Computer side elevation reconstruction of Blackfriars ship 1.

This study shows that a considerable amount of detailed knowledge exists about the ship, but that in many respects it is only possible to guess at how the ship was best handled. For example much more information is needed about the methods of loading and unloading heavy cargoes, particularly from tidal beaches, perhaps by using the yard; how close to the wind could the ship sail, bearing in mind that voyages in such vessels were commonly from the Rhine to London and therefore against the prevailing south-westerly wind; how long would the ship take to be loaded with a cargo of building stone, and then for this to be carried from the Medway to London; and how much would leeway (ie being blown sideways) affect the ship with alternatively one or two quarter rudders, and how effective would these rudders be in steering the ship?

The solution to these and other research questions can only be found by building a full-size working reconstruction; although many details will be uncertain, the general pattern of performance should be valid. This would be a valuable guide not only to understanding this example of a seagoing Romano-Celtic sailing ship, but also would enable an assessment to be made of the efficiency of the earliest ports in Britain with their tidal beaches. In this way it would complement the working reconstructions of Viking ships built in Denmark and Norway (Brogger and Shetelig 1951, 141–5; Neerso 1985), of a medieval merchantman or *cog* recently built in Germany, and of an ancient Greek merchant ship (the Kyrenia II ship) and a warship (*Olympias*) built in Greece (Katzev 1989, Coates *et al* 1990). Except for the Greek warship all of these working reconstructions are based upon archaeological discoveries of sunken ships.

The loss of the ship

The Blackfriars ship sank in the mainstream of the River Thames, opposite the mouth of the River Fleet, probably about the mid second century AD (Fig 18). It is conceivable that it might have been deliberately sunk to form the foundation of some port construction, as was the ship sunk at Portus, at the mouth of the Tiber, which formed the foundation of a Roman lighthouse (Meiggs 1960, 155). However, as the excavations around the ship did not reveal other Roman structures, and the vessel had

such a list that much of its bottom after sinking was unsupported and liable to the accumulation of driftwood, this explanation is not tenable.

Sinking

The ship was found heeled over to port, with the bulk of the ragstone cargo lying on that side holding the hull at an angle of 11 degrees from vertical (Fig 39). Since it is extremely unlikely that the stone would have been stowed off centre, and it is difficult to imagine how it could have moved after the ship had sunk, it is probable that it had shifted during the sinking process. This is, therefore, a clue to the cause of the loss of the ship.

The most common causes of ships sinking in recent times are foundering in severe weather, stranding, contact with or striking a fixed structure, collision with other ships, fire, war loss, and hull failure (Couper 1983, 162–9). Of these, striking a fixed structure such as a waterfront or a submerged object, or colliding with another vessel are likely to cause a ship to heel over sharply in the sheltered conditions of a river, though it is just possible that a severe gale or even an attempt to raise the ship after it had sunk could have heeled the vessel. The River Thames at London does present shipping hazards, as is demonstrated by the four historic shipwrecks found in the Blackfriars area, and recently by the *Marchioness* which was sunk nearby in a collision with a considerable loss of life. Whatever the cause in the case of Blackfriars ship 1, the heeling force must have been great, for its natural stability, as measured by the Metacentric height of 0.76m and by the very considerable righting lever of the ship as reconstructed, would have offered a strong resistance. Because of this, and the location of the ship far from both the Roman London bridge and the river bank, the most likely cause of sinking would seem to have been a collision. As it came to rest across the flow of the river with the bow facing southwards away from the city waterfront, it is likely that the ship drifted on the current while sinking and came to rest on the riverbed some distance from the site of the accident, either upstream or downstream depending upon the tide.

Since the bottom of the Blackfriars ship, beneath the mast-step, lay at 3.59m below OD, this was about the level of the river bed at the time of the sinking. With a tidal range probably from about 0.5m above to 1.0m below OD (see Chapter 1) the ship was therefore lying in about 2.6 to 4m of water at that time, depending upon the state of the tide. No human remains were found and there is no reason to believe that there was any loss of life, though the possibility cannot be ruled out; Roman sailing fatalities did occur in Britain as is demonstrated by a tombstone found at Chester which records the death of a soldier in another shipwreck (Collingwood and Wright 1965, no 544).

The estimated tide levels show that it would have been possible for a salvor to have walked upon the submerged deck at low water and to have removed items of value such as the mast, rudders and anchors. However, the

ragstone cargo was probably not considered to be of great value since such stone was rarely robbed from the ruins of buildings in London during the Roman period. For some time after the sinking, therefore, the ship would have been a shipping hazard until it broke up and its sides collapsed.

Break up and burial of the ship

Evidence in the alluvium deposited in and around the vessel makes it possible to reconstruct the most likely sequence of break-up and burial of the ship (Fig 87). The river bed on the wreck site at the time of the sinking was grey silt (Fig 39, level 4), in which, a short distance to

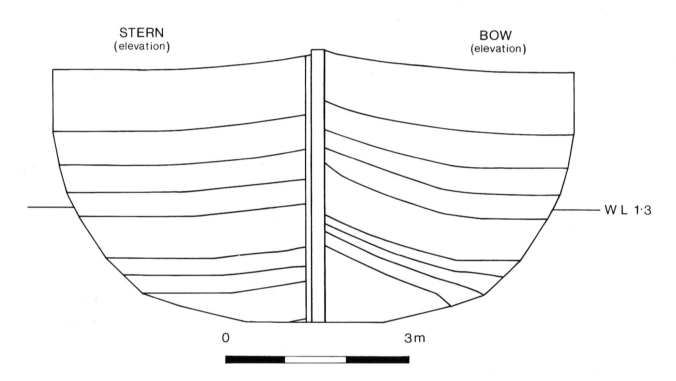

Fig 82   Computer-drawn end elevation (ie body plan) of Blackfriars ship 1.

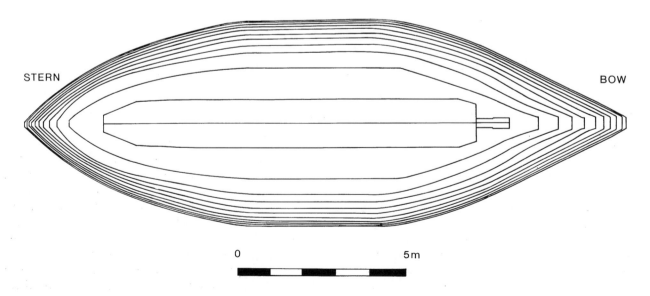

Fig 83   Waterlines at vertical intervals of 0.28m. Computer reconstruction of Blackfriars ship 1.

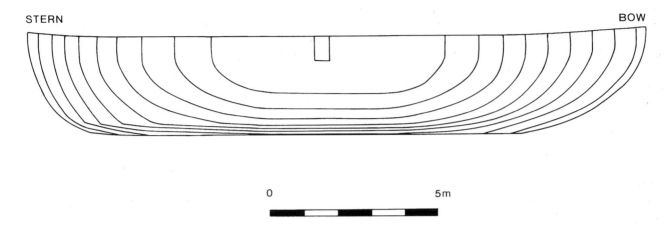

Fig 84   Buttock lines (ie vertical longitudinal profiles) of the hull. Computer reconstruction.

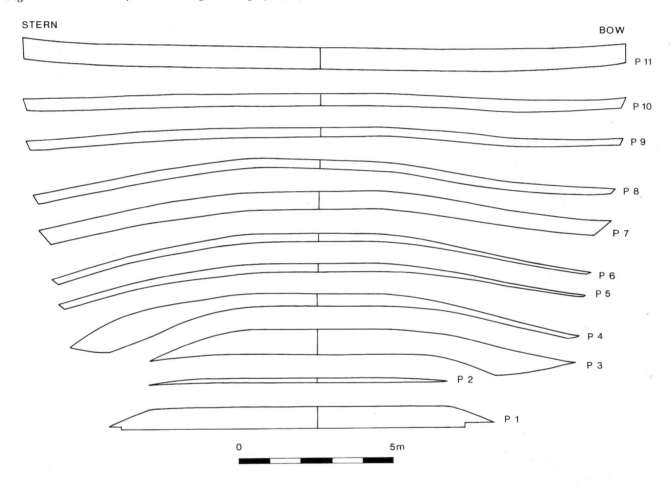

Fig 85   The shape of each strake when laid flat, from the computer reconstruction of Blackfriars ship 1.

the west, was found a sherd of samian ware, showing that it was deposited during the Roman period. The first sign of alluvial deposition after the sinking was an accumulation of gravel and tree branches, evidently driftwood, caught under the upward sloping bottom of the ship on the starboard (upstream) side. These branches were aligned north-south, parallel with the axis of the vessel, and were tightly held against its underside and presumably reflect a strong downstream flow. By the time the sides of the ship had collapsed about 0.5m of gravel had accumulated around the wreck. The gravel below the

forward part of the ship evidently prevented the bottom from collapsing downwards, but at the stern the hull timbers appeared to be lying horizontally as if that end might have collapsed downwards. If this assumption is correct this would have occurred before the gravel accumulated under that part of the vessel, and may indicate that the stern portion had partly fractured away from the rest of the ship, perhaps as a result of the accident.

In the forward half of the ship the starboard side had collapsed inwards, and the port side outwards, the direction of the collapse downstream no doubt having been

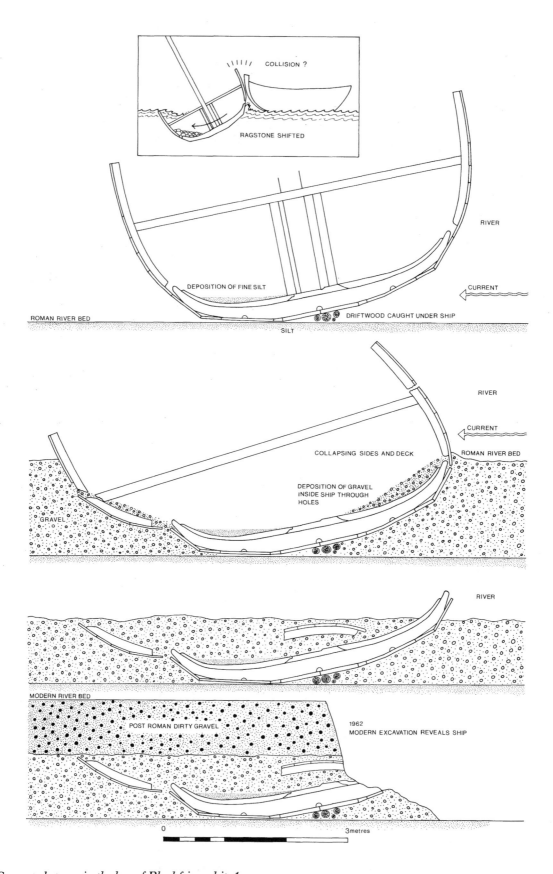

Fig 86   Suggested stages in the loss of Blackfriars ship 1.

caused both by the force of the river current and by the inclination of the ship. The starboard side overlay two basic deposits of alluvium within the ship: a fine grey silt (Fig 39, layer 3), and above that river sand and gravel (layer 2).

The fine stiff grey silt (Fig 39, layer 3), the primary deposit, was the layer most likely to contain objects used in the ship. It lay between the floor-timbers in the bottom, and was at its thickest amongst the cargo in the hold, thinning out towards the bow. This suggests that the hatch, or open hold was the entry point of silt-laden water into the sunken ship, and that once in the comparatively still water inside the bow there was less fine silt to settle out. The silt was up to 0.33m thick at floor-timber 7, but how long this took to accumulate cannot now be judged. It contained relatively few objects, all of which were Roman (Excavation Register 860; Marsden 1967, 48–57). These include a number of broken wooden barrel-staves probably deposited as driftwood since there was no indication that they were once joined and part of the cargo. Other objects could have been used on board, including a wooden mallet, possibly used for caulking (Fig 71); a piece of leather decorated with a fish (Fig 71); the tibia of an adult horse; a wooden wedge 0.19m long, 0.38m thick at one end, and more than 0.05m wide; and two fragments of a single coarse grey sandy ware bead-rimmed bowl (Fig 71a) of a type made in the first or second centuries (Appendix 1). These two sherds, broken in antiquity, were the only fragments of pottery found in level 3 and they immediately overlay the bottom of the ship. Since they were fragments of the same pot, and they occurred in isolation from other pottery, it is likely that the pot was in use on board before the ship sank.

The river gravels forming layer 2, which overlay the clay, contained many broken pieces of the ship, including the sides which had collapsed. This gravel could only have been washed into the wreck after the sides had begun to collapse at river bed level. Once the sides collapsed the deck and its beams also must have collapsed (Fig 86), and as both sides apparently survived to a similar height it seems likely that the deck lay just above that level, and that the hull above had been washed away.

Dating evidence

The date at which the sinking occurred depends mostly upon an analysis of the pottery found in the clean yellow river gravel deposit (Fig 39, level 2) that had been washed into the wreck (Marsden 1967, 48–55). Most of the dateable material was found in the upper half of this layer with many broken timbers of the ship containing cone-headed iron nails (Excavation Register 854).

During the emergency excavation in 1962 it seemed likely that the speed of work might cause some contamination of the dating evidence by finds from later deposits. Consequently, several undisturbed parts of the deposit of clean yellow gravel, layer 2, were carefully excavated by trowel. One of these comprised the gravel immediately above strake P6 of the collapsed port side, and beneath the end of floor-timber 8 (Excavation Register 855). Another area marked the point where the gravel was sealed by part of the inward collapsed starboard side (Excavation Register 871). Since most of the pottery was in the upper half of level 2, with the broken ship's timbers, the date of the latest pieces indicate the period when the wreck broke up rather than when it sank. This pottery points to a mid second-century date for the sinking (see Appendix 1).

This is consistent not only with the dendrochronological study of some timbers which indicate that the ship was built about the middle of the second century, but also with the absence of repairs which suggest that the vessel had not been in use for too long. It is important to remember that the stern half of the hull remains still survive in the former river bed, now beneath the new roadway. Judging from the floor-timbers found in the forward half, these stern timbers should include sapwood, and that from these it may well be possible to obtain a very close tree-ring date for the construction of the ship.

3 The New Guy's House boat, 1958

Discovery

Part of this second-century boat was found by the writer on 8 March 1958 as workmen dug a trench (Fig 87, trench 1) for a foundation near the south-west corner of New Guy's House, the then new surgical wing of Guy's Hospital in Southwark, close to the south end of London Bridge (Fig 1). The vessel lay in a silted creek of Roman date, east of the modern street called Great Maze Pond. There was little opportunity to record it *in situ*, but information was recently recovered from pieces of frames and planks cut away in 1958 and preserved in the Cuming Museum, Southwark, (acc no 1959.1) and in the Shipwreck Heritage Centre, Hastings.

From the start it seemed that the vessel might date from the Roman period because it lay at a depth of about 4.9m, at which level Roman pottery had been found a few metres away. For confirmation a small excavation (Fig 87, trench 2) was carried out by the writer in 1960 to recover some dating evidence, and to study the construction and state of preservation of the boat (Fig 89). The ancient timbers and iron fastenings were in an excellent state of preservation because they lay in water-logged clay overlying sandy gravel, though the remains of the vessel in trench 2 were vandalised during the excavation and part of its west side was destroyed. This small excavation, which included areas just north of the boat, revealed pottery which dated its abandonment to the end of the second century AD.

Once recognised and dated it was clear that the vessel was worthy of protection, particularly as the hospital authorities had a major building programme in the area which might have endangered it further. An application for legal protection was made to the Department of the Environment, whose reply was that this was not possible under the then existing ancient monuments legislation because the vessel was classed as a chattel, since it was originally designed to move. Had there been any form of fixed structure adjacent to the boat, even a post, that structure could then have been scheduled with a surrounding protected area that included the boat. Unfortunately, no such fixed structure was found.

A report on the vessel was published in 1965 (Marsden 1965c), though it is now evident that the boat belongs to the Romano-Celtic family of shipbuilding traditions, and is the only known example definitely built in Britain, since it is just possible that Blackfriars ship 1 could have been built in northern Gaul to give a tree-ring pattern like that of the London area. A further small excavation was later carried out by M Maitland Muller of the Cuming Museum, Southwark, at an unspecified location close to the southern part of the vessel, which recovered a loose piece of its timber.

When discussions were taking place during the 1970s to revise the ancient monuments legislation, repre-

sentations were made by the writer and others in the hope that ancient ship sites like that at Guy's Hospital could in future be protected. This was accepted, and the Ancient Monuments and Archaeological Areas Act 1979 included the necessary provisions. Following a new application by the writer to the Department of the Environment the boat site was scheduled under the Act as a protected monument on 22 June 1983.

Even so, the quality of long-term protection for the vessel is still uncertain, for new hospital buildings have recently been constructed over part of the protected area and the vessel is becoming inaccessible. Moreover, the water-table is now below the boat and only the residual water in the surrounding silts keep it wet. Since the new buildings are also restricting the ingress of rainwater into the ground, it seems likely that in time the deposits will dry out and the boat will decay away. The experience of the gradual dewatering and drying of the natural deposits in the reclaimed parts of the former Zuyder Zee shows that action is needed soon to assure the survival of the boat (de Jong 1979, 253–5).

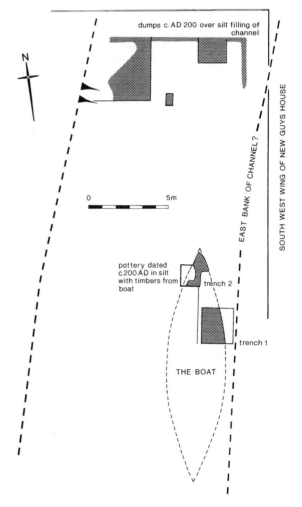

Fig 87 The position of the New Guy's House boat adjacent to the south-west wing of the hospital building.

The boat

Materials used in its construction

The planks, frames and the end-post (ie stem or stern-post) were all of oak (*Quercus* sp), and the caulking in the seam between some planks was of crushed hazel wood (*Corylus avellana*) in the form of shavings, see Appendix 3 (identification by the Director and David Cutler of the Royal Botanic Gardens, Kew). Iron nails were used to fasten the planks to the frames, and traces of a pine tar coating were found on the exterior of some of the planks (identified by John Evans, University of East London). The caulking and pine resin were identical to that used on Blackfriars ship 1 (Appendix 4).

Description of the vessel

Excavations revealed the northern part of a broad barge-like vessel, whose south end has yet to be found. The excavations were in two trenches, one of which, trench 1, was dug roughly by the site contractors so only limited details of the boat were recorded, near the middle of the vessel (Fig 88). More detail was available from trench 2, which was archaeologically excavated at the north end, though the vessel was only viewed from inside.

For the purpose of this description the frames have been numbered from the north end southwards, and the planks have been numbered from the endpost outwards. The term 'endpost' has been used in relation to the curving timber found in trench 2 that was either the stempost or the sternpost.

The north end

The hull was found to be curving inwards horizontally to the north end throughout the whole 6.7m recorded length of the vessel, and consequently it is possible to reconstruct the general shape of that end. It is not known if it was the bow or stern, for the main clue, the step for a mast or towing post, was not found.

Endpost

At the north end the upper part of the stempost or sternpost was 0.152m wide, and narrowed to 0.127m near its lower end (Fig 89). Below frame 2 it was 0.114m thick, and had been cut with a rabbet on each side to accommodate the ends of the planks fastened in place by means of iron nails with flat heads and square shanks. These rabbets were at an angle of 47° to the flat upper surface of the endpost at frame 2.

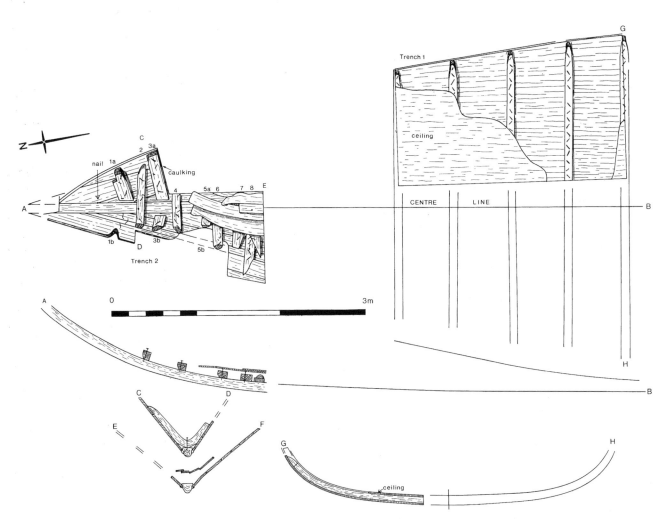

Fig 88   Plan, long-section, and cross-sections of the New Guy's House boat.

Fig 89   The north end of New Guy's House boat. Scale in inches.

Planks

The planks throughout were about 0.025m thick and were laid edge-to-edge. Judging from fragments recovered from trench 1 they were tangentially cut, presumably by saw though no saw marks could be seen on the dried timbers. At the north end, in trench 2, the planks narrowed towards the endpost to about 0.3m wide. There were no scarf joints. It is presumed that in trench 1 many of the planks were wider since they were nearer the full beam of the vessel. There were no fastenings holding the planks to each other edge to edge, though through the thickness of plank fragments recovered from trench 1 were a few small drilled holes up to about 5mm across that were filled with wooden pegs or bungs, as if nails and trenails had once been located there. Their purpose is not clear.

Samples of planks 4E and 5E in trench 2 had tar adhering to their outboard surface, and fragments recovered from trench 1 also had a similar surface coating. Analysis showed that this was a pine resin that had probably been applied at a low heat (Appendix 4).

Against the outboard surface of the planking on the west side of the boat in trench 2, was found a timber rectangular in section, 0.076m wide and 0.038m thick. This was originally thought to have been a fender (Mars-den 1965c, 120), but as no fastenings were found and fenders of this form are unknown on Romano-Celtic barges this timber is more likely to have been a piece of shaped driftwood lying hard against the hull.

Caulking

The seam between planks 4E and 5E in trench 2 was found to have been caulked with hazel shavings (Corylus avellana) lying across the seam. Recent analysis indicates that these shavings and a warmed pine resin had probably been placed into position before the next plank was fastened (Appendix 3, 4). The caulking was not restricted to this end of the vessel since amongst the broken pieces of planking recovered from trench 1 was a portion with a similar caulking adhering to its seam edge. Other pieces of plank edge from trench 1 bore no trace of caulking and no other caulked seams were noted in trench 2, suggesting that not all seams were caulked. It is possible, therefore, that the caulking was only applied when there were gaps between the planks, and that such gaps did not always exist.

The junction where the planks were fastened to the rabbet in the endpost below frame 2 contained traces of the epidermis of a root whose internal tissues had become so disorganised that the root could not be identified. It is most unlikely that this insubstantial material was a caulking, but instead it probably comprised the roots of plants growing after the boat was abandoned in the creek.

Frames

In trench 1 the frames were flat on the bottom and curved 0.52m upwards to the surviving top of the side. Traces of probably five frames were uncovered in the trench, four appearing to have been spaced c 0.432m apart and two were c 0.533m apart. Each frame was rectangular in cross-section measuring 0.146m wide and 0.076m deep, and their upper ends at the sides of the vessel appeared to narrow on the fore-and-aft sides.

The frame fragments recovered from trench 1 had been cut from a quarter of a tree branch, and two pieces retained sapwood along one edge. Two of the dried fragments had shallow limber holes, now 30 and 38mm wide and up to 5mm deep, on their undersides. They formed an inverted V in section, and still retained the marks of the blade of the cutting tool at their apex. Although the frames had become shrunk and distorted on drying, their original size was preserved as impressions on the iron nails still within the dried timbers. This shows that these frames were originally about 0.065m thick (moulded), and that originally the limber holes were a little more than the size mentioned above. Of particular interest were the limber holes which crossed the frames diagonally at angles of 62° and 75° to the frame sides. As limber holes in Blackfriars ship 1 and in the County Hall ship tended to follow the alignment of seams between planks it is possible that this also occurred in the New Guy's House boat. This would explain the odd angles of the limber holes, particularly if they followed the tapering end of a keel-plank similar to those in Blackfriars ship 1. Had this postulated keel-plank in the Guys Hospital boat been much thicker than the hull planking, it should have been seen in the sections of trench 1, but no such plank was noted.

At the north end of the boat, in trench 2, there were two forms of frame (Figs 88 and 90). There were three pairs of side-frames (1A, B; 3A, B; 5A, B) lying at an angle to the endpost and nailed opposite each other to the inside of the outer hull planks. Also, U-shaped crooks (frames 2, 4, 6, 7, 8) fashioned from naturally grown trees, approximately 0.114m broad and 0.076m deep.

Two scarf joints seem to have existed in frame 8, one on the west side and one (a possible scarf) over the endpost (Fig 93), and as they were so close together and roughly fashioned it is likely that they represent repairs to the frame. The western scarf was vertical, 0.28m long in a frame 0.1m wide. The scarfed timbers were fastened together by a nail driven horizontally through the scarf from the north side, and by a nail hooked over the top of the two timbers. This is exactly how a second scarf was fashioned in a loose frame fragment found in trench 1. This scarf was probably about 0.5m long, of which 0.36m survives, in a frame now 0.11m wide. One ordinary sized iron nail, with a shank about 8mm square in section, had been driven horizontally through the scarf, and there was the impression of a hooked nail holding the two timbers together on the inboard face. In contrast the possible scarf in frame 8, over the endpost, was horizontal and more rounded, suggesting that it was a repair patch strengthening the frame.

Fastenings

The planks were held to the frames by hooked iron nails which had flat heads and shanks about 8mm square. The wood was hardly deformed where the nails passed through the outer planks and frames, and it seems that holes had been drilled through both prior to the insertion of the nails. The point of each nail was turned at 90° to the shank, and the shank itself was turned through a further 90° so that the point was embedded in the top of the frame (Fig 46). In general each nail was bent in a herring-bone pattern, downwards towards the keel and across the centre of the frame, presumably to distribute stresses.

Ceiling planking

In trench 1 the inner surface of the frames was covered with a ceiling of oak planks 0.02m thick (Fig 93). They were fastened to the frames by iron nails with flat heads and shanks about 0.102m long and 4mm square.

The U-shaped frames at the north end of the boat incorporated a central vertical nail, whose head stood about 0.025m proud of the upper surface over the end-post. This indicated that a plank had originally been fastened along the centre-line above the endpost (Fig 89), but had rotted away leaving the nails in position. This missing plank gave access to that end of the vessel, and had been replaced by some loose oak planks also 0.02m thick, and between 0.076m and 0.177m in width, lying on the top of the frames.

Fig 90   Frames on the east side of the north end of New Guy's House boat.

Reconstruction of the boat

As only one end and part of one side of the New Guy's House boat has been investigated, it is only possible to make a tentative reconstruction of the entire vessel.

Length

Although it is certain that the north end was pointed, the form of the south end could have been either pointed or squared, since both shapes occur in Romano-Celtic barges on the Rhine. However, in the Rhine vessels the opposite ends were normally of similar shape, and on this basis it seems probable that the south end of the Guy's boat was pointed too. This enables an estimate to be made of the length of the vessel, for, as all of the 6.7m length of the north end was curving in to that end, it seems likely that there was a similar length of curved hull at the south end. By allowing for a section in the middle of the vessel, it would seem that the boat had a minimum length of 16m.

Beam

Since the endpost gave the central longitudinal axis of the boat it is possible to establish that the width of the vessel, at the south end of trench 1, was about 3.8m. However, the side of the boat seems to have suffered some distortion, for in trench 1 it sloped outwards (Fig 88), whereas it seems more likely that the upper ends of these frames would have stood vertically. Moreover, the inward curve of the sides of the vessel in plan to the north end shows that the section at the south end of trench 1 lay close to the maximum width of the boat. Therefore, if it is assumed that the sides were originally a little more upright, taking account of their distortion, this would give the vessel a little more freeboard, and a probable width of about 4.25m (Fig 94).

Height

The surviving side of the boat was only 0.52m high in trench 1, but as the upper ends of the frames seemed to be tapered on the fore and aft sides, it seems likely that only the gunwale was missing. By adjusting the vertical

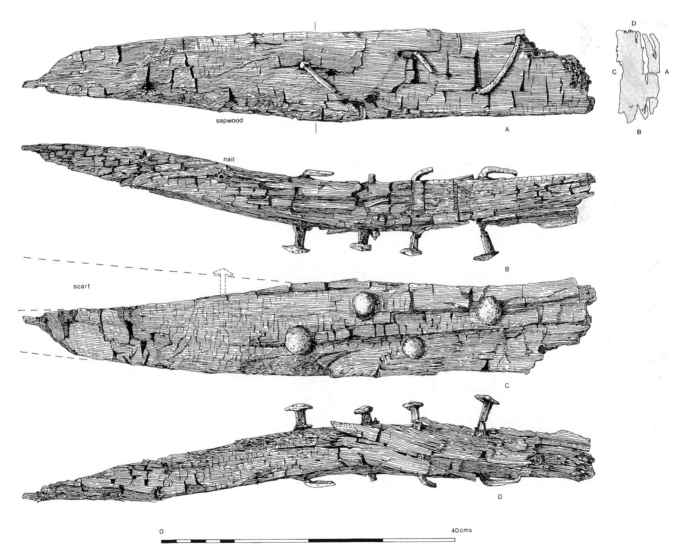

Fig 91 Drawing of a scarfed frame of the New Guy's House boat, found in trench 1. This timber was drawn in its dried and shrunken state.

Fig 92   The inner planking of the New Guy's House boat, at the north end.

curve of the side so that the ends of the frames were more upright, and by assuming that the top of the sloping faces of the frames represented the top of the side, it seems that the boat was originally a little over 1m deep amidships. The run of the planks at the north end shows that there was some sheer, with the gunwale rising upwards towards that end (Fig 94).

Propulsion and steering

No evidence was found for propulsion and steering.

Sequence of construction

The building sequence of the vessel was similar to that of Blackfriars ship 1. Frames had probably been fastened to a keel or keel-plank, and the stem and sternposts were added presumably before most of the planking. The caulking of hazel shavings and warmed pine resin were placed on the plank edges before the next plank was attached (see Appendices 3, 4). Finally, a ceiling of planks was nailed on top of the frames inboard, and the outboard plank faces were coated with a pine resin.

The small isolated bored holes containing pegs in the planking, were similar to those noted in Blackfriars ship 1, and may represent temporary fastenings, such as cross-battens, holding the planks in position before being attached to the frames. This suggestion, however, can only be checked by further excavation.

There are various uncertainties which do emphasise the need for a very careful study of the hull when further excavation is possible, and in particular the importance of recording the exact location of all pegs, trenails and iron nails.

Where and when was the boat built?

As the freeboard of the boat was so low it is clear that the vessel could not have been used at sea; it must have been built on the Thames or on one of its tributaries. A

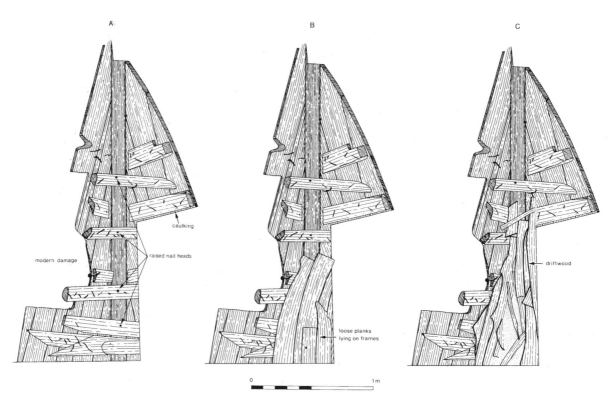

Fig 93   The construction of the north end of the New Guys House boat: (A) raised nail heads indicate the position of a (missing) central plank; (B) loose planks on the frames; (C) driftwood that had accumulated in the boat.

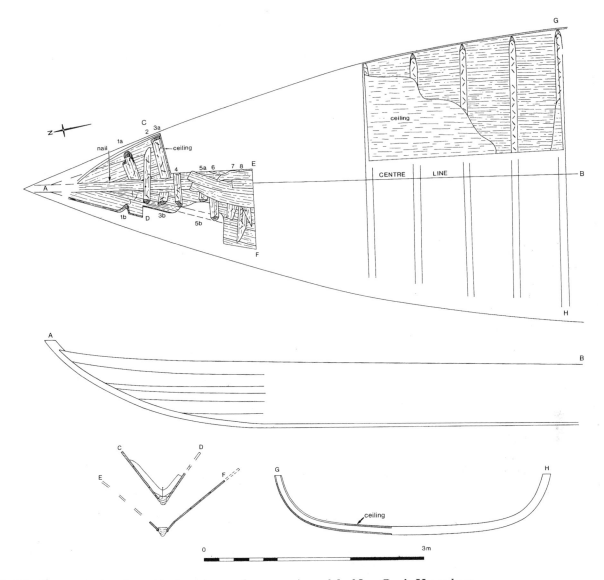

Fig 94   Reconstruction plan, side elevation, and cross-sections of the New Guy's House boat.

tree-ring analysis of some dried plank fragments gave inconclusive results. Dating evidence in the silt deposits around the vessel (Marsden 1965c, 123–31) indicates that it was probably abandoned at the end of the second century AD. Damage and repairs show use over some considerable time, though the life-span of more recent wooden barges suggests that it had been built during the second half of the second century AD.

How was it used?

It seems safe to assume that this shallow, open, beamy vessel, at least 16m long, about 4.25m wide, and about 1m high, was a river barge designed for use in the shallows of the river Thames and its tributaries. The ceiling in the midships region presumably indicates that this was part of the hold that was designed to carry cargo. The pointed end shows that it was not well suited to the transportation of cattle and waggons as were some of the Rhine barges of the Roman period which had broad sloping ends, 'swim heads', down which vehicles could be wheeled and cattle walked (de Weerd 1988, 205), as indeed occurred in barges used on the Thames in more

recent times (Chaplin 1982, 40; Wilson 1987, 41). In fact it was more likely that loading was effected from the sides into the hold amidships, and that the vessel was serviced from low quays. Excavations at Guy's Hospital in 1990 revealed such a quay in the creek in which this vessel was found abandoned (Fig 17), and it seems very likely that the barge was used there (Heathcote 1990, 193, cover). This barge, therefore, was ideally suited to carrying goods up and down the river between settlements, and future excavations may find evidence of former cargoes in the silt in the bilge of the boat, particularly under the ceiling planks.

Although only a minimum reconstruction of this vessel has been attempted, and much remains uncertain about its length, propulsion, steering and the weight of its fittings (eg anchors and cable) and crew, nevertheless it is possible to obtain an approximate indication of its lightload draught (ie without cargo, crew or fittings), and of its possible load. These can be calculated on the Boatcad program on the basis that the hull had a density/weight of 35kg/square metres. This is based upon the weight of the frames, the iron nails, the outer planking and the inner ceiling planks, and it is assumed that the discovered parts of the hull are typical of the whole vessel. On calculating the hull area, Boatcad gives a total weight of 1.862 tonnes and a lightload waterline of 0.144m. This is ideal for working in the shallows at the edge of the Thames; and with a waterline of 0.4m, which gave a freeboard of two-thirds the height of the sides, the vessel would have had a displacement of 9 cubic metres and could carry a load of about 7.14 tonnes. As some of this weight would include fittings and crew it is likely that the cargo weight was about 6 tonnes. It is important to stress that this is only a very rough approximation but it is a useful guide, though further excavation would make possible a much more accurate assessment of the performance and stability of the craft.

Damage and repairs during use

There was considerable evidence of damage and repair, indicating that this was a much-used vessel. The long central plank over the frames at the north end had been replaced by loose planks about 0.15m wide (Fig 93). Frame 6 was found to be split in three places above the endpost. Frame 8 had a roughly made scarf and a possible strengthening piece inserted in the centre, probably after the central plank had been removed for there was no central nail with a raised head there as was the case in frames 4, 6, and 7. Moreover, the small plugged holes in plank fragments from trench 1 may represent the former position of frames that had been replaced. Side-frame 1B was missing and bent iron nails still in place show that it had been wrenched out, presumably by some impact, as is indicated by the hole in the plank behind. The plank above this too was missing.

The loss of the boat

The boat lay in a shallow creek in the marshes on the east side of the Roman bridgehead settlement in Southwark, near London Bridge. It lay roughly NNE-SSW, its bottom at about 0.15m below OD, and was covered by some 2.1m of silt and 2.75m of post-medieval rubbish.

Damage to the vessel indicates that it had been abandoned there due to old age. For some time driftwood had accumulated inside and around the vessel together with fresh-water molluscs, the deposit inside the hull near the middle of the vessel being 0.152m thick in trench 1. At the north end, there was more driftwood, and also some outer planks which had fallen off (Fig 93).

The dating evidence for the abandonment of the boat is derived from two sources. Firstly, thirty-three small sherds found in the silt around the north end, were dated to about AD 190 – 225 (Marsden 1965c, 124, 128–9), and secondly, dumps of rubbish in the creek just north of the boat, that probably cut off access to it from the river and should therefore be later than its abandonment (Fig 87), date from the end of the second and the early third centuries (ibid, 126). Taken together, this indicates that the vessel was probably abandoned at the end of the second century AD.

4 The port in the later third and fourth centuries

Historical context

London evidently considered itself threatened during the late third and fourth centuries. Not only was a riverside wall built in the later third century to complete the defensive circuit already built on the landward side of the city (Fig 4) earlier that century (Miller *et al* 1986, 72; Sheldon and Tyers 1983, 358), but also a possible look-out tower was erected beside the river downstream at Shadwell, perhaps to monitor a threat from seaborne Germanic raiders (Merrifield 1983, 191–4). To these pressures must be added the economic and political difficulties of the closing years of the third century, particularly the rebellion of the Roman usurpers Carausius and Allectus in 286 and the reclamation of Britain in 296 by the legitimate Roman ruler in the West, Constantius Chlorus, and his entry into London (Fig 95) (ibid, 200–206). London's administrative role in the fourth century is suggested by the minting of coins there until about AD 326, the presence of the official in charge of the provincial Treasury (Royal Commission on Historical Monuments 1928, 7) and by the city's status as the seat of a bishop in the newly established Church (ibid, 4).

However, the archaeological evidence suggests a city that had changed fundamentally from its earlier character, for not only are there few traces of any significant new building activity, except for defence, but also the quayside was allowed to fall into decay. The population of the city was apparently small in relation to the area enclosed by the defences, for houses within the city seem to have been scattered, with large open areas between them (Marsden 1980, 148–9).

After the middle of the fourth century Britain was under increasing barbarian attack, and in the 360s it succumbed to raiders on two occasions. When Count Theodosius restored Roman rule in AD 367–8 he may have been responsible for building the system of bastions on the exterior of the landward city wall, though as these occur around less than half of the defensive circuit it seems likely that the scheme was unfinished. At that time building stone was apparently no longer obtainable from the ragstone quarries in Kent, possibly because the organisation for quarrying and transporting the material no longer existed. Instead, existing buildings and monuments in London, fine tombs particularly, were demolished and the stones reused. Moreover, in the late fourth or early fifth centuries the riverside defensive wall was strengthened with further construction work (Parnell 1985, 13–22), with the building stone obtained from the demolition of religious buildings (Hill *et al* 1980). There is no evidence to indicate a final battle for the survival of the Roman city, since the few known very late Roman buildings appear to have been abandoned rather than deliberately destroyed (Marsden 1980, 163–86).

Indeed the remaining population of Roman London appears to have deserted the city during the fifth century, and the discovery of a Saxon saucer brooch in the ruins of the late Roman bath at Billingsgate suggests that by about the middle of the fifth century Saxon settlers in the countryside near London had unimpeded access to the abandoned Roman city (Merrifield 1983, 236–68).

Types of ships and boats in London

Local river boats

Barges were presumably used to transport pottery down the River Thames from Oxfordshire (see p 107), but as the river upstream from London was mostly not tidal and had shoals and rapids, it is likely that towing was necessary against the river flow, as in medieval times (Wilson 1987, 30–2).

Fishing boats

That these were used in the Thames estuary is indicated by fish bones found on a waterfront site at Peninsular House, Lower Thames Street. A reused Spanish amphora of the second century AD had been smashed and was found surrounded by thousands of fish bones in a deposit dated on coin evidence to the end of the third century. The bones were mostly of young whole herring (84%), with sprat and individual bones of bass, flatfish and sandeel comprising the rest; all of them probably caught off Britain. The sprat almost certainly required a fine-mesh net, and although the fish could have been

Fig 95 Reverse of a gold medallion commemorating the arrival of Constantius Chlorus in London in AD260.

105

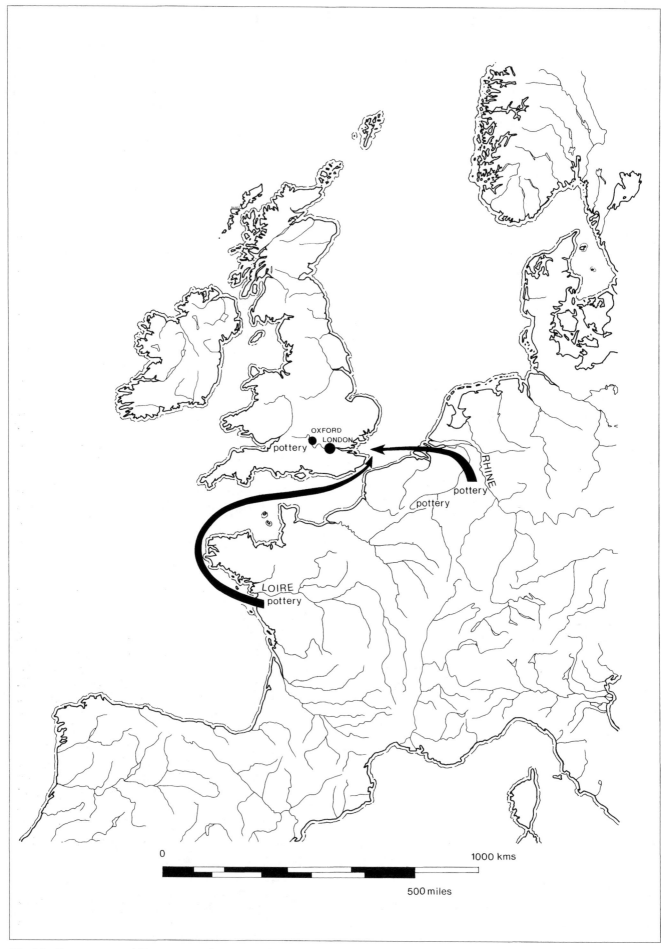

Fig 96   Some suggested European trade routes to London, late third to fourth century

preserved elsewhere by smoking or salting, it is likely that they had been brought to London soon after having been caught, for around the deposit were traces of a timber building, a tank, and drain, suggesting that this was a fish-processing plant for a local fish sauce (Milne 1985, 87–91).

Seagoing merchant ships

That such vessels visited the port is indicated by pottery imported from the Rhineland and Gaul, even though the quantity seems small relative to the first and second centuries (see below).

Warships

These were evidently present on the Thames from time to time, particularly in AD 295 on the arrival of Constantius Chlorus. A warship is depicted on the reverse of a commemorative gold medallion which also shows a woman, personifying Londinium, kneeling at a city gate while greeting Constantius (Fig 95). Since this medallion was minted in Trier it is unlikely that its designer had seen either Londinium or the warships used (Merrifield 1983, 200), and none of this detail can be taken as a true representation of the actual scene.

Cargoes

Four waterborne trade routes to London seem to have been particularly important in the latter part of the third and fourth centuries (Fig 106): the cross-Channel route bringing goods from the Rhineland to south-east Britain (Fulford 1977, 39–46), the Atlantic route from western Gaul to southern Britain (ibid, 45–7), the route down the River Thames from the Oxfordshire area to London (Richardson 1986, 130–1), and finally the coastal routes around eastern and southern Britain, between the Humber and Dorset, to the Thames estuary (Milne 1985, 115). Occasional discoveries in London of coins from distant mints, such as Thessalonica in northern Greece, of amphorae from the eastern Mediterranean, perhaps carrying olive oil or dates, and of pottery from north Africa, show that links with distant parts of the Empire were not broken, even though they were tenuous by earlier standards (Fulford 1977, 56; Milne 1985, 124–5; Richardson 1986, 129).

Gaul

The Atlantic trade route from Gaul to Britain, presumably using the river Loire, is indicated by pottery believed to have been manufactured in the Poitiers region of Aquitania in western Gaul. Known as 'ceramique à l'éponge', it is mainly found in Britain within 50 miles of the port of *Clausentum* (Southampton), as well as in late Roman deposits in London (Richardson 1986, 130).

Germany

Two types of pottery imported into London during the fourth century reflect the Rhine-Thames shipping route. German coarse pottery, particularly Mayen wares manufactured in the Eiffel Mountains between the rivers Rhine and Moselle, and fine orange Argonne ware manufactured east of Rheims between the rivers Meuse and Aisne, are mostly found in south-east England, on coastal and riverbank sites like London (Fulford 1977, 41–5).

Britain

It is possible that the rise of the Oxfordshire red-slipped pottery industry was a response to the reduction in imported pottery from Gaul and Germany, caused by barbarian raids which damaged the East Gaulish samian ware factories in the middle of the third century. This Oxfordshire pottery was widely distributed around south-eastern Britain, particularly in London and Kent, during the late third and fourth centuries, and was even exported to northern Gaul where sherds have been identified at Boulogne and Etaples. It is likely that it was barged down to London and trans-shipped for seaborne voyages (ibid, 50). At New Fresh Wharf, London, the Oxfordshire pottery was mostly no later than the first half of the fourth century, suggesting that the trade continued for some time after the quay on that site had become derelict, though how it was brought through the line of the riverside wall is not clear (Miller *et al* 1986, 64; Richardson 1986, 130–1). Sherds have even been found beyond the Roman frontier, at Traprain Law, Scotland, and one possible fragment has been found at Tara, Co. Meath, Ireland, but it may be that these were the result of barbarian raids rather than trade (Fulford 1977, 55).

The transportation of goods down the Thames is also indicated by an important discovery in 1859 in the river near Battersea Bridge. The circumstances of the find are not known, but six pewter ingots, weighing a total of 15.8kg were given to the British Museum, a further two are now deposited in the Museum of London, and two more are in the Yorkshire Museum. These seem to have been part of a shipment of raw pewter which was lost in the Thames during the fourth century AD. The 'hoard' may represent a wreck site, for it is otherwise difficult to understand how the collection was lost in the river. Analysis of the ingots at the British Museum shows that they were of tin, probably mined in Cornwall, and of lead, probably from Somerset or Derbyshire. Of considerable interest are the stamped impressions of a Chi-Rho, 'Spes in Deo', and the name SYAGRIVS which was presumably that of an official responsible for the production of the ingots (Hughes 1980).

Conclusion

Although pottery can reveal patterns of trade, it is best seen as an indicator of the more common shipping routes by which other, more perishable, goods were also carried. The quantity of pottery being carried across the

Channel in the late third and fourth centuries was much smaller than was carried during the first and second centuries (Fulford 1977). Nevertheless, London was evidently a viable port exerting a focal role in maritime trade even as late as the fourth century AD. There is no certain evidence for heavy packaged goods, such as amphorae, barrels of wine, or stone blocks, being shipped to London, and this may be as much a reflection of the decaying waterfront and the absence of bulk cargo handling facilities as of the economic difficulties of the late Roman empire.

Berthing

Waterfronts

Excavations at a number of waterfront sites in Thames Street have cast doubt upon the importance of shipping and trade to London during the fourth century. The massive second- and third-century quays found there were decaying and had been separated from the rest of the city by a riverside defensive wall (Brigham 1990, 140–1). At New Fresh Wharf the wall lay only 3m back from the quayfront (Miller *et al* 1986, 50–1), and is believed to have been built *c*255–70 AD (ibid, 72). The disuse of the quay is also suggested by silt deposits up to 0.7m thick against its front, for these were allowed to accumulate during the mid or later third century, and subsequently the quay was robbed perhaps in the early fourth century (ibid, 50, 64; Tatton-Brown 1974, 127–8). If such circumstances were general along the late Roman waterfront it is hard to understand how London could have functioned as a port (Miller *et al* 1986, 72). Nevertheless, as some trade goods clearly were still being imported into the city there must have been some fa-cilities for berthing and unloading which have not yet been found.

Mooring

One possible explanation of this problem is that seagoing ships were being moored in the river and unloaded their cargoes into barges with a shallow draught. This could explain the use of the County Hall ship, since Roman merchant ships of Mediterranean-style construction were built for a tideless environment in which they normally stayed afloat. The existence of patched leaks and repaired frames in the bottom of the County Hall vessel shows that the master was aware of the dangers of frequent grounding which might in particular damage the mortice-and-tenon joints, and it is unlikely that he would knowingly increase these difficulties. The level of high tide in the late third century is not known, but as the base of the riverside wall lay between 0.4m and 1.2m OD it is likely that high tide lay below 0.4m OD (Brigham 1990, 144).

Warehousing

There is no evidence of new warehouses being built in London during the late third and fourth centuries, though the probable trans-shipment of Oxford ware into seagoing ships at London implies their existance. Although the first century warehouse buildings at Pudding Lane continued in use during the fourth century, each room was by that time different in plan and construction, suggesting an uncoordinated use of the buildings which would not be expected if they were still employed as warehouses (Bateman and Milne 1983, 219–24).

5 The County Hall ship, 1910

Discovery

The central part of a ship of the late third – early fourth century AD was found in February 1910 during the building of County Hall on the south bank of the River Thames, between Westminster Bridge and Hungerford Bridge (Fig 1). It was excavated and recorded by London County Council officials, and an excellent booklet describing the vessel was published by the LCC (Riley and Gomme 1912). As this had long been out of print a new account of the ship was published in 1965 (Marsden 1965a), and subsequently, when additional information was found, particularly a full-sized copy of the original large-scale plan of the vessel, it became desirable to publish a more detailed description (Marsden 1974). However, this has now been superseded by new information mainly derived both from dismantling the reassembled remains of the vessel, and from a study of its story since 1910 (Sheppard 1991, 31–2, 52–4).

The ship was not removed from the site until August 1911, by which time the wood was becoming shrunken and brittle as it dried (Fig 97). Attempts were made to preserve it by painting it with glycerine, but without much success. A recent study of the pieces of planking show that the inboard face, on which the glycerine was painted, was rather less damaged than was the outboard surface which had remained in contact with the wet sand. The ship was removed as a single object, on a huge wooden cradle, to the new London Museum at Kensington Palace, and was placed in a new temporary exhibition shed called the Annexe. Moving the vessel was a spectacular occasion, for it had to be jacked up on its cradle slowly to street level (Figs 98 and 99), and on 24th August it was carried on an eight-wheeled wagon pulled by twelve powerful carthorses through the streets of London, past the Houses of Parliament, to its new home (Fig 100). The traffic of London was disrupted, but as a means of gaining publicity for the new museum it could not be bettered. A large tarpaulin covering the ancient vessel announced: 'Roman boat, London Museum', and the museum's director, Guy Laking, led the procession on horseback, while officers of the museum and the LCC followed in a motorcar. The procession reached its new home by 5.30 pm, the arrival of the unique treasure being witnessed by a large crowd of the public.

By then the Roman timbers were in a poor state for display and a museum official was commissioned to replace much of the damaged timber with painted plaster. It was probably then that the plaster and the inboard face of many timbers were coated with tar to simulate the ancient oak. A report by an official of the Museums Association a few months later stated that the vessel had been 'transformed into some sort of gluey composition', and he concluded that 'we cannot regard its future with equanimity'. The ship was displayed in a large pit lined with sand, and enhanced with simulated pools of water, a scatter of seashells, and a stuffed seagull (Fig 101). The exhibition was highly praised, and in March 1912 was viewed by King George V, Queen Mary, and other members of the royal family (Fig 102).

Guy Laking was happy with the outcome, but in 1912 privately wrote of the man who 'restored' the vessel, 'I do not know who else could have assisted me to fake it in the manner I directed'. He added that 'We have now finished with the Roman boat. Another is not likely to be found, we will take good care of that. This echoes the sentiments of all the officials of the London County Council who have been bothered with this white elephant' (Sheppard 1991, 53–4). Their attitude reflects the problem encountered by many museums subsequently when faced with trying to accommodate the substantial waterlogged remains of an ancient ship, or the many objects that have been recovered from a early shipwreck – all needing conservation. The task can be overwhelming, with the result that the safest action on the part of a museum has normally been to do nothing. With this in mind the efforts of the London Museum are to be applauded, since they have ensured that at least some pieces of the ship are still available for study eighty years after the discovery.

In about 1913 the vessel was moved to the basement of Lancaster House nearby and was displayed in a similar sunken area. However, during the 1939–45 war the basement was occupied by War Reserve Police who used it as a dormitory, and are said to have bowled some large stone cannonballs from the museum store into the vessel, and to have used the sunken area as a rubbish dump. This resulted in further damage, and after the war, when the rubbish was removed, it was found that the surviving frames had been piled up at one end of the vessel and that even the earlier plaster restoration needed considerable repair. The result was that further restoration followed, this time using three-quarters of a ton of plaster painted black.

The true state of the ship was not generally known, and just how much of the original still existed was not clear until 1978, when it was decided by the Museum of London, successor to the London Museum, to dismantle the remains and place them in storage. The author was given this responsibility, and found that very little of the hull had survived; most of what was on exhibition in the basement of Lancaster House comprised a variety of plasters mixed with wire, rags, small fragments of ancient oak planking, and even a bone, all of which had been coated with tar or painted black on the inboard face to simulate the ancient wood. Indeed, apart from the frames very little of the rest of the ship had survived in any meaningful form, and there was no guarantee that any of the timbers, apart from the keel, were in their correct positions. The broken frames and several slabs

Fig 97   The County Hall ship being excavated in 1910.

of planking were worth saving, but everything else was too fragmentary and unrecognisable. Even the keel timber had exfoliated at its tree-rings and no longer retained any of its original carved shape.

Finding that so little of the ship had survived was a mixed blessing. On the one hand what remained of the vessel was no longer exhibitable, but on the other hand it was still possible to carry out research on the surviving pieces and study clues to its method of construction and date, particularly by the analysis of the tree-rings. Moreover, the construction of an accurate scale model for exhibition in the Museum of London helped to clarify certain details of its construction. All of the frame fragments were drawn 1:1 by tracing them on film, and all sections of planks cut to show the tree-ring patterns were similarly traced on film, and of these a few representative examples are published here. The remainder are in the Museum of London archive under accession numbers B.708 and B.709. While remaining the property of first the London County Council and then its successor the Greater London Council, the ship's remains have now been given to the Museum of London and the Shipwreck Heritage Centre, Hastings.

Since the County Hall ship was the first Roman vessel in the world to be studied and published in detail, no parallels were available in 1910, and the excavators were unable to understand its importance. Many ships of this Mediterranean tradition have since been found and the significance of the vessel is now much clearer. The recent research has enabled the originally published description to be greatly enlarged, more fully understood and duly placed in a wider context.

Location of the ship

No plan contemporary with the discovery is known which shows exactly where the ship was found, together with its precise orientation, on the County Hall site. However, its position was given in the 1912 report as 350 feet (106.68m) north of the Westminster Bridge approach road, and 300 feet (91.44m) east of the then new Embankment retaining wall beside the River Thames (Riley and Gomme 1912, 5). Also, its position is marked with a cross on the 25 inch Ordnance Survey map published in 1914. The vessel was noted as lying NE–SW with the north end towards the shore, and at a depth of 21 feet 6 inches (6.55m). With this information it is now possible to plot this position on a plan of the foundations of County Hall, and, with the aid of photographs of the vessel in situ, to establish its alignment relative to the foundations of the building (Fig 104). Although the plotted position is only approximately correct, its location on the site is particularly important because it helps to understand the relationship of the vessel to the river during the Roman period.

The ship

The interpretation of the remains of the County Hall ship partly depends upon the degree of accuracy and completeness of the drawings made in 1910. It is clear that the plan made then (Fig 105) does not include all structural features, for it only shows a selection of the mortice-and-tenon joints (ie draw-tongued-joints). A few others were shown in the small sketches in the text of the report published in 1912. However, because nobody in Britain had then recorded and published an ancient ship in such detail, it was evidently deemed

Fig 98   *The County Hall ship being boxed-up ready for transportation to the new London Museum in August 1911.*

unnecessary to record all these features. Nowadays all such details would be recorded as clues to how the vessel was built. Some small discrepancies in the dimensions of planks and frames exist between the plan and the sections, in which case the dimensions shown on the plan are assumed to be correct because it is there that their relationship to other components is defined.

Since it was not clear from the remains as excavated which end was the bow, in the description that follows the timber elements are coded with reference to the points of a compass. The vessel was lying north-east to south-west, with the south end of the remains roughly coinciding with the maximum beam of the ship, and with the north end near the former stem or stern. The strakes are numbered outwards from 1E next to the keel on the east side, and 1W outwards on the other side. The frames are numbered from 1 at the surviving north end to 41 at the surviving south end. Other elements, such as the keel, stringer, wale, and deck beam, are named.

Interpretation also depends in part upon establishing exactly where the collapsed east side originally fitted onto the bottom. The break occurred between strakes 8E and 9E at the south end of the remains, and between strakes 7E and 8E in the middle (Fig 106). There appears to have been little fore-and-aft movement of the collapsed side, for the lines of frames, shown by trenail positions and the location of the frames themselves, continued across the bottom of the ship and onto the collapsed side. Indeed, the small trenails holding both sides of a mortice-and-tenon joint between strakes 8E and 9E still survived between frames 19 and 20. The major scarf joint

in strake 9E had clearly opened up before the ship was buried, and may have been the cause of distortion in strakes 11E–13E.

Materials used in its construction

The preserved portion of the ship was built throughout of oak (*Quercus* sp, but this alone cannot be taken to indicate that the ship was built in central or northern Europe, as was previously thought (Marsden 1974, 55). Iron nails were occasionally used to strengthen or replace trenail fastenings, and there is evidence that the outboard face of the planks had been coated with pine resin that had been only slightly heated (see Appendix 4).

Description

The part of the ship which survived constituted the midships area extending towards the north end, but both ends of the vessel had been destroyed. The investigators in 1910 believed that the north end was the bow, though their reasons were not given. When *in situ* the remains were approximately 13m in length and 5.5m in width, with the bottom and one collapsed side being preserved. Although the collapsed side had not survived to gunwale level, it did extend above the deck. A total of twelve strakes, plus one wale, remained on the east side, and seven strakes on the west side.

The keel
This had been cut from a long, fairly straight oak log

Fig 99 The County Hall ship being raised to street level.

Fig 100   The County Hall ship being taken from the site to the London Museum, 24 August 1911.

whose pith lay in the centre of the keel. The surviving part of the keel was about 10.3m long and almost straight, and measured 0.215m in width, 0.165m in thickness, and was chamfered on both lower edges to 0.076m on the flat underside (Fig 107). The slight sideways bend in the keel may have been an original feature of the ship since it is unlikely that it was bent after the ship was abandoned.

Throughout most of its length the keel was level, except for 2.13m at the north end which rose 0.019m towards the stem or sternpost. Since this slight upward curve corresponded with a closer coincidence of mortice-and-tenon joints than elsewhere in the ship it would seem that it was intended to impose a curve on the end of the keel. This might suggest that the keel originally had a slight 'rocker', or curve, throughout its length, but that this had been flattened by the pressure of overlying alluvium. A rocker was not unusual in ancient times, for example the Greek ship found off Kyrenia showed evidence of one (Steffy 1985), its purpose being to concentrate bilge water in the centre of a ship, and to simplify beaching operations. Moreover, in soft mud it would help to ensure that the ends of the ship could be more easily released from seabed or riverbed suction by a rising tide (McGrail 1987, 116). There was a row of trenails, each about 13mm in diameter and spaced at intervals of between 0.127 and 0.178m along the centre of the upper face of the keel at its north end. At the time of the discovery these were apparently considered to have penetrated the keel, though this was not specifically stated, and originally to have secured a false keel to its underside, so that, if the vessel grounded unintentionally, the force of the impact would break this timber away and so free the vessel (Riley and Gomme 1912, 6). This may be correct, for a false keel has been found on the Greek ship found off Kyrenia, dating from the fourth century BC (Steffy 1985, 75–6), and such a feature is also recorded in Greek literature (Casson 1971, 208n, 221). No trace of any trenails or pegs could be found recently in the surviving remains of the keel, though only a relatively short length of the keel had survived.

The planks and fastenings

Thirty fragments of planks were sectioned, and their tree-rings showed that all had been tangentially fashioned from oak logs, all close to the pith as if it was intended to obtain the maximum breadth of plank in the heartwood (Fig 108). None was found to be radially cut. There were no traces of the cutting tools because the surfaces of the timbers are now dried, split and otherwise damaged, but presumably they were originally sawn to the correct thickness. It was possible to judge which was the inboard face in each fragment from the layer of black tar that had been painted on it for display purposes, and so establish that in 24 samples the pith of the tree lay close to the outboard plank face, and in only 6 samples was the pith laid close to the inboard face. As these can be considered as a random sample of planking fragments it seems that the shipwright probably preferred to place the pith outboard. The reason for this may be concerned with the way a plank bows or warps when it becomes repeatedly dry then wet. Also noted in this connection was the fact that the tree-rings near the pith were usually wide, but that near the edges of the planks the rings were very narrow. This, it seems, would tend to give the plank edges more strength than the middle, particularly as the edges contained the mortice-and-tenon joints.

The records of the ship made in 1910–12 show that some of the planks used were substantial. Amongst the largest were the garboard strakes next to the keel, one of which was 10.5m long between its broken ends, and up to 0.38m wide and 0.076m thick.

The ship was carvel-built, its planks fastened edge to edge by mortice-and-tenon joints (Fig 107A), as was characteristic of shipbuilding in the Mediterranean region in Greek and Roman times (Casson 1971, 201–8). These joints, without any caulking, fastened the garboard strakes to the keel at intervals of about 0.152m at the north end, and the rectangular oak tenon of each was 0.127 x 0.064 x 0.007m and was secured with trenails

0.016m in diameter (Fig 107). This relatively close spacing was not general in the ship, and was probably due to securing firmly the timbers towards that end of the vessel. The spacing of the joints away from the north end was not recorded in detail, but the few examples noted in 1910 as holding the garboard strakes to the keel had spacings with centres of 0.20m and 0.46m. If there was a regular spacing then the former measurement should apply, placing them further apart than the mortice-and-tenon joints at the north end.

The other strakes forming the bottom of the ship were also tightly secured edge-to-edge with mortice-and-tenon joints so that caulking of the seams was apparently unnecessary. A few damaged fragments of planking recently studied at the Museum of London contained traces of mortice-and-tenon joints. Since shrinkage longitudinally along wood grain would be relatively small (McGrail 1987, 27, 41–3), the present spacing between the mortice-and-tenon joints should be a rough indication of their spacing before the timbers dried out. In the edge of one plank fragment were two mortice holes 0.484m apart. In another, mortice holes were 0.37m apart, and in yet another the distance between joints was more than 0.41m.

A larger plank fragment contained the remains of several mortice-and-tenon joints on each edge (Fig 109). On one edge the joints were 0.97m apart, and more than 0.61m apart. On the other edge they were 0.43m and

Fig 101   The partly reconstructed County Hall ship on on exhibition at the London Museum, about 1912.

Fig 102   King George V, Queen Mary, and other members of the Royal Family visit the County Hall ship, March 1912.

Fig 103   The County Hall ship as excavated, 1910.

more than 0.52m apart, as well as 0.73m between the nearest possible joints. In this case they were not placed opposite the joints in the other edge, and the distances apart show that there was no regular pattern of spacing.

The surviving mortice holes in the plank edges were carefully examined in their warped state to determine how they were originally made. In the few surviving cases the sides, and in two cases the inner corners, were angular and seemed to have been chiseled. There was no suggestion that the mortice holes had been drilled. The mortices themselves were normally held by a small oak peg in each plank, but in one surviving fragment no peg was found at the surviving end.

Strakes averaged 0.267 to 0.381m in width, and in thickness those near the keel were 0.076m, thinning down to 0.051m at the collapsed east side. They were long planks, commencing with a feather heading (Fig 107B), widening to the centre and scarfed in places (Fig 107C). The feather headings pointed towards the north end of the vessel, where the hull narrowed. Although little iron was used in the construction of the ship, it was noted that where each strake started with its feather head a large-headed nail was driven into the strake already in place (Fig 107B). This also occurred at scarf joints in the

strakes. The nail gave extra strength at what could have been a weak point, for the feather head of one scarf joint had been repaired. Nails in this position are also found in the Lake Nemi ships, Italy, of the first century AD (Ucelli 1950, fig 153), in the Yassi Ada ship, Turkey, of the fourth century AD (Doorninck 1976, 121), and in a small boat of the first century BC – second century AD found on the shore of Lake Kinneret (the Sea of Galilee), Israel (Steffy 1987, 326).

Since the hull shape on each side of the keel must, for stability, have been the same, it is not surprising to find that the first seven strakes on the west side of the vessel were mirrored by the strake pattern on the east side, though there was some difference in their widths. Indeed, the duplicated pattern even extended to include a scarf in strake 6 on both sides. Since there were a further seven strakes (including one wale) on the surviving east side, the symmetry and balance of the hull demanded that these should be mirrored on the destroyed west side. Although strake widths varied, it is clear that the height of the top of the wale, 12E, must have been the same on both sides of the hull because it carried the cross-beams.

Only the east side of the ship above the turn of the bilge had survived, the planking being 0.051m thick, and was fastened edgeways with mortice-and-tenon joints. The spacing between the centres of the recorded joints was irregular and could have been as short as 0.28m, but on a rough average it seems that the spacing was often about 0.53m. A fragment of planking believed to be from this side still exists (it contains a modern nail showing that it was fastened to the side of the reconstructed hull as preserved in Lancaster House), and has mortice-and-tenon joints 0.388m apart. One of the dried mortice holes is 0.11m wide along the strake, and 0.065m deep. The surviving width of the other mortice slot from top to bottom is 7mm, but both mortice holes suffered from distortion on drying in 1910.

A careful examination of the many surviving fragments of planking made it clear that, although the inboard faces were coated with modern black tar, plaster, and other recent materials, the outboard faces were not so coated. Instead many were covered with a thin layer of sand showing that they had never been cleaned, and on some the wood surface was also covered with a thin layer of brownish material that was undoubtedly an original deposit and not of recent date. Similar brown deposits are often found on the planking of ancient ships and boats where analysis has shown that they are the remains of a tar coating. A sample was removed for analysis and was found to be a dressing of pine resin (see Appendix 4).

The frames and fastenings

The frames were about 0.114m broad, 0.165m deep, and had generally been cut from grown crooks, the curvature of which generally matched the form of the hull, though judging from some of the surviving frames the grain did not always exactly follow the required frame shape. Bearing in mind the U-shaped cross-section of the ship, it is interesting to note how long, apparently, were some of the frames as continuous pieces of timber, indicating that the trees had been carefully chosen. Some curving frames were over 3.3m long, but frame 18 appeared to be over 4.8m long. Scarf joints that were not repairs were found only in frames 8, 12 and 28, out of a total of 41 frames. The scarfs in frames 16 and 20 were apparently repairs to the centre sections over the keel, as was probably the scarf in frame 36. V-shaped limber holes 0.04m wide and 0.02m high were cut into the underside of the frames on either side of the keel to permit bilge water to flow towards the centre of the vessel where the water could be pumped out. Fragments of frames still preserve limber holes (Fig 110) in which there are traces of the edged cutting tool, probably an axe, by which they were shaped.

There were two groups of frames in the main part of the hull: the 'lower' frames that ended at about strake 8 on the east side, and the longer frames that mostly alternated with the lower frames and crossed the bottom of the ship and extended up the side. Strake 8 lay at the

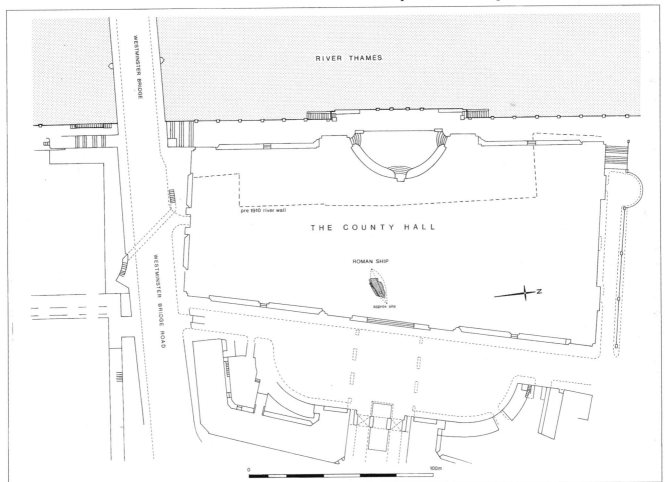

Fig 104　Approximate site of the County Hall ship.

turn of the bilge, and it is possible that the shipwright may have stiffened the bottom with the lower frames before building the sides of the hull. However, because only one side had survived it is not known if there were short bottom frames alternating with longer frames that extended up both sides of the hull (Fig 111A), or if each frame started at about strake 8 on opposite sides of the ship, and, after crossing the bottom, alternately extended up opposite sides of the hull (Fig 111B). Whichever was the case, the effect was to create a hull bottom stronger than the sides.

Although most of the frames were missing from the north end, the broken trenails in the strakes recorded their former position. The usual distance between the frames in the main part of the ship was about 0.533m from centre to centre, but this dimension decreased at a distance of 1.83m from the north end, where the frames averaged 0.254m from centre to centre. This spacing generally applied, except at a distance of about 7m from the north end where there was a space of 0.38m on the west side. No trenails were found in the strakes to indicate that a frame had been fixed there. The gap appears to have been deliberate, for a short length of frame 24 had been fastened to the east side to support the keelson above. A smaller gap at frame 28 is not mentioned in the 1912 report, but the record of a 'splay' or lap joint in the frame (Fig 105) indicates that a section of the frame crossing the keel may have become detached and lost, and that its trenails in the planking were not recorded.

Frames and strakes were fastened together by oak trenails 0.032m in diameter, averaging about 0.15m from centre to centre, and usually with two trenails through each strake. Where it was possible to examine them in the surviving frames, the trenails often had an oak wedge on the inboard end of the frame. This must mean that they had been driven from the outboard side as is usual in ships, the purpose of the wedge being to expand the slightly narrowed inboard end of the trenail.

Scarf joints were found in frames 12 and 28, their purpose evidently being to join lengths of timber end-ways to create single frames. The overlap scarfs were usually held by a single trenail. The scarf in frame 12 was 0.193 long in a frame 0.152m deep. No doubt other scarf joints existed on the collapsed east side, but those frames were missing. The scarf joints in the frames were all of the same basic lap form, except in frame 8 where the ends of two frames roughly overlapped side by side. Drawings of the surviving frames were recently reduced to the scale of the 1912 plan of the ship in the hope that the pattern of trenails, the limber holes, and the scarf joints might match up and allow the frame fragments to be identified. Unfortunately, only fragments of frames 14, 15, 17, 19, and 27 could be matched, since most of the other frame pieces were either too small or probably too distorted, but the exercise was enough to show that the original plan was an accurate representation of the ship.

A length of curved frame discovered loose in the bottom of the ship (Fig 107H) had been pierced by a row of trenails from end to end, indicating a variation in the framing pattern, and may have derived from the ship's superstructure. One end was feathered off to a point, with a straight face 0.508m long, suggesting that it had been fastened to a straight timber.

The cross-beams

'Strake' 12E was a wale, a heavy fore and aft strengthening timber 0.152m square, with its lower outer corner chamfered off (Fig 107D). It was fastened by mortice-and-tenon joints to the strakes below (11E) and above (13E), and its purpose was to receive the ends of the cross-beams set in notches cut into its upper inboard corner (Figs 107D and 112).

Strake 11E was surprisingly narrow (c 0.15m) when compared with all other strakes found, and, judging from the Kyrenia ship which had a similar narrow strake (Steffy 1985, 93), it seems likely that it was an adjustment strake to level off the side so that the wale (12E) which supported the cross-beams was at the same height as the missing wale on the other side of the ship.

The ends of cross-beams, indicated by notches in the wale at the side of the ship, were found spaced irregularly at distances apart of 0.60m, 0.72m, 0.73m, and 0.88m. Each was 0.165 to 0.19m long fore-and-aft, 0.089m deep, and 0.039m wide vertically (Fig 107E). The surviving end of one cross-beam, held by two iron nails which fastened it to the wale, was 178mm wide and 38mm thick. A sketch in the 1912 report (Fig 107D) shows that the two nail heads were proud of the surface of the end of the cross-beam just outside the ship, suggesting that a piece of timber had covered the upper outboard end of the joint.

The stringer

A stringer was housed on the frames on the east side of the bottom of the ship, between 0.61 and 0.914m. from the keel (Fig 107E). It was presumably one of a pair, but the one on the west side of the vessel was missing. The surviving stringer measured 0.14m wide by 0.089m thick, and iron nails fixed it to the frames. Only two nails were recorded so that this construction may not have been very secure. Rectangular mortice holes about 0.063m long, 0.038m wide and 0.038m deep, were spaced along the top of the stringer, but these were not always situated fully over the frames. The spacing of the mortice holes from the north end of the stringer was 0.81m, 0.96m, 0.83m, 0.96m, 0.87m, and 0.99m.

The gunwale

The upper end of a loose frame (Figs 107D and 112) found lying on the collapsed side is an important clue to the position of the gunwale. The end curved round and terminated with a tenon 0.15m long, showing that it had been fastened into a timber more than 0.15m thick, presumably the gunwale or sheer strake. The spacing of the recorded trenails which once held it to the planking did not coincide with any trenails recorded in the planks, though the accuracy of the recording in 1910 may not have been sufficiently precise to allow the original position of the frame to be established.

1 Iron nail
2 19mm sinking
3 Coin found, Carausius
4 16mm oak pins
5 5mm dowel
6 Paste bead found
7 Coin found under rib, Tetricus
8 Iron nail
9 32mm oak pins to rib
10 Piece of pottery wedged under rib to cover hole in plank
11 Iron nail
12 Iron nail
13 Patch over leak with thin packing of clay, covered with 25mm oak
14 Iron nail
15 Iron nails
16 Patch
17 Pins half covered by rib
18 2 iron nails
19 Oak block (pulley) found under rail
20 178mm x 38mm cross beam
21 Splay joint
22 Patch [under rib] 51mm up
23 Housing 51mm deep x 51mm x 31mm
24 Cross beam broken off
25 Pin under rib
26 Iron nail
27 Splay joint, ram's horn found
28 Splay joint
29 Fractured [planking]
30 Piece of pottery found, fragments of small vessel
31 Sinking 76mm deep
32 Piece of pottery (bottom) found
33 Coin found, Allectus
34 Part of brooch found in limber to rib
35 Splay joint
36 Splay joint
37 Belaying pin found
38 Iron nail
39 Crushed by modern foundation
40 Large iron nail found resting on bottom
41 Coin of Carausius beneath rib
42 Housing 76mm x 38mm x 38mm
43 Iron nails [3], 76mm sinking
44 Iron nail
45 Rib evidently drifted here (89mm wide)
46 Planking indented and fractured with large flint embedded in same
47 63mm x 38mm x 38mm
48 Sinking, 76mm deep
49 Iron nail
50 Splay
51 Iron nail
52 25mm x 38mm x 38mm
53 Point of iron nail
54 Iron nail
55 Joint
56 Mortice or pin hole
57 63mm x 38mm x 44mm
58 Splay joint
59 Iron nail

60 16mm oak pins to dowels to planks
61 SS limber holes to ribs
62 44mm [?gap between nail head and beam]
63 2 iron nails
64 76mm [plank thickness]
65 12mm shoulder
66 32mm oak pins to ribs

Fig 105 *All imperial measurements have been changed to metric. Dates of coins have been omitted since some were incorrect. The pulley block (19) was of ash, not oak. The symbol* **ᔕ** *on the plan indicates a limber hole cut in the underside of a rib for the flow of bilge water. 'Pin' refers to a wooden peg or trenail. 'Splay joint' is a scarf. 'Sinking' is a mortice hole. Words in [ ] are added to clarify meaning.*

Fig 105 *The County Hall ship as excavated (after Riley and Gomme 1912).*

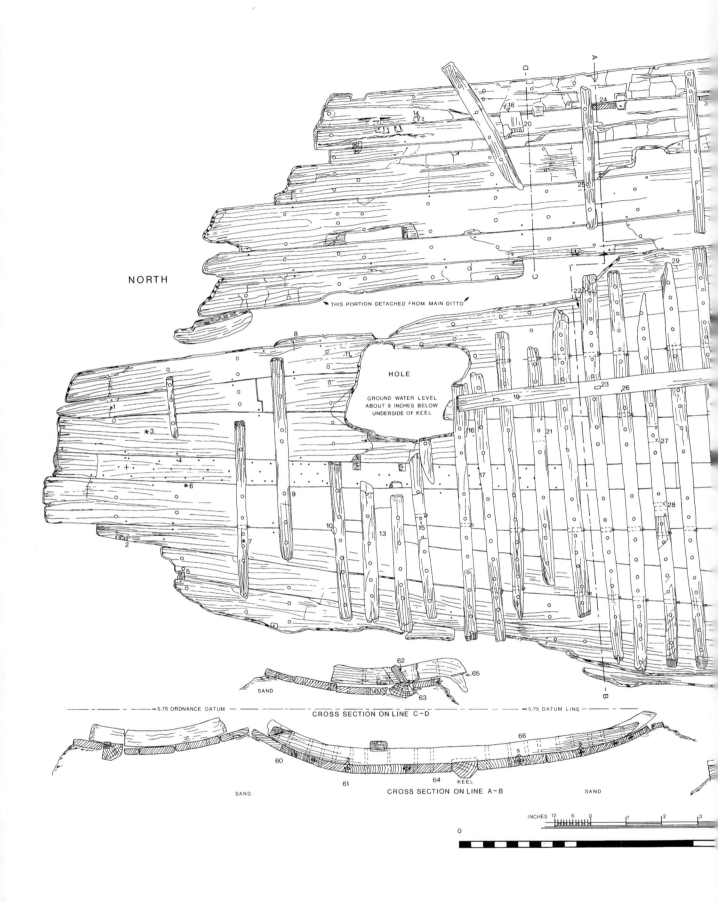

NORTH

THIS PORTION DETACHED FROM MAIN DITTO

HOLE

GROUND WATER LEVEL
ABOUT 9 INCHES BELOW
UNDERSIDE OF KEEL

SAND

CROSS SECTION ON LINE C-D

—5·75 ORDNANCE DATUM—   —5·75 DATUM LINE—

SAND   SAND
KEEL
CROSS SECTION ON LINE A-B

INCHES 12 6 0   1   2   3

0

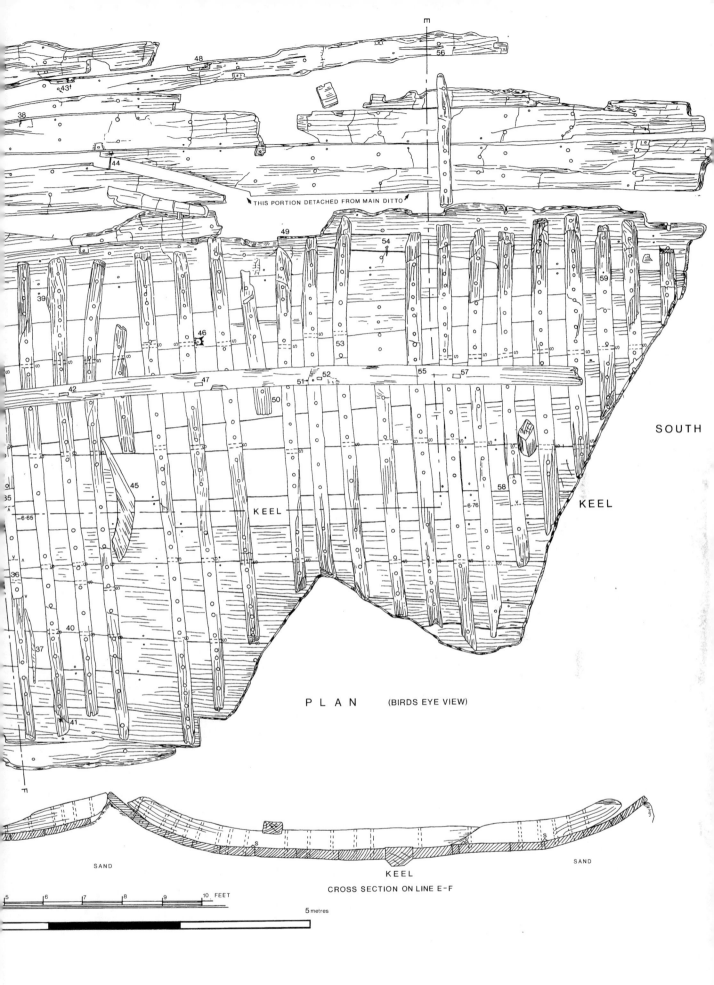

THIS PORTION DETACHED FROM MAIN DITTO

SOUTH

KEEL

KEEL

PLAN   (BIRDS EYE VIEW)

SAND

KEEL

SAND

CROSS SECTION ON LINE E-F

5   6   7   8   9   10 FEET

5 metres

Fig 105   The County Hall ship as excavated (after Riley and Gomme 1912).

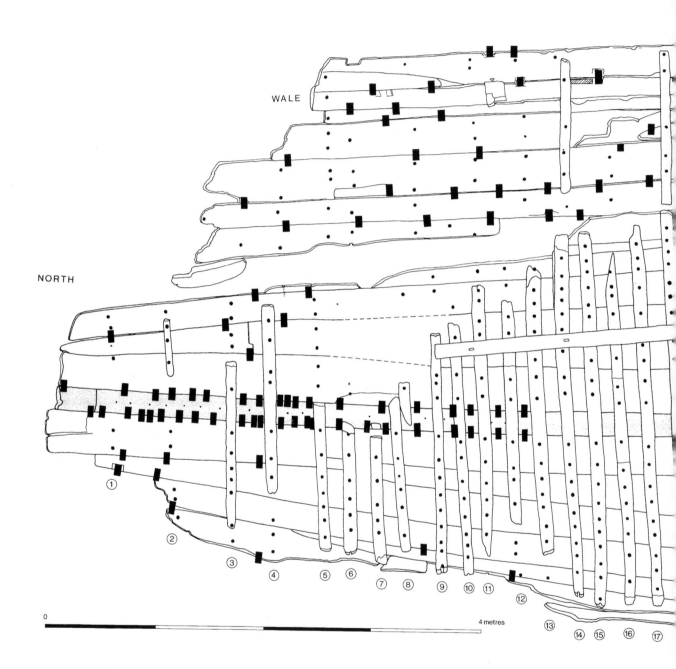

WALE

NORTH

0   4 metres

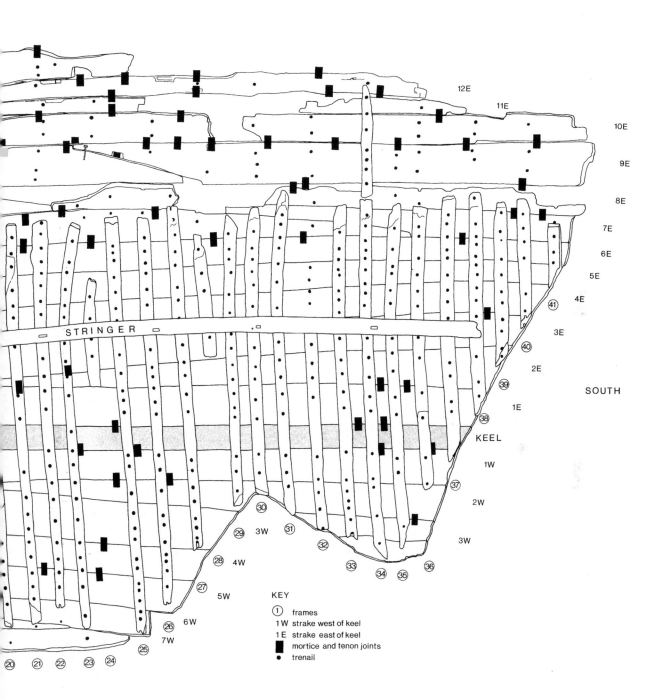

Fig 106 *Significant features of the County Hall ship, including all recorded mortice-and-tenon joints.*

Reconstruction of the ship

Aims and limitations in the reconstruction

As neither end of the County Hall ship had survived, and there was no trace of the mast-step, it is not clear in which direction its bow lay. In spite of this limitation, a sufficient length of its hull was recovered, from the midship position towards one end, to allow a rough estimation of its original length to be made. Moreover, as the construction of the ship was in the Mediterranean tradition, it is assumed that its form was also consistent with vessels in that tradition, and that Roman pictorial evidence and contemporary shipwrecks in the Mediterranean are valid for use in its reconstruction.

How the reconstruction was achieved

Before attempting to reconstruct the form and construction of the ship it is necessary to correct the distortion to the hull resulting from the weight of overlying silts. Several sections were recorded across the ship in 1910, and of these section A-B (Fig 113) was the most complete. The curve of the frames seems to give a fairly accurate profile of the vessel, though the break between the bottom and the collapsed side leaves some doubt about whether the highest surviving part of the side was originally upright or had an outward sloping flare. The actual arrangement is suggested by the angle of the rebates for the cross-beams in the wale 12E, for they would originally have had to accommodate the beams almost horizontally. They indicate that the top of the side was approximately upright. Moreover, as the end of each beam was only resting on the wale and was fastened by just two nails there was nothing to hold the sides in position had they been flared, and the downward weight of the deck might have tended to force the sides further outwards. On balance, it seems that the correct profile of this ship was one with the top of its sides upright.

By reconstructing the side onto the bottom at section E (Fig 113x) it is clear that there had been considerable flattening of the collapsed side at frame 34, for the hull shape there was splayed out at the level of the wale. This is in sharp contrast to the hull profile in section A–B only 4.57m away (Fig 113, A and B), and cannot be original. In the reconstruction it is necessary, therefore, to increase the curve of the side in section E to match that of section A–B (Fig 113y).

Dimensions of the ship

Having reconstructed the probable original transverse form of the discovered part of the ship, it is necessary to consider the original size and form of the vessel as a whole. In attempting to reconstruct the dimensions of the ship it is necessary to assume, for reasons of stability, that both sides of the vessel were of exactly the same shape and size, even though it is clear from the surviving sections and from the horizontally curved shape of the keel that this was not exactly so. Consequently it is

necessary to average out the inequalities. This problem is not peculiar to this ship for it applies to others too (Steffy 1985, 99). Since the most complete part of the hull was its east side this must be used as the basis for reconstruction.

Beam

The reconstruction of the cross-section of the hull at section E (Fig 113y) gives a half beam of 2.46m taken to the outboard face of strake 13E immediately above the wale. However, judging from the plan of the ship, the maximum beam of the vessel was about 0.9m to the south where the bottom planks were 0.07m wider. This would make the half beam of the ship 2.53m, and its whole beam 5.06m.

Height

The reconstructed cross-section at E shows that the highest surviving edge of the wale 12E was at 1.55m above the bottom of the keel. This was not the original top of the side since only a little to the north the full width of strake 13E had survived with mortice-and-tenon joints along its upper edge, showing that it was originally fastened to another timber, 14E.

The position of the gunwale is indicated by the loose upper end of the curving frame which terminates with a tenon (Fig 107D and 112). The shape of this frame fits the curved side of the ship and indicates that the missing timber 14E was probably the gunwale, whose top lay at a height of about 2m above the bottom of the keel amidships. It is of course possible that this uppermost wale supported other constructions but this must remain mere speculation.

Length

The length of the ship is more difficult to assess because the obvious indicators, such as the stem and stern posts and the mast-step, had not survived. However, the hull was at its widest just south of section E (5.06m), and at 4.57m to the north at section A-B it was only 4.16m wide, and was clearly narrowing towards the north end of the vessel. Moreover, the wale and planking were clearly rising upwards towards that end (Fig 114).

The overall form of the surviving part of the hull can be further reconstructed since the upper part of the hull shape was partly determined by strake 5 at the turn of the bilge. As the relationship between strake 5 and the side of the ship is known at sections A-B and E it is possible to deduce the shape of the rest of the side relative to the known part of strake 5 nearer the north end of the ship. This, then, gives the curve of the sides of the hull from the midship position towards the north end of the vessel, and it enables the position of that end to be estimated roughly, particularly bearing in mind that the final two metres of the keel had begun to rise upwards as if it was soon to be scarfed onto the endpost. Indeed, the frequency of mortice-and-tenon joints holding the garboard strakes to the hull at that end suggest that the garboard strakes were beginning to take the form of the end. This is also suggested by the absence of limber holes

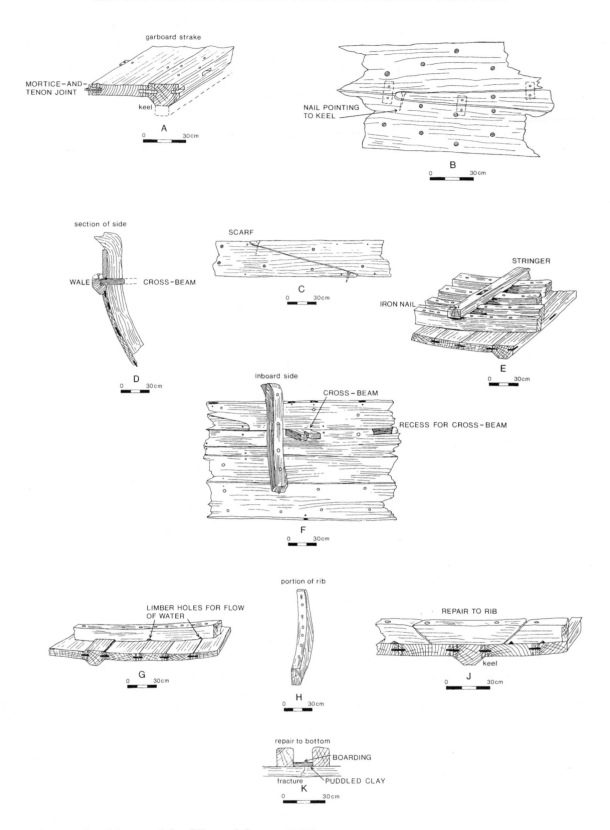

Fig 107   Constructional features (after Riley and Gomme 1912).

in frames 4–7. An important clue to the original length of the County Hall ship are the remains of the bottoms of other classical ships which preserve the shapes of the hulls at the turn of the bilge (Table 12). The relationship of length to breadth at the turn of the bilge in these other ships is difficult to fix precisely since the turn of the bilge is not a fixed point, but nevertheless it occurs roughly as shown in Table 12.

Although the ships and boats of the Mediterranean shipbuilding tradition listed in this table range from rowing boats to imperial barges, and include seagoing merchant ships, the ratios of length : breadth are remarkably consistent and should be valid for determining the approximate length of the County Hall ship. The average ratio suggests that the length of the bottom of the County Hall ship should be 3.04 x 3.5 = 10.64m. It is clear from

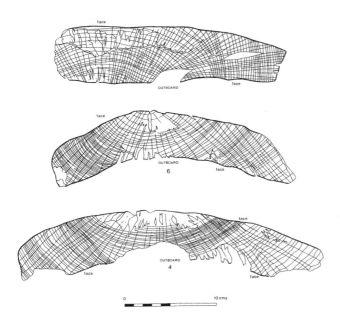

Fig 108 Cross-sections of planks showing the tree-ring patterns, the tangential cutting, and plank distortion due to drying-out in 1910.

the plan (Fig 106) that the County Hall ship was much longer, but if it is assumed that the widest part of the hull, just south of section E, was at the mid-point of the ship then the plan of the vessel shows that the ship could have been 26m long overall. Since this would give a breadth to length ratio of 1:8.5, which is far greater than that of any of the eleven vessels compared in Table 12, this is most unlikely to be correct. The length of the ship should lie between these limits, though the plan shows that the minimum practical length should lie at a ratio of about 1:6.3. This would give a length of 3.04 x 6.3 = 19.1m. It is possible to draw a reconstruction of the ship at this length in which all the known features are incorporated. However, the widest part of the hull, at about section E, would lie at roughly 67% of the length of the vessel from the north end and would give the plan of the vessel a distinct pear shape. This hydrodynamic shape would give the north end a much sharper entry into the sea than the comparatively rounded south end, from which it would seem that the north end was more likely to have been the bow (as the excavators thought in 1910, though they did not give their reasons). Such a plan is not impossible and is believed to have occurred in the Yassi Ada ship of the seventh century AD (Steffy 1982a, 67) and in the Kinneret boat (Steffy 1987). Although the ship seems to have been longer relative to its beam than was usual, comparison has only been possible with a few classical vessels: too small a number from which to judge whether or not it lay outside the full range of ship proportions.

Fig 109 Recent drawing of one of the best-preserved fragments of the County Hall ship, with a reconstruction of its original appearance.

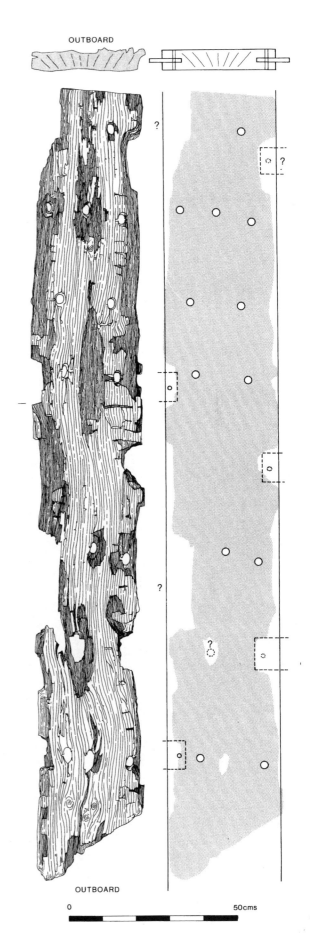

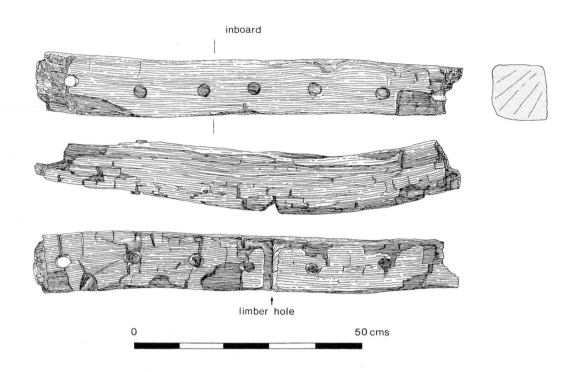

inboard

limber hole

0   50 cms

Fig 110   Frame fragment with a limber hole and oak trenails, from the County Hall ship.

Deck

The County Hall ship preserves rare evidence of a deck, since normally only the lowest parts of ancient vessels survive, often because they are buried under the cargo. The deposition of alluvium over the collapsed side of the County Hall ship was undoubtedly responsible for its preservation.

As the ends of the cross-beams originally lay at 1.3m above the upper surface of the lowest frames it is clear that they could not have been rowing benches. Indeed, as they were not strongly fastened to the side of the hull their primary purpose was evidently not to hold the sides of the hull in place though they evidently contributed to transverse strength by helping to hold the sides at a constant distance apart. They must therefore have been deck beams.

Although the deck beams were fastened into slots in the wale 12E, as each beam was only about 38mm thick they clearly needed the additional internal support of stanchions to enable them to span the ship from side to side for up to 5m. The stanchion positions were indicated by mortice holes in the top of the stringer overlying the bottom frames, but as these did not accord with the spacing of the deck beams, indicated by the slots in the wale, it is clear that the stanchions must have supported a horizontal longitudinal beam upon which the deck beams lay (Fig 115). These longitudinal beams could have given the deck beams a little camber to allow water to drain off the deck into the sea. However, it is worth noting the absence of any scupper holes just above the level of the deck in the 4.5m surviving length of strake 13E. These were surely essential at some point along the

side of the ship so that water caught on the deck could be discharged into the sea. Their absence presumably implies a deck sheer or downward slope towards the middle of the vessel where scuppers were no doubt situated.

This deck construction is not entirely unique, for the remains of deck structure have been found in two other seagoing Roman ships found in the Mediterranean. The first was in a merchantman, at Laurons, off Martigues, Bouches-du-Rhône, France. In this case the deck beams, rectangular in section with their long sides placed vertically, were fastened to a wale by a dove-tailed joint. The deck planking that lay above was edge-joined by mortice-and-tenon joints, as was the hull, and in a wash-strake immediately above the deck were groups of three rectangular scupper holes, 0.1m long and 0.03m high, at intervals along the vessel (Gassend *et al* 1984, fig 3). The deck surface lay about 1.8m above the top of the lowest

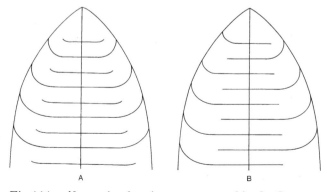

A   B

Fig 111   Alternative framing patterns used in the County Hall ship.

Table 10   Approximate dimensions of strakes as found

strake	max width found (m)	thickness (mm)
1W	0.34	76
2W	0.30	
3W	0.39	63
4W	0.30	56
5W	0.29	51
6W	0.23	51
7W	0.27	51
1E	0.38	76
2E	0.37	69
3E	0.30	56
4E	0.30	56
5E	0.28	51
6E	0.25	51
7E	0.28	51
8E	0.27	51
9E	0.36	51
10E	0.27	51
11E	0.13	51
12E	0.15	140
13E	0.25	51

frames. Part of yet another deck has been recorded in a wreck near Punta Ala, off the island of Elba (ibid, 87). The deck beams here too were fastened into a wale, and although there was some variation the basic deck construction was very similar in all three vessels.

Gunwale

The upper end of a loose frame which terminated with a tenon (Fig 112) is the only clue to the position and size of the gunwale in the County Hall ship. Since the lower half of the frame was curved, as was the hull below the wale 12E, it is possible to establish its position relative to the turn of the bilge with a fair degree of accuracy (Fig 117, section A–B). Assuming that the upper ends of the other frames were similar, the tenon would indicate that the gunwale probably lay immediately above strake 13E. The upper edge of this strake contained mortice-and-tenon joints by which it was fastened to the lower edge of the gunwale, just as strake 11E was attached to the surviving wale 12E below. The tenon at the end of the frame shows that the gunwale was at least 0.15m wide, and was about 0.23m high, and it seems reasonable to expect that it was of the same shape as the wale 12E.

In the County Hall ship the height of the gunwale above the deck amidships can be established by allowing for a deck 0.02m thick. Subtracted from the probable height of the top of the gunwale this gives a height of 0.7m, and compares with 0.68m which was the height of the gunwale above the deck of the Laurons ship (ibid).

Propulsion and steering

Although the size of the County Hall ship indicates that it was propelled either by oar or by sail, the height of the deck and the absence of any fittings for rowing make it unlikely that it was rowed. Judging from discoveries of Greek and Roman ships in the Mediterranean, such as the Chretienne 'A' wreck, France (Dumas 1964, 120–7), it seems likely that the mast-step would have been situated in a longitudinal timber above the keel. No trace of this or of its fastenings either to the keel or to the frames were noted in the County Hall ship when it was excavated in 1910, and it is likely that they had been eroded away, as was the stringer on the west side. However, the excavators did note that there was a gap in the frames over the keel at frame 24, which could be explained as allowing a mast-step timber to rest upon the keel. As a matter of coincidence the centre of this gap occurs half way along the reconstructed length of the ship (Fig 114), in the ideal position for a square sail where the Centre of Effort of the sail would lie close to the Centre of Lateral Resistance of the hull as reconstructed.

As the ship was of Mediterranean-style construction its method of propulsion and steering was probably the same as used in Mediterranean ships, and so it is likely that it had a single square sail, and was steered by two quarter rudders, though there is no evidence that these were so. A small pulley block (Fig 116B) with two wheels was found, but if this was part of the rigging it could hardly have carried rope of much weight for the wheels allowed for a rope circumference of only about 27mm. Also found was part of a rounded wooden object, perhaps a belaying pin (Fig 116A). Both were made from ash (*Fraxinus* sp), though the drawings are based upon the dry shrunken remains, which in the case of the pulley block are much distorted. A loose portion of timber

Table 11   Frame spacing along keel of Blackfriars ship 1

between frames	m	between frames	m
* – 1	0.33	18 – 19	0.10
1 – 2	0.43	19 – 20	0.14
2 – 3	0.48	20 – 21	0.15
3 – 4	0.25	21 – 22	0.14
4 – 5	0.37	22 – 23	0.13
5 – 6	0.16	23 – 25	0.40
6 – 7	0.15	25 – 26	0.18
7 – 8	0.09	26 – 27	0.19
8 – 9	0.20	27 – 29	0.31
9 – 10	0.10	29 – 30	0.10
10 – 11	0.13	30 – 31	0.12
11 – 12	0.13	31 – 32	0.18
12 – 13	0.13	32 – 33	0.15
13 – 14	0.13	33 – 34	0.13
14 – 15	0.13	34 – 35	0.13
15 – 16	0.11	35 – 36	0.14
16 – 17	0.13	36 – 37	0.16
17 – 18	0.16		

* denotes limit of remains, and no frame found

Fig 112   The loose upper end of a frame found in 1910. Note the end of a deck beam.

0.73m long and 0.25m in diameter, believed to have been part of the mast, was found under the ship 0.6m from the large hole near the north end of the hull. As there was no actual evidence that it was part of the mast, other than its relationship to the ship, it should be discounted. It could have been a piece of driftwood caught under the wreck.

Sequence of construction

The pattern of fastenings in the planks and frames is the main clue to the stages in building the ship, the method of which can be paralleled in the Mediterranean tradition of construction. It is recognised that the shell of planks of ships with mortice-and-tenon joints were generally constructed before the frames were added (Casson 1971, 203–6). This was evidently the case in the County Hall ship, particularly as one of the surviving plank fragments shows that at least one frame had been pegged to the plank through a mortice-and-tenon joint which was already in place.

It seems that initially the keel was laid down on stocks in the shipyard and the garboard strakes were fastened to it by mortice-and-tenon joints. The scarf joints in the other strakes show that strakes 7W, 7E, 8E, 9E, 13E were constructed from the north end towards the midships area. There were two exceptions, however, for parts of strakes 6E and 10E were first fastened amidships and laid towards the north end. Also, as strakes 2E, 3E, 4E, 2W, 3W, and 4W were feathered off towards the north end

of the ship they were presumably laid in the centre of the ship first.

The wale (12E) was then fastened by mortice-and-tenon joints to the topmost strake below (11E), and rebates were cut in the top of the wale to take the ends of the deck beams. Strake 13E was then fastened in place by further joints above, and the gunwale was probably fastened on top. The stringers and their stanchions must have been fastened into position before the deck structure was constructed.

Where and when was the ship built?

Since the method of constructing the County Hall ship is characteristic of shipbuilding in the Mediterranean area in classical times (Throckmorton 1987, 92), it is theoretically possible that the vessel was built there and sailed to London. However, a ship built entirely of oak would be unusual in the Mediterranean, and in any case a recent dendrochronological study by Ian Tyers of the remaining plank samples shows a tree-ring pattern typical of south-east England, and it is clear that it was built from trees growing in that region. Although it was definitely not built in the Mediterranean area, the shipwright was certainly experienced in Mediterranean techniques and even knew how to construct hidden details such as the nail holding the feather end of a strake or scarf in the planking, and was also familiar with mortice-and-tenon construction. There can be little doubt that the shipbuilder had been trained in the Mediterranean region.

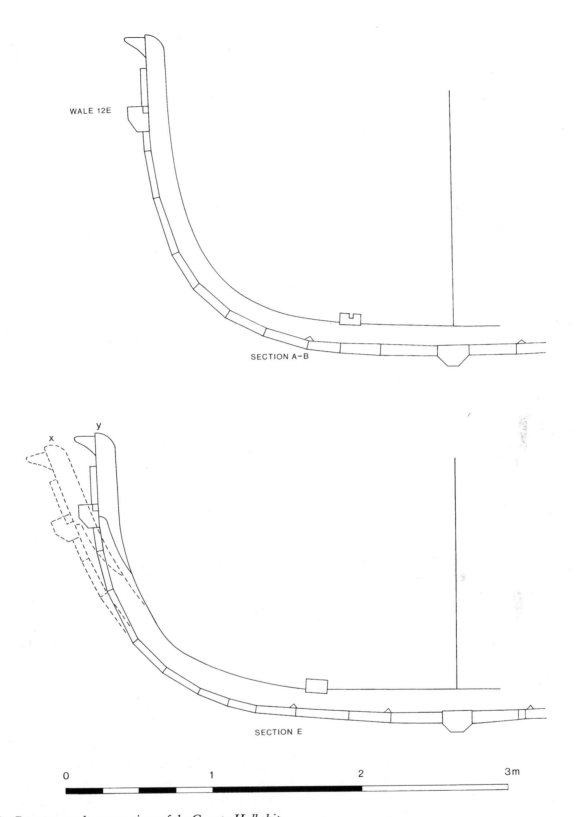

WALE 12E

SECTION A–B

x   y

SECTION E

0   1   2   3m

Fig 113 Reconstructed cross-sections of the County Hall ship.

The dendrochronological study of ten samples of oak planking gives a probable felling date after AD 287 (see Appendix 6). Bearing in mind that the coin evidence (see p 131) indicates that the ship was in use by the end of the century, a construction date of *c* 290–300 seems likely from the archaeological evidence alone. However, this coincides with the period when Britain was ruled by the usurpers Carausius and Allectus (AD 287–96), when there was no 'official' control from Rome. For this reason

a building date after AD 296 seems likely, when Britain was restored to the Roman Empire under Diocletian. A date of *c* AD 300 seems probable.

How was the ship used?

Soon after the ship was found it was suggested that it was a warship, 'one of Allectus's vessels that endeavoured to escape in the fight of London, but was overtaken and

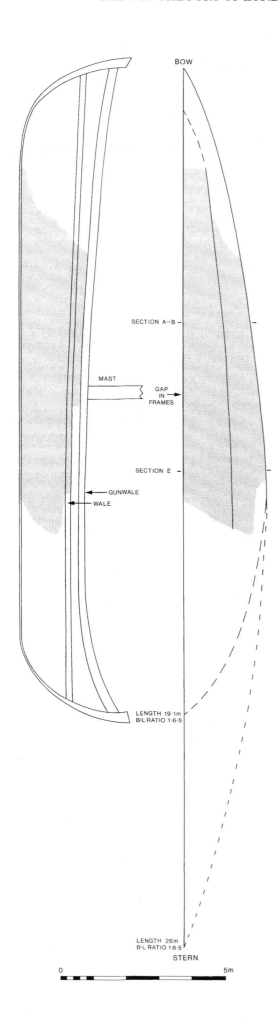

destroyed' by the fleet of Constantius in 296 (Riley and Gomme 1912, 22). Although Mortimer Wheeler (1946, 154) later pointed out firmly that this was a conjecture entirely unsupported by the evidence, it did not much alter the popular public perception of the function of the vessel as a 'galley'. This may be due partly to the fact that in 1910 the Director of the London Museum, Guy Laking, described it as 'a single-decker war galley propelled by oars and sails' which had been built in Gaul, and the newspapers of the day which gave it prominant coverage as 'one of the saucy ships that flouted Imperial Rome in the Channel' (Sheppard 1991, 52). No attempt was made to show how what was found could be interpreted as a warship, and it did not seem to matter either that there was an absence of any clear evidence for its purpose, or that no other substantial parts of Roman ships of any type had then been found anywhere and were available for comparison.

It is important to remember that the remains of the County Hall were very fragmentary and that its original length is unknown, so the evidence upon which an interpretation can be based is extremely limited. The fact that no Roman warships have been found anywhere makes it is impossible to make a comparison, though the absence of classical finds has not restricted speculation about what warships were like. Indeed, a full-sized working reconstruction of a Greek warship has recently been built and successfully use at sea (Morrison and Coates 1986), but in spite of the enormous care that has been taken in making this reconstruction fit what is known, its structural validity has yet to be demonstrated. But even if a Roman warship were to be found in the Mediterranean caution would still be needed since it may not be entirely valid for northern Europe where the maritime environment was very different.

What does seem clear is that there is no evidence of the rowing fittings, such as footrests and oarports, that would have been necessary had it been a warship. It is of course possible to conjecture much additional structure onto what has been found so as to suggest a warship, but this can also be done with the incomplete remains of most ancient craft, including some that are known to have been merchantmen. Therefore, it is important to keep to a 'minimum reconstruction' for this restricts conjecture closely to what is known, and allows caution rather than unsubstantiated imagination to determine the limits of interpretation.

Its reconstruction as a civilian ship of some kind also presents problems, for there are no good parallels, amongst the many Mediterranean merchantmen wrecks of this period, for its elongated form, its framing pattern, and its stringers with mortice holes. Moreover, the fact that the four other plank-built vessels of Mediterranean-type construction that have been found in central and northern Europe were all associated with forts, and were presumably military craft, must cast some doubt on interpreting the vessel as a merchantman. Perhaps the

Fig 114   Reconstructed plan and side elevation of the County Hall ship.

solution is that the County Hall ship had an official use of some form, possibly associated with the restored Imperial government after AD 296. The parameters for reconstructing the ship are far from clear, and it is hoped that the study of other finds in the Roman world might clarify the picture in due course, but until then the ship will remain an enigma.

The working life of the ship is reflected by evidence of damage and repair. Three frames (frames 16, 20, and 36) may have had their centre portions renewed, perhaps because they had become rotten from contact with bilge water, though this may have been simply how the shipwright joined lengths of timber to make continuous frames. The planks in many places showed signs of

Table 12   Approximate dimensions of Greek and Roman ships and boats at turn of bilge

ship	length (m)	breadth (m)	B/L ratio	source
Fiumicino 1	2.70	0.84	1:3.2	Scrinari 1979, fig 4
Fiumicino 2	4.50?	1.40?	1:3.2	Scrinari 1979, fig 9
Fiumicino 3	4.20	1.26	1:3.3	Scrinari 1979, fig 11
Fiumicino 4	7.20	2.12	1:4	Scrinari 1979, fig 16
Fiumicino 5	6.80	2.70	1:2.5	Scrinari 1979, fig 19
Nemi 1	60.40	17.60	1:3.4	Ucelli 1950, tav II
Nemi 2	67.50	22.00	1:3	Ucelli 1950, tav VI
Nemi 3	8.00	2.30	1:3.5	Ucelli 1950, 235
Kyrenia	12.30	3.00	1:4.1	Steffy 1985, 100
Kinneret	7.70	2.10	1:3.6	Steffy 1987, 328
Yassi Ada 7c	15.26	3.15	1:4.8	Steffy 1982a, 67
County Hall	?	3.04		

average B/L ratio 1:3.5

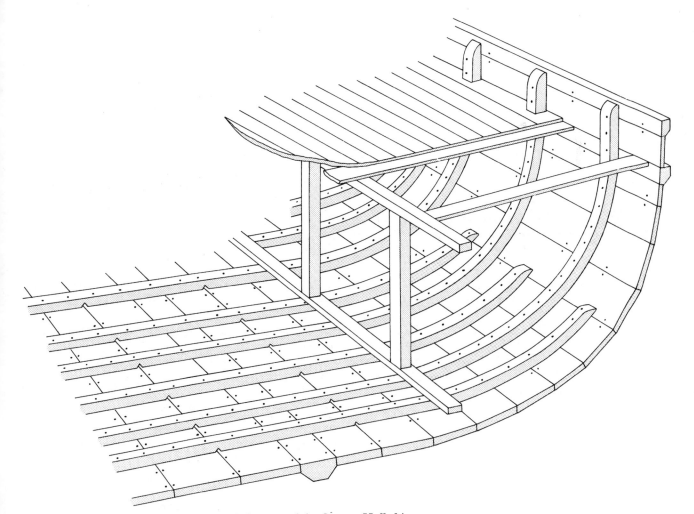

Fig 115   Reconstruction of the structural elements of the County Hall ship.

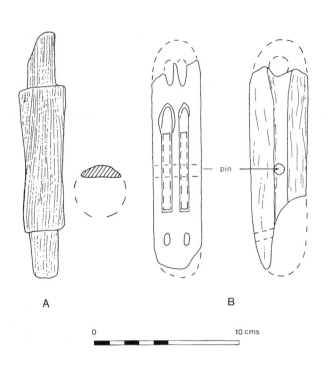

Fig 116   (A) Possible belaying pin; (B) pulley block (reconstructed from its shrunk and distorted shape).

fracture, but much of this may have been due to the weight of overlying clay long after the ship was buried. However, between frames 6 and 7 a leak in the hull had been covered by a packing of clay and by a piece of oak 0.025m thick which seems not to have been otherwise fastened in place (Fig 107K). There was another patch by frame 14, but this was not described in detail by the excavators. A leak in the feather-head of strake 3W had been repaired with a sherd of Roman black pottery tightly wedged and embedded in stiff clay below frame 5. Apart from this, several large iron nails were found driven through the strakes into frames (eg in frame 31), presumably to replace broken trenails, and as only some trenails in frames had been wedged from inside the ship, these may have replaced earlier unwedged trenails.

The loss of the ship

The date of the use and loss of the ship is indicated by four bronze coins lying on the bottom of the vessel: a coin of Tetricus the Elder (Emperor in Gaul), AD 270–73, discovered beneath frame 3 at the north end; a bronze coin of Carausius (Emperor in Britain), AD 287–93, beneath frame 21; another bronze coin of Carausius, between frames 1 and 2; and a bronze coin of Allectus (Emperor in Britain), AD 293–96, between frames 18 and 19.

It is clear from these that the ship was abandoned after AD 293, but as all the coins date from the last thirty years of the third century it seems likely that the ship was abandoned soon after AD 300. This is also suggested by a fragment of a Roman grey coarse ware flanged bowl also found in the wreck (Marsden 1965a, 113–4).

The cause of the ship's loss is not so clear since only a few repairs had been made to the bottom of the ship. It seems, therefore, that it was not abandoned because it was old and derelict, a view which is borne out by the condition of the outer face of the few surviving planks which had no obvious sign of erosion or wear, and no *Teredo* borings. This is fully consistent with the tree-ring dating and the coins which together suggest that the vessel was not old when abandoned.

The circumstances of the loss of the County Hall ship have been the subject of some discussion (Riley and Gomme 1912, 17–22; Merrifield, 1983, 201–3), and it has been suggested that it sank during the battles in AD 296. In support of this view Gomme mentioned that in the ship was found a number of large rounded stones, one of which is now identified as a septarian nodule from the London Clay, each weighing about 3 lbs (about 1.5kg) (ibid, 18). Indeed, one was found partly embedded in a strake as if it had been thrown from a considerable height.

Although this interpretation is possible, there are alternative, less dramatic, explanations to account for the stones, for example that they were the remains of ballast. Indeed, a stone embedded in a strake need not have been a projectile for its weight under the pressure of overlying clays could well impress it into the waterlogged planking long after the burial of the ship. Pressure marks such as this are commonly found on buried waterlogged wood, and occurred, for example, on the New Fresh Wharf boat timbers (see Chapter 8). It is possible that part of the ship had been damaged beyond repair in an accident, for it was noted in 1912 that there was 'some slight indication that fire has destroyed the upper portions of the gunwale down to the water's edge' (ibid). No trace of the burning has survived, and this view is at variance with the fact that the side of the ship had survived above deck level.

The position of the ship is perhaps also an indicator of the cause of its loss, for it was sunk close to the marshy south bank of the River Thames away from the Roman port of London (Fig 1). This is exactly the kind of area close to modern ports in which can be seen nowadays the rotting hulks of unwanted and abandoned ships. Whatever the cause of the abandonment of the County Hall ship, whether lack of trade, accident, or the death of the owner – but not, in view of the ship's apparent short life, old age – its position close to the shore suggests that it was deliberately placed there away from the activity of the port.

Break-up and burial of the ship

As the remains of the ship were overlaid firstly with sand and then by silt it was evidently lying on the bed of the Thames at the time of its abandonment. The condition of the river following the abandonment is reflected first by the erosion of the hull, then by the deposition of sand, and finally by the deposition of fine silt, all pointing to a reducing flow of water over that point, perhaps due a build-up of alluvium at the edge of a meander of the river.

Thus, when the vessel was abandoned the river flow was considerable and caused the sides of the vessel to collapse, and large parts, including its north end, to erode away (Fig 121). A large hole at the north end, and several smaller holes in the bottom of the hull, were presumably also caused by underwater erosion at that time. Although the south end of the remains of the ship was destroyed in the building operations of 1910, it seems unlikely that much was lost since the eroded south end of the collapsed east side was still intact.

It is not surprising to find that the south end had been eroded for the vessel was lying north-east to south-west with the south end nearest the main stream of the river where the flow from south to north was strongest. This flow could also account for the erosion of the west side of the ship, but the survival of the east side, which would have faced the force of the river, is difficult to explain, and may have been due to the protection of a small sandbank just south of the wreck. The subsequent covering of the hull by silt saved what remained, just in time to preserve a large portion of the collapsed east side that had already broken away from most of the hull. The considerable strength of flow of the river at the time the ship was lost is indicated by the erosion of the timbers, by the deposition of shelly sand under the curved portions of the hull, and by the deposit of about 90mm of sand inside the ship.

Only a handful of objects were found in the wreck, and of these it is probable that the coins found under the frames were lost during the use of the ship. Apart from these the finds comprised several pieces of pottery, portions of brick, two light-blue gaming counters, a number of iron nails, fragments of a leather hob-nailed shoe, two oak pins one of which had a burnt end, and several animal bones, as well as the tusk of a boar and part of an antler. The heavy items may well have been lost while the ship was in use, but the other objects could have been washed into the wreck by the river after the sinking.

Following the erosion fine grey silts were deposited over the remains for a considerable period, and it is due to this and the waterlogged environment that the ship was preserved. The silts were 2.1m thick above the vessel, and were in turn overlaid by 4.2m of man-made deposits of 'made ground'. At that point the upper part of the silt layers had been destroyed by a recent building, but their true thickness of 4.4m was preserved nearby. Judging from other sites in Southwark these fine silts seem to represent a period when the main flow of the River Thames had moved to its present position west of the wreck site, leaving a low-lying marsh over the ship. Flooding of the marshes over more than a thousand years deposited successive layers of silt which raised its surface in tandem with the post-glacial rising level of the river (Devoy 1980).

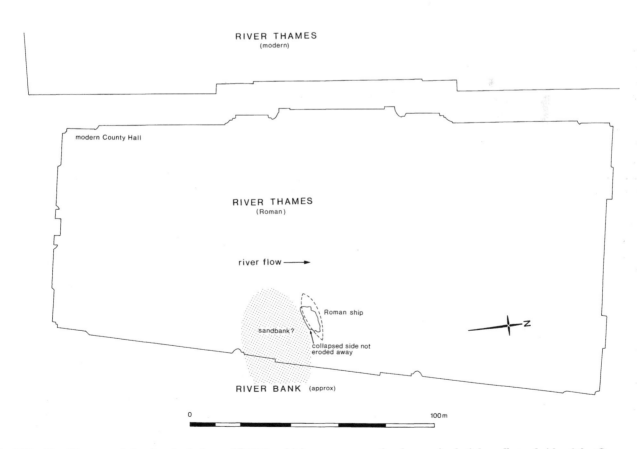

Fig 117 Possible state of the river bed about AD300, which may account for the survival of the collapsed side of the County Hall ship.

6 The port in the seventh to ninth centuries

Historical context

There is no archaeological or historical evidence to indicate that London existed in the fifth and sixth centuries as a port and an organised urban centre after the collapse of the Roman Empire (Merrifield 1983, 255–9; Vince 1990, 12). Throughout the seventh and eighth centuries the site of London was under the successive control of the kings of Kent and Mercia, amongst others, and its emergence from obscurity is marked by a record of the year 604 when the church of St. Paul's is said to have been first built (Bede II, 3). By c 685 the Laws of Hlothhere and Eadric indicate that *Lundenwic* was a trading centre with a king's hall and a reeve to regulate transactions. Moreover, a charter dating from 672–4, conveying to the abbot of Chertsey land 'by the port of London, where the ships come to tie up' ('iuxta portum Londonie ubi naves applicant'), shows that the port was in existence by then (Dyson 1980). As it was under Saxon control it is presumed that the ships were clinker-built, though it is possible that an older Celtic population was living in the region and was still using vessels with a different construction.

Seafaring trade is indicated by Bede who, in the early eighth century, described London as 'a trading centre for many nations who visit it by land and sea' (Bede II, 3). This is also indicated by coins (silver *sceattas*), dating from the seventh and eighth centuries, which have been found in south-east England, in the northern Netherlands and around the mouth of the Rhine, particularly at Domburg and Duurstede, suggesting trade conducted by Saxon and Frisian merchants (Hill 1958).

During the eighth century the king received an income from the customs on trade at the port of London, and in 734, c744 and 747 he gave the bishops of Rochester and Worcester and the abbess of Minster in Thanet the right to receive the tolls on certain ships to the port (Dyson and Schofield 1984, 293). In 842 there occurred the first of the recorded Danish raids on London, and the history of the city was to change fundamentally as it met the Viking threat.

Although historical references to Middle Saxon London are few they do reflect a growing urban settlement and a developing trade. There is a marked absence of pottery and other objects of the period AD 500–900 from within the Roman walls of London, though objects and buildings of this period have now been found on an increasing number of sites in the Strand area, about a mile west of the city (Fig 1), and it would seem that this was the location of the Middle Saxon settlement of *Lundonwic*, still remembered as Aldwych – the 'old town' (Vince 1990, 13–25).

Users of the port

There is no evidence to suggest the appearance of the ships that visited London at this period. The only evidence for Anglo-Saxon ships at this period are those found in south-east England, particularly at Snape and Sutton Hoo, dating from the seventh century AD (Evans and Bruce-Mitford 1975). These were clinker-built with planks fastened by iron rivets, and were of the shipbuilding tradition represented in northern Europe and Scandinavia by the Nydam boat, of the fourth century AD (Akerlund 1963), and the Kvalsund ship of the seventh century AD (Brogger and Shetelig 1951, 52–7).

Coin evidence suggests that some of the seafaring traders visiting London were Frisian (Hill 1958), perhaps trading in slaves and other commodities (Bede, IV, 22), and it is suspected that they may have had a somewhat different shipbuilding tradition from that of the Celts and Saxons, though no certain remains of seagoing vessels of this type and period have been found anywhere (Ellmers 1985b, 81–4; 1990; Lebecq 1990).

Cargoes

Only a small quantity of Middle Saxon pottery has been found in London, probably due to a lack of archaeological investigation of the Strand settlement site until very recently. Existing finds may therefore not be representative of imports generally to London.

Of the two most common types of pottery found in the Strand area only Ipswich-type ware had been imported, presumably by water from the Thames estuary (Vince 1990, 107). That there was a substantial trade in this pottery is shown by its distribution not only on the coastal and riverside settlements of Suffolk and Norfolk (Hurst 1976, 301–2), but also from the Thames valley to Yorkshire (Vince 1984, 432–3). Additionally, just a few sherds of Continental imports (Fig 118), Tating ware and sherds of Badorf-type amphorae and cooking pots (ibid, 433–5), have been found in London, suggesting trading contact with the Low Countries consistent with some coin evidence (Vince 1988, 88–9). No trace of containers for the pottery, such as boxes or barrels, has been found. Other types of trade goods are suggested by the discovery of querns of Niedermendig lava from Germany, and by grapes, figs, and lentils (Vince 1990, 96–7).

Berthing

No Middle Saxon waterfront has been found within the walled area of London, though a row of stakes and possibly an embankment of the seventh–eighth centuries was found at 18–20 York Buildings, WC2, south of Aldwych, and on the same site an oak structure was

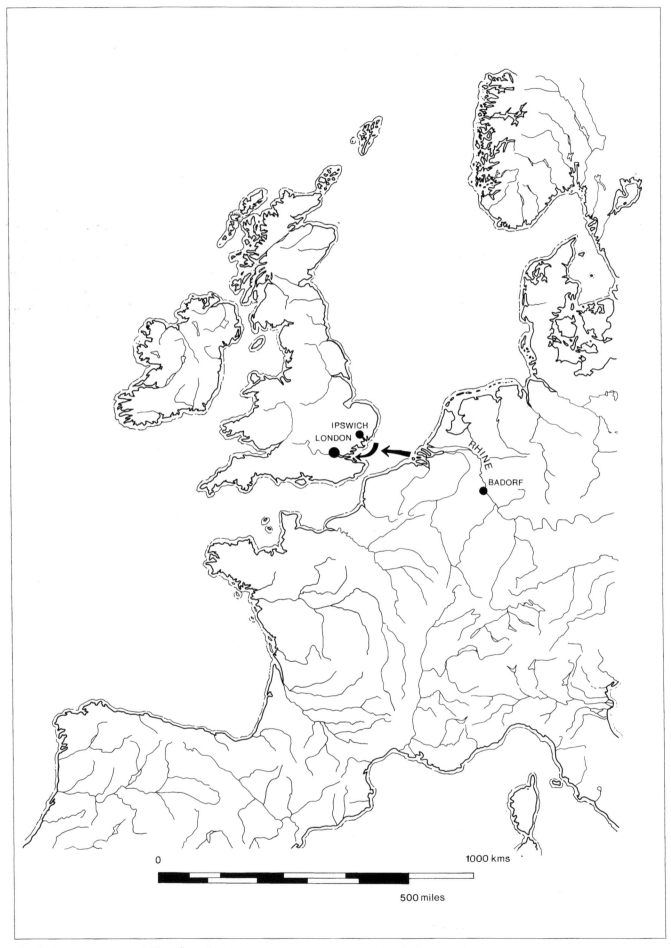

Fig 118 Some suggested European shipping routes to London, seventh to ninth centuries.

dendrochronologically dated to the late seventh century (Girardon and Heathcote 1989, 80). There was no clear indication that this was more than a riverbank revetment to stop erosion, and there is no evidence to show how ships may have berthed in London.

Remains of ships and boats

Although no ship or boat structure of the fifth–ninth centuries has been found in London, an iron rivet (Fig 119), possibly from a ship, was found in 1986 in the filling of a ditch of the ninth century, which had cut a pit containing a coin of Coenwulf (AD 796–805), at 21–2 Maiden Lane, just north of the Strand (Fig 1). The rivet is heavily corroded and the shape of its nail shank could not be established. An X-ray showed that the shank was 8mm across, and the distance between the nail head and the rove was about 42mm. This would be the thickness of the two overlapping planks that it presumably once fastened.

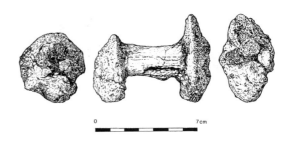

Fig 119   Iron rivet from Maiden Lane, Strand, ninth century.

Similar rivets occur in the Nydam boat of the fourth century AD and in the Sutton Hoo ship, but unless they are actually found in boats they should be treated with caution for they are also known to have been used in doors (Geddes 1982, fig 17.4), and in buildings as early as the sixth–seventh centuries (Hope-Taylor 1977, 192–3). This means that the rivets from *Hamwic*, Middle Saxon Southampton (Holdsworth 1980, 75), also need not have been from ships and boats.

7 The port in the tenth to eleventh centuries

Historical context

By the beginning of the tenth century the Saxon city was being constructed within the walled area of the former Roman city, and the Middle Saxon Aldwych settlement site to the west seems to have been abandoned, presumably because Viking raids were making it too dangerous to live there. The earliest recorded raids on London, mentioned in the *Anglo-Saxon Chronicle*, date from 842, when there was 'great slaughter' in London and Rochester, and in 851, when Rorik the Dane captured London with 350 ships. Although there was extensive Viking settlement in England, Alfred was able to recover London in 886. By 918 eastern England had been recaptured and relative peace was maintained until the end of the tenth century when Viking attacks were renewed (Page 1923, 35–43; Vince 1990, 26–37). London grew rapidly during the late tenth and eleventh centuries and was governed for the king by a 'portreeve'. Houses and churches were built, streets laid out, and trade and industry developed (ibid, 217).

In 994 Viking attacks on London began again but the city held out until 1016 when it and the English throne were seized by Cnut, the Dane. London's wealth was such that it was then taxed 10,500 pounds of silver – nearly 5 tons of bullion, and one-eighth of the total for the whole of England (Brooke and Keir 1975, 24).

In 1042 the Saxon King Edward 'the Confessor' assumed the throne, but when on his death in 1066 Earl Harold took the crown he was challenged and defeated by William of Normandy, whose coronation occurred at Westminster on Christmas Day 1066 (Page 1923, 43–69). William built castles in London, and elsewhere, to subdue the English population and made Westminster his headquarters. He confirmed London's rights given under the Saxon kings, and during the next 150 years the city continued to grow rapidly. In spite of all the political and economic difficulties throughout the late Saxon and Norman periods trade remained central to London's wealth, and amongst the population foreign traders are recorded, particularly from northern France, the Low Countries, Germany, Denmark, and Norway. Nevertheless, a very high proportion of London citizens in the early twelfth century still had English names, presumably indicating that the major part of its population was English and that it was largely they and not the Normans who controlled trade (Stenton 1970, 42).

Users of the port

Local river craft

That barges were used to carry Late Saxon Shelly ware down the Thames from Oxfordshire to London, is suggested by the distribution of the findspots of this pottery mostly near the river (Vince 1985, 36). It is not clear how such vessels were able to pass upstream, particularly through areas of natural rapids, though documentary records do refer to vessels using the upper Thames in the eleventh century, and to the existence of mills, and presumably mill dams, between Oxford and Bray. Those dams could have included flash locks thus enabling barges to pass through as in later times (Thacker 1914, frontispiece, 45–6).

Fishing vessels

The variety of trading vessels that were to be found in the port is indicated in a law code dating from *c*1000 AD, part of which relates to the public landing place at Billingsgate (Loyn 1962, 93–94). Archaeological evidence from eleventh-century deposits in London show that cod and ling, as well as oysters were brought to the city (Vince 1990, 96).

Seagoing merchant ships

According to this law code, small ships would have had to pay a toll of one half-penny, and larger vessels with sail would pay one penny. A keel (*ceol*) and a hulk (*hulcus*) would pay fourpence, suggesting that they were much larger; a ship with a cargo of planks would pay a toll of one plank; and a boat containing fish would be charged one half-penny, and a large ship one penny. Men of Rouen would pay a duty of six shillings plus a percentage of their cargo. A 'law of the Lorraine merchants' of *c*1130, and later port regulations of London in the early thirteenth century, also mention the presence of types of vessel known as keel and hulk (Bateson 1902, 496).

These references to the keel and hulk are the earliest specific historical record of ship types in London, but what these vessels looked like is unknown, though their later meaning is known and may be indicative of their former aspect.

In recent times the keel was traditionally 'a low flat-bottomed vessel' used off the east coast of England (Falconer 1815, 210). Until 1860 keels carried a square sail and other primitive features, particularly heart-shaped deadeyes, which suggested that they may not have been very different from their medieval namesakes mentioned in fifteenth- and sixteenth-century documents (Burwash 1969, 140–1). References to keels have otherwise been traced back to 1319 (Sandahl 1951, 66), thus the mention of keels in the London records of the eleventh and twelfth centuries are the earliest known. It is possible, therefore, that the keel of that time was also a flat-bottomed vessel with a thick plank-like keel suited to beaching, rather like that found at Fennings Wharf, Southwark (see p 160). Unger (1980, 77) has suggested that the keel was like the Late Saxon boat from Graveney,

Fig 120   Seal of New Shoreham depicting a 'hulc'; late thirteenth century.

though no reason is given and this view cannot be substantiated.

The London reference to a *hulc*, dating from about AD 1000, is the earliest known for this type of ship too, and it is fortunate that such a vessel is depicted on the seal of New Shoreham (Fig 120), dating from 1295 (Crumlin-Pedersen 1972, 187). It was a clinker-built banana-shaped craft with a single mast and a square sail (Fliedner 1969, 94–6; McGrail 1981, 38–40). Documentary evidence shows this type of ship to have been particularly important in the fourteenth and fifteenth centuries (Greenhill 1976, 283–5). There has been considerable discussion concerning how these ships might have been built, and it has been suggested that a logboat found in Utrecht in 1930 might have been an early form of hulk (Johnstone 1980, 119–20; Unger 1980, 58–60), but this view has, with good reason, been discounted (Vlek 1987, 143–5). Until a hulk has been found it will not be possible to resolve the many questions that surround this important type of merchant vessel.

Warships

The *Anglo-Saxon Chronicle* frequently refers to Viking raiders, and discoveries of Viking ships of this period at Roskilde in Denmark show what they looked like, and how they were built and used (Olsen and Crumlin-Pedersen 1967). They were long open vessels, sharp at both ends, and were clinker-built with fastenings of iron rivets. Of particular importance is the discovery in London of a group of Viking weapons and tools of the early eleventh century, in the former bed of the Thames near the north end of London Bridge. The group, thought to have been lost from a Viking ship, includes seven battle-axes, a smaller woodsman's axe, six spearheads, a pair of tongs, and a grappling-iron (Wheeler 1927, fig 1, 18–23). Moreover, a broken anchor of Viking type was found

in the Thames at Blackfriars, suggesting a mooring site (see p 163). Although no Viking ships have been found in London, it is relevant to mention in this context the discovery some years before 1890 at Benfleet on the north bank of the Thames estuary in Essex, of 'many ships deep in the mud, several of which on exposure had evidently been burnt, as their charred remains showed. Indeed, about them lay numerous human skeletons', and it was suggested that these may be the remains of a Danish fleet destroyed in 893 by the citizens of London (*Essex Naturalist* 1890, 153). This is potentially a site of exceptional importance which is worthy of future archaeological attention, particularly as the ships were found during the construction of a railway bridge, and their location can probably be fixed exactly as only one pier of the bridge was built in the bed of the creek.

Cargoes

Documentary evidence describes seaborne trade at the end of the tenth century as bringing to London some exotic goods including silks, precious stones, gold, wine, (olive) oil, ivory, bronze, and glass (Loyn 1962, 96). To a very limited extent archaeology confirms this, in that Syrian glass has been found (Clark 1989, 23). A law code of Ethelred II, of *c* 1000, mentions more prosaic cargoes on which customs duty had to be paid at Billingsgate: timber, cloth, fish, chickens, eggs, and dairy produce. Although much of this trade (Fig 121) was imported from Normandy, northern France, Flanders, and Germany (Loyn 1962, 93–4), it is likely that the more perishable items, particularly eggs, were brought from nearer sources.

Excavations have produced a valuable view of some trade goods entering late Saxon and Norman London, though its scope is conditioned by the ability of objects to survive in the ground. These imports include figs, grapes, and silk, as well as hones from Norway (Vince 1990, 97).

Pottery, a useful clue to some trade routes to London, includes tenth-century sherds of domestic ware manufactured in Oxfordshire, but this shelly pottery stopped being produced in the early eleventh century, perhaps due to the sack of Oxford by the Vikings in 1010 (Vince 1985, 34, 42). Its distribution at Thames-side settlements between Oxford and London at that period indicates that it was brought down the river. From the later eleventh to the late twelfth centuries there were many pottery imports, particularly from the Rhineland, Low Countries, northern France and south-east England, from an area which coincides with that described in Ethelred's law code (ibid, 42–3).

Of particular interest is the size and volume of individual types of packaged goods that were imported by ship, for, judging from excavated examples, these appear to have been less than a tonne in weight, as if it was important that they could be easily manhandled. This may be a reflection of the modest cargo-handling facilities believed to have been generally extant in ports at that time. It is later in medieval times that the weight of

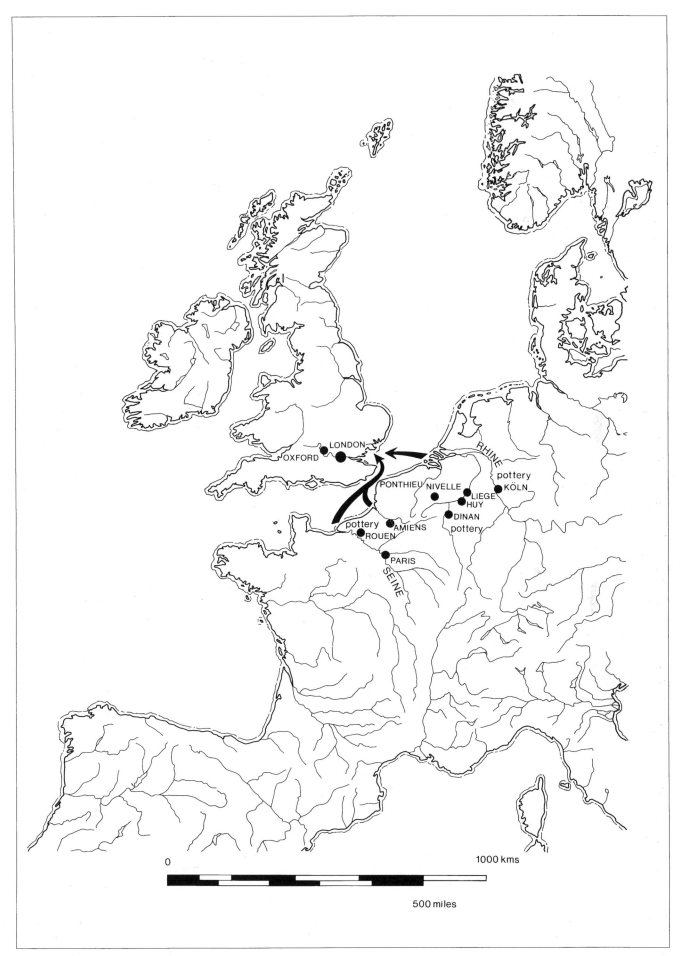

Fig 121   Some suggested European trade routes to London, tenth to eleventh centuries.

individual packaged items of cargo seems to become larger and more common, perhaps due to improved port facilities. Although this is a tentative suggestion, it does illustrate the importance of recording and weighing imported goods that have been found. Such goods include querns of Niedermendig lava from the Rhineland (Vince 1990, 97), but particularly important are the sizes of barrels, of which only fragments have been found, and which presumably once contained wine. Ethelred's law code of cAD 1000 refers to the men of Rouen who brought wine, presumably in barrels (Loyn 1962, 93), and in the early twelfth century some London port regulations refer to the men of lower Lorraine who are specifically described as bringing wine in barrels (Bateson 1902, 496–500). Archaeological evidence is all that is available to establish their sizes and capacity.

Berthing

Documentary evidence shows that during the tenth to twelfth centuries there were several berthing places in London where customs duties on a variety of goods were collected for the king (Dyson 1985). It is likely that there was some form of beach market (Milne and Goodburn 1990) at such locations as Dowgate and Vintry (Fig 122) which were primarily used by German and French merchants. Although it is not clear how these berthing places functioned, excavations at Dowgate show that it had an artificial embankment with a low angle of slope, perhaps forming a stable area for ships to beach thus facilitating the loading and unloading of cargoes. Also there were three 'common quays', at Billingsgate, St Botolph Wharf, and Queenhithe, and parts of the first have been excavated. Like Dowgate, it too comprised an artificial embankment that may have been built to enable boats to be run ashore, though traces of revetments and a possible jetty have been found. A major study of the late Saxon and Norman waterfronts in the London Bridge area was published in 1992 (Steedman et al 1992).

Billingsgate, first mentioned in the law code of cAD 1000 (Dyson 1985, 20) had an embankment of stones laced with rough-hewn logs aligned east-west with the flow of the river. At what may have been its west end were some upright posts that might have formed the supports of a jetty (Fig 123) (Hobley and Schofield 1977, 37; Dyson and Schofield 1981). Recent consideration of the archaeological dating evidence for the embankment suggests that it was constructed in the late tenth to early eleventh century (Vince 1988, 84). To the east was found a timber revetted inlet 5m wide with a sloping pebbly clay bottom at between about 0.3 and 1.5m below OD, below banks at least at 1.8m above OD. The high water level is estimated to have been a little above 1m OD, so the inlet could well have enabled small vessels to berth there, made fast to two possible mooring posts found nearby (Steedman et al 1992, 53; T Brigham pers comm).

At Dowgate, first mentioned in the 1140s, but apparently in existence at the time of Edward the Confessor (Dyson 1985, 20), there was a similar Saxo-Norman artificial embankment of clay and timber logs, upon which lay a considerable quantity of discarded pottery of the Norman period, believed to be cargo breakages imported from the Rhineland (Dunning 1959, 73–7). It is probably significant that this embankment lay close to a centre of German traders from the twelfth century, and was to become the London headquarters of the Hanse merchants (Harben 1918, 549–51).

Queenhithe, originally called *Ethelredeshythe* after Ethelred the son-in-law of King Alfred, seems to have been the earliest public landing place, first mentioned in a grant of King Alfred in 898 or 899. Extending to the north was a plot of land upon which a waterfront market was established in 889. Profits from the market were given to the bishop of Worcester, and he and the archbishop of Canterbury had the right to moor ships there. The types of goods then handled there are unknown, but Dyson (1985, 20) has pointed out that from the early thirteenth century the record of grain, salt, and freshwater fish suggest that it dealt mostly with inland goods brought by river. In this way it contrasts with Billingsgate and Dowgate which dealt with goods from downstream,

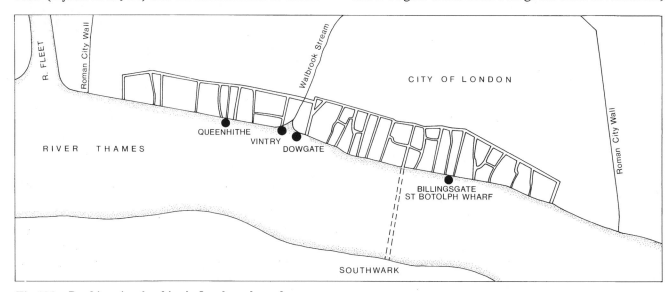

Fig 122   Berthing sites for ships in London, eleventh century.

both English and foreign, and, although in the eleventh, twelfth, and thirteenth centuries other hithes and wharfs were established along the London waterfront to handle various types of goods (Dyson 1989, 22), it seems that later medieval berthing was generally restricted to the quays of Queenhithe, Dowgate, Billingsgate, and nearby St Botolph Wharf (Dyson 1981).

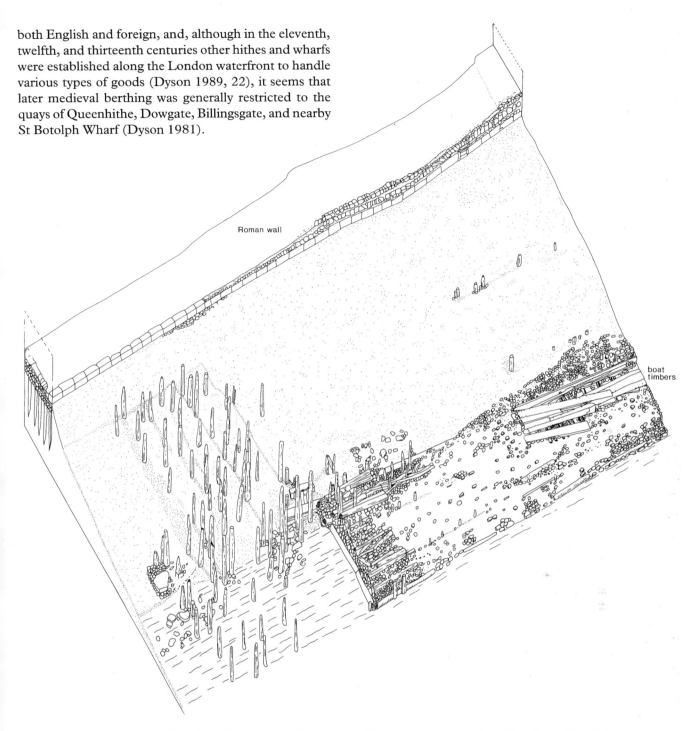

Fig 123 Partial reconstruction of a rubble bank and posts, probably to support a jetty, from New Fresh Wharf, late tenth or early eleventh century.

It is not clear how ships berthed at the artificial embankments. They were up to a metre thick and were broad with a low angle of slope, suggesting that at least the smaller or flatter-bottomed vessels were beached so as to be unloaded at low tide. Traces of a probable jetty and revetments do indicate that larger vessels, possibly hulks and keels which are known to have reached London (p 137), may have had a deeper water berth. But before the berthing methods can be established it is necessary to know what were the high and low tide levels then relative to OD, and also the draught of various types of ship. It is thought that in the eleventh century high water was at about 1.40m OD (Steedman *et al* 1992, 99).

The 'law of the Lorraine merchants' (Bateson 1902, 496–500) of soon after 1200, is believed to have originated *c*1130 and may reflect the long established practice that attended the berthing in London of any ship brought by the merchants of Lower Lorraine. Their main cargo was barrels of wine, but other goods could include cloth, gold, and silver tableware and precious stones from as far afield as Constantinople. Their trade was via the rivers Danube and Rhine, and then across the narrow seas to the Thames and the port of London. On arrival at London they were required to raise their ensign, no doubt to identify themselves, and then sing 'Kyrie eleison'. They could also broach their first barrel of wine, perhaps as a sample of their trade, which would be sold at one penny a stoop. Having passed London Bridge and reached a hithe, presumably Dowgate because this was used by foreign traders, they would wait two ebbs and one flood tide when no trade was allowed. During this time the ship could be visited by the king's chamberlain and the sheriff, as the king's representatives who had the exclusive first opportunity of buying part of the cargo, which must be paid for within two weeks. After this the Lorrainer could sell to others, first the merchants of London, next those of Oxford, then those of Winchester, and thereafter to anyone. If the ship was a keel the sheriff and chamberlain could take two barrels of wine from the hold below the mast and one from before the mast-head at a reduced price, and if the vessel was a hulk or some other type of ship then they could take one barrel from before and one from behind the mast. On the assumption that the numbers of barrels reflect not only the distribution of volume in the holds but also the capacity of the vessels, it seems that this 'law' suggests that the hulk was a little smaller than the keel, and that whereas the mast of the hulk was central in the hold, the mast of the keel was forward of the centre. The Lorrainer who sold his goods on board only needed to pay the wine custom, but if he sold it ashore then he would pay further customs duty to the King (Bateson 1902, 496–7).

8   Ships and boats of the tenth and eleventh centuries

Fragments of several vessels have been found in London dating from the tenth and eleventh centuries, and, although they do not show what the vessels themselves looked like, they do indicate how they were constructed and suggest to which shipbuilding tradition they belonged. They have been found in waterfronts at New Fresh Wharf and Billingsgate in the City, and at Fennings Wharf in Southwark. Recently, more ship or boat timbers were found at Thames Exchange in the City (Milne and Goodburn 1990), but these are not included in this study. A few other items are important: a possible oar or paddle blade from Hibernia Wharf, Southwark, and a broken anchor from the river at Blackfriars, probably at a mooring position. Published elsewhere is part of a possible logboat of unknown date from Chamberlains Wharf, Southwark (Heal and Hutchinson 1986, 205–10), and a group of Viking weapons of c 1000 found near London Bridge (Wheeler 1927, 18–23, fig 1).

Timbers from New Fresh Wharf, City of London, 1974

Site and context

An area of broken boat timbers of the tenth century, found on top of a late Saxon foreshore embankment immediately west of Billingsgate, was archaeologically excavated in 1974 at New Fresh Wharf, Lower Thames Street, in the City of London (Miller 1977). Exposed timbers had suffered from some water erosion before being buried in grey silt, and it seems that they indicate the place where a boat had been broken up. The timbers are preserved in the Museum of London and the Shipwreck Heritage Centre, Hastings.

Although the timbers were mostly planks, there were also a few frame fragments, a knee, and pieces of what may have been a sheerstrake. No keel was found. The recovered timbers did not constitute the entire remains for they extended beyond the trench, but enough was found to indicate the constructional features of the vessel. The similarity of construction and the fact that the timbers were found together indicate that they are from the same vessel.

When and where was it built?

The tree-ring study shows that this boat was built of oak probably grown in south-east England (see Appendix 6). The analysis suggests felling of the trees between AD 920 and 955.

Log conversion

The planks had been radially cut from straight-grained oak (*Quercus*) with narrow rings (Fig 124), and there were few traces of knots. As the plank faces did not always exactly follow the rays in the wood it is clear that the surfaces had been trimmed, as would be expected. In almost every case the sapwood had been removed, though one plank still retained the sapwood interface.

In spite of the surface erosion by the river, many planks bore traces of tool marks (Fig 125), roughly parallel narrow cuts in the wood surfaces, perhaps made by an axe or scraping tool (Olsen and Crumlin-Pedersen 1967, fig 68).

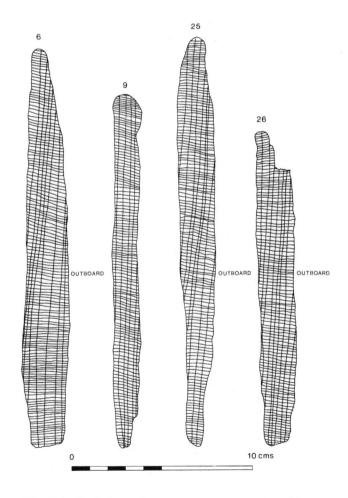

Fig 124   Radial tree-ring pattern on cross-section of boat planks from New Fresh Wharf.

Fig 125 Plank fragment from New Fresh Wharf showing pegged laps and eroded peg holes.

Description

Planks

The boat was clinker-built, and its overlapping planks had a variety of widths, mostly in the range of 0.25–0.325m (actual reconstructed widths are *c* 0.25, 0.265, 0.27, 0.297, 0.30, 0.32, and 0.325m). One plank was more than 0.37m wide. The thickness of the planks ranged from 14 to 27mm, but was mostly 20–24mm.

The clinker planks overlapped each other by about 32mm (Fig 128, no 3; Fig 132, no 21) and were fastened together with small wooden pegs, their centres spaced between 80 and 152mm apart, but mostly between 105 and 125mm. Each peg was of willow/poplar (*Salix/Populus*) type, about 15mm in diameter, and was cut following the grain. It was wedged with oak at one end only (Fig 129). Each wedge was of oak (*Quercus*), *c* 35mm long, was about 6.5mm thick at the end (Fig 126), and had been driven across the line of the plank's grain so as to avoid splitting away the plank edge. This was particularly important since the row of lap pegs normally lay only about 7–9 mm from the plank edge.

The angles at which the peg holes had been drilled through the planks varied from at right angles to the plank faces to pronounced angles, and presumably reflected the changing form of the hull as it curved down from the gunwale to the keel.

Moss caulking lay between the overlapping strakes to make the joints watertight (Fig 127). One undisturbed lap (Fig 128, no 3) was found to comprise three superimposed layers of moss. There were no hollows or grooves cut in the faces of any planks to accommodate the caulking. It was noted that in a few instances the action of driving pegs into the lap had carried a little of the moss caulking with it into the peg hole, thus confirming that pegs had been driven into position from the unwedged end after the caulking was in place.

The moss itself has been identified by Peter Boyd, Environmental Department, Museum of London, as *Neckera crispa* Hedw, *Neckera complanata* (Hedw) Hub, *Thuidium tamariscinum*, (Hedw) Br Eur, and *Eurhynchium striatum* (Hedw) Schimp. All of these species have a widespread distribution in Europe, including southeast England, and both *Neckera complanata* and *Eurhynchium striatum* were used as caulking in the Bronze Age boats from North Ferriby, Yorkshire (Wright and Wright 1947, 138).

Some of the planks had scarfed ends, most of which were so eroded or broken that their fastenings were not generally clear. Only one end of each scarf contained fastenings, and traces of one, two, and three peg holes survived, suggesting that up to three fastenings held those ends. The scarf of only one plank was well preserved, though still damaged. It was about 0.185m long in a plank 18mm thick, and in the scarf were traces of moss caulking which, when pegs had been driven through to hold the joint, seem to have been carried down around the pegs on the wedged end, which was presumably the inboard side of the scarf. Thus it is clear that these pegs had been driven from the unwedged end, presumably outboard. Several plank fragments with scarf joints were found (Fig 130, nos 10, 12; Fig 131, nos 13–16; Fig 132, nos 19–23) of which four were about 0.18m long. These were simple overlap joints. It is presumed that the pegged end of each scarf lay on the outboard side of the plank towards the stern, as was and still is the normal practice in clinker-built boats (Lienau 1934, 23; Smolarek 1969, 402; Madsen 1984; Christensen 1985, 202; McGrail 1987, 127), for the practical reason that this reduces the possibility of the scarf leaking below the waterline.

A small wooden patch for a plank (Fig 134, no 33) lay amongst the timbers, and was only 80mm wide, over 0.35m long, and 6mm thick. It had been fastened to its parent timber by four wooden pegs, each 12mm in diameter, one of which had survived and still contained a wedge. The patch was of radially cut oak, like the rest of the planking.

Frames

The only clue to the spacing of the frames in the boat were the trenails in the planks. These were 15, 16.5 and 17mm in diameter and were of willow/poplar (*Salix/Populus*) and were mostly unwedged in the planks. This accords with more recent ships in which it was normal for trenails to be driven from outboard through the plank and through the frame, so that only the inboard end in the frame was expanded with a wedge. However, in the New Fresh Wharf boat two trenails were found to have been wedged in the plank rather than in the frame, probably with oak, the thickest part of the wedge being 4.5mm across (Fig 132, no 20; Fig 133, no 28).

The 'frame' trenails had spacings of 0.214m (Fig 133, no 28), 0.23m and 0.29m (Fig 130, no 11), 0.51+m (Fig 132, no 20), 1.07+m (Fig 131, no 16) and 1.235+m (Fig 133, no 24). These presumably reflect the distance between the frame centres and are an important clue to the framing of the boat, for the spacings fall into two groups: 0.19–0.29m, and those greater than 1m.

In Scandinavia and along the southern Baltic it was usual in clinker-built ships and boats of this period to fasten each plank to the frame that passed across it with one trenail (Olsen and Crumlin-Pedersen 1967, 168), and for the frame centres to be less than one metre apart (Lienau 1934, 15; Olsen and Crumlin-Pedersen 1967, 167). This pattern seems to differ from the New Fresh Wharf boat, where some spaces were apparently well in excess of a metre. Rare occasions of greater spacing occur in Scandinavia and in the southern Baltic and include a boat from the Gokstad site (McGrail 1974, fig 3), and from Ralswiek 2 (Herfert 1968).

However, the Graveney boat, also of late Saxon date, had alternate strakes fastened to each frame (Fenwick 1978, 240), and such a pattern may account for the greater spacing of some frames in the New Fresh Wharf boat. On the present evidence it is not possible to reach a firm conclusion on the frame spacing of the New Fresh Wharf boat. The best explanation of the two groups of trenail spacings is that there were closely spaced frames in the bottom of the boat, and more widely spaced frames

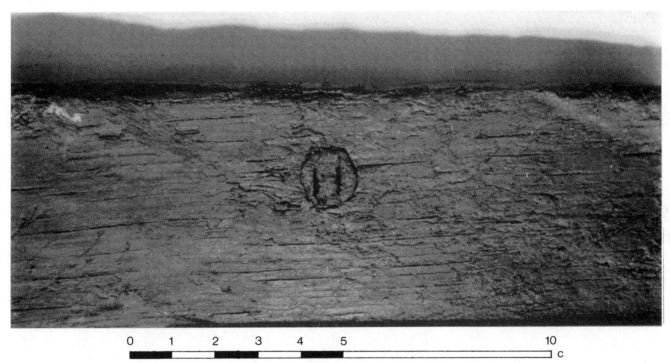

Fig 126 A wedged lap peg on a plank from New Fresh Wharf.

Fig 127 The lap of a plank originally held by pegs, from New Fresh Wharf. The adjacent plank protected it from erosion.

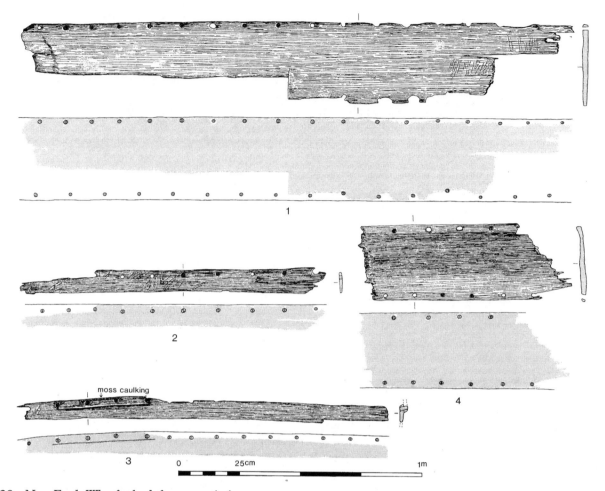

Fig 128   New Fresh Wharf: plank fragments 1–4.

higher up, an arrangement that occurs in some recent clinker-built boats (McKee 1983, 110, 175).

Two fragmentary frames were found. One (Fig 134, no 36) was 0.394m long and broken at both ends. It was rhomboid in section, 47mm wide, and 52mm high at one end and 90mm high at the other. It was pierced by two trenail holes, each 14mm in diameter, which were spaced 0.345m apart centres. One unwedged trenail remained. The underside of the frame was not stepped for clinker planking and had no impression of plank edges.

It is probable that the fore and aft sides of the frame were approximately upright in the boat, and that the angle of the top and bottom faces relative to the sides reflected the angle of the outer planking of the vessel. If correct, this suggests that the frame was situated close to a narrowing, presumably sharp, end of the boat. Also, it is likely that the thickest part of the frame was closest to the centre-line of the vessel.

A tight U-shaped, almost V-shaped, timber of fruit wood, *Pomoideae* (eg apple, pear, hawthorn, etc, Fig 134, no 37) with trenail holes, one of which was 13mm in diameter, at its broken ends, was probably a small frame, for the angle was not square enough for it to have been a knee. It was 33–40mm wide, and up to 140mm deep, and had been fashioned from a tree branch of this shape, with one 'vertical' face following the rounded shape of a branch, and the other face having been formed by splitting the branch down the centre.

If its use is correctly identified there are two places in which it could have been used: over the keel, thereby giving a V-shaped bottom to the vessel; and over the stem or sternposts near one end. However, no close parallels for such a frame have been found, except possibly in the 'faering' or small boat found with the ninth century Gokstad ship, Norway (McGrail 1974). It is not possible to judge between these possibilities, though the narrow space allowed for a keel in the first interpretation does make this seem less likely.

Knee

An L-shaped oak knee (Fig 134, no 34), forming an obtuse angle, was found with the planks, and is of a type that is characteristic of Scandinavian and Slavonic ships of the Viking period. It had not been cut from timber growing to the curving shape, but instead from a fairly straight log. Originally it possessed three trenails, one at each end and one at about the middle. The knee was 0.61m from end to end, about 70mm wide, and 70mm thick. The end trenails were missing, though their holes showed that they had fastened the knee to other timbers. The middle trenail, still in place, was 17.5mm in diameter, and had been wedged from inside the angle of the knee (ie from inside the boat). Knees of this form were normally used to fasten horizontal cross-beams or thwarts to the sides of a boat, and it is possible that this

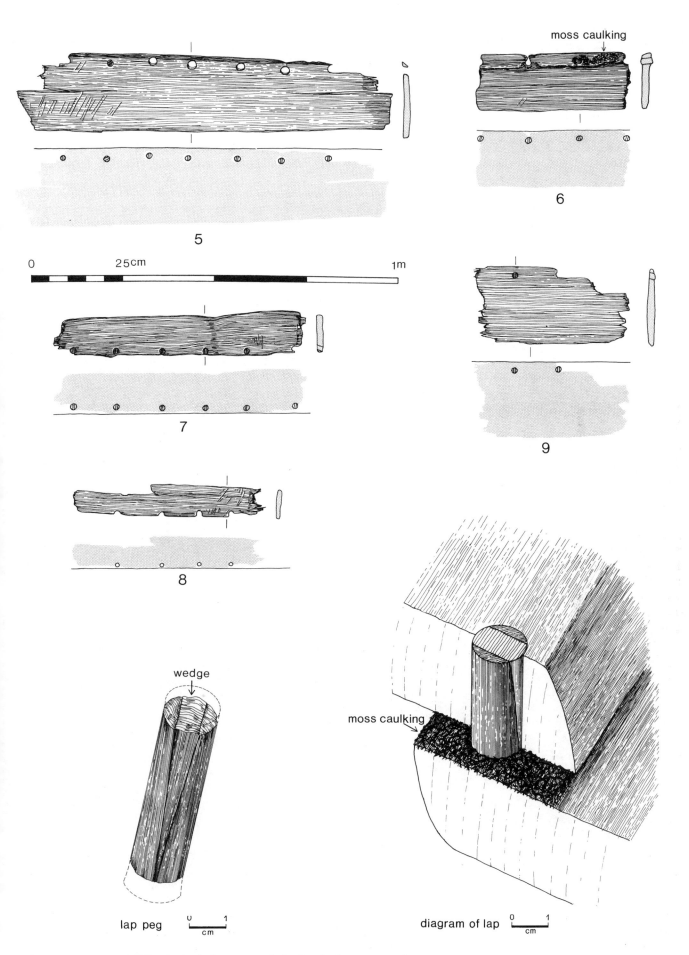

Fig 129 New Fresh Wharf: plank fragments, 5–9, also the lap construction.

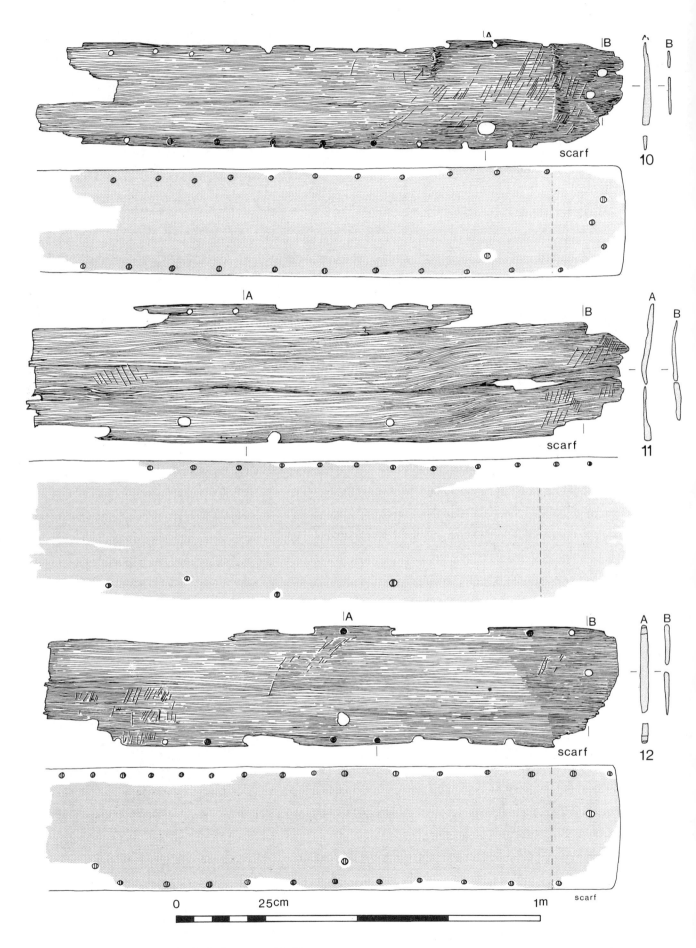

Fig 130   New Fresh Wharf: plank fragments 10–12.

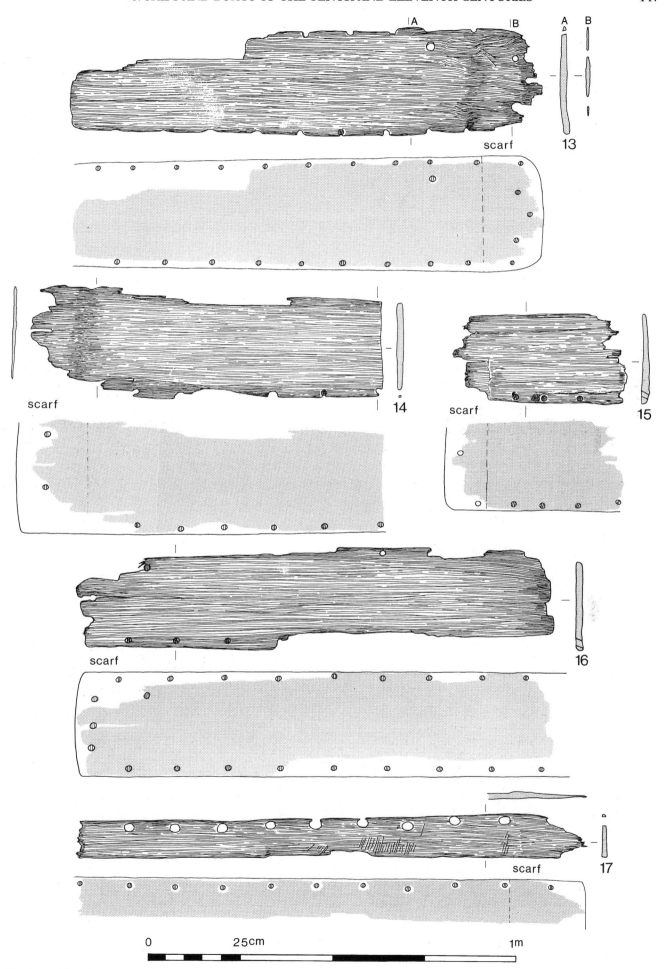

Fig 131   New Fresh Wharf: plank fragments 13–17.

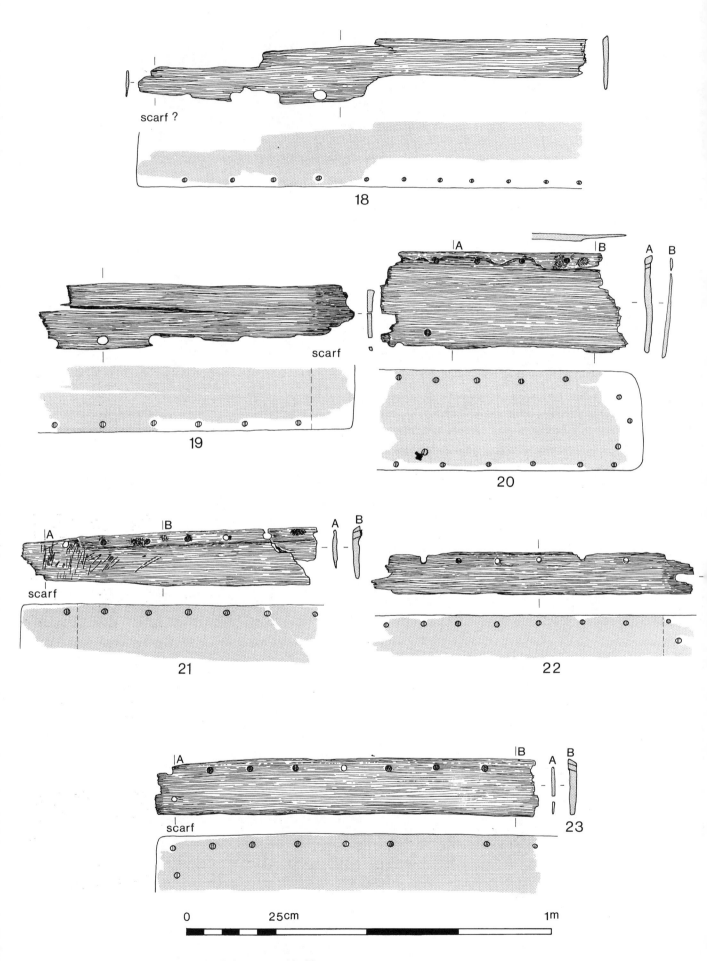

Fig 132 New Fresh Wharf: plank fragments 18–23.

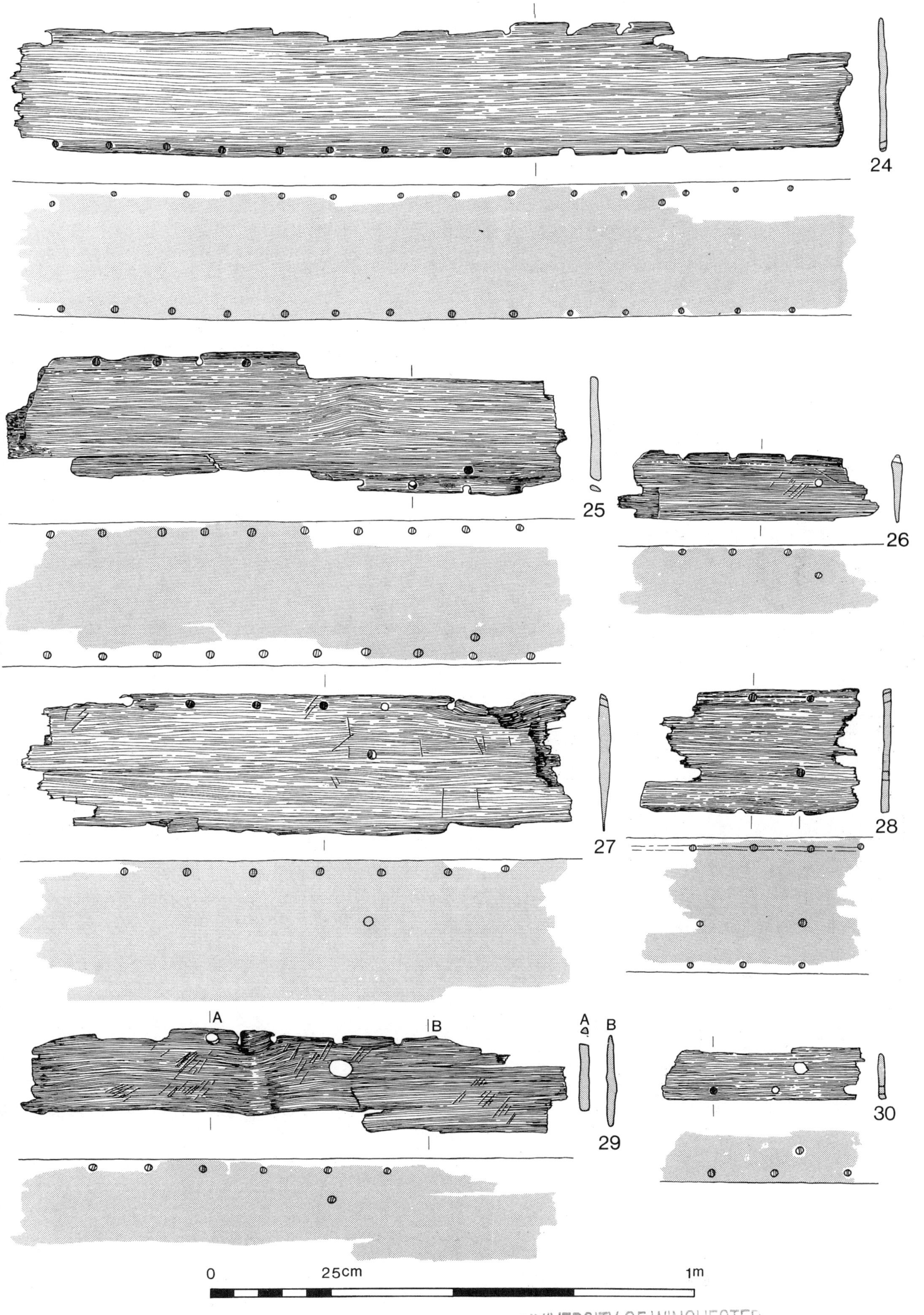

Fig 133   New Fresh Wharf: plank fragments 24–30.

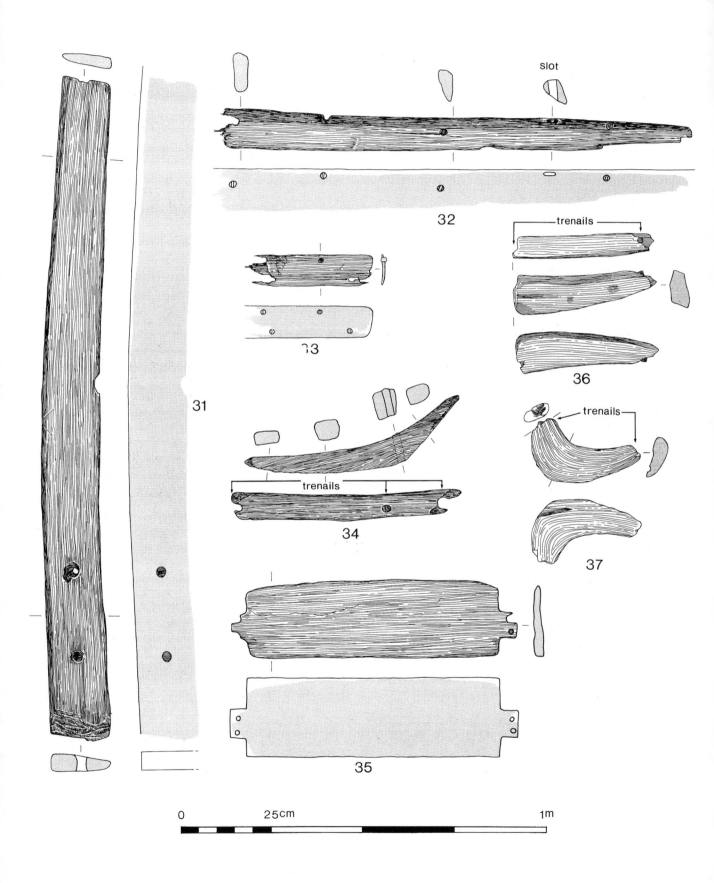

Fig 134   New Fresh Wharf: miscellaneous timbers as found and reconstructed.

was the case here (Fig 136, no 4). One face was curved, and presumably reflected the form of the side of the vessel; and the other, shorter, arm was straight as if it had been fastened to a horizontal cross-beam. The curve of the outer face of the knee suggests that it was a standing knee passing over two strakes rather than a lodging (ie horizontal) knee, but the absence of a notch to fit the overlapping clinker planking is interesting, since in Scandinavian and Slavonic vessels at this time it was normal for frames and knees to be 'joggled' (ie notched). The absence of notches may be indicative of Anglo-Saxon shipbuilding, as most of the frames in the Graveney boat were not notched either (Fenwick 1978, 240). The outer face was at a slight angle, suggesting that the knee lay towards one end of the boat.

A possible stringer

Two lengths of partly eroded timber, probably rectangular in section originally, were amongst the finds. One (Fig 134, no 31) was 47mm thick, and the other (Fig 134, no 32) 40mm thick. Some trenails passing 'horizontally' through the timber had wedges on one side, showing that they had been fastened on the unwedged side to another timber. These trenails were 16.5, 18.5, 26, and 28mm in diameter, and it is possible that the two timbers were stringers, longitudinal beams fastened to the side of the boat for added strength. In the edge of one of the timbers (Fig 134, no 32) was also a slot 23mm across and 32mm along the timber which had been enlarged by water erosion. Had this timber been a stringer then the slot would have been vertical and could have held a pin or oar pivot enabling the boat to be rowed. It is possible that these timbers were not from a boat, but the fact that almost all other timbers in the group were certainly from a vessel makes it probable that the same was the case with these timbers too.

A possible bottom board

A rectangular oak plank (Fig 134, no 35), 0.68m long, 0.205m broad, and 26mm thick, and radially cut, had small water-eroded rectangular flanges about 48mm long by 65mm wide at each end. Each flange appears to have had two holes for pegs, but part of only one peg remained. It was 14.5mm in diameter and not wedged, and showed that the ends of the plank had been fastened to other timbers. As almost all the other timbers in this group were apparently from a boat and had similar pegs, it is likely that this was too. Ole Crumlin-Pedersen (pers comm) has suggested that in the absence of ancient parallels it might be the paddle from a waterwheel. However, similarly shaped boards are nowadays used as decking on the bottom frames of modern local fishing boats in Tenerife (pers obs), the rebates on either side of the flanges accommodating the frames. If this is correct then the flanges represent a gap of 0.065m between the frames, which is consistent with the frame spacing suggested by some 'frame' trenails described above.

Reconstruction of the boat

Enough broken boat structure was found to suggest the type of vessel that this boat might have been. The planks, the knee, the moss caulking, and the stringer are all paralleled in Slavonic plank-built vessels of the same period found around the southern Baltic (Fig 135). When this is considered with the fact that ships and boats of both Scandinavian and Slavic type at this period were mostly open vessels, sharp at both ends and clinker-built, it seems likely that the New Fresh Wharf boat was as well. The major constructional difference between the Scandinavian and Slavic vessels is that in the former the overlapping planks were held together by iron rivets, but in the latter they were held by small wooden pegs.

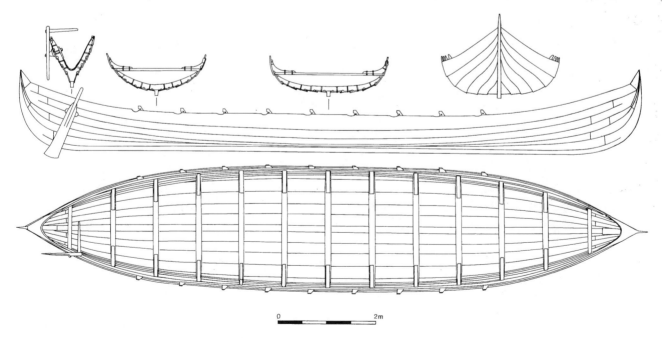

0   2m

Fig 135   Reconstruction of boat 1 from Danzig Ohra (Gdansk), Poland.

Table 13   Plank size relative to vessel size

boat	length	beam	strake width	strake thickness (cms)
New Fresh Wharf			25–32.5	2–2.4
Skuldelev 2	28m	4.5m	24–29	1–3
Skuldelev 5	18m	2.6m	25–38	1.5–2.5
Skuldelev 1	16.5m	4.6m	23–29	1.2–3.4
Skuldelev 3	13.5m	3.2m	28–36	1–3.5
Danzig-Ohra 3	13.3m	2.46m	25	2.2
Danzig-Ohra 1	12.76m	2.37m	25–28	1.5–2.2
Skuldelev 6	12m	2.5m	25–40	2.2–4
Danzig-Ohra 2	11m	2.27m	30	2.2

(Olsen and Crumlin-Pedersen 1967; Lienau 1934, 15)

The possible stringer with the hole for a possible oar pivot, if correctly identified, would suggest that this was a rowing boat, and the knee may give the angle between the end of a thwart or seat and the side of the boat. The frame fragments indicate a vessel with sharp ends. It is not possible to judge the size of the craft, for on the present published evidence there seems to have been little correlation between the sizes of vessels at that time and the dimensions of their planking (see Table 13). However, the frame size is small indicating that this was probably a small local river vessel.

Sequence of building the boat

The fragments of timber give some indication of the stages in building the boat. Particularly important are the trenail holes in the planks which would normally indicate frame positions.

After being split radially, the logs were trimmed, probably by axe, to provide the planks, as is shown in the Bayeux Tapestry (Olsen and Crumlin-Pedersen 1967, 155). This could result in the tool marks to be seen cut on the surfaces of the planking.

This boat was 'shell-built', as were all Scandinavian-Slavic clinker built vessels (McGrail 1987, 102–3), for its planks were fastened together before the frames were inserted (Fig 136). This is clearly demonstrated by projecting the lines of frames onto the plank fragments at the 'frame trenail' positions, for it will be seen that some frames (eg Fig 133, nos 26–28) must have crossed lap pegs. Since those lap pegs had been wedged, presumably from inboard, they could only have been fastened and wedged before the frames were in position. It is also clear that entire strakes were formed from several planks joined endwise with simple overlapping scarfs pegged at the outboard end only.

Loss of the boat

The breaking-up of the boat was presumably due to its old age. Not only was a repair patch found (Fig 134, no 33), but also many of the planks appear to have split

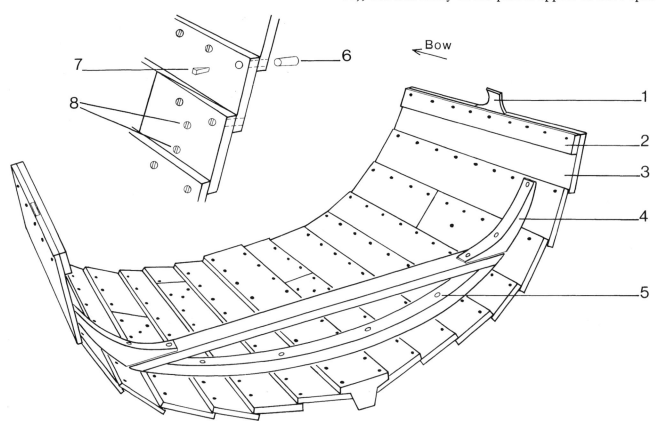

Fig 136   Possible reconstruction of the New Fresh Wharf timbers to include all known features: (1) oar pivot; (2) inwale; (3) gunwale/sheerstrake; (4) standing knee; (5) frame held to planks by trenails; (6) lap peg; (7) wedge of peg, inboard; (8) pegs wedged inboard holding a plank scarf.

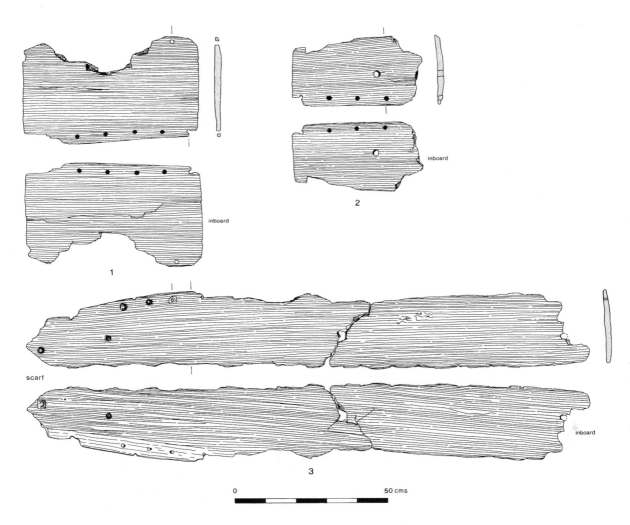

Fig 137 Billingsgate: (1), (2) pegged planking; (3) riveted plank; tenth to eleventh centuries.

along the grain. All of the planks lay east-west with the flow of the river, and no other evidence was found to suggest that the planking was left for any other purpose. Instead, the timbers had been exposed to river erosion, and peg holes had become enlarged by eddy action, though where planks were covered by other timbers they

were protected from such erosion. Had they been used to help slide boats ashore it seems likely that there would have been some evidence of this, particularly in the form of breakages across the planks, but none was found. In due course the timbers were covered by silt.

Planking from Billingsgate, City of London, 1982

Site and context

Small fragments of two boats were found in waterfront deposits dating from the eleventh and the first half of the twelfth centuries (Steedman *et al* 1992). Tree-ring analysis indicates that the vessels were built in the tenth and eleventh centuries.

Pegged planks

Two small pieces of boat planking (site object no 6697, Fig 137, no 1; site object no 6698, Fig 137, no 2) were found in the construction of an artificial embankment that had been built, according to tree-ring dating, in 1039–40. This embankment lay on the west side of a small contemporary inlet leading into the River Thames

(Trevor Brigham pers comm).

The tree-ring analysis indicates that the planks are derived from the same tree felled after AD 970. Also, as the lap peg positions matched, it is clear that the planks were once fastened together, and probably became detached when excavated. The planks had evidently been reused in the tenth or eleventh centuries, as they were only 0.572m long, and had saw-marks at the transverse edges. There is no indication of their reused purpose.

Both planks were of radially cut oak (*Quercus*), one originally being 0.324m wide and up to 20mm thick in the centre, and 15mm at the laps. The adjoining plank was incomplete, but was 19mm thick in the middle and 14mm near the laps, and probably of similar width.

They were held together clinkerwise by a row of wooden pegs, each 12mm in diameter. The lap was

Table 14   Shipbuilding characteristics

ship	sh/sk	cv/ck	plank	fasten	clk	material	age
Blackfriars ship 1	sk	cv	tang	none	clk	hazel	R
New Guy's House boat	sk	cv	tang	none	clk	hazel	R
County Hall ship	sh	cv	tang	m & t	none	none	R
New Fresh Wharf	sh	ck	rad	peg	clk	moss	S–N
Fennings Wharf planks	sh	ck	rad	rivet	clk	hair	S–N
Fennings Wharf keel	sh?	ck?	rad	nail	clk	hair	S–N
Billingsgate pegged	sh	ck	rad	peg	clk	?	S–N
Billingsgate rivetted	sh	ck	rad	rivet	clk	hair	S–N

sh	shell	material	caulking material
sk	skeleton	tang	tangentially-cut plank
cv	carvel	rad	radially-split plank
ck	clinker	m & t	mortice-and-tenon
fasten	plank-to-plank fastenings	R	Roman
rivet	rivetted	S–N	late Saxo-Norman (ie tenth to eleventh century AD)
clk	caulking		

48mm wide, and there was no surviving trace of caulking. The lap pegs, probably of willow/poplar (*Populus/Salix*) type, had been driven from one face, presumed to be outboard, so leaving the ends projected slightly from the plank and resembled a champagne cork. The other end, presumably inboard, was wedged, probably with oak (*Quercus*), across the grain of the plank so as not to split its edge. Each wedge was about 20mm long and 6mm across the top. The pegs generally lay 18mm from the plank edges, and were spaced between 84 and 96mm apart at the centres.

Near the centre of one plank (Fig 137, no 2) was a trenail hole 19mm in diameter, presumably for a frame, but as there was none in the adjoining plank it seems that the frame had not been fastened to every plank.

The riveted plank

During the first half of the twelfth century two pieces of boat planking had been used as cladding in the relining of the embankment on the east side of the inlet. One piece was retained (site object no 6873) and gave a terminal tree-ring date of AD 1041. Since the sample does not retain any sapwood a felling date after AD 1050 is indicated.

The surviving length of the retained plank (Fig 137, no 3) was 1.845m, but it was originally *c* 260mm wide at one end, and *c* 280mm wide at the other. It had been radially cut from from straight-grained oak, and it was 15mm thick in the centre, but thinned towards the lap edges. One intact lap was 50mm wide, and was held to the adjacent plank by iron rivets spaced between 76mm and 104mm apart at their centres. The rivets at the other, damaged, lap were spaced between 89 and 134mm apart. The rivet shanks were 5mm square. At one end there was a damaged scarf with an iron rivet in its centre. It had a rhomboid-shaped rove measuring 23mm by 28mm. Judging from the 'clinker rules' this would probably place the fragment on the starboard side of the vessel. There were also two trenail holes, presumably for frame fastenings, which were 16mm and 17mm in diameter and 1.502m apart at their centres. One hole contained part of a trenail 17mm in diameter, of willow or poplar (*Salix/Populus*). It is possible that the modern break in the middle of this fragment represents a further trenail position.

Planks from Fennings Wharf, Southwark, 1984

Site and context

Six small pieces of clinker boat planking (Fig 138) of *c*AD 1100, recovered from Fennings Wharf, Tooley Street, Southwark, at the south end of London Bridge (Fig 1), are assessed together since they are from the same context and may be from the same boat. George Dennis, the excavator, reports that 'the planks numbered 2157 and 2238 had been reused in a waterfront revetment at right angles to the river bank and therefore were possibly part of the "pre-Colechurch" timber bridge structures (ie before AD 1176). The planks stood vertically in a rebated rectangular beam lying horizontally to form a base plate. The dating is principally from the timbers themselves' (site archive report, Museum of London).

When and where was the boat built?

Four of the pieces have been tree-ring dated (see Appendix 6) and were felled after AD 1055. The similarity of the last surviving ring dates supports the conclusion that they are from the same boat. The dated pieces are (Fig 138) B, FW84, II (2238); C, FW84, (2157) [544]; D, FW84, (2157) [545]; and E, FW84, (2157) plank A.

Log conversion

All the fragments had been radially cut/split from straight-grained oak.

Description (Fig 138)

(A) This was from site context 2256. Although not confirmed by tree-ring analysis, this is believed to be of the same date as the other pieces since it was part of the same group of timbers. The plank was of oak 24mm thick, thinning to the lap with the adjacent strake. The lap itself was 58mm wide, and was held by iron rivets with nail heads 27mm and 30mm across, and shanks 5–6mm square. There was a diamond-shaped rove 24mm by 25mm, and 6mm thick. No caulking had survived. There was a trenail 23mm in diameter and of willow or poplar (*Salix/Populus*).

(B) This fragment comprised the remains of three articulated planks from two strakes. Two of the pieces were the remains of planks scarfed endways to form a strake

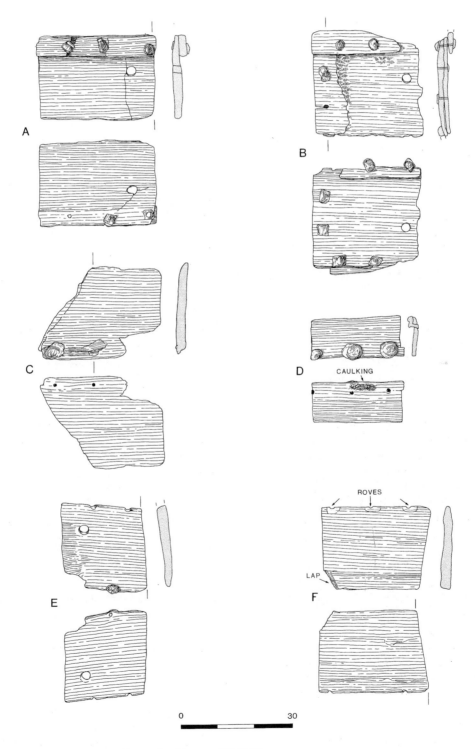

Fig 138 Fennings Wharf fragments of boat planking, c AD1100.

which was probably originally 0.29m wide and up to 30mm thick. It thinned to 15mm at the edges, and was attached to adjacent strakes clinkerwise by iron rivets. The surviving complete strake lap was 43mm wide and was held by iron rivets with nail heads 20mm–25mm wide, nail shanks 7mm square, and diamond-shaped roves 25mm by 30mm and 26mm by 38mm, and 2mm and 4mm thick. The rivets were spaced at 93mm at their centres. In the central plank was a trenail hole 25mm in diameter. The outboard end of a scarf was held by two iron rivets near the middle of the plank and in the scarf were traces of a hair caulking of sheep's wool (see Appendix 7). The laps and scarf indicate that this fragment may be from the port side of the boat.

(C) This fragment of plank was up to 21mm thick, thinning to 11mm near the lap. The lap itself was 28mm wide, and was held by rivets (which had not survived but had left an impression) with square shanks spaced 106mm apart. There was one trenail hole about 25mm in diameter in a small separate piece of plank.

(D) This small piece of planking had a maximum thickness of 15mm, but narrowed to 12mm by the lap. The lap itself was 46mm wide, and had rivet nails about 6mm square spaced at intervals of 100mm and 110mm centres.

(E) Another fragment of planking with a maximum thickness of 21mm bore traces of rivet nails along one broken edge, at centres 95mm apart, and part of a rivet along the other broken edge. This plank was about 0.28m wide originally, and had a trenail hole 22mm in diameter.

(F) A small piece of plank with a maximum thickness of 28mm, retained the impressions of rivet nails along both broken edges, indicating that the plank was originally about 0.28m wide. The rivet centres were at 100mm and 110mm apart, and there were the slight impressions of roves.

Conclusion

The use of iron rivets is typical of vessels of this period, especially in Scandinavia, though the iron nails were square in section in the Fennings Wharf planks, unlike those used in Scandinavian vessels which were then round (Muller-Wille 1974, 189). This may be because, according to the tree-ring analysis, the boat was built in south-eastern England. There is no clue to the form of the vessel. In each case the lack of compression in the wood around the rivet nails indicates that holes had probably been drilled before each rivet was inserted.

Boat keel from Fennings Wharf, Southwark, 1984

Site and context

Part of the keel of a boat with a length of the garboard strake attached to one side (Fig 139), was found on the Fennings Wharf site. George Dennis, the site excavator, reports that: 'This is a 2.50m length of stout boat timber from site context FW 84 (156). Unfortunately it was removed by the contractors' machine and so was not examined or recorded *in situ*. It came from the same foreshore deposits as did further rebated baseplates (ie like that from which came the riveted boat planking), and so the keel could be part of another waterfront structure. The timber itself is the only evidence for its date.'

When and where was the boat built?

The keel was unsuitable for tree-ring analysis but part of an attached plank, the 'garboard strake', is tree-ring dated after AD 985 (see Appendix 6). Only part of the plank width remained, but as there was no trace of trenails that should have held the plank to the frames it is likely that these would be in the missing part of the plank, and that the plank was at least twice its surviving width. The missing part could, therefore, account for another hundred rings and, assuming that they remained equally narrow, would bring its date to the late eleventh century. This is consistent with what little is known about the date of its possible context on the site.

Log conversion

The keel had been tangentially cut from an oak log, the flat upper and lower faces suggesting that it had been sawn. The centre of its upper or inboard face lay close to the heart of the tree, although the chosen timber was rather knotty. The plank, in contrast, had been radially cut from an oak log, and was of straight-grained timber with narrow rings.

Description
The keel

When recorded recently this fragment was only 2.145m long, one end having been sawn off when excavated, and the other having been broken by the mechanical excavator. The keel had flat upper and lower surfaces and was 0.365m wide and 0.096m thick at one end, and 0.324m wide and 0.078 thick at the other end; thus it was becoming narrower and slightly thinner towards one end. Rabbets, 0.065m wide and about 0.03m deep, had been cut into the lower sides of the keel to hold the garboard strakes. At the broader end of the keel the rabbets held garboard strakes horizontally, but at the narrow end the rabbets were cut so that the garboard strakes were held at an angle of 14° on one side, and 21° on the other. It is clear from this, therefore, that the keel was narrowing towards one end of the vessel, and that

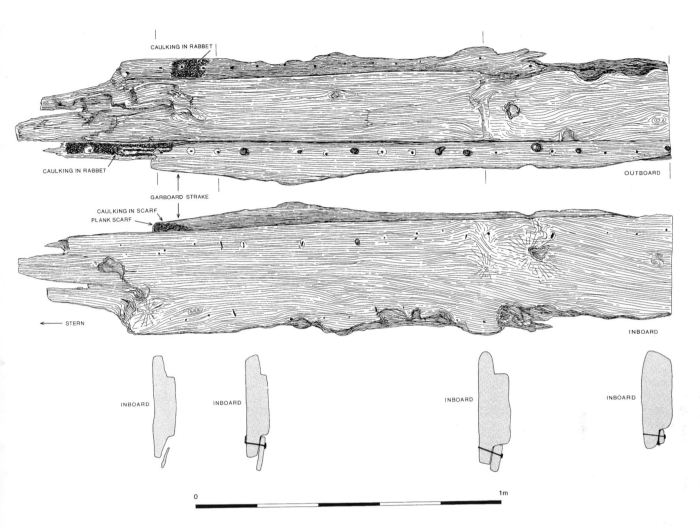

Fig 139   Keel from Fennings Wharf, probably late eleventh century AD. The garboard strakes were held by hooked nails.

the lower part of the hull was changing from a flat bottom amidships to a V-section near the end of the vessel.

The garboard strake

The maximum surviving width of the garboard strake was only 0.14m, its outer edge having been cut away during recent excavation, so it was originally wider. The strake itself was about 0.025m thick, and had a simple overlap scarf which was originally about 0.17m long. This gave a ratio of scarf length divided by plank thickness (0.17 ÷ 0.025) of 1:6.8.

The caulking

A layer of ox hair caulking (see Appendix 7) lay between the garboard strake and the keel. This had been laid along the rabbet in four or five ropy twists.

The hooked nails

Iron nails, now mostly corroded, had been used to fasten the garboard strakes to the keel. These were about 61mm long, and had been hooked towards the centre of the keel. They had shanks 6mm square near the head and 4mm square near the point, and their flat heads were roughly 20mm in diameter.

Each nail had been driven into place from outboard, first through the garboard strake, then through the caulking and the keel itself. The point of each was turned 90° before the remainder of the nail was hammered down onto the face of the keel so that the point was embedded in its surface. These hooked nails were between 60 and 108mm apart, but their spacing averaged about 92mm.

The frames

There were no frame fastenings in the surviving 2m length of keel, or in the garboard strake, though the changing angle of the garboard strakes indicates the likelihood that frames had originally crossed this part of the keel.

Conclusion

The scarf in the garboard strake indicates that the narrow end of the keel was probably the stern of the vessel, and the varying angles of the rabbets in the keel show that the bottom was changing from a fairly flat profile near amidships to a V-shaped profile at the stern, as if this vessel had a pointed stern instead of an inclined flat punt-like 'swim-head'.

The absence of fastenings in the keel to hold the frames that would have crossed it, indicates that the

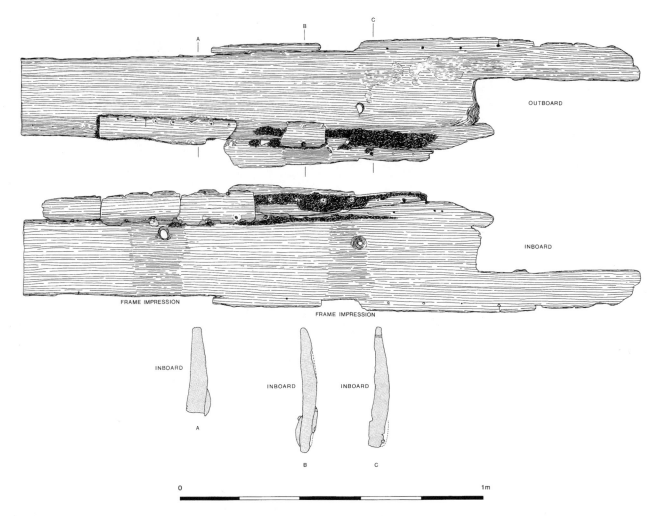

Fig 140   Fennings Wharf wale, eleventh century.

vessel was probably shell-built as was normal in clinker vessels. Although there is no certain evidence that the vessel was clinker-built, the strake did have two clinker characteristics: it was radially cut, and the overlapping form of the scarf is typical of a clinker vessel of that time.

The hooked nails suggest the method which might have been used to fasten the strakes together, as was used in the Bremen and Dutch cogs of the thirteenth and fourteenth centuries (Ellmers 1985b, 80–1; Reinders 1985).

Wale from Fennings Wharf, Southwark, 1984

Site and context

This item, a timber 2.4m long with one end broken by a mechanical excavator and the other sawn off after excavation, may have been a wale from a ship (Fig 140). George Dennis reports that: 'This was recovered from context II, (2124), 5–7–84, within waterlaid fills on the former Thames foreshore, and was possibly part of a collapsed revetment since it was adjacent to some posts. The fills may be medieval' (pers comm).

Date

The wale is of oak and is tree-ring dated to after AD 1030 (see Appendix 6). It is possible that it is contemporary with other ship timbers from this site.

Log conversion

The timber had been tangentially cut from a fairly straight-grained log.

Description

Broken along one edge, the timber had a maximum surviving width of 0.437m, but, because one face was flat and the other curved, it is possible to calculate the missing shape of both sides, and to establish that its original width was about 0.47m. It had a maximum thickness of 0.06m. The timber had split longitudinally during use, and had been repaired with long wooden patches about 0.01m thick and 0.096m wide fastened with square-shanked iron nails over the split on both faces. Under each patch was a layer of hair caulking, that on the flat side being sheep's wool, and that on the curved side being ox.

There were originally two trenails 30mm in diameter passing through the timber at an oblique angle, one of which has survived and was of willow or poplar (*Salix/Populus*). These are presumed to have fastened the timber to frames. This trenail was covered by a repair patch on the curved face, thus indicating that this face probably lay outboard. Indeed, the flat 'inboard' surface was slightly darker in a strip about 0.3m wide at each trenail, suggesting an impression of each frame. The trenails were 0.66m apart indicating the separation between frame centres.

On the curved face were traces of a pale yellow/brown substance which might have been tar, and there were slight traces of a red substance, possibly paint. Close to one edge of the timber, where it was about 0.02m thick, was a row of iron nail holes, each about 7mm or 8mm square, but there was no impression of nail heads or roves on the wood surface.

Interpretation

The caulking of hair in the repairs, the possible coating of tar, and the possible impressions of frames all suggest that this timber is a wale from a ship with the flat face inboard. The oblique angle of the trenails suggests that at the wale position the side of the vessel was flared. However, no trace of roves could be found, and there was no impression of any strake lap at the edge of the wale, so that it is not clear how the wale was attached to the rest of the hull. The patches are particularly interesting for they are thin with little strength, and their purpose was evidently only to make the split watertight.

Wales of various shapes were fitted in early medieval ships to give longitudinal strength. By itself the Fennings Wharf wale cannot be linked to any particular type of vessel, for similar wales have been found in Bergen amongst ship fragments of the Scandinavian tradition (Christensen 1985, 100, no 33, 110, no 90460) as well as in the eleventh-century extended logboat from Utrecht (Vlek 1987, 105, 120).

Possible oar or paddle, Hibernia Wharf, Southwark, 1979

Site and context

The oak blade and part of the shaft perhaps of an oar or paddle, was found in a ditch at Hibernia Wharf (Fig 1), Southwark, in 1979 (Fig 141). The excavation was carried out by the Museum of London, under the direction of George Dennis. When found the wood surfaces were very friable.

A report by George Dennis describes the site context: 'The blade was found lying on the base of a man-made inlet or canal which connected with the Thames and may well have been navigable. The channel, containing a good group of early–mid eleventh-century Saxo-Norman pottery, had been cut across a timber-lined pit with a later tenth-century tree-ring date. The channel is thus quite well dated, probably to the early eleventh century' (pers comm).

Description

The blade had been radially cut from an oak tree, though the choice of timber was probably not ideal for across the upper part of the blade and across the shaft were transverse knots which must have weakened it.

Because of the degraded condition of the wood it is not now possible to judge the exact original shape of the object. Variations in its shape are mainly due to differences in decay, but although the thin edges of the blade have not survived what does remain suggests an original oval shape. The blade was about 0.515m long, at least 0.135m wide, and had a maximum surviving thickness of 22mm.

The shaft was roughly oval, almost rectangular in section with rounded corners, and had a maximum surviving dimension of 42mm by 21mm. It is far from clear that this reflects the original size and form of the cross-section, but bearing in mind the direction of the grain this is likely.

The blade has been subjected to fire, the surface of its lower half on one side only having been charred black to a depth of at least 2mm. The extent of the charred surface is not clear.

The oval shape of the blade and the nautical context in a waterway, indicate that this may be part of an oar or paddle, though the burning might indicate a non-nautical use, perhaps as a shovel used in a bread oven.

Anchor, River Thames, Blackfriars, City of London, 1969

Site and context

An iron anchor with a broken shank (MoL acc no 25389) was found by workmen in 1969 in the bed of the Thames near Blackfriars in the City of London (Fig 142). It lay about one hundred metres east of the Mermaid Theatre, where excavations were taking place in the bed of the river, within a large coffer-dam, for the construction of a new embankment wall (Fig 143).

Description

The anchor, of wrought iron, measures 0.907m between the ends of the flukes. The arms are triangular in section, about 30mm thick and 68mm deep. The flukes are small and leaf-shaped, about 90mm long and 48mm wide. A hole at the crown contains a wrought iron ring 162mm in diameter and 15mm thick. The shank is rectangular in section, 30mm thick and 65mm wide at the bottom, narrowing to 50mm at the surviving top. A smooth, slight thickening of the shank perhaps reflects the wrought method of construction. As the shank was broken in antiquity, presumably when being raised at a mooring site, no trace of the stock remained.

Dating

The surface of the anchor had a natural concretion adhering to it when found, which preserved traces of the surrounding deposits in which the anchor was lying. This showed that it lay in clean sands and gravels with small pieces of wood and a piece of blackened leather. The clean sand and gravel is particularly significant because archaeological observations in the coffer-dam showed that there were two distinct groups of deposits in the river. The lower comprised layers of clean sand and gravel in which only Roman objects had been found; and above this was black silty gravel containing objects of fifteenthth-century and later date. On this basis the anchor is believed to be of medieval or earlier date.

The distinctive form of the anchor is an important clue to its age for it does not have the large flukes that are so typical of medieval and post-medieval anchors (Peterson 1973, 120, pl 46–50), and this alone suggests an earlier date. A note on its discovery was published by the author (Marsden 1971, 10–11) who then concluded that it might be Roman. This view was based upon the absence of early medieval finds from the site, and the presence of a swelling in the shank, which may be paralleled with Roman anchors from Pompeii and in the Boreli Museum, Marseilles (Frost 1963, 60). On closer examination, the swelling in the shank is clearly a feature of construction, rather than a design feature, so this cannot be regarded as dating evidence.

The Blackfriars anchor has been compared with a wrought-iron anchor found in a late Iron Age hoard of

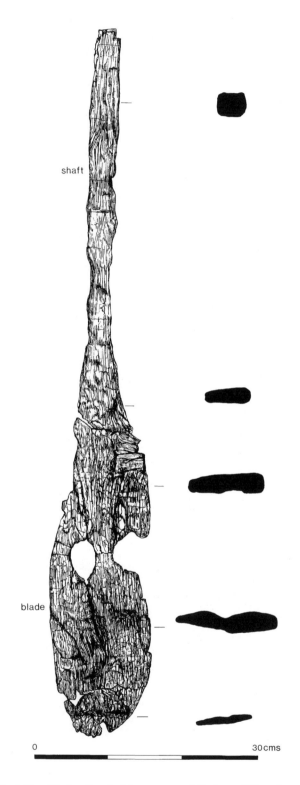

shaft

blade

0   30cms

Fig 141 Blade of probable oar or paddle from Hibernia Wharf, eleventh century.

metalwork found at Bulbury, Dorset (Cunliffe 1972, 300–2), but the arms of the Bulbury anchor are square in section, ending in points without any flukes and consequently, there is no real similarity. However, an

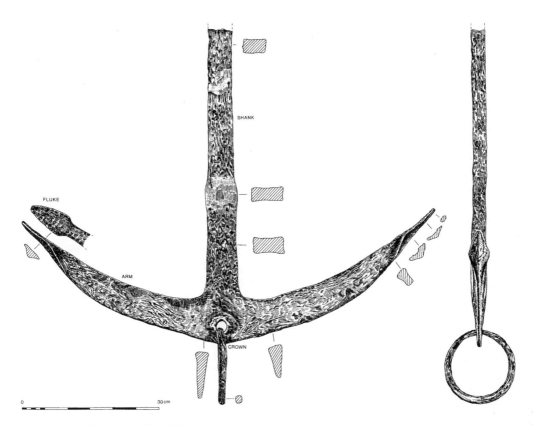

Fig 142   Iron anchor of Viking type, Blackfriars.

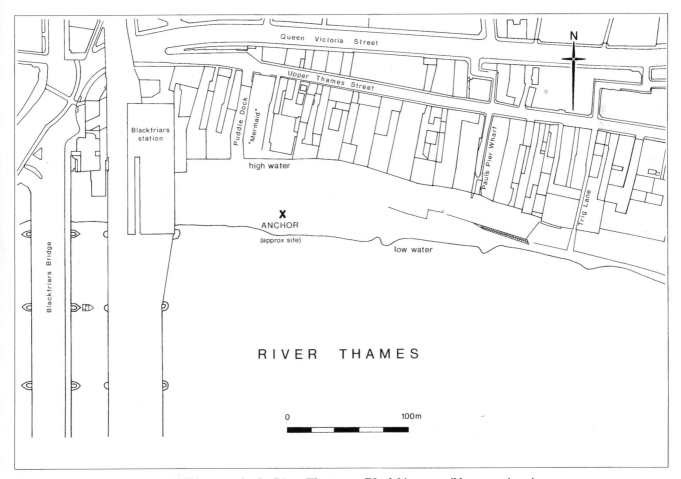

Fig 143   Site of the anchor of Viking type in the River Thames at Blackfriars, possibly a mooring site.

almost identical anchor to that from Blackfriars was recovered from the ninth-century Viking ship burial at Oseberg, Norway (Ucelli 1950, fig 27; Brogger and Shetelig 1953, 98). Its arms are also triangular in cross-section, though they terminate with blunt points, instead of small leaf-shaped flukes. However, leaf-shaped flukes, like those in the Blackfriars anchor, do occur on an iron anchor found in the tenth-century Viking ship burial at Ladby, Denmark (McGrail 1987, 255), and as the characteristics of the Blackfriars anchor are only known in Viking anchors it seems likely that it dates from the ninth to eleventh centuries AD. Although no deposits belonging to Saxon, Viking, or earlier medieval times were noted in any of the Blackfriars coffer-dams, despite attempts to locate them, the conditions under which the investigation of the site was carried out did not enable anything other than the most obvious features to be recorded, and there is no reason why the anchor should not be of Viking period. It is important to remember, though, that at that time London was essentially Anglo-Saxon and that Saxon anchors have not been found to give a comparison. The Blackfriars anchor, therefore, could also have been lost by a Saxon ship moored in the port of London.

The presence or absence of flukes on anchors may be an approximate indication of age, suggested by the absence of flukes in the Bulbury anchor, and the presence of incipient flukes in the Ladby and Blackfriars anchors. It was only after about 1000 AD that large flukes seem to become normal in northern Europe, for an early representation of substantial flukes appears on the Bayeux Tapestry in a scene depicting a ship sailing from England to France bringing news of King Harold's coronation (McGrail 1987, 255, fig 12.35). In contrast flukes are not present on Roman anchors found in the Mediterranean (Casson 1971, 253). It is possible, therefore, that the Blackfriars, Ladby and Oseberg anchors represent an intermediate stage in the development of flukes, from Roman and Celtic anchors which had none, to medieval anchors which had large shovel-like ones.

9 Conclusions

The aim of this study has been to reconstruct the types of ships and their use in the port of London from Roman times to the eleventh century. Inevitably, this means that the history of London as a port for inland and overseas trade has had to be examined as the background against which to set the various shipbuilding traditions represented by the remains of vessels found. These appear to have roots in various parts of Europe and Scandinavia, though there is considerable evidence to suggest that the merchant ships of the Roman period sailing between ports like London in the northern provinces of the Roman empire were normally of 'native' Celtic type. Such a strong native tradition might have survived into the Saxon and Norman periods, and the early ship remains of London have been assessed with this possibility in mind. The development of the port's berthing facilities, enabling vessels to be loaded and unloaded, has proved to be particularly important, and the action of tides appears to have been a central factor. Finally, since the early history of the port and its shipping was the foundation upon which its later development relied, it is relevant to conclude this study with a very brief outline of the later history of the port.

It is important to remember that the River Thames had long been a highway for water transport and trade before London was created in the mid first century AD. The Bronze Age riverside embankment of the eighth to ninth centuries BC found at Runnymede (Needham and Longley 1981), and another possible one of late Bronze Age to early Iron Age date at Whitehall (Andrews and Merriman 1986, 17–21), although not necessarily for boat use, do attest the importance of the river to some settlements. The riverine distribution of many Bronze Age (Ehrenberg 1980) and Iron Age objects suggests that transportation by water was particularly important before the Roman invasion of AD 43, though concentrations of artifacts at some places, such as at Brentford, are more likely to reflect fords for land transport (Kent 1978, 60).

There is reason, therefore, to believe that traditions of shipbuilding, berthing and marketing of goods were already established in the Thames valley when the port of *Londinium* was founded *c* AD 50 (Merrifield 1983, 41–52; Marsden 1987, 17–19). What the boats themselves were like is unknown, and indeed the only local type of prehistoric plank-built vessels that can be associated with any British river system at present are the Ferriby and Brigg boats from the Rivers Humber and Ancholme, which have been dated *c*1500–650 BC (McGrail 1981, 17–19), part of a Bronze Age boat found at Caldicot, Gwent, beside the estuary of the River Severn (McGrail pers comm), and a boat of somewhat similar construction found in 1992 at Dover. These were sewn vessels which were shell-built, unlike the skeleton-built Romano-Celtic vessel from New Guy's House,

close to London Bridge, and Blackfriars ship 1, which must have been built locally and probably reflect a local Iron Age tradition (Chapter 3).

The creation of Roman *Londinium* established a focus for land and waterborne transport, and brought trade on such a vastly increased scale and variety that the economic potential of the River Thames and the site of the new port could now be fully exploited. But the extent to which local 'native' ships and boats, such as that from New Guy's House, were modified as a result will remain unclear until pre-Roman examples of local plank-built vessels have been found.

Shipbuilding traditions

A remarkable feature of the parts of probably eight ships and boats that have been considered in this study is their variety of construction methods, for they seem to represent several shipbuilding traditions. Although the timespan under study is great, it is important to bear in mind that shipbuilding traditions were then slow to change. On the Rhine and its tributaries, for example, the existence of certain types of vessel has been traced from the Bronze Age to the present (Arnold 1977, 296; Ellmers 1978, 1–7). Similarly, in Scandinavia there was only a slow development in ship design and construction between the fourth and the eleventh centuries, and these early methods of boatbuilding still persist today (Greenhill 1976, 257). Thus it is only by examining the London vessels as a group that it is possible to ascertain whether they provide evidence of any comparable continuity of tradition on a single major river.

Ships and boats are the buildings of the sea, rivers, and lakes. They function as houses, warehouses, banks, markets, and castles, and their architectural forms and construction methods often represent their cultural background, even when they sometimes operate a long way from their place of origin. Vessels of the Roman period in London included classical as well as native types of nautical architecture giving a native – classical mixture that also occurred amongst buildings on land (eg Salway 1981, 671). Although there is no generally agreed system of classifying methods of ship and boat building (Christensen 1977), there is some agreement on the characteristics of certain traditions (eg McCaughan 1978) (see Table 14).

Defining what is meant by 'shipbuilding tradition' is not simple for it embodies aspects of construction and shape. Ellmers (1984, 153) has defined it as 'traditions of handicraft' whereby the methods used to make a boat are handed down from generation to generation, and, although certain changes can occur over time and constructional details of one tradition might be incorporated into another, there is nevertheless a basic shipbuilding system which separates it from others. It is sometimes

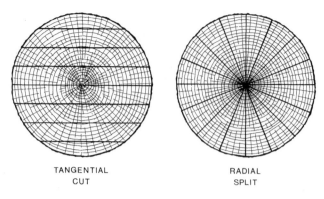

TANGENTIAL
CUT

RADIAL
SPLIT

Fig 144 Sections of logs showing tree-rings and rays, and radial and tangential log splitting.

felt that the form of a ship need not be a factor in determining a shipbuilding tradition, for this will vary with function and environment (Ellmers 1984, 153; McGrail 1985, 291), though in certain circumstances form too is also important (Crumlin-Pedersen 1983).

The most recent and comprehensive classification of ships and boats has been carried out by McGrail (1985), who describes planks as one of a number of types of building material used. Within this the London vessels fall into the two classes C7, in which vessels were 'shell-built by reduction, transformation, and construction', and C8 in which they were 'skeleton-built with a waterproofing envelope made by reduction, transformation, and construction'. The term reduction means that the logs were reduced in volume by shaping to make parts of a ship, transformation means that the parts of a ship, particularly its planks, were bent to the required shape, and construction means that several elements were joined together. McGrail has followed a generally agreed classification according to whether boats were shell- or skeleton-built. Shell-built essentially means that the watertight envelope of stems, keel, and planking was constructed before the frames and other internal strengthening members were fitted, and skeleton-built means that the framework of stems, keel, and frames were built or partly built before being clothed in a skin of planking (Greenhill 1976, 311; McGrail 1987, 98–111).

Although these classifications are helpful they are not specific enough, and it has been necessary to define further the possible shipbuilding traditions of the London vessels by assessing them in accordance with five important surviving constructional characteristics, which reflect the methods by which each shipwright built the vessel.

Were they shell-built or skeleton-built?
This is discussed above.

How were planks shaped?
There were two fundamentally different methods of converting an oak log into planks in the London ship timbers: (i) by splitting the log into wedge-shaped radial segments and working each into a plank, in which case the plank faces would tend to follow the rays of the oak (Fig 144); and (ii) by sawing, probably, the log tangen-

tially into planks, in which case the plank faces would generally be at a marked angle both to the rays and rings of the tree (Fig 144). It is possible, but difficult, to obtain tangential planking by splitting oak. It is usually obtained in oak by hewing.

Was the planking carvel- or clinker-laid?
In this case carvel-laid means flush-laid with the flat edge of one strake laid against the flat edge of the next. Clinker-laid here means that each strake is so placed that the edge of one partly overlaps the edge of the next. There are other definitions, but these are the ones used in this study (See Appendix 8).

Was there a caulking?
This is a substance placed in the plank seams to make the boat watertight. It seems likely that it was not always necessary for a ship to have this (Appendix 8).

What was the caulking material?
Various waterproofing materials have been used in the past and it is possible that the choice was as much due to tradition as to availability (Arnold 1977).

The vessel's age places it in the broad political, cultural, and economic context of the Roman, Saxon, or Norman periods. On the basis of this analysis the ship and boat finds appear to fall into three distinct groups or shipbuilding traditions:

Group 1: Blackfriars ship 1 and the New Guy's House boat, which were skeleton-built carvel vessels
Group 2: the County Hall ship, which was a shell-built carvel vessel
Group 3: the New Fresh Wharf, Fennings Wharf and Billingsgate vessels, which were shell-built clinker craft

The definition of these traditions is further suggested by the fact that whereas Groups 1 and 2 are Roman, Group 3 is much later in date.

Blackfriars ship 1 and the New Guy's House boat

These vessels are characterised by being primarily skeleton-built, their planks having been added to a pre-erected skeleton of frames which gave the vessels their shape and support. They were carvel-built (in the sense given above), with a caulking of hazel shavings and tar, and the planks were tangentially cut from the logs. The shapes of the Blackfriars and New Guy's House vessels were different from each other in as much as one was a seagoing merchant ship, and the other a river barge for inland waters.

As Blackfriars ship 1 was a seagoing ship it is not surprising to find that traces of similar vessels have been found elsewhere in Europe, all dating from the Roman period (Fig 145). One of its most distinctive features was the mast-step frame with a central socket and raised surround, and medial ridges leading away along the upper face. Similar mast-step frames occur in the Bruges and St Peter Port vessels, also of the Roman period

(Marsden 1976a; Rule 1993), but although distinctive they do not by themselves show where the vessels were built because all three craft were probably capable of sailing at sea, and they may have been found some way from where they were built. However, the discovery of yet another mast-step frame of this type in a river craft of the fourth century AD at Mainz (vessel fragment no 9) is sufficient to show that vessels with this distinctive

feature were being built in the Rhineland (Hockmann 1982, abb 2, 4; Rupprecht 1985, 81). This is probably not where Blackfriars ship 1 was built, for its tree-ring pattern fits that of London and indicates that it was probably built in or near south-east England. Its caulking of hazel shavings and tar, otherwise found only in the New Guys House boat which must have been built in the Thames valley, supports this view.

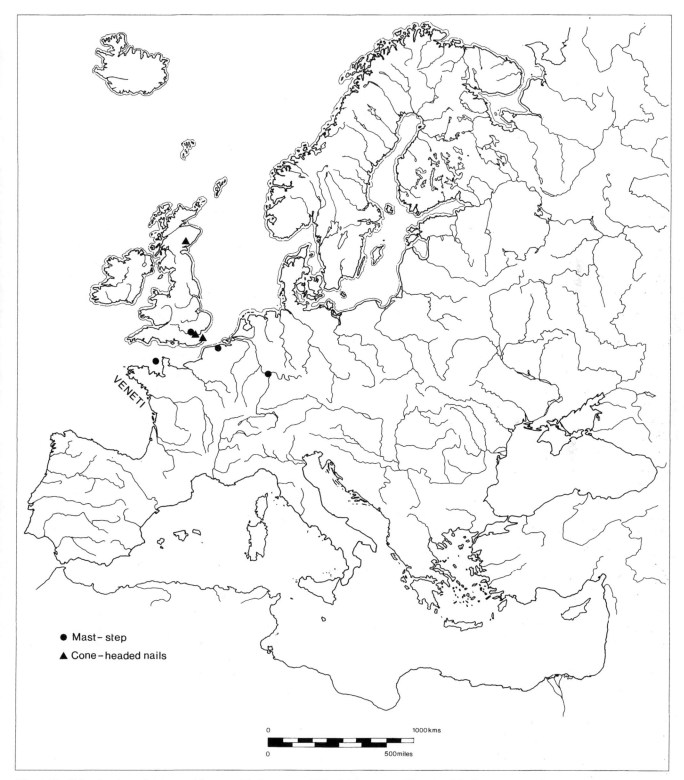

Fig 145   Distribution of ships and boats with features of Blackfriars type. Vessels with the mast-step frames have been found at London, St Peter Port, Bruges, and Mainz. Cone-headed nails found loose have been found at London, Richborough, and Inchtuthil.

Although only four vessels with this type of mast-step frame are known, the distribution of craft with Black-friars characteristics can be enlarged by studying the find-spots of another distinctive feature – their iron cone-headed nails. Two were found on the Roman fort site at Richborough, in eastern Kent (Uncatalogued nail, shank broken, in the Richborough site museum; another, complete, illustrated in Cunliffe 1968, pl LVII, no 284), another in the first century AD legionary fort at Inchtu-thil, Scotland (Healy 1978, pl 64b), and another in London. The head of the London nail is about 25mm in diameter, and therefore smaller than those used in Black-friars ship 1. It was found on an unspecified site in London, 'from a pile' in the Thames (Guildhall Museum 1908, 55, no 139–40, MoL catalogue no 1643). A further nail was found in the third century quay dump at New Fresh Wharf, London (see Fig 5). Such nails are rare, and as their heads were carefully made to contain a caulking intended to prevent the seepage of water into the hull, it seems that their sole use was in ships.

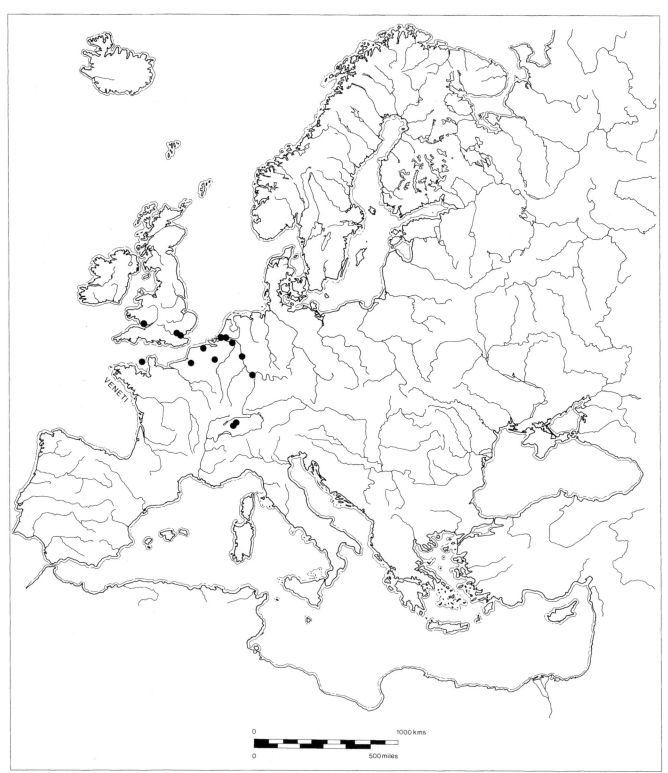

Fig 146   Distribution of plank-built ships and boats of Romano-Celtic type.

Vessels of Blackfriars 1 type are unlike any contemporary craft then used in the Mediterranean or in Scandinavia, and, as they only seem to occur in north and north-western Europe it is reasonable to suppose that they represent a shipbuilding tradition of the native people of that region. Those native peoples were the Celts (Powell 1980), and it is generally agreed that Blackfriars ship 1 and various other vessels with some similar characteristics, found on the inland waters of central and north-western Europe (Fig 146), should be termed Romano-Celtic (Marsden 1967, 34–5; Ellmers 1969; Christensen 1977, 274).

This Celtic attribution is supported by Caesar's description of the ships of the Veneti (Caesar III, 1), a Celtic tribe inhabiting the north-west coast of Gaul in the first century BC (Fig 145), whose vessels seem to have had features similar to ships of Blackfriars 1 type. Caesar wrote that they were built and rigged in a different manner from Roman ships (Casson 1971, 339–40), and that they had flatter bottoms enabling them to sail across

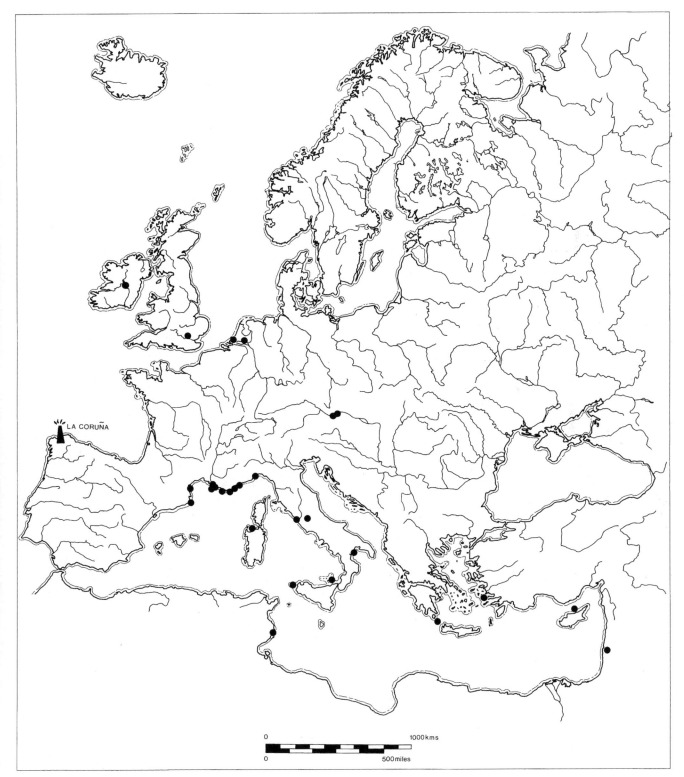

Fig 147   Distribution of ships and boats of 'Mediterranean type' construction, ie with mortice-and-tenon joints.

shallows. They also had sails of leather, as well as exceptionally high bows and sterns to enable them to weather heavy seas, and in this respect were much better suited to northern waters than were the Roman ships. Indeed, when the Romans erected turrets on their warships, so as to fight the Veneti better, they found that they were still overtopped by the lofty sterns of the enemy – a comment which might suggest that the native sterns were higher than the bow. It is known that the height of the Veneti ships made them difficult to board. Their hulls were made entirely of oak, and they had cross-timbers (*transtra*) a foot (304mm) thick which were fastened with iron nails an inch (25mm) thick. The result was an extremely solid hull that could not be damaged by ramm-

Table 15 Plank-built ships and boats with mortice-and-tenon fastenings, Mediterranean tradition (Fig 147)

ship site	reference
1 Grand Congloué, France	Benôit 1961
2 Antikythera, Greece	Throckmorton 1972, 70
3 Nemi 1, 2, 3, Italy	Ucelli 1950
4 Dramont, France	Throckmorton 1972, 68
5 Marsala 1, 2, Sicily	Frost 1973; 1974; 1975
6 Kyrenia, Cyprus	Katzev 1987
7 Marseilles 1864, France	Benôit 1961, 144–5
8 Madrague de Giens, France	Pomey 1975
9 La Roche Fouras, ?France	Joncheray 1976
10 Yassi Ada 2, Turkey	Doorninck 1976
11 Jeune-Garde B, France	Carraze 1977
12 Capistello, Sicily	Frey et al 1978
13 Cap del Vol, Gerona, Italy	Foerster 1980
14 Palamos, Spain	Laures 1983
15 Los Ullastres, Spain	Laures 1983, 219
16 Caesarea Maritimer, Israel	Raban 1985, 174–6
17 Kinneret, Israel	Steffy 1987
18 Mahdia, Tunisia	Throckmorton 1972, 68
19 Titan, France	Throckmorton 1972, 68
20 Torre Sgarrata, Italy	Throckmorton 1972, 70
21 La Chretienne, France	Parker 1980
22 Martigues, France	Gassend et al 1984
23 Fiumicino 1,2,3,4, Italy	Scrinari 1979
24 Marseilles, France	Gassend 1985
25 Oberstimm 1, Germany	Höckmann 1989
26 Oberstimm 2, Germany	Höckmann 1989
27 Laurons, France	Gassend et al 1984
28 County Hall, London	see Chapter 6
29 Vechten, Netherlands	de Weerd 1988, 184–94
30 Zwammerdam, Netherlands	de Weerd 1988, 180–3
31 Lough Lene, Ireland	O Eailidhe 1992

ing. Strabo (4.195) adds the important fact that the Veneti caulked the seams with a material that is usually translated as sea-weed, but which E Wright, who excavated the prehistoric boats at North Ferriby, believes has been wrongly translated and should read as moss (Wright pers comm).

If correct this takes on a considerable significance, not only because it is difficult to envisage seaweed as an effective caulking material, but also because moss has been found as a caulking material in the cone-shaped nail heads of the St Peter Port ship (Rule 1990). An even more relevant reference is given by Pliny (16.158) who in the first century AD describes the caulking of ships built in the Low Countries as being of reeds (*harundines*) which when 'pounded and inserted in the seams of ships, solidify the structure, being more tenacious than glue and, for filling cracks, more reliable than pitch' (Casson 1973, 210, n 39). This may be how the hazel shavings were treated as caulking in Blackfriars ship 1, though they were apparently applied with resin as the planks were being assembled, rather than afterwards. The similarities between the Veneti and the Blackfriars types of ship are very striking, particularly the massive beams, the thick planking, the large nails which held the timbers together, the fact that both were designed to sit on the bed of a tidal shore, and that they were built in a different way from the Roman ships of the Mediterranean region.

Although dating from the second century AD, Blackfriars ship 1 represents a type of shipbuilding that probably had a considerable ancestry in north-west Europe before the arrival of the Romans. But to what extent the size, form and construction of these ships might have been altered by the arrival of the Roman economy is far from clear (Doorninck 1974, 311). Before the Roman invasion the trade in wine contained in Dressel 1 amphorae, from Italy to south-west England and particularly to Hengistbury Head (Cunliffe 1990), may well have been carried in ships of this type. This trade to south-west England is thought to have been in the hands of the Veneti for it apparently stopped about 50 BC, after Caesar had opened up of the whole of northern Gaul to trade with southern Britain (Cunliffe 1978, 78–9). The ancestry of these ships may be reflected by the ships on the coins of the Belgic king Cunobelin found at Canterbury and Colchester (Muckleroy et al 1978), and by ships on Iron Age coins from Gaul (Allen 1971) (Fig 61).

There are similarities between the construction of the Blackfriars type of vessel and various other river craft on the Rhine, Schelde and Somme, and it is thought that collectively these constituted a family of Romano-Celtic shipbuilding traditions since they were generally partly skeleton-built and had massive timbers (de Weerd 1988; Arnold 1977). In this respect they were not unlike the New Guy's House boat which was also part of the family of Romano-Celtic shipbuilding traditions.

The County Hall ship

The County Hall ship, in contrast, was shell-built, and therefore the shipwright had planned its construction around a hull form determined mainly by the planking, the strakes having been fastened together edge-to-edge with mortice-and-tenon joints. This construction technique, known to be characteristic of ships in the Mediterranean basin not only during the Roman period but also at least as early as the fourteenth century BC (Bass 1985; Throckmorton 1987, 92–6), was very different from that in group 1.

A large number of Greek and Roman shipwrecks with the mortice-and-tenon construction have been found in the Mediterranean, and a few in central and northern Europe (Fig 147). A list of finds is now available (Parker 1992), and many are published in various journals. The list given below (Table 15) is not comprehensive, though useful descriptions occur (Throckmorton 1972; Parker 1973; Bass *et al* 1980; Gianfrotta and Pomey 1981; Throckmorton *et al* 1987).

The construction technique of the County Hall ship is rarely found in the northern provinces of the Roman Empire, and it was evidently introduced there by the

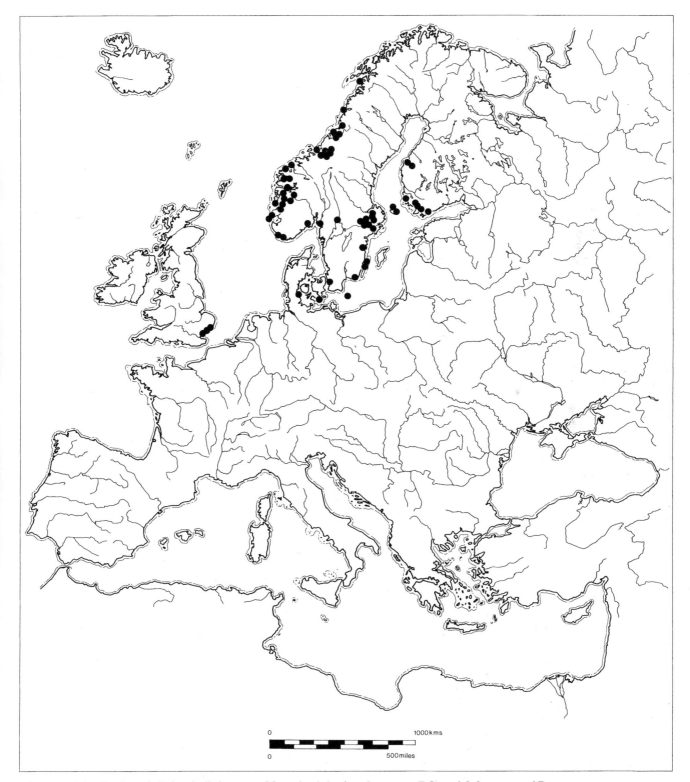

Fig 148   Distribution of clinker-built boats and boat burials, fourth century BC to eighth century AD.

Romans, though a small boat with a dugout log bottom and planked sides fastened with mortice-and-tenon joints has been found in Lough Lene, Ireland and may be a local tradition (Farrell 1989). This boat has a Carbon 14 calibrated date range of 400–100 BC, and allowing for the possible age of the wood sample used for dating, might be as late as the first century AD. It has been suggested that it may have been built by a Mediterranean shipwright (Brindley 1991).

The County Hall ship fits rather well into what is known of the change from the shell-construction of ancient times to the skeleton-construction used in Mediterranean shipbuilding nowadays. The study of various wrecks in the Mediterranean indicates that the change occurred between the seventh and eleventh centuries, and was characterised by a gradual reduction in the use of the mortice-and-tenon joints (Throckmorton 1987, 94). Up to the first century AD such joints were rarely more than 100mm apart (eg the wrecks at Antikythera, Grand Congloue, Titan, Torre Sgarrata, and Lake Nemi, Throckmorton 1972, 70–1). But by the fourth century AD they were much more widely spaced, as is shown by the Yassi Ada wreck of that date off Turkey in which some joints were 70–120mm and others 170–240mm apart (Doorninck 1976). In wreck F from Cape Dramont, France, also dated to the fourth century AD, the mortice-and-tenon joints were not only widely spaced but were particularly badly finished (Joncheray 1977, 5–6). The decreasing dependance upon the joints by that time meant that the frames were becoming more important elements in forming the hull. In a wreck of the seventh century, also off Yassi Ada, Turkey, the mortice-and-tenon joints were spaced almost one metre apart, and had no small trenails locking the mortices into the planks (Bass 1971, 23). The mortice-and-tenon joints of the County Hall ship were locked by pegs and were irregularly spaced, not less than 150mm at the north end, and sometimes probably in excess of a metre, indicating that the shipwright was aware of shipbuilding changes taking place in the Mediterranean, and that he himself was probably trained in that region.

The New Fresh Wharf, Fennings Wharf, and Billingsgate boats

Fragments of probably five boats from these three sites have characteristics which suggest that they formed part of a single clinker shipbuilding group of traditions of the tenth and eleventh centuries AD, but with different methods of holding the overlapping strakes together, by rivet, by wooden peg, and probably by hooked nail. Tree-ring analysis indicates that the vessels were all built in or around south-east England.

Whether or not these different methods of post-Roman clinker fastening represent one or more shipbuilding traditions is not clear at present. The root of the clinker technique of shipbuilding may have been in Scandinavia where parts of such vessels have been found, the earliest known dating from the fourth century BC (Fig 148). This was found at Hjortspring on the island of Als in Denmark, and its planks had been sewn together (Greenhill 1976, 118; Akerlund 1963, 135). The earliest clinker-built vessel with iron rivets dates from the late fourth century AD and was found at Nydam in northern Germany (Akerlund 1963), in the region on the border with Scandinavia from which peoples migrated to south-eastern England in the fifth century. It seems likely, therefore, that this migratory people introduced the 'Scandinavian' clinker shipbuilding tradition into southern Britain, the best example of such a vessel being the Sutton Hoo ship, found in a grave of the seventh century AD (Evans and Bruce-Mitford 1975, 104, 127–8, 345–435), though a form of overlapping planking was not unknown in prehistoric Britain (Wright 1990, 139). The continuing use of clinker shipbuilding in Britain is best represented by the late Saxon boat from Graveney, north Kent (Fenwick 1978), and by later medieval illustrations and discoveries of such vessels (Landstrom 1961, 66–79). The vessels found at New Fresh Wharf, Fennings Wharf, and Billingsgate in London can best be understood when the wider distribution of the various methods of clinker fastening in Europe and Scandinavia is considered from the ninth to the thirteenth centuries (Fig 154).

Three methods of fastening clinker boats from late Saxon-Norman London have been found.

Iron rivets

Fragments of oak planking from Fennings Wharf and Billingsgate are characterised by having oak planks radially cut, and held clinkerwise by iron rivets with nail shanks between about 5mm and 7mm square and with diamond-shaped roves. There was a caulking of hair between the overlapping planks, and they are tree-ring dated to about AD 1050–1100.

The wide extent of the clinker shipbuilding tradition with iron rivets before the ninth century is reflected by the distribution of surviving parts of vessels found in Norway, Sweden, Denmark, Britain, and the southern Baltic coastland, and also by boat graves which show a somewhat similar distribution (Fig 149) (Muller-Wille 1974, 188, 196). Many of these are Viking and are identified by the presence of iron ship rivets. However, the tree-ring analysis of the Fennings Wharf planking reflects an origin in south-east England, and the shanks of the rivet nails were square in section, in contrast to the rivet nails in Scandinavian ships which were then generally round in section (Muller-Wille 1974, 189). The Fennings Wharf and Billingsgate riveted planking, therefore, seems to represent a local Anglo-Saxon variety of the clinker shipbuilding tradition, with ultimate roots in Scandinavia and north Germany, or perhaps a different blacksmith tradition.

Wooden pegs

The New Fresh Wharf and Billingsgate pegged boats were characterised by oak planks, radially cut, and held clinkerwise with pegs of willow or poplar expanded by wedges of oak, with moss caulking. Tree-ring analysis indicates that the boats were built during the tenth century in or around south-east England. Fragments of similarly pegged and locally constructed late Saxon boat planking, not yet published, have been found on one other waterfront site in London, at Thames Exchange, Upper Thames Street (Milne and Goodburn 1990, 633), and must be from yet another boat.

The pegged construction with a moss caulking is identical to that of contemporary boats found only on the southern Baltic coastland mainly in Poland (Fig 150), and it is possible that there was some relationship between the two groups. The southern Baltic boats date

from about AD 1000, and were found at Danzig-Ohra, Mechlinken, Charbrow, Czarnowsko, Ralswiek and Szczecin (Smolarek 1969) as well as at Falster in Denmark (Madsen 1984). It is believed that this pegged clinker construction was a characteristic of Slavonic shipbuilding, and, although Crumlin-Pedersen (1972, 189) suggests that the Slavs copied aspects of form and construction from Scandinavian ships, Smolarek (1969, 405–7) considers that the Slavonic shipbuilders were following a separate tradition. There were differences in

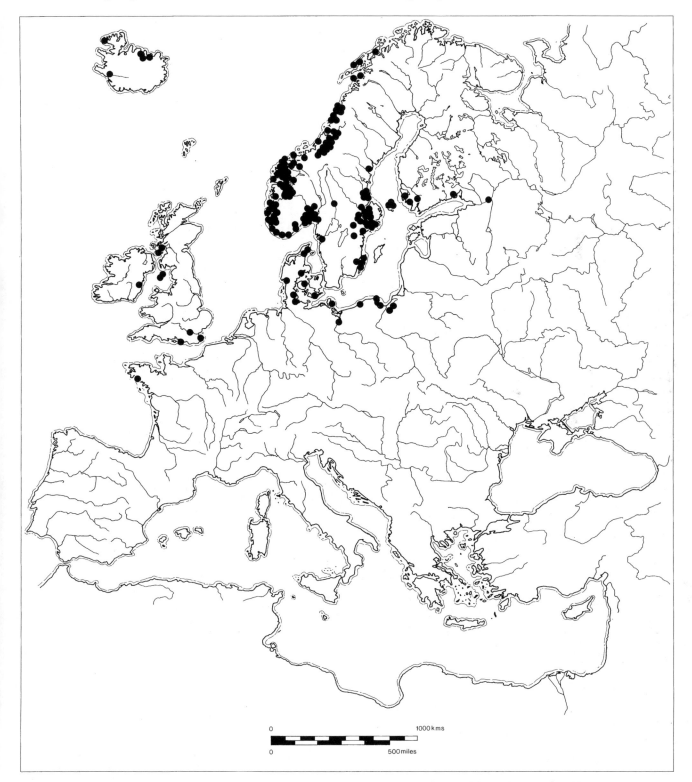

Fig 149 Distribution of clinker-planked ships, boats, and boat graves of the ninth to thirteenth centuries AD.

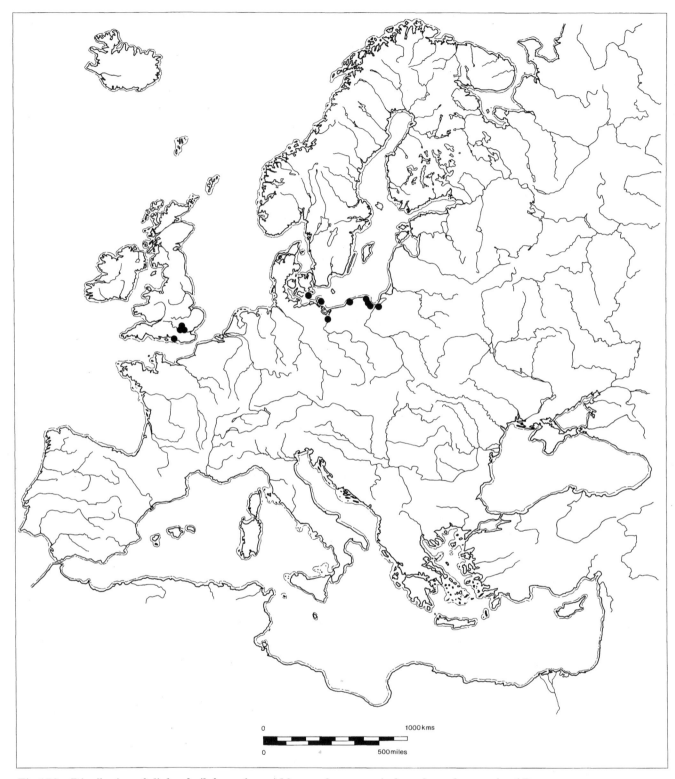

Fig 150   Distribution of clinker-built boats fastened by wooden pegs, ninth to eleventh centuries AD.

form and construction between Scandinavian and Sla-vonic ships, the latter being generally more flat bottomed, having a different mast-step fitting, and their planks were pegged and not riveted together (Madsen 1984). But in addition to the clinker construction there were some similarities, such as the the *bite* or cross-beam between the tops of the frames (Crumlin-Pedersen 1981). The existence of such a timber in the New Fresh Wharf boat is suggested by the knee (Fig 134, no 34).

The discovery of both pegged and riveted boats of this period in southern England complicates this Scandina-vian-Slavonic planking division, for it shows that both traditions existed in Anglo-Saxon England. This, then, reinforces Crumlin-Pedersen's view that they were vari-ants of a linked family of traditions.

It has been pointed out that wooden lap pegs were not exclusive to the Slavonic ships at that time (Fenwick 1978, 224), for they also occur in Skuldelev ships 1 and

6 where they were used in hulls that were otherwise iron-riveted (Olsen and Crumlin-Pedersen 1967, 108, 147, 152). They also occur in Kalmar boat XXII, possibly of Viking period, and were used to fasten the upper planking of Kalmar ship I, which dates to the thirteenth century and was otherwise fastened by iron rivets (Aker-lund 1951, 152, 155). Moreover, they were used in some

medieval ship planking from Bergen in Norway (Christensen 1985, 202). But in all of these instances the wooden lap pegs were secondary to the main fastening technique of iron rivets, and were therefore fundamentally different from the New Fresh Wharf and Slavonic boats in which the primary fastenings were pegs. It is appropriate to mention here Utrecht boat 1, found in

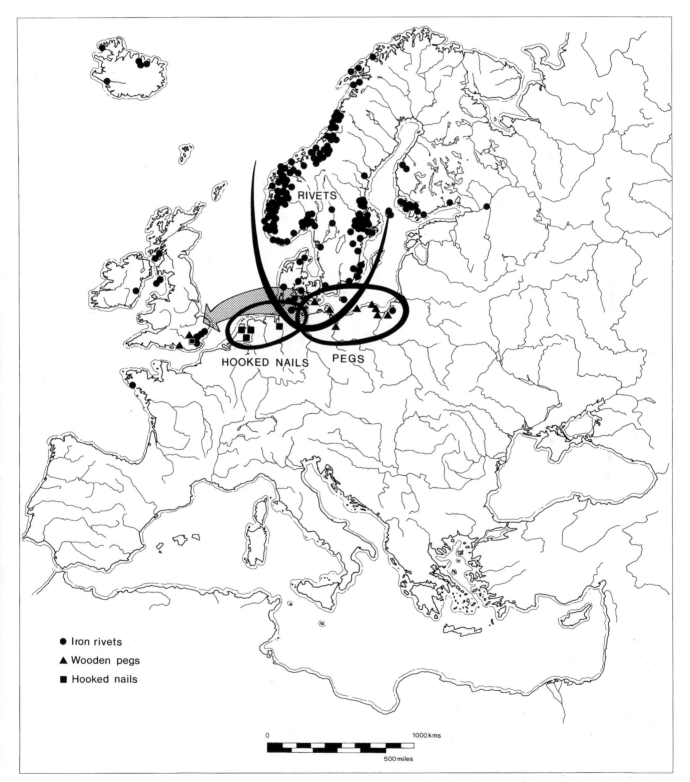

● Iron rivets
▲ Wooden pegs
■ Hooked nails

Fig 151 All types of clinker plank fastenings, seventh to thirteenth centuries AD. Iron rivets occur in Scandinavia, pegs in northern Poland and north-east Germany, and hooked nails in the Netherlands. All fastenings were used in south-east England. It is possible that the use of these varied fastenings in England was due to the Saxon migrations from northern Germany, to Frisian traders, and to Viking settlers.

1930 in the Netherlands, whose strakes overlapped and were held by trenails (Vlek 1987). Although dated to the eleventh century, this vessel has none of the characteristics of Scandinavian clinker shipbuilding.

Doubts have rightly been expressed about a possible direct link between London and southern Baltic pegged shipbuilding (McGrail 1987, 130), for there is little specific evidence of trade between London and that area during the Saxon period (Brooke and Keir 1975, 263–5). Nevertheless, Slavs were settling in north-eastern Germany during the sixth century AD (Brachmann 1983, 90–1), and it is possible that they were using pegged fastenings then, in an area where iron rivets, represented by the Nydam boat, were also in use. Both techniques could then have been introduced into southern England during the migration period of the fifth to sixth centuries (Fig 151). The earliest published evidence for pegged planking around the southern Baltic dates from about the tenth century AD, though a recently discovered pegged clinker-built vessel at Puck, near Gdansk in Poland, has provided three Carbon 14 dates in the sixth century AD (Stepien forthcoming), and supports this view. The interval between the fifth and tenth centuries in England is only slightly closed by a fragment of Saxon boat planking with peg holes along its edge, from a site in southern England. This was at Medmerry, in West Sussex, and was associated with objects dated by dendrochronology to AD 770–810 (Goodburn 1987).

The recognition of pegged clinker fastenings in Anglo-Saxon boats throws new light on the Graveney boat, found less than 50 miles (80 km) from London, whose precise late Saxon date (Fletcher 1984, 151) is currently being reassessed (Tyers forthcoming). The vessel had been fastened by iron rivets with square shanks, some of which had been driven through small wooden pegs. Where pegs were not found, apparently due to damage caused by driving in the iron rivet nails, it seems that the nails lay within circular drilled holes 8mm in diameter. These may be explained by their having been drilled for pegs that have since decayed (Fenwick 1978, 221–224). Fenwick believed that the rivets and the pegs had been fastened at the same time, perhaps to overcome the possible problem of lap fastenings working loose. A similar construction has been found in a late Saxon clinker built boat from the Thames Exchange site, London, whose iron rivets had been driven through pegs of alder (Milne and Goodburn 1990, 633). However, the absence of pegs in Scandinavian riveted planks, and the identification of an Anglo-Saxon pegged construction technique gives reason to think that the Graveney and Thames Exchange boat fastenings might conceivably represent two separate stages in the history of the boat: when first built it was fastened with lap pegs, and after some use it was refastened more strongly with iron rivets which used the old pegs like a rawlplug.

Hooked iron nails

The characteristic feature of the Fennings Wharf keel were the hooked nails holding the garboard strakes to the keel. There is reason to think that this was a clinker-built vessel (see Chapter 8), and as plank fastenings in both pegged and riveted clinker boats generally used the same types of fastenings to hold the strakes to the keel, it seems that hooked nails may have held the strakes together in the Fennings Wharf boat also.

None of the many pre-thirteenth century clinker-built vessels found in Scandinavia or in the southern Baltic is known to have had hooked nails, and as the tree-ring analysis shows that the Fennings Wharf vessel was probably built in south-eastern England, it is likely that the hooked nails reflect a local method of boat fastening.

Conclusion

The overriding feature of this random group of ship remains dating from the second to the eleventh centuries AD is that they were all built locally with a considerable variety of construction methods. The proximity of London to regions of Europe and Scandinavia in which similar methods of construction were prevalent does show that London was a meeting point of various shipbuilding traditions.

The cosmopolitan perspective on the port of London given by its early ships and boats is fully in accord with other archaeological evidence, and with early writers. In the first century AD Tacitus (XIV, 33) described the city as being 'crowded with traders and a great centre of commerce'. Bede (II, 3) in the eighth century said that it 'is a trading centre for many nations who visit it by land and sea'. And in about AD 1000 Ethelred's law code (Loyn 1962, 92–3) shows that there was a concentration of trade between London and ports on the Continent between Rouen and the Rhine. Therefore, although this group of ships and boats is mostly very fragmentary, it does enlarge the view of the early history of seafaring, and helps to give the future study of early shipping in southern England a sense of direction.

Roman European merchant ships

The tree-ring analysis of the Blackfriars and County Hall ships, representing two different shipbuilding traditions, shows that they were built fairly locally, and raises questions about the 'normal' type of merchant ship to be seen in northern waters during the Roman period. Indeed, were ships that had been built in the Mediterranean to be seen sailing in northern seas?

The County Hall ship is one of five plank-built vessels of the Mediterranean tradition of shipbuilding that have been found on Roman sites in central and northern Europe (Fig 147); the others being found at Vechten and Zwammerdam, on the Rhine in the Netherlands (de Weerd 1988, 162–73), and two boats found at Oberstimm on the Danube in Germany (Hockmann 1989). Moreover, a curious steering oar was also found at Zwammerdam which had been constructed with mortice-and-tenon joints in the Mediterranean tradition, though its shape and probable use over the stern seems to have been Rhenish (de Weerd 1988, 162–73). But as these five vessels represent only a small proportion of the number of ships and boats of the Roman period that have now been found in central and northern Europe (see Table 16), they suggest that Mediterranean-type ships were comparatively rare there.

This view is strengthened by an examination of the five mortice-and-tenoned plank-built vessels, for a tree-ring analysis of the two Oberstimm boats shows that they were built locally on the Danube, and, like the County Hall ship, did not sail from the Mediterranean. Moreover, the Vechten boat, only about 3m wide and 1.5m deep amidships, was too small for use on an ocean voyage and also could not have sailed from the Mediterranean, though it is just possible, but rather unlikely, that it was carried on the deck of a sea-going ship sailing out of the Mediterranean and around Spain, Portugal, and France to the Rhine. This leaves only Zwammerdam boat 2a, a fragment of planking that is too small to determine its source or the size of the vessel. The Lough Lene boat is extremely puzzling, but is excluded from this list since it was a logboat and its Carbon 14 date seems to be more pre-Roman than Roman. Moreover, as it was found in an inland lake, it was presumably locally built. Thus as none of the many ship and boat finds of the Roman period in central and northern Europe can be shown to have been built in the Mediterranean, and most are of a local Celtic tradition, it seems probable that vessels of Mediterranean-type construction were rare in northern waters, and that shipping rarely sailed direct from the Mediterranean to the northern provinces. Indeed, had there been a strong Mediterranean shipbuilding tradition in the north, the fact should have been manifest in the construction methods of many more local vessels on inland waters there.

This supports the view that most goods from the Mediterranean region were carried north on the inland rivers of Gaul and Germany (Peacock 1978; Parker 1980, 56; Cunliffe 1984). The alternative sea route around Spain had little to commend it, not only because of the dangers of an exposed Atlantic coastline, and delays caused by trying to round headlands with unsuitable winds, but also because of the limited trading market on the Atlantic coast compared with that on the inland rivers. Although there is evidence that some Mediterranean shipping did reach Britain via the Atlantic before the Roman invasion (Boon 1977, 21–5), there is little indication of much shipping and trade along the Atlantic seaboard of Portugal and northern Spain during the Roman period. That there was some is shown by the discovery of a Portuguese amphora at *Vindolanda* in northern Britain (*Britannia* 5, 467, n 41; de Alarcao 1988, 88–90), and by the concern for the dangers to shipping off the Atlantic coast indicated by a Roman lighthouse, still standing 33m high, at La Coruna on the north-western tip of Spain (Fig 147) (Hague 1973).

The Iberian peninsula was a deterrent to shipping between the Mediterranean and northern Europe, and since much of the Atlantic coast of Portugal, northern Spain, western France, and the other northern provinces was settled by Celtic peoples (Powell 1980; Duval 1984; de Alarcao 1988, 2–4; Keay 1988), it is likely that their own types of ships, rather than those of the Mediterranean, dominated trade outside the Mediterranean basin as the Celtic ships were better suited to the tidal conditions.

This means that there is no justification for the use of Mediterranean representations of Roman merchant

Table 16   Plank-built vessels of the Roman period found in central and northern Europe (Fig 146)

ship site	reference
England	
1 County Hall (Mediterranean-type)	see Chapter 5
2 New Guy's House	see Chapter 3
3 Blackfriars ship 1	see Chapter 2
4 Goldcliff, Gwent	
France	
5 Abbeville	Traullé 1809
6 Wanzenau	Höckmann 1989, 322
7 Strassburg	Ellmers 1972, 106
Belgium	
8 Bruges	Marsden 1976a
9 Pommoroeul 1	de Boe 1978
10 Pommoroeul 2	de Boe 1978
11 Ostende	Höckmann 1989, 106
Netherlands	
12 Vechten (Mediterranean-type)	de Weerd 1988, 185–94
13 Zwammerdam 2	de Weerd 1988, 93–148
14 Zwammerdam 2a (Mediterranean-type)	de Weerd 1988, 180–3
15 Zwammerdam 4	de Weerd 1988, 148–55
16 Zwammerdam 6	de Weerd 1988, 155–61
17 Woerden	de Weerd 1988, 240–3
18 Druten	Hulst and Lehmann 1974
19 Kapel-Avezaath	de Weerd 1988, 229–36
Germany	
20 Mainz 1	Höckmann 1982
21 Mainz 2	Höckmann 1982
22 Mainz 3	Höckmann 1982
23 Mainz 4	Höckmann 1982
24 Mainz 5	Höckmann 1982
25 Mainz 6	Höckmann 1982
26 Koln	de Weerd 1988, 303
27 Kalkar	Höckmann 1989, 322
28 Rindern	Höckmann 1989, 322
29 Oberstimm 1 (Mediterranean type)	Höckmann 1989
30 Oberstimm 2 (Mediterranean type)	Höckmann 1989
Switzerland	
31 Bevaix	Arnold 1978
32 Yverdon	Arnold 1978
Channel Islands	
33 St Peter Port	Rule 1993

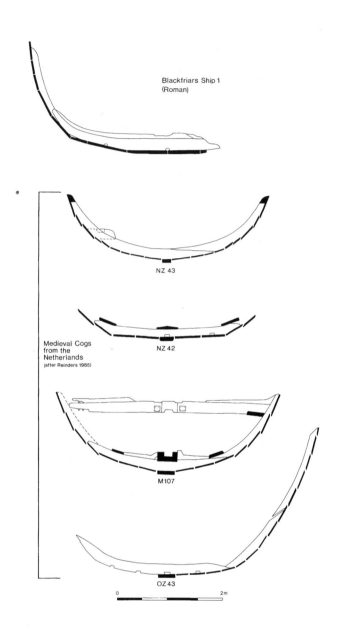

Fig 152   Cross-section of the Romano-Celtic ship from Blackfriars compared with cross-sections of medieval 'cogs'. It is possible that the Blackfriars type of vessel was the ancestor of the 'cog'.

ships as examples of the appearance of ships in northern Europe. This study has shown that Romano-Celtic sea-going ships were significantly different, though to what extent is not always clear. The curious forms of Roman craft, some with unusual rigs, that are depicted in the Rhineland region (Ellmers 1978) should be a sufficient caution. Unfortunately, contemporary representations of northern ships and boats are rare, and, although this author has argued elsewhere (Marsden 1990) that caution should be exercised in interpreting the ships on pre-Roman Celtic coins as necessarily representative of northern native vessels, the discussion above does nevertheless strengthen the view (Muckleroy *et al* 1978; McGrail 1990) that the ships depicted were indeed of Celtic type.

The strong native tradition of Celtic shipbuilding in the northern provinces begs the question, why was it necessary to build some Mediterranean types of vessels

in central and northern Europe? The answer is suggested by the fact that four of the five vessels in question (ie all but the County Hall ship) are of the first to second centuries AD and are associated with Roman military forts. There seems little doubt, therefore, that these were official boats built according to Roman military regulations presumably established in Rome (Höckmann 1989).

The County Hall ship was different from the other four plank-built vessels in three ways; it is of late third to early fourth century date, it was much larger than the boats, and it was not associated with a fort. But as its builder was probably from the Mediterranean it is possible that it too had an official use, though it is not clear if it had been built during the period under the British usurpers Carausius and Allectus (AD 286–96) or under the emperor Diocletian (after AD 296) when

Britain was divided into four small provinces, one of which probably had London as its provincial capital (Merrifield 1983, 197–206). A building date for the ship after AD 296, when Britain was being reorganised by Diocletian, could explain the presence of a ship with this construction in London, and it is possible that the suggestion that it was associated with events in AD 296 (Riley and Gomme 1912, 17–22) may have been closer to the truth than has been thought in recent times (Wheeler 1946, 154; Marsden 1965a, 109).

Celtic ship building

The use of hooked nails in the Fennings Wharf keel of the eleventh century is so different from the use of iron rivets in Anglo-Saxon and Scandinavian vessels that it raises the question of the possible source of this technique. The thirteenth to fourteenth century cogs found at Bremen and the Netherlands (Fig 153), whose clinker-built sides were fastened by similar hooked nails instead of rivets have been discussed by Ellmers and Crumlin-Pedersen (Crumlin-Pedersen 1979; Ellmers 1985b, 80–1; Reinders 1985).

Cogs appear to have been developed in the north German region and have also been found in Denmark, and both Ellmers and Crumlin-Pedersen see in their method of hooked-nail fastening, in their full-bodied hull form, in the shape of the mast-step frame of the thirteenth century Kollerup cog from northern Jutland (Crumlin-Pedersen 1979, 28–30), and in their edge-to-edge bottom planking (Ellmers 1985b, 81), a form of shipbuilding derived from the Romano-Celtic shipbuilding tradition, represented by Blackfriars ship 1 (Fig 152). They suggest that there was a merging of the Celtic and Scandinavian shipbuilding traditions (Crumlin-Pedersen 1965; ibid 1985, 90–1), and both Crumlin-Pedersen (1965; ibid 1972, 186–7; 1983) and Ellmers (1985b) believe that this occurred under the Frisians, whose trade was so important in the seventh to ninth centuries, and that it was they who may have created the cog. Reinders (1985, 19) doubts the view that the Blackfriars and Bruges vessels are of the same family as the Kollerup cog and cogs generally, for this theory is 'based upon the assumption that there were no parallels from other medieval ship finds in northern Europe'.

Ellmers (1985b, 84) has pointed out that about sixty hooked cog-nails were found in a tenth-century deposit, with many rivets, at Birka near Stockholm, and he suggests that these were derived from a foreign cog. Reinders (1985, 18) urges caution with this interpretation, for unless actually found in association with a ship or boat there is no certainty that such fastenings were so used. This is a fair comment for they, like rivets, were also used for non-nautical purposes, hooked nails having been found in England, for example, on the middle Saxon site of Shakenoak, Oxfordshire, several miles from a navigable river (Brodribb et al 1973, fig 54, nos 352, 353), and on an eleventh-century site at Aylesbury, Buckinghamshire, also several miles from a navigable river (Farley 1976, fig 39, no 16).

The finding of hooked nails in the eleventh-century keel from Fennings Wharf may support the Frisian theory, though it does not prove it. Nevertheless, there is no avoiding the fact that this group of medieval cogs and the Fennings Wharf keel existed in a region in which during the Roman period there had been a Romano-Celtic shipbuilding tradition that had also used hooked nails and had vessels of cog-like form (Fig 151). It is of course possible that shipbuilders in Roman times and the Middle Ages independently created similar ship forms and construction methods to suit the environmental conditions of the south-east England – Low Countries area. But this is unlikely, for culturally there were always very strong cross-Channel trade links. During the Roman period much of London's seaborne trade was through the Low Countries, as witness the dedications at the shrines of Nehalennia at Domburg and Colijnsplaat at the mouth of the Scheldt (Fig 9) (Hassall 1978, 43), and the earliest known list of traders to London, dating from about AD 1000, describes a concentration of its most important seafaring merchants also from the region between Rouen and the Rhine (Fig 121) (Loyn 1962, 93–4). In conclusion, then, it seems likely on the present very limited evidence, that there was a form of continuation of Celtic shipbuilding tradition, and that it was gradually absorbed into the clinker tradition during the Middle Ages. However, it is important to remember that there is a gap of eight centuries between Blackfriars ship 1 and the Fennings Wharf keel which is not bridged by any 'Celtic' ship finds in Britain, so this conclusion can at best be only tentative.

Development of berthing methods

It is significant that the same stages that occurred in the development of facilities in the Roman port of London – initially a prepared hard for beaching, followed by the construction of quays and jetties – also occurred in Saxon and Norman times when the port was re-established after some centuries. Moreover, when other factors are taken into consideration, particularly the flat bottoms of Blackfriars ship 1, the New Guy's House barge and Fennings Wharf (keel) vessel, together with the fairly small size of individual items of packaged cargo which rarely exceeded a tonne or so, a pattern emerges in which the most important factor determining the use of the port was the tides. Tides carried ships upstream to the port, tides enabled ships to be beached for loading and offloading, and it was the depth of water at high tide beside the quays and jetties of London that restricted the draught of ships and consequently their cargo capacity.

Roman beaching

Beaching, the most elementary form of berthing, is of pre-Roman origin and occurred at the Bronze Age site at North Ferriby (Wright and Wright 1947). Caesar (III, 1) mentions it in connection with the Veneti of northwest Gaul. Moreover, it seems likely that it was used at Hengistbury Head, Dorset, where a native port of the first century BC has been found (Cunliffe 1990). Beaching on the shore of the river at London, rather than elsewhere at sea, gave safety from storms. Beaching in shallow water near half tide to avoid being stranded, the ability to pass over shoals, and the need to carry the maximum possible cargo safely, probably determined the flat-bottomed form of the Blackfriars ship and the New Guy's House barge, and also the flat bottoms of the Romano-Celtic barges found on the rivers of central and northern Europe. At low tide cargoes could be transferred into waggons, as so often happened in later times in northern Europe (Ellmers 1985a).

The Roman quay or jetty

Beaching as a method of berthing was soon to change in London in favour of a more suitable arrangement, presumably based upon the Roman experience of

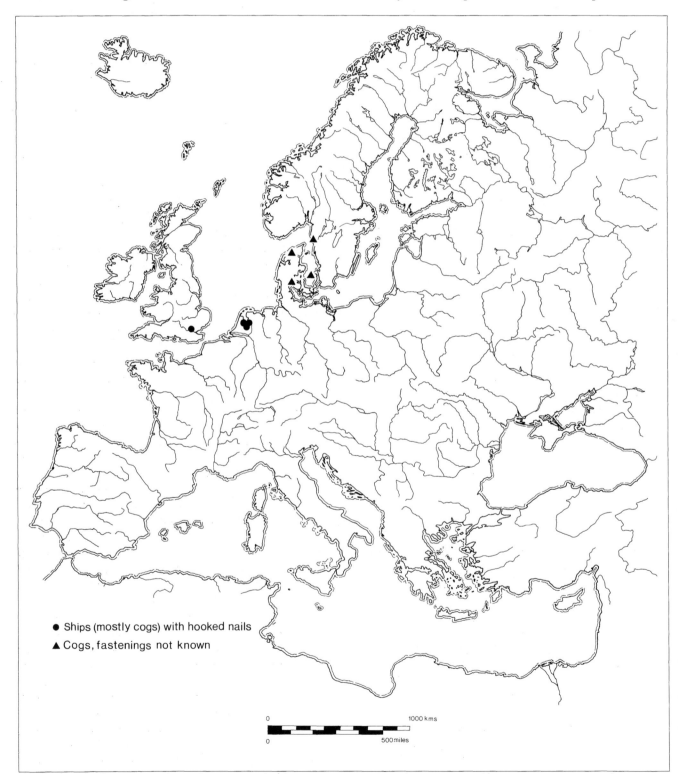

● Ships (mostly cogs) with hooked nails
▲ Cogs, fastenings not known

Fig 153   Distribution of medieval ships with hooked nails holding clinker planks. The 'cog' form of most of these vessels and their hooked nails suggests that they developed from Romano-Celtic seagoing shipping.

constructing ports in the tideless Mediterranean. Around the Mediterranean they built great masonry moles out into the sea and on these supported warehouses and loading equipment, as at Portus (Shaw 1972, 98–9). At some ports located on rivers ships could moor alongside quays, as at Rome (ibid, 107). So in the Mediterranean region generally there were facilities which would enable enormous loads to be transferred into ships (Throckmorton 1972, 75), like the 40 tonne marble block found in a third-century wreck off Marzamemi, Sicily, (Throckmorton et al 1987, 76). Thus, although ships could only berth alongside the London waterfronts near the time of high water, investing in quays and jetties would give dry access to ships by providing a working surface for loading and unloading whenever it was needed, rather than when tides allowed. Also, the security of cargoes, the use of lifting equipment, the proximity of warehouses, and the regulation of port dues by the political authorities were all much better controlled by having a properly constructed quay beside which ships could berth.

These were perhaps some of the reasons why in the latter half of the first century AD quays were built in London. But even these were probably unsatisfactory, however, for judging from the laden draught of Blackfriars ship 1, which would require about 1.5m of water beside the quays, the first quays did not give very deep water even at high tide. Although vessels could only berth on an incoming tide or set sail on a falling tide, the jetty found at Miles Lane (see Chapter 1) shows how ships could have berthed in deeper water, though as the end of the jetty was not found it is not possible to judge how deep into the Thames it would have reached. However, the landing stage at Peninsular House indicates that it was intended that light draught vessels should berth along the shore parallel to the flow of the river. By the late second and early third centuries the waterfront may have been improved by building quays farther out into the river, as at Custom House and at New Fresh Wharf, presumably to give access to deeper water.

Saxo-Norman beaching

The Saxon solution to the problem of berthing in the tenth century was to build low-angle embankments mainly of timber and clay along the shore for beaching. Parts of the embankments at the public berthing sites at Dowgate and Billingsgate have been excavated, and show a careful construction of clay, timber, and stones one metre thick. However, berthing may not have been as simple as this, for at New Fresh Wharf there were the timber supports of a probable jetty, and at Billingsgate there were revetments holding back the river bank as well as a dock inlet (Steedman et al 1992), suggesting that here were the beginnings of the quays and docks that were to become so important later in the medieval period and would ultimately make it possible for larger vessels with a deeper draught to berth at London's waterfronts.

The few fragmentary remains of boats of late Saxon and Norman London, together with the documentary records mentioning the type of ship called a *keel*, suggest that vessels visiting the port were of fairly light draught and had flat bottoms for berthing in shallow water.

Later port development

These stages in the development of the waterfronts laid the foundation for the subsequent development of the port of London which is better documented elsewhere (eg Milne and Milne 1982, 62–68). During the Roman, Saxon, and Norman periods the shallow depth of high water beside the waterfronts, usually less than 2m, meant that only ships with a shallow draught could berth there when laden, and to be economical the vessels had to be broad and flat bottomed .

During the later medieval period the greater size and weight of cargoes carried meant that ships required higher sides, rounded bottoms, and also a greater depth of water when berthing. Moreover, it seems clear that although in the fourteenth century quays were frequently of timber, during the fifteenth century there was an increasing amount of more permanent waterfront building in stone (ibid). Tides continued to carry ships upstream to London, and river vessels, such as Blackfriars ship 3 of the fifteenth century, continued to need flat bottoms to carry them over shoals (Marsden 1972). In the fourteenth and fifteenth centuries docks probably became more common with warehouses nearby (Schofield 1981; Marsden 1981, 14–15), enabling the port of London to handle better a whole range of ships and boats. The ship and boat remains of this later medieval period, studied by the present author (Marsden forthcoming), indicates that local vessels were clinker-built and fastened with iron rivets.

By the sixteenth and seventeenth centuries, the Upper Pool of London, the old port area of the City, was too small and restricted to handle the volume and size of shipping and their cargoes, and a new docklands area began to develop downstream where it was possible to create deeper water berthing facilities. By the nineteenth and early twentieth centuries the lower reaches of the Thames had become the main port of London (Jackson 1983). During the 1950s the port was in decline for various reasons, and soon the docklands area downstream of the City became disused. Nowadays the remaining docking facilities are at Tilbury, with much seaborne trade having moved to Rotterdam. The last merchant vessels to dock regularly at the City's waterfront were two ships that carried tomatoes from the Canary Islands. They moored at New Fresh Wharf, immediately downstream of London Bridge, opposite the site of the first century hard, and were often seen there by the present author in the early 1960s. They would arrive on a flood tide, and at low water lay aground on the river bed, much as sailing ships had done close by nineteen centuries earlier. The main difference is that one day they sailed away and never returned to the City. For a time they berthed downstream at West India Dock until that too was closed, but by that time the ancient port of London had died.

Appendix 1   The pottery dating evidence from Blackfriars ship 1

by Jo Groves, Museum of London

Acknowledgments

Thanks are due to Barbara Davies and Roberta Tomber for their help and advice in the preparation of this report.

Introduction

The purpose of this report is to present the dating evidence from the pottery for the sinking of the Blackfriars ship. The pottery is from three contexts. ER 860, the earliest layer, was composed of grey silt and contained material which may have been carried on board. ER 855 was a sandy deposit on the planking of the collapsed starboard side and below the top of the side frames. ER 854 consisted of gravel and sand which had accumulated over the bottom of the ship during the period when the sides collapsed. This layer was partially disturbed in a few places during the post-medieval period. Many of the finds and their contexts are illustrated in the original report by Marsden (1967).

The total assemblage of pottery available for study consists of 66 sherds (2167g). This was analysed by the standard system of pottery recording used by the Department of Urban Archaeology, Museum of London (Department of Uurban Archaeology 1984). This discussion, arranged by context, is based on the quantified data which is preserved in the Museum of London Archaeological Service archive.

ER 860

The pottery consists of two abraded joining fragments (70g) of a bowl (Fig 71A).

Form

The vessel is a wheelmade bead-rimmed bowl (125mm diameter) with a high shoulder and decorated by horizontal grooving beneath the rim. There is a slight groove on top of the rim which is possibly intended as a lid-seating. Close parallels for the vessel have not been found, although the high shoulder is reminiscent of Gallo-Belgic tradition.

Fabric

The fabric (DUA fabric code Sbw 4114) is sandy (rounded grains, mostly 0.4–0.6mm) with occasional inclusions of iron and flint. A moderate amount of white mica is visible on the surface. It has a light grey core (2.5YR 7/0), brown margins (5YR 5/4) and mainly brownish grey surfaces (7.5YR 6/2) but with areas of darker grey (2.5YR 4/0) and reddish orange (2.5YR 5/8). The fracture is irregular and the surfaces are harsh and

abraded, but there are traces of burnishing over the rim and on the exterior.

This fabric is similar to, but less coarse than, an early Roman sandy fabric (DUA fabric code Sw 2873) which occurs as a bead-rim jar in a Hadrianic fire deposit (c120 AD) at the General Post Office site, Newgate Street, London (GPO75, context 7374, phase VIIf). Although the Blackfriars and GPO75 sherds are superficially similar to Rhineland granular grey ware (RGGW) which is dated c43–80 AD in London (Anderson 1981, 94) they both contain flint inclusions which RGGW lacks. Thin-section analysis of fabric 2873 suggests instead that the possible sources are Kent, Essex, and the south-east Midlands, excluding the Oxford clays (A Vince pers comm). The forms also differ from those in RGGW apart from the use of multiple grooving (Anderson 1981, fig 6.2, nos 10–11).

ER 855

The quantity of pottery from ER 855 is very small (2 sherds) forming only 1.19% of the total assemblage by weight. Nevertheless it provides important dating evidence for the sinking of the ship because it is fairly unabraded, unlike the sherds from ER 854.

Both sherds are second century: a samian conical cup (Dr 33) from Lezoux, and a Cologne rough-cast beaker with a cornice rim. Samian production commenced at Lezoux c125 AD, and Cologne rough-cast beakers are in use in London c120–60 AD. These sherds together are indicative of a mid second century date.

ER 854

All the pottery from ER 854 (62 sherds, 2071g) is abraded. It constitutes the largest part of the total assemblage (95.56% by weight).

Most of the closely dateable material belongs to the second century (22 sherds) and the late first to second century (10 sherds). There is very little pottery which is confined to the first century (4 sherds) and similarly there is only a small quantity belonging to the late Roman period (2 sherds). There is a single sherd of post-Roman pottery which is post-medieval. Since a large proportion of the material is second century it is perhaps reasonable to suggest that the sinking of the ship occurred sometime during the second century. The first-century pottery is probably residual, and the late Roman and post-medieval sherds are possibly intrusive.

Closer analysis of the second-century material indicates that several of the vessels represented emerged in the Antonine period (samian Dr 45; samian Dr 38; Verulamium region coarse white slipped ring-necked flagon with a cup-shaped mouth; and bead and flange mortarium) and most of the others were current *c*120–60 AD. This tends to highlight a mid-century date for the second century group.

Conclusions

Unfortunately the pottery which might have provided the most reliable dating evidence for the ship, the bowl from ER 860, is neither closely identifiable nor dateable. Any attempt to date the sinking of the ship by the material from ER 854 and ER 855 must be tentative due to the nature of its deposition. Residuality and redeposition have to be borne in mind. It is not possible to determine, for instance, how long the sherds had been washed around in the Thames before their final deposition in the ship, or indeed what their history was prior to being dumped in the river.

The pottery from ER 854 and ER 855 has a concentration of second-century sherds and a scarcity of first-century and late-Roman types which indicates that the second century is the most likely date for the sinking of the ship. The fresher condition of the pottery from ER 855 lends support to this suggestion. Closer examination of this second-century material makes it possible to refine the date further and point to the mid second century as the probable date of the sinking of Blackfriars ship 1.

Appendix 2   Metallographic analysis of nails from Blackfriars ship 1

by Brian Gilmour, Royal Armouries

Longitudinal sections of three large hooked iron nails and transverse sections of another nine nail shanks were examined metallographically at the Royal Armouries. The main purposes were to find out what iron or steel alloys had been used, to establish how the nails were made, and to understand better how the nails had been driven into the hull.

Each nail was fairly thickly encrusted with iron corrosion products below which the iron was well preserved. Three of the nails were embedded in polyester mounting resin and were cut longitudinally. These sections were polished and etched using 2% nitric acid in alcohol (Nital) to show the structure of the metal. The remaining nail shanks were only cross-sectioned for analysis.

Nails longitudinally sectioned

1   Tall cone-headed nail

This large nail from a side-frame had a slightly tapered shank up to 16mm in diameter. Analysis showed that the shank and the cone-shaped head were made from a medium-high carbon steel bar which had been heated and forged to the required length and diameter. The wider end of the bar was then reheated and forged a number of times until the desired cone-shaped head was achieved (Fig 154).

Repeated reheating resulted in the cone-shaped head becoming largely decarburised (ie the carbon having become oxidised) with a carbon content mostly down to about 0.1–0.2% (ie little more than a low carbon wrought iron) (Fig 155). The differing alignments of the non-metallic slag inclusions show how the metal at the end was forged to form the cone (Fig 155), and it is clear that the head was part of the same metal bar as the shank and was not welded on later. Some decarburisation along the shank had also occurred during the reheating and forging, but the effect was limited to the part of the metal near the surface. The shank mostly consisted of a high carbon steel with a carbon content of about 0.6 – 0.7%. The nail had not been quenched but was evidently air-cooled after final reheating and forging, for this had resulted in giving a pearlithic structure to the steel (Fig 156). Three hardness values were obtained from across the conical head and part of the shank (Fig 154). The first, 245 HV (0.1), was obtained for part of the high-carbon steel shank, but the values 158 HV (0.1) and 139 HV (0.1) were obtained on parts of the decarburised cone-shaped head with carbon contents of approximately 0.2 and 0.1% respectively.

There was very little distortion of the grain structure of the metal at the top of the cone-shaped head, as would have occurred had it been subjected to violently ham-mering into the ship. This implies that the nail head had been protected in some way, perhaps by a cone-shaped dolly which was itself struck by the hammer. Moreover, the need to strike the nail head very hard may have been reduced by the nail having been driven into slightly undersize pre-drilled holes in the planks and frames.

2   Semi-cone-headed nail

This nail from a floor-timber had a shank 16mm in diameter near the head. The head itself was only partly cone-shaped (Fig 157) when compared with the previous example. The rim of the head was about 46mm in diameter.

Unlike the previous example, this nail consisted almost entirely of low carbon wrought-iron, but with a few areas of slightly higher carbon unevenly distributed along the shank, but even here the carbon content was less than 0.1%. Etching of this specimen proved very difficult, apparently because of the very variable nature of the iron used. A great deal of two-phase non-metallic slag was visible across the central part of the nail head, and in it were some massive inclusions which were irregular in shape towards the centre (Fig 158). They were more flattened near the surface where it had been forged out to give the partial cone shape. The pale grey (possibly Wustite) dendrites in a darker grey Payalite glassy matrix looked typical of smithing slag (Fig 159).

Across the head of the nail, including the areas where the slag concentration was greatest, the iron consisted of

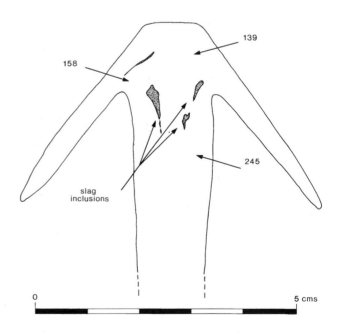

Fig 154   Section of cone-headed nail showing hardness values and slag inclusions.

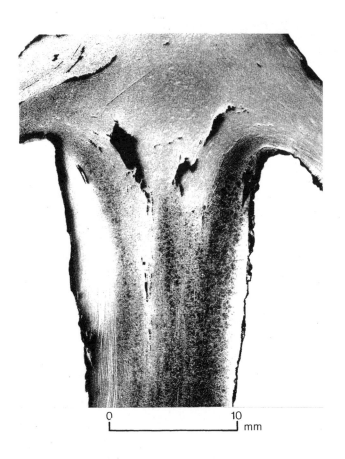

Fig 155   The nail shown in Fig 154; (left) photograph of section; (right) structure of the wrought iron.

medium grain (ASTM 4–5) equiaxed (ie not flattened) ferrite (Fig 159). Three hardness values were obtained from across the nail head; 79, 91, and 116 HV (0.1), which show that this part is a fairly pure soft wrought-iron (Fig 157).

There appeared to be four main zones or bands visible across the shank (Fig 158). These consisted predominantly of ferrite although the grain size and hardness varied between the zones. The outer zones gave hardness values of 164 and 147 HV (0.1) and had a medium to large grain structure (ASTM 3–4). One of the wider bands appeared to be continuous with part of the soft iron of the head. The remaining band was harder, 209 HV (0.1), than the rest and also had a massive ferrite grain structure (> ASTM 1).

Traces of probable welds are visible as linear concentrations of slag inclusions between the different zones. The most probable explanation for these variations in the form of the iron, as well as the likely presence of welds, is that this nail was made from a bar which itself was made of five or more pieces of scrap iron. The widely varying hardnesses and grain sizes of the different parts suggest a widely differing phosphorous content between these parts, with the harder parts being higher in phos-

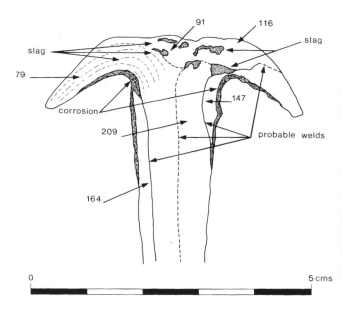

Fig 156   Section of semi-cone-headed nail from a floor-timber, showing hardness values and probable welds.

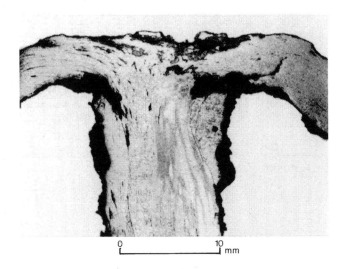

Fig 157 Section of the nail shown in Fig 156.

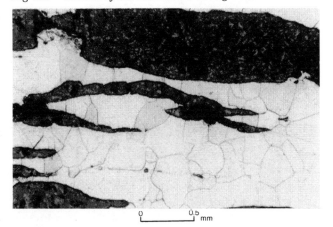

Fig 158 Detail of the structure of the nail head in Fig 156.

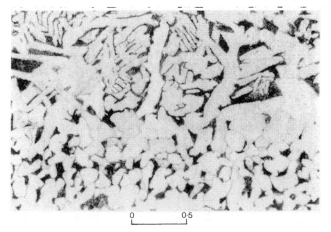

Fig 159 Structure of the nail shank shown in Fig 156.

phorus. The massive two-phase slag inclusions visible near the nail head were probably trapped during the welding of irregular pieces of scrap iron to form the bar from which the nail was forged.

3 Nail shank, head missing

This broken portion of a nail shank was 0.279m long and 11mm in diameter. In contrast to the previous specimens, it consisted of a fairly homogeneous low carbon steel, the structure of which was similar along the whole

length of the specimen. The longitudinal section examined in detail spanned the part of the shank where the corrosion products showed a curious dog-leg appearance, rather like that of a broken long bone that has re-knit out of position (Fig 159). Upon etching, it became clear that this dog-leg bore no relation to any damage that might have happened to the metal of the nail, and the apparent kink must relate to differences in the wood through which the nail passed.

The etched section had a slightly banded appearance which continued undistorted down the shank (Fig 159). The metal consisted mainly of fine grain ferrite (ASTM 6–7) with pearlite fairly evenly distributed through it, and with a carbon content which, although it varied slightly with the banding, was mostly about 0.2%. The metal was rather similar in appearance to modern mild steel.

The hardness values of 166, 152, and 153 HV (0.1), obtained from across the section, are fairly typical of a fine grain low carbon steel. The metal was also quite clean with only a few small predominantly medium-grey (?fayalitic) slag inclusions. These had become very elongated by the forging out of the starting bar from which the shank was produced.

Nails cross-sectioned

Transverse sections of nine nail shanks, chosen at random, were metallographically examined to clarify whether or not the varied nature of the three nails already described was a constant factor. The nail sections were all roughly circular and between 8mm and 12mm in diameter, although varying amounts of the surfaces had been lost to corrosion. None of the shanks appears to have had an original diameter of more than about 15mm.

4

This section of nail showed a basic wrought-iron structure consisting of large grain ferrite (ASTM 3) with some small slag inclusions, mostly of one medium grey phase. A few massive three-phase slag inclusions were also visible. Vickers micro-harness values of 108 and 109 HV (0.1) were obtained confirming a basic wrought iron structure.

5

Three parts visible in this section formed a distorted sandwich of pieces which seemed to have been welded together before the shank was forged out. The central part was a medium carbon steel consisting of medium grain (ASTM 4) spheroidised pearlite with a maximum carbon content of about 0.4–0.5%, although this was less where extensive carbon diffusion had taken place across the welds into the outer iron pieces during the final forging of the shank. Parts of the steel showed signs of grain growth with a Widmanstatten structure, a probable indication of overheating during the forging. There were also signs of decarburisation having taken place before the pieces were welded together.

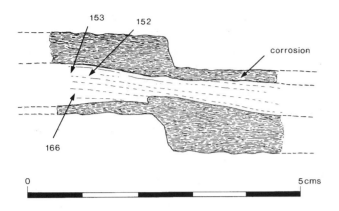

Fig 160   *Section of a nail shank showing dog-leg in corrosion products at the junction of the planking and frame.*

The outer pieces were both wrought-iron consisting of medium grain ferrite with a scattering of small slag inclusions. Vickers micro-hardness values obtained were consistent with the structures observed. The spheroidised steel gave a value 167 HV (0.1) compared with 117 and 118 HV (0.1) for the wrought-iron parts.

6

This shank had a wrought-iron structure right across the section consisting of medium grain (ASTM 3–4) ferrite with a few small slag inclusions. Hardness values of 121 and 125 HV (0.1) were obtained, again consistent with wrought-iron.

7

At first glance the section of this shank appeared to be made of a plain wrought-iron. The section, however, could be divided into two halves each with a different structure. Both parts showed up as a quite clean ferrite structure with a few small slag inclusions.

In one half the ferrite structure was very variable (ASTM 7), although it was mostly very large (ASTM 3), with the effect of phosphorus 'ghosting' showing up in the larger grained areas. This effect showed up as a network of raised areas independent of the ferrite grain structure and seemed to represent a variable phosphorus content in the iron. Hardness values of 187 and 189 HV (0.1) were obtained which were consistent with a fairly high phosphorous content.

The other half of the section showed up as a variable grained (ASTM 2–5) ferrite with no sign of the phosphorus ghosting effect. Hardness values of 137 and 141 HV (0.1) were slightly higher than for the wrought-iron seen in other shanks.

This part of the shank appears to have been made from two separate pieces of iron, one with a high phosphorus content. There are no welds clearly visible between the two pieces.

8

This nail had a very large grained (ASTM 2) wrought-iron structure consisting of ferrite with many large three-phase slag inclusions. The hardness tests, 160 and 195 HV (0.1), showed that this was not a plain wrought-iron, and, together with the large grain size, a variable phosphorus content is probable. Although this metal is still a coarse wrought-iron, it is one which must have been smelted from a high phosphorus ore.

9

The section of this nail shows that the shank was possibly made from up to four or five pieces varying between low-carbon iron and medium-carbon steel, although the junctions between these areas are very unclear. This suggests welds of a high standard. Over half the shank at the section seems to consist of a medium-carbon steel with a carbon content of approximately 0.4%. This may have consisted of two or three similar pieces welded together. The structure of these pieces varied between a small grained (ASTM 8), partially spheroidised pearlite and ferrite, and much larger grained areas which showed a Widmanstatten structure indicating localised overheating during forging.

The rest of the section consisted of low-carbon iron, with a carbon content mostly of 0.1–0.2%, and with small areas of ferrite near the edges. These appear to represent decarburisation during forging.

Hardness values of 210 and 162 HV (0.1) were obtained for one of the fine-grained steel areas. A mean value of approximately 190 HV is consistent with the fine-grained pearlite structure. Hardness values of 169 and 192 HV (0.1) for two of the mainly ferrite or very low-carbon iron parts was unusually high and probably indicates the presence of phosphorus.

10

This nail appears to have been made from three similar pieces of medium-carbon steel with a carbon content of

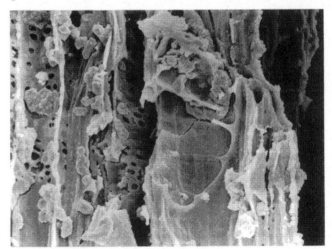

Fig 161   *Scanning electron microscope view of the hazel wood caulking from a nail head in Blackfriars ship 1.*

approximately 0.3 – 0.4%, welded together, the weld lines marked by corrosion along lines of slag inclusions. There appears to have been extensive decarburisation mainly down one side of the shank where the structure has a fine grain (ASTM 7), mainly of low-carbon iron or ferrite. A typical low-carbon iron hardness value of 129 HV (0.1) was obtained for this decarburised area. One of these pieces was much more variable in composition than the others, and ranged between fine grained (ASTM 8) pearlite plus ferrite and fine grained ferrite (ASTM 7) with grain boundary carbide. The metal was fairly clean with a few small slag inclusions.

Hardness values of 150 and 180 HV (0.1) were obtained for the pearlite parts of the section compared to a value of 120 HV (0.1) for one of the ferritic areas.

11

This nail was very variable in composition suggesting that possibly four different pieces may have been welded together. There are hints of distorted welds in the form of a few slag inclusions plus some linear highlighting (traces of a diffuse white line) suggesting a small degree of trace element enrichment. This is an end-product of forging and welding that is sometimes found where elements such as arsenic are present.

One of the parts to one side was a low-medium carbon steel with a carbon content of approximately 0.3%. This mostly consisted of fine grain pearlite (ASTM 7–8) with some larger grain patches showing the distinctive Widmanstatten formation, probably caused by localised overheating during forging. There also seems to have been carbon diffusion into the adjacent piece.

This adjacent piece was a low-carbon iron which mostly varied in carbon content between 0.2 and 0.1%. There was little slag visible in either of these two parts. Most of the remaining part of the section, about half in all, consisted of fine grain ferrite (ASTM 7) with a few small slag inclusions. Alongside one edge opposite to the steel part was an area of very large grain (ASTM 1) ferrite, the grains of which included many short rod-like carbide or nitride needles'.

Hardness testing gave consistent values of 183 HV (0.1) for the low carbon iron. The ferrite areas, however, gave hardness values of 152 and 157 HV (0.1) which suggest that they contained a small but significantly higher proportion of phosphorus than the other parts.

12

This nail appeared to comprise of three pieces welded together and was similar in appearance to the previous sample. There were no clear traces of welds although the different structures observed strongly suggest their presence. As in nail 11, the smaller part of one side consisted of a piece of medium-carbon steel, this time with about 0.4% carbon. It also comprised fine grain (ASTM 8) pearlite and ferrite with larger grain patches showing a Widmanstatten structure, the likely result of localised overheating during forging.

There appears to have been considerable carbon diffusion from the steel part into the adjacent part, a wrought-iron consisting mainly of fine grain (ASTM 7 – 8) ferrite. The remaining half of the section also comprised wrought-iron, but this time it had a variable, but mostly very large grain (ASTM 4) ferrite which in places also included short rod-like carbide or nitride needles. Patches of fine grain (ASTM 7-8) ferrite were also present. Patches of two-phase, pale, and medium-grey slag were visible near the probable weld boundary between the two wrought-iron parts. The rest of the metal was quite clean with only a few small inclusions of slag.

A typical hardness value of 189 HV (0.1) was obtained for the steel part. The adjacent ferritic part into which some carbon had diffused gave hardness values of 136 and 139 HV (0.1), whereas the variable grain ferrite gave a hardness value of 121 HV (0.1) which is fairly typical of a plain wrought-iron.

Conclusions

It is clear from these twelve samples that the nails vary fairly widely in composition between wrought-iron and medium-carbon steel. There seems to have been no consistent effort to use steel for these nails, and whereas steel seems to form the major part of some nails, in other examples only a small piece of steel exists, having been welded to either low-carbon or wrought-iron. Some of the wrought-iron pieces included in some nails were larger grained and harder than the rest, suggesting that they were quite high in phosphorus. It seems clear, therefore, that the nails were generally made from scrap iron and steel forged out to produce the bars from which the nails were made. The cone-shaped nail heads were interesting for they had been hammered and repeatedly reheated from the same piece of metal as the shank, rather than been applied to the shank.

The smiths making the nails appear to have been aware that they were using both iron and steel because after forging the nails were left to cool slowly. No quenched structures were found in any example, and these would have been avoided presumably because quenching makes steel brittle and inflexible. The varying characteristics of the metal from which the nails were made unfortunately provides no clue to where the nails were manufactured.

Appendix 3   Romano-Celtic ship caulking

by David F Cutler, Royal Botanic Gardens, Kew

All of the caulking material seen in the sample provided is of hazel, *Corylus avellana*. The characteristic short, scalariform perforation plates and relatively coarse vessel wall pitting are shown in Fig 161, taken with a scanning electron microscope, from nail-head caulking in the Blackfriars ship. Features of the rays and the short radial chains of vessel elements seen in transverse section helped to confirm the identification. There is a considerable proportion of bark associated with the wood, particularly in that from between planks.

Blackfriars ship 1

Nail caulking

The material appeared to be from strands prepared by splitting twigs or small branches longitudinally. Individual strands are c 2–5mm in section. The bulk of the material is wood, with a little bark. The strands were wound round the shank of the nails, and compacted into the concavity of the nail-heads. This appears to have produced a washer-like seal when the nails were driven in.

Plank caulking

The material consists of bark fragments with a small proportion of the outer growth rings of the wood from just inside the bark; individual fragments are between

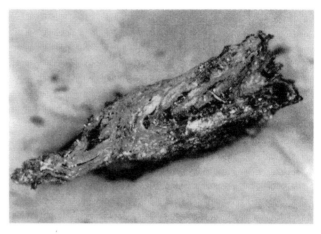

Fig 162   Close-up end view of contorted hazel caulking

2–4mm thick, with the longest axis at 25mm, and the widest about 10mm. They have irregular outlines, and may represent the size of the fragments originally used, or could have broken into smaller pieces when they were detached for examination; they are strongly compressed.

In one sample fractured at 90 degrees to the long axis (which corresponds to the long axis of the branch or trunk from which it was prepared) the structure appears contorted (Fig 162), suggesting that a wider strip or strips had been folded several times to build up thickness.

The individual fragments showed little or no distortion along their long axis. This suggests that they were

Fig 163   View of hazel wood shavings applied to the edge of a plank in the New Guy's House boat.

not forced into the joints between the plank edges. Hazel bark is very pliable when fresh, and would be expected to distort if forced into a narrow space. The caulking could have been applied to the edge of a plank before the adjacent plank was offered to it. The edges of the planks could have been butted tightly together and then secured to make the joint.

The New Guy's House boat

The caulking method appears to be similar to that for the Blackfriars ship. Portions of the caulking were found adhering to the inboard edge of the plank specimen examined. Most are aligned at 5–15 degrees from the perpendicular to the plank surface but some are inclined at up to 45°. Some portions overlie others, at different angles, frequently crossing (Fig 163). There is little sign of axial distortion, and the pieces could have been applied to the edge of the plank as described above.

Appendix 4 Analysis of resin
by John Evans, University of East London

Two dried fragments of wood caulking from between the planks of Blackfriars ship 1 were submitted for analysis, together with the cone-shaped head of a nail in which there were traces of further caulking. In none of these was there any obvious evidence of resin that could bind the caulking together. Also pieces of planking from the New Guy's House boat and the County Hall ship were submitted upon which there was a brown deposit on the outboard face which might have been tar.

Initially the samples were subjected to infra-red spectroscopy followed by both thin-layer and gas chromatography, in order to establish their chemical identities. Next the samples were investigated by X-ray fluorescence spectroscopy to identify the suite of elements present. This information served a two-fold purpose. It would establish the use of additives such as lime or clay, and it would detect the use of mineral bitumens that tend to have a characteristic metal presence. Finally, the samples were examined by differential scanning calorimetry to determine their melting/softening temperatures and the possible presence of secondary organic additives.

The data obtained showed that all of the samples had traces of resin of a very similar nature (Fig 164). None involved the use of mineral additives or bituminous materials and all were of a wood origin, soft wood tars derived from the *Pinus* species. All showed the presence of abeitic acid and palustric/isopimaric acid as well as the expected dehydroabeitic acid. In all cases the latter substance was the major component. However, the presence of the former substances suggests the use of a relatively low-heated resin. Possibly the resin was mixed with a wood tar to make the latter thinner and therefore more easy to work. Alternatively a relatively low-heated resin was used directly.

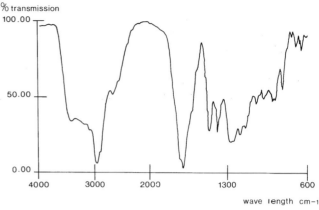

A. Blackfriars nail caulking

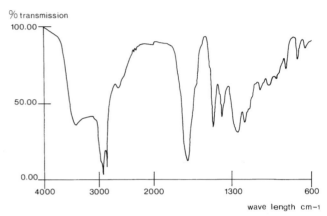

B. Pine resin

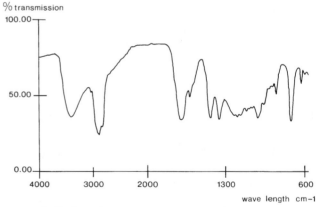

C. Birch resin

Fig 164 (A) Gas chromatograph analysis of the resin in the nail head caulking from Blackfrairs ship 1. It shows a similar chemical identity to pine resin (B) and is different from other tree resins, such as birch (C).

191

Appendix 5   Theoretical stability of Blackfriars ship 1

by Peter Marsden

Weight distribution in the ship

Before considering the theoretical stability and perform-ance of Blackfriars ship 1 it is necessary to reconstruct both the overall weight of the ship and the distribution of the weight. This is done by calculating the weight of an average square metre of the hull surface so that the computer program Boatcad can multiply this by the total area of the hull. As an average square metre of the bottom of the hull below strake 5 was heavier than an average square metre of the sides, the extra weight was found by calculating the 'actual weight' per square metre of the bottom below strake 5 and subtracting from this the 'average weight' per square metre of the side of the hull. The difference was then treated as 'ballast' in the sub-sequent computer calculations. For establishing the weight of the hull the specific density of oak was taken to be 800kg/cubic metres (McGrail 1987, 20).

Actual weight of the hull below strake 6

Floor-timbers 1–26 were measured and estimated to contain 5.711 cubic metres of oak. To obtain their weight this was multiplied by 800 to give a total weight of 4568 kg. Similarly the outer hull planking up to strake 5 was found by the computer program to have a 'wetted surface' of 64.7 square metres. This was multiplied by 0.05m, its average thickness, and then by 800 to obtain the total weight of 2588 kg. The inboard ceiling, the stempost, and the sternpost were estimated to have about 50% of the outer hull surface area, ie 32 square metres, and this was multiplied by the ceiling thickness of 0.025m and also by 800 to give the weight of 640 kg. The total weight of nails holding the planks to the floor-timbers was estimated at 350 kg, or 5.4 kg per square metres This gave a total 'actual' weight of 4568 + 2588 + 640 + 350 = 8146 kg for the lower hull, and by dividing this by its 64.7 square metres surface area the density of one square metre was 125.9 kg.

Weight of the sides above strake 5

It was necessary to find the average weight of one square metre of the upper hull, and for this a typical area of one square metre of the collapsed side was taken.

Two side frames each measuring 0.203 x 0.110 x 1m, and each having a volume of 0.022 cubic metres, crossed the square metre. Multiplied by 2 this gave 0.045 cubic metres, and multiplied by 800 this gave a total weight of 36kg for the frames.

The planking measured 1 x 1 x 0.05m, giving a total of 0.05 cubic metres. Multiplied by 800 this gave a weight of 40kg per square metres of hull area. There were on average fifteen nails per square metres of the collapsed side, giving a weight of about 5.1 kg per square metres in the upper hull. The ceiling was estimated to have 50% of the hull planking area, and was 0.025m thick, giving 1 x 1 x 0.025m x 800 = 20kg. Thus the average weight of one square metre of the upper hull was 36 + 40 + 5.1 + 20 = 101.1 kg.

The ballast weight

These calculations show that up to and including strake 5 there was a difference between the actual hull bottom weight (8146 kg) and the weight for the same area based upon 101.1 kg per square metres (6541 kg). This dif-ference of 1.605 tonnes was treated as ballast for the purpose of the calculations, and enabled the standard density of the entire hull to be fixed at 101.1 kg per square metres (ie that of the upper hull).

Weight of the superstructure

An estimate was needed of the weight of elements that probably existed above deck level. The volume of oak comprising the mast and yard, as already described, was calculated to weigh about 3.8 tonnes. The sail and rigging were estimated at about 0.700 tonnes, thereby giving a total weight of about 4.5 tonnes.

Weight of the fittings

In order to compare the stability of the Blackfriars ship as reconstructed with various cargoes an estimate of the weight of the ship's fittings, equipment, and the crew has been added to that of the vessel. Although no evidence for the ship's fittings etc was found it is necessary to speculate on their nature so as to arrive at a minimum total weight for the ship without its cargo. The ship is likely to have had two anchors (*c* 0.5 tonne), a ship's boat (*c* 0.5 tonne), a crew of three men (*c* 0.18 tonne), their possessions and provisions of food and fresh water (*c* 1 tonne), and tools and spare rope, tackle, and sail (*c* 1 tonne). This gives a total of about 3 tonnes.

> Weight of the ship: 29.7 tonnes
> Crew and fittings : 3.0 tonnes
> Total : 32.7 tonnes (Role B in Table 17)
> Any additional weight would be cargo.

Stability

A measure of the stability of a ship is its ability to right itself when heeled (Hind 1982; Taylor 1984; Kemp and Young 1987; McGrail 1987, 12–22). This righting lever is proportional to the transverse metacentric height (or

GMt), which is the distance between the Centre of Gravity (G) and the transverse Metacentre (Mt) (Fig 79). For a ship to be stable the righting moment must be positive, that is M must always be above G. However, a large metacentric height can make an uncomfortably stiff vessel that pulls itself upright too quickly, but a small one makes the vessel tender with a possibly dangerously weak righting moment (McGrail 1987, 15). It is difficult to judge what was an ideal metacentric height in an ancient ship, but nowadays in sailing ships a large GMt separation is needed to counteract the heeling force on the sail, while in large modern powered ships it is considered desirable that it should not exceed about 3–4% of a ship's beam (Kemp and Young 1971, 65). Much more study is needed of the theoretical stability of ancient ships before it is possible to generalise, and ideally such vessels should be tested with full-size working reconstructions. Consequently it is important to recognise that although the computer answers given below are theoretically correct for the ship as reconstructed, how far they can be applied to the actual ship will depend upon the accuracy of the reconstruction.

An initial test of the validity of a reconstruction is whether or not the vessel would have been stable when launched in its 'lightship' or empty hull state, but with its mast, sail and rigging in place (Table 17, Role A). The Boatcad program shows that with no cargo the vessel would have a displacement of 29.7 tonnes and a draught of 0.71m, and that the ship would have had excellent initial stability (GMt = 0.77m) when launched.

Throughout most of its working life the ship was no doubt loaded with cargoes, equipment, stores, and crew, and it is essential to establish both its normal working draught and its stability. There are three alternative methods of examining the load and stability of the ship, by various waterlines, by the strength of the righting moment on the hull, and by designated loads.

Waterlines and righting moment

There are several clues to what the draught of Blackfriars ship 1 originally was. The *Teredo* borings in the hull at 1.22m above the bottom suggest a waterline at about 1.3m or higher (Table 17, Role G). A medieval Icelandic law states that the minimum freeboard of a cargo ship should be 2/5 the depth of the hull near amidships (McGrail 1987, 13), which would give the Blackfriars ship as reconstructed a draught of 1.71m (Table 17, Role I). The Boatcad assessment of the heeled righting moment of the hull (Table 17, Role H), as reconstructed,

Table 17   Theoretical performance of Blackfriars ship 1

role	state	load (t)	disp (cu m)	draught (m)	fbd (m)	GMt (m)	dr/D	GMt/Bm
A	light	0.0	29.7	0.71	2.14	0.77	25%	13%
B	fitted	3.0	32.7	0.77	2.09	0.76	27%	12%
C	wine	18.3	48.0	1.02	1.84	0.99	36%	16%
D	grain	21.3	51.0	1.07	1.79	1.01	37%	16%
E	rag	39.4	69.1	1.34	1.52	1.14	46%	18%
F	26 ton	29.0	58.7	1.18	1.68	1.11	41%	18%
G	1.3mWL	37.2	66.7	1.30	1.56	0.77	45%	12%
H	momt	61.0	90.5	1.63	1.23	0.81	57%	13%
I	2/5Fbd	66.7	96.4	1.71	1.15	0.82	59%	13%

Role A is a 'lightship' condition
Role B is the ship fitted out with the ship's equipment, the crew and their possessions
Role C is 12 barrels of wine filling the hold
Role D is 18.36 tonnes of grain filling the hold
Role E is 34 tonnes of ragstone filling the hold
Role F is 26 tonnes of ragstone found in the hold
Role G is a draught of 1.3m suggested by the Teredo *borings in the hull*
Role H is just below the point of maximum righting moments
Role I is a freeboard at 2/5 the midships hull depth

disp   displacement
d   hull depth amidships
bm   beam
fbd   freeboard
dr   draught
GMt   distance between the Centre of Gravity of the ship and the Metacentre.

The ship is calculated to weigh 29.7 tonnes without load (cargo etc). Except in C, D, E, and H (where the load is mainly situated in the hold amidships) the load is considered to be evenly distributed in the vessel.

reaches its peak at a draught of about 1.63m (Fig 165). Above and below that, the ability of the ship to right itself when heeled diminishes. A waterline below this peak, at about 1.5m, would be particularly desirable so that the vessel could safely recover from transient additional buoyancy forces on the hull caused by rough seas.

Load

A further clue to the waterline is the weight of the cargoes carried by the ship as reconstructed, for this would increase the draught from the 'lightship' waterline. Since the size and position of the hold are known, the Boatcad program makes it possible to isolate the hold in this reconstruction and to establish that the volume of Blackfriars ship 1 was about 28 cubic metres. It is then possible to estimate the quantity of cargo that in practice could fill the hold by using stowage factors which take into account the volume and weight of the cargo, as well as the interstices between the containers and space lost to the containers and to dunnage (McGrail 1989, 356). Stowage factors are a practical rule-of-thumb developed by ship masters for assessing how much cargo can be used to fill a hold. On this basis it is estimated that the hold could contain a cargo of 12 barrels of wine weighing a total of 15.33 tonnes (Table 17, Role C), or 27 one cubic metres sacks of grain weighing 18.36 tonnes (Table 17, Role D), or 28 cubic metres of ragstone weighing 36.4 tonnes (Table 17, Role E). However, when found the ship was not carrying the cargoes described above, but instead a consignment of building stone estimated to weigh about 26 tonnes (Table 17, Role F).

Although this is only a rough estimate these calculations show that a tonne of weight at a waterline of 1.3m only alters the waterline by about 14mm, and that for there to be significant changes the hull and cargo weights must be substantially greater. Since the length and beam

Table 18 Total weight of Blackfriars ship 1

hull and deck	23.6 tonnes
'ballast' of frames	1.6 tonnes
superstructure	4.5 tonnes
crew and supplies	3.0 tonnes
total	32.7 tonnes

of the ship are approximately known such changes can only be at the expense of reconstructing the ship with higher sides. But as it seems that the depth of water in front of the second-century quays was generally less than 1m it is most unlikely that the ship had a greater draught.

Stability with various cargoes

Total weight of the ship

With these calculations, and by using Boatcad, the weight of the ship as reconstructed, excluding cargo, is estimated to have been as shown in Table 18.

A graph showing the height of the transverse Metacentres above the keel at various displacements is shown in Fig 166, and draught relative to displacement in Fig 167.

Barrels of wine

One type of cargo that the ship might have carried was wine in barrels. One barrel, found reused in a well of the late first century AD, was 1.83m high, with a maximum diameter of 0.96m. It is calculated as weighing 1.278 tonnes when full (p 22). Barrels of wine have a stowage factor of 1.78 (McGrail 1989, 356). In order to discover how many barrels would fit into the hold it is necessary to multiply 1.278 by 1.78 which gives a total of 2.27 cubic metres volume to be occupied by one barrel for stowage.

This total is divided into the volume of the hold (28 divided by 2.27 gives 12.33), showing that the hold would take 12 barrels. Their total weight would be 15.33 tonnes (1.278 x 12). Allowing for the weight of the ship and crew (32.7 tonnes) plus this weight of cargo (15.33 tonnes) this gives the vessel a total weight/displacement of 48 tonnes. Boatcad calculates that this would give a waterline of 1.02m.

The transverse metacentric height of the ship with this cargo was calculated using Boatcad as follows:
- (1) The centre of gravity (CoG) of the ship (2.48m) multiplied by the weight of the ship (32.7) gives 81.10
- (2) The CoG of the cargo (0.84) multiplied by the cargo weight (15.33) gives 12.88
- (3) Add (1) and (2) together, which gives 93.98
- (4) Divide (3) by the the weight of ship (32.7) and cargo (15.33), giving 93.98, and then divide this by 48.03, giving 1.96. The CoG of ship and cargo is 1.96m

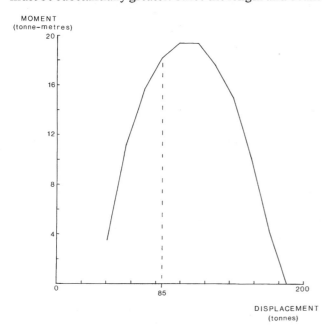

MOMENT
(tonne–metres)

Fig 165   Graph of righting moments, Boatcad.

- (5) Find the height of the Metacentre (KMt) on a graph (Fig 166) at a displacement of 48 tonnes, which equals 2.95m
- (6) The metacentric height (GMt) is 2.95 minus 1.96, giving 0.99m

Sacks of grain

Since sacks of grain were probably a common cargo in ships it is appropriate to examine the vessel on this basis. They have a stowage factor of 1.50 (McGrail 1989, 356). In order to establish how many cubic metre sacks of grain would fit into the hold the weight of one sack (0.68 tonnes) is multiplied by the stowage factor (1.5), giving 1.02. This total is divided into the hold volume (28 cubic metres) giving 27.45 (ie 27 sacks). 27 sacks of grain weigh 27 multiplied by 0.68, giving 18.36 tonnes.

The weight of the fitted ship (32.7 tonnes) plus the weight of this cargo (18.36 tonnes) give a total weight/displacement of 51.06 tonnes. Boatcad calculates that this will give a waterline of 1.07m.

The transverse metacentric height of the ship with this cargo is calculated as follows:
- (1) The CoG of ship (2.48) multiplied by the weight of the ship (32.7) gives 81.10
- (2) The CoG of cargo (0.84) mulitplied by the cargo weight (18.36) gives 15.42
- (3) Add (1) and (2), giving 96.52
- (4) Divide (3) by the weight of the ship (32.7), plus the cargo weight (18.36), which gives 99.46. Divide this by 51.06, giving 1.89, the CoG of ship and cargo
- (5) Find the height of the metacentre (KMt) on the graph (Fig 167) at a displacement of 51.06, giving 2.9
- (6) The metacentric height (GMt) is 2.9 minis 1.89, giving a height of 1.01m

Loose ragstone

For a full hold of ragstone it would be necessary to carry 28 cubic metres, which would weigh 36.4 tonnes, since one cubic metre of ragstone weighs 1.3 tonnes. The weight of the ship (32.7 tonnes) plus the weight of the cargo (36.4 tonnes) would give a total weight/displacement of 69.1 tonnes. Boatcad calculates that this would give a waterline of 1.34m.

The transverse metacentric height of the ship with this cargo is calculated as follows:
- (1) The CoG of ship (2.48) multiplied by the weight of the ship (32.7) gives 81.10
- (2) The CoG of cargo (0.84) multiplied by the cargo weight (36.4) gives 30.57
- (3) Add (1) and (2) to give 111.67
- (4) Divide (3) by the weight of the ship (32.7) plus the cargo weight (36.4) to give 114.61, then divide by 69.1 to give 1.62m, the CoG of ship and cargo
- (5) Find the height of the metacentre (KMt) on the graph (Fig 166) at a displacement of 69.1 which is 2.76
- (6) The metacentric height (GMt) is 2.76 minus 1.62, giving 1.14m

Stability of a ship with cargo partly filling the hold

26 tonnes of stone

This is established by dividing the total weight of the cargo by the weight per cubic metre of the cargo to give the number of cubic metres (ie 26 divided by 1.30 gives 20 cubic metres). The weight of the ship (32.7 tonnes) and cargo (26 tonnes) give a total weight/displacement of 58.7 tonnes. Boatcad calculates that this would give a waterline of 1.186m.

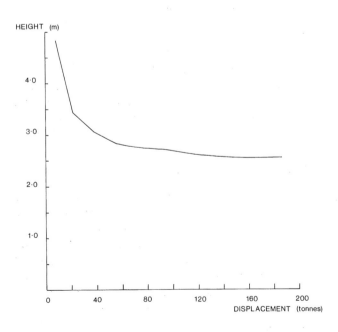

Fig 166   Height of transverse metacentres, Boatcad.

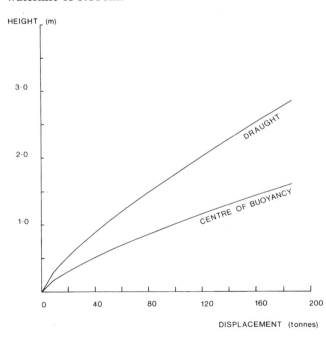

Fig 167   Draught and the Centre of Buoyancy related to Displacement, Boatcad.

Table 19   The deadweight coefficient of Blackfriars ship 1

role		dwt	divided by	disp (tonne)	=	dwt coeff
A	(empty)	0		29.7		0
B	(fitted)	3.0		32.7		0.09
C	(wine)	18.33		51.03		0.36
D	(grain)	21.6		51.06		0.42
E	(full rag)	39.4		69.1		0.57
F	(26 tonnes)	29.0		58.7		0.49
G	(1.3m WL/*Teredo*)	36.8		66.5		0.55
H	(Rt Mom 1.5m)	5 9		80.6		0.63
I	(2/5 Fbd 1.15m)	6t.		96.0		0.69

It is necessary to use a separate computer graph which plots buoyancy relative to draught and displacement in the hold, by pretending that the hold is filled with water. This shows that the centre of gravity (buoyancy) relative to cargo level (draught) and volume (displacement) in the hold, at a volume (displacement) of 20 cubic metres has a CoG (buoyancy) at 0.92m. This is the CoG of the stone in the hold. Next, these calculations for the metacentric height are made:

- (1) The CoG of the ship (2.48) multiplied by the weight of the ship (32.7) gives 81.10
- (2) The CoG of the cargo (0.92) multiplied by the cargo weight (26) gives 23.92
- (3) Add (1) and (2) together to give 105.02
- (4) Divide (3) by the weight of the ship (32.7) plus the cargo weight (26) to give 105.02, and then divide by 58.7 to give 1.82, the CoG of ship and cargo
- (5) Find the height of the metacentre (KMt) on the graph (Fig 166) at a displacement of 58.7, which gives 2.93
- (6) The metacentric height (GMt) is 2.93 minus 1.82, giving 1.11m

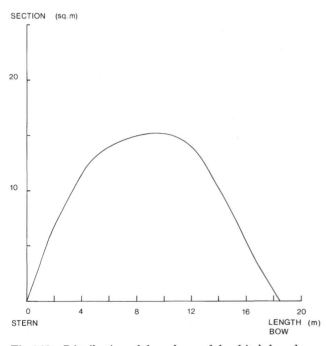

Fig 168   Distribution of the volume of the ship below the gunwale as reconstructed, Boatcad.

Cargo capacity

Deadweight coefficient (McGrail 1987, 198–9)

This is based upon the weight of the crew, equipment, cargo, and victuals, but not the ship (Table 19). This may be used for comparison with other ship reconstructions (McGrail 1987, table 11.4), but as the assessment of the weights of crew etc is most uncertain in the case of Blackfriars ship 1 there is considerable doubt about the usefulness of these deadweight coefficients in this particular instance, except perhaps in the most general terms.

Hold index (McGrail 1987, 201, table 11.6)

Since the approximate size of the hold of the Blackfriars ship has been calculated it is possible to give a rough indication of the relative importance of cargo-carrying in this ship by dividing the length of the hold by the overall length of the ship:

- L hold divided by L ship
- 5.8m divided by 18.5m = 0.31 hold index.

Distribution of hull volume

The distribution of volume in the hull between the lowest parts of the ship (ie the stempost, keel, and sternpost) and the gunwale is probably a reflection of the purpose of the ship, since much of the hull is intended to carry a cargo. This volume is calculated by Boatcad (Fig 168).

Speed

The underwater body of a ship will set up waves as the vessel moves forward, and beyond a certain speed the resistance from these greatly increases as the stern sinks into the trough behind the bow wave (Fig 169). Beyond that point more propulsive force is required per knot of speed than is needed at slower speeds for the ship has not only to push through the water resistance but also has to climb the bow wave. A rule for calculating maximum theoretical speed is given by McGrail (1987, 196–7). The Boatcad graph (Fig 170) shows that at a

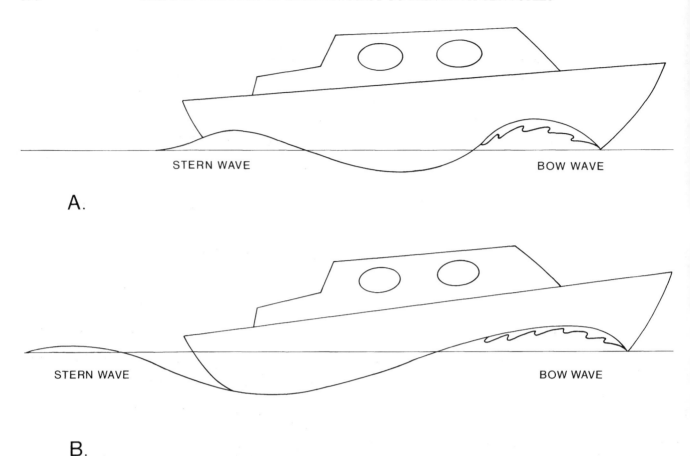

A.

B.

Fig 169   One wave speed. At a slow speed (A) the wave resistance is small, but at a fast speed (B) the stern sinks into the trough behind the bow wave and the vessel has to increase its propulsion power to climb the bow wave. Consequently the wave resistance has increased. This is shown in graph form for Blackfriars ship 1 in Fig 170.

draught of 1.3m this point occurs at about 7 knots, and that at 9 knots there is a second point beyond which considerably more force is required. These are therefore likely to reflect the maximum theoretical speed of the ship, as reconstructed, but to achieve this the vessel would need to have an appropriate sail and sailing conditions, as well as good handling by the master.

Speed is also indicated on the basis of coefficients (see Table 20) which may be compared with other ancient

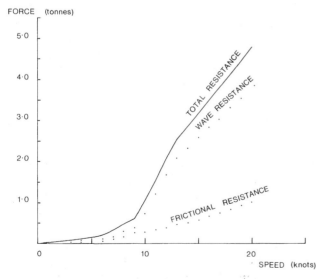

Fig 170   Total wave resistance to Blackfriars ship 1, Boatcad.

ships (McGrail 1987, 196–198). Comparison with other early northern European ships and boats shows that the Blackfriars ship was rather slow. It was potentially faster than Ferriby boat 1 and Brigg boat 2, though these were probably not sailing vessels. It was probably a slower speed design than the following vessels: Hjortspring, Sutton Hoo 2, Gokstad 1 and 3, Skuldelev 1 and 3, and the Graveney boat (McGrail 1987, 198). These potentially faster vessels are all of the Scandinavian clinker shipbuilding tradition which appear to have been designed for greater speed, whereas Blackfriars ship 1 was apparently designed to carry considerable loads relatively slowly.

Heel angle

On the assumption that the side limber holes in the floor-timbers were intended to drain the bilge water when the ship was sailing heeled, they indicate that the ship was expected to heel to a maximum of about 12 degrees in a beam wind. On the Boatcad program it is possible to calculate the wind force needed.

On a graph of righting levers find the GZ for 12 degrees (ie 0.151m). Multiply the displacement of the ship at a draught of 1.3m (66.5 tonnes) by 0.151 to give 10 tonne-metres (as a moment on the sail). Find the approximate centre of effort of the sail above the centre of lateral resistence of the ship. CoE is estimated to be about 8m above the hull bottom (from Fig 64), and

Table 20   Speed potential coefficients at a waterline of 1.3m

slenderness	midship	block	prismatic
3.08	0.78	0.5	0.67

Boatcad calculates that the CoLR is 0.68m above the bottom. Thus the CoE is at 8 minus 0.68, giving 7.11m.

Divide the moment (10) by the CoE (7.11) to give 1.4 tonnes on the sail to heel the ship 12°. On the total resistance graph (Fig 170) read off 1.4 tonnes to find the speed of 10.4 knots.

Alternatively, should the ship travel at the maximum one-wave speed of 10.1 knots calculated by Boatcad, it is possible to calculate how much the ship would heel with a side wind. On the total resistance graph (Fig 170) the speed of 10.1 knots requires a force of 1.1 tonnes. Multiply the CoE (7.11) by 1.06 tonnes to give 7.5 tonne-metres. Divide this by the displacement (7.5 div. by 66.5 to give 0.11). Find 0.11m on a righting levers graph to give the heeling angle of about 8°. This shows that it would in theory be difficult to heel the ship, and that the vessel would be very stable. How this would happen in practice cannot be calculated, though the side limber holes suggest that the ship could heel that far.

Speed assessment coefficients

Slenderness

Length divided by breadth gives 18.5, divided by 6 to give 3.08.

At a waterline of 1.3m. the following coefficients apply (Table 17, Role F):

Midship

- A divided by (B multiplied by T)
- 5.7 divided by (5.62 multiplied by 1.3)
- 5.7 divided by 7.3 to give 0.78

Block

- Displacement volume divided by (B multiplied by L multiplied by T)
- 66.5 divided by (5.62 multiplied by 17.34 multiplied by 1.3)
- 66.5 divided by 126.68 to give 0.5

Prismatic

- Displacement volume divided by (A multiplied by L)
- 66.5 divided by (5.7 multiplied by 17.34)
- 66.5 divided by 98.8 to give 0.67

In the coefficients the following apply (Table 17, Role F):

- A = Area of underwater volume (midships), 5.7 square metres
- B = Breadth at waterline, 5.62m
- L= Length at waterline, 17.34m (56.89 ft)
- T = Draught, 1.3m
- Displacement volume = 66.5 cubic metres

Speed is calculated on the basis of the following (McGrail 1987, 196):

- Maximum velocity is approximately equal to the square root of the length of the waterline (in feet) multiplied by 1.4
- V max = 1.4 x square root L
- V max = 1.4 x square root 56.89ft
- V max = 1.4 x 7.54 = 10.55 knots

Appendix 6   Dendrochronology of Roman and early medieval ships

by Ian Tyers, Museum of London

This appendix provides details of the tree-ring analyses and timber identifications carried out upon the ship and boat timbers described elsewhere in this volume.

Dendrochronology, or tree-ring dating, has been routinely carried out on excavated timbers in Britain for 20 years (see Baillie 1982; Schweingruber 1988). The technique involves the precise measurement of the sequence of annual ring widths within a timber and then the matching of this pattern of wide and narrow rings to reference sequences. These reference sequences have been built up by starting with old living trees, thus fixing in time the chronology. They are then extended backwards by matching successively older ring series on to the sequence.

Requirements for tree-ring dating

A reliable tree-ring date depends upon several factors. Firstly, it is important that the timbers contain enough rings to find a reliable cross-match with another sequence: ideally a piece of timber should contain at least 50 rings. Secondly, it is helpful if a structure contains more than one usable timber since if several timbers from the same object can be dated better interpretations can be made from the results. Thirdly, reference chronologies for the period, area, and species of interest should be available for comparison. In this respect there are many oak (*Quercus* spp) sequences from northern, western, and central Europe that cover the last millenium, but rather fewer back to the Roman period. These sequences vary from region to region due to differences in local climatic conditions. As a result, had a Roman ship been found which was not constructed of British or north-western European timber it is extremely unlikely that a tree-ring date could be produced at present. It is expected that future work, for instance in the Mediterranean region, will eventually resolve such problems by establishing appropriate local sequences. Few extensive chronologies exist for other native timber species at present. The cross-matching of tree-ring sequences demands appropriate computer programs to find possible positions, as well as graphs to enable visual checking of these matches. To this end most tree-ring laboratories in Britain and Europe use similar programs and graphs, and almost all laboratories use one statistical measure to report the validity of their work. Throughout the results described below, reference will be made to 't' values. These are a measure of similarity between two tree-ring sequences at a particular relative position and are based on Baillie and Pilcher's (1973) program CROS. Significant 't' values are usually over 3.5. Visual checking of the positions found by the computers is vital since they can be wrong or measurement errors may exist in the sequences.

Reliability

The advantage of dendrochronology is its independence of other dating methods, since it is a biological system that does not rely on archaeological assumptions. Thus in the event of suitable timbers being found and dated in a rigorous fashion the tree-ring date produced can be assumed to be correct. The problems that occur which may reduce the reliability of a tree-ring date are few, but they are important to note to avoid misunderstandings. Firstly, there may be errors in the tree-ring chronologies used to date an object. For the periods and the species with which we are concerned here, Roman and early medieval oak, errors are unlikely. This is because there are many independent sequences from different parts of Ireland, from south, central, and northern England, Belgium, north and south Germany, and Switzerland that can be shown to be synchronous throughout this period (Sheldon and Tyers 1983; Pilcher *et al* 1984). As long as techniques are adopted which rely upon significant correlation values for a new sequence against three or more independent chronologies, then reliability will be maintained. Another issue that has to be addressed is one of some consistent error existing between tree-ring 'years' and the true calendrical scale, that could lead to a Roman tree-ring date being inaccurate by a year or even a decade or more. In this instance the widespread independent yet synchronous sequences from across Europe enable us to be confident that this error is not present.

The more important difficulties to be faced come in converting a tree-ring date into useful archaeological information. Here we cease to be involved in hard facts and have to rely instead upon observation and interpretation. Tree-ring dates that are 'wrong' will result from problems as diverse as unrecognised repairs or from the use of second-hand timber for a construction. Here the first instance gives a date later than the true construction date whilst the other gives an earlier date. Other problems will arise where a timber is assumed to be associated with a structure but in fact is not, and when samples are muddled by mis-labelling. Most of these problems can be minimised by adequate observation and tight procedures for both sampling on site and analysis in the laboratory.

Types of information provided

Tree-ring analysis of boat timbers may be expected to provide information of five different types. Firstly, it gives a date for or after which the tree was cut down, and therefore potentially the date of construction (see sapwood discussion below). Secondly, if it dates, it may provide some indication of the source area of the timbers; since boats are intended to travel from their source this may be important. Thirdly, it may indicate if some timbers are derived from the same tree, which, in combination with structural analyses, may provide information about the techniques employed to manufacture the vessel. Fourthly, it may indicate the ages of the trees used in shipbuilding, and therefore may indicate the availability of certain types of timbers as well as the choices of timbers made by the shipbuilders. Lastly, it may be possible to identify the useful lifespan of the vessels reported here. This is only considered feasible where they are subsequently re-used in another tree-ring dated structure, and in the sections below observations of this nature are confined to the medieval fragments found in waterfronts.

The wood

Sapwood

In the analyses reported below the boats have been dated by multiple samples having been measured and cross-matched with each other and a mean ring series created from them. These series were then exhaustively checked against a number of reference sequences to attempt to date each boat series. Where this has been achieved the end-date of the sequence is not the date of the boat for in all cases reported here the oak timbers do not retain all the outermost (ie most recent) rings of the original tree, the sapwood. These rings are usually readily recognisable on timbers and were frequently removed during the construction of wooden structures because sapwood is significantly less resilient than heartwood. In other cases these rings may have been lost due to one or more of the following reasons; abrasion during the use of the boat, or during its excavation, or rotting away during the time the boat was in use, buried, or stored. Additional years thus have to be added to the date of the last surviving ring to allow for the missing rings. If some sapwood survives a range of possible dates can be calculated; if no sapwood survives only a *terminus post quem* can be produced. The sapwood estimate used here is a range of 10–55 rings, used as 95% confidence limits (Hillam *et al* 1987).

Source of timbers

The specific instance of attempting to locate the original source of timbers used for a vessel reported here is dealt with below. However, it should be mentioned that the degree of cross-match between two trees that were growing next to each other, all other things being similar, is expected to be higher than that between two trees that were growing some distance apart. This can be checked using modern trees from around Britain and Europe. These empirical observations allow models of tree growth and tree-ring cross-matching behaviour to be built that show that a tree's growth pattern over time combines regional climatic information and a variable amount of background 'noise', presumed to be influences from local site conditions. Using this observable

behaviour it is theoretically possible to locate the original geographical source of timbers on the basis of the pattern of their correlation values to a grid of tree-ring chronologies. Difficulties arise for archaeological material since the grid of reference sequences we have built for the Roman and early medieval periods is not as geographically extensive as those for modern data sets and, of course, relies on assumptions that the timbers were grown relatively close to the site on which they were found. There is therefore a lack of precision built into any interpretations of the locality in these periods and they have to be confined to statements like 'local to' an area, or from 'southern England', or from 'northern Germany'. It is usually possible to say where timbers do not originate from rather more precisely than it is possible to say where they do come from. Hence in the analyses reported below where the term 'local to London' is used, this phrase may be taken to exclude areas such as Ireland, Scotland, Wales, Northern England, and Germany. It is likely to include all the areas that were probably exploited for timber in the Thames basin, the Wealden and Essex forests for example. Unfortunately the inability to be more precise, at present, leads to the probable inclusion of all areas within 100km of London, and possibly includes areas further away.

'Same tree' identifications

The identification of timbers originally derived from the same tree is based on high correlations (t values over *c*10) backed up by similar medium-term growth trends in the series. These qualified identifications may assist in estimates of the number of trees consumed in the building of different vessels, though the data has to be used with care since it is unfortunately not usually possible to say that timbers are from different trees. This is because some trees growing in stressed or unusual situations exhibit very different growth trends on opposite sides of the tree and could not, on the criteria used, be recognised as 'same tree' in origin.

Fresh or seasoned?

The use of freshly felled timber for the construction of vessels and most other archaeological structures is usually assumed, though it is difficult to be certain. It is usually accepted that freshly felled timber is considerably easier to work with hand tools, although the timbers themselves are heavier. However, if seasoned timber was used a mixture of felling dates within a single structure would be expected, all earlier than the true construction date.

Methods used

Sampling

The samples consist of 30–50mm sections cut across the grain of a timber in such a way as to maximise the number of rings, or to include any surviving sapwood.

The samples were cut with an electric rotary saw by Peter Marsden and Caroline Caldwell where they felt it would be most appropriate after initial discussion of tree-ring requirements with the author. They were not necessarily considered representative of the entire construction. Samples were also taken after due consideration of any possible repairs. They were bagged and labelled and submitted for tree-ring analysis in groups from individual boats. In addition each vessel usually had several other small wood samples taken for identification only. These included pegs, trenails, or wedges, and some otherwise unsampled planks.

Identification

The first step in the laboratory was to identify the wood type of the sample. The identification of the pegs etc was carried out by making microscope slides of radial, tangential, and longitudinal sections and comparing them with reference slides and appropriate wood identification keys (Schweingruber 1982; Wilson and White 1986) using high magnification microscopes.

For the tree-ring samples examination using a low magnification binocular microscope was usually sufficient to distinguish the wood type concerned. If not the methodology outlined above for the pegs was adopted. The primary hardwood species (oak, ash, elm, and beech) are easily distinguished in this quick fashion and in this case all the tree-ring samples reported below are of oak (*Quercus* spp).

Sample preparation

Prior to tree-ring measurement the samples were cleaned so that the entire tree-ring sequence was clearly visible. It is necessary to distinguish clearly where each ring begins and ends along a radius or series of connected sub-radii. The samples reported below fall neatly into two groups of material in that each had to be processed somewhat differently.

The first group consisted of the three Roman vessels (Blackfriars ship I, the New Guys House boat, and the County Hall ship), which were the three groups of samples originally excavated longest ago (1962, 1958 and 1910 respectively). All of their timbers had air- dried decades ago. These are, as far as the author is aware, the first group of dried timbers of archaeological origin (as opposed to bog-oaks) that have been analysed for tree-ring dating. They had dried very hard and the central dense part of each section when initially cut had resulted in a very shiny surface, in which it was impossible to see the ring boundaries. The outer parts of most of the samples were friable and prone to breakage when handled. It was necessary to cut small fragments off the surfaces using scalpel blades and double-edged razor-blades flexed to form a curved cutting edge. Extensively brushing with stiff or soft toothbrushes and occasionally dabbing the surface with a wet paint-brush helped to emphasise the rings sufficiently for successful measurement. During measurement itself the high surface reflectivity had to be circumvented by using fibre-optic lamps pointing at right angles to the cut surfaces. Clearly shrinkage of these timbers probably occurred during the drying and the dimensions and average ring-widths do not truly reflect the original timbers. The tree-ring dating is unaffected by this since it works by using relative changes in ring-widths, not their actual size. It is pleasing to note that these dry samples have worked as effectively as the more typical recently excavated wet samples, and this raises the possibility that the investigation of other dry material held in museums around the country, for instance the many logboats in small provincial museums (such as those catalogued in McGrail 1978), may well be worthwhile.

The second group of material reported here was in a wet state having been excavated relatively recently from deposits below the water-table. These samples were frozen in ordinary domestic freezers. The surfaces were then smoothed using planes, surforms, and razor blades until the ring sequence was completely visible. The surfaces were cleaned by rinsing them under hot water while still frozen. They were then left to thaw out prior to measurement.

Measurement

The sequence of rings in each tree-ring sample was measured using a low-power binocular microscope and a travelling stage connected to a computer that enabled the ring-widths to be recorded automatically. Measurement was carried out to an accuracy of 0.01 mm and the resulting computer file also recorded the site and context information for the timber and a number of other details. In some cases more than one radius was measured.

Analysis

The sequence resulting from each sample was then plotted out, either by hand onto standard semi-log roll paper, or by the computer using a plotter. These enabled both visual checks of the ring-sequence matches to be made and errors in the sequences to be recognised.

When all the timber samples from each boat had been measured and plotted, cross-matching between individual timbers was carried out using computer programs and checked for validity using the graphs. Where acceptable matches were found a new 'mean' series was built by averaging the patterns at the appropriate relative positions. The timbers not in the new means were compared with the new mean and the process repeated until as many of the timbers as possible were incorporated into the working mean sequence. All the individual timbers and the working means were then compared with reference sequences of Roman and later dates from London and elsewhere in order to find significant correlations (t values over 3.5) for each of these sequences. These positions were again checked by comparing the graphs and where acceptable resulted in a tree-ring date for the individual timbers. After appropriate interpretation a date for the boat was produced.

Individual vessel details

The following sections detail the tree-ring results from the various boats reported in this volume. Additional information is lodged in the archive reports stored with the bulk of the records.

Blackfriars ship 1

Although excavated in 1962 a total of 17 samples from dried timbers were taken in 1988 for tree-ring analysis. These samples are numbered here 1 - 17 inclusive. Samples 1 - 16 are planks while 17 is part of a floor-timber. The timbers had all been air-dried in fluctuating conditions for much of the 25 years since their excavation. They had suffered damage as a result of shrinking, cracking, warping, and physical breakage caused by their fragility.

All the submitted samples were of oak (Quercus spp). Fourteen of the samples were measured, the other three samples having insufficient rings to be considered suitable. Eleven samples cross-matched with each other and/or to reference chronologies, all of which were planks. A mean chronology of 167 years was produced that dates to 49BC–AD118. Fig 171 shows the relative positions of the dated samples.

The poor condition of the timbers made it difficult to identify the heartwood/sapwood boundaries but otherwise the tree-ring analysis appears to be unaffected.

As shown in Fig 171 one of the two samples with the latest (AD118) ring, 13, has a probable heartwood/sapwood boundary at its outer edge. Sample 12 (end ring AD95) has an unmeasurable sequence of some 20–30 more rings before reaching a probable heartwood/sapwood boundary. Applying sapwood ranges and rounding to the

nearest half-decade suggests felling between AD130–175. The absence of sapwood and the difficulty of identifying heartwood/sapwood boundaries precludes tighter dating of the construction of the ship.

It should be noted that no sample had more than 100 rings present, which is relatively unusual for a Roman timber group from London. This is likely to reflect either the state of the available timber, the conversion methods adopted, or even the post-excavation mis-treatment of the ship. There is a fairly wide range of end-dates to the individual samples. There is some possibility of re-use, although only slight, particularly of samples 15 and 16 since they end much earlier than the other sequences. Only two of the submitted samples seem likely to be derived from the same tree (15 and 16). This low figure is perhaps due to the incomplete recovery and sampling of the ship. No repairs, or re-used timbers, were noted in the structural recording. The individual timbers and the mean sequence all cross-match well with other London chronologies, and there is therefore no evidence to suggest that the wood is other than local in origin.

The New Guy's House boat

This Roman boat was partly excavated in 1958 and 12 of the surviving timbers were sampled in 1991 for tree-ring measurement. All the samples were of oak (Quercus spp). They had air-dried over the previous 30 years leading to shrinkage, warping and cracking. All the samples were measured. Several 'pairs' of timbers were identified from the cross-matching. Nevertheless it was impossible to match the sequences uniquely either to each other or to reference chronologies. Thus no tree-ring date is available at present for this vessel. It is unlikely that this problem was caused by their condition.

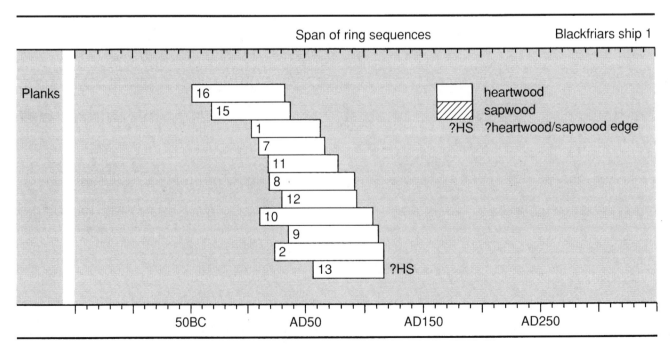

Fig 171   The relative positions of dated tree-ring samples from Blackfriars ship 1.

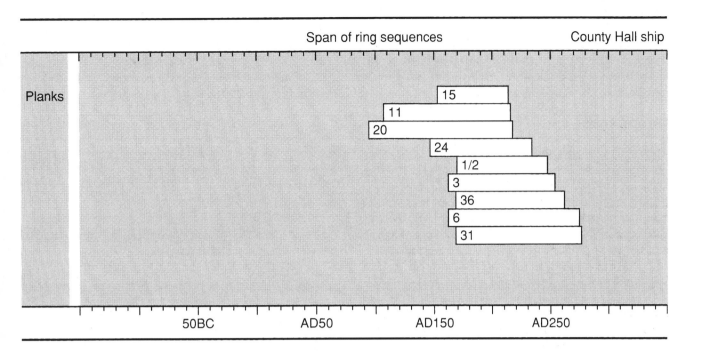

Fig 172   The relative positions of dated tree-ring samples from the County Hall ship.

The sequences were short and exhibited strong medium-term fluctuations, a pattern that is rarely datable.

The County Hall ship

The County Hall ship was discovered in 1910 and 30 of the surviving timbers were sampled between 1988 and 1991. The timbers had all dried about 80 years before the analysis was undertaken and shrinkage had occured, though this does not seem to have affected the dendrochronological analysis. All the samples were oak (*Quercus* spp), but only 12 contained enough rings for tree-ring dating to be considered. Ten of these were cross-matched with each other to form a 183 year mean sequence, the relative positions of the timbers are shown in Fig 174. This sequence is dated to AD95–277. The last ring is present on sample 31. Sample 6 ends at AD276. Other individual sequences end between AD215 and AD263. Although the end dates of the individual series do not cluster particularly well (as shown in Fig 172) there seems no reason to doubt that the craft is of a single construction date. No sapwood was identified, the minimum expected sapwood figure was added to the last ring and the result rounded to the nearest half-decade to produce a *terminus post quem* of AD285 for the construction of the vessel. Several of the samples were apparently derived from the same tree (identified pairs are; 3 and 6; 11 and 20; and 31 and 36). The timbers appear to be local in origin since they cross-match closely with other London chronologies.

The New Fresh Wharf boat

The boat timbers had been kept wet in tanks since excavation, and the entire assemblage was examined with a view to sampling for tree-ring analysis. The fragments exhibited unusual constructional features for which there are parallels from Poland. The main aims of the analysis, therefore, were to determine a likely construction date for the vessel and to isolate the area of origin of the vessel. Since other tree-ring evidence exists for the waterfronts in which the boat timbers were incorporated it was also possible to determine the maximum lifespan of the vessel.

Eight planks were selected for analysis, each of which contained reasonable ring sequences and three retained some evidence of sapwood. All the selected samples were oak (*Quercus* spp). The sequences from the eight samples were found to cross-match, the relative positions being shown in Fig 173. A 262-year mean sequence was constructed and correlations were examined between it and the main north-western European sequences. Significant correlation values were only apparent for the position AD654–AD915.

Two samples retained some sapwood (9 with 8 sapwood rings, and 13 with 5 sapwood rings), while one also retained a possible heartwood/sapwood transition (5). These three samples are those that have the latest end dates from this group, ending respectively at AD909, AD915, and AD907. Using British Isles sapwood data and assuming that a single phase is present the samples produce a combined felling range of AD920–AD955. With a tree-ring date for the boat's construction, and a tree-ring date for its re-use as a landing stage, it should be possible to provide a reasonably precise estimate of the length of time this boat was in use.

The tree-ring analysis of the Saxon embankments from this site is reported by Hillam (1992). The boat timbers were excavated from the foreshore in front of a jetty published as Period 2.2. Unfortunately none of the primary timbers from this phase are datable. The earliest primary timber dated comes from Period 2.4, providing a *terminus post quem* of AD1020. With this information and the complexity of the foreshore stratigraphy it is difficult to be confident about the life-span of the vessel, but less than 100 years seems likely.

All samples had fairly long tree-ring sequences, varying between 96 and 170 rings. All were relatively slow grown and are derived from very straight-grained trees. This reflects an intentional sample bias. All the faster grown samples and those with smaller numbers of rings were avoided for the dating exercise.

The likely origin of the boat in view of the Polish parallels was an important question. The tree-ring sequence was compared with all available chronologies of similar date in Europe in order to assess the variation in the level of cross-matching across a wide geographic area. This technique has proven viable when applied to modern chronologies of precisely known origin, though it needs to be applied with some care to excavated wood.

There are three main potential pitfalls when this technique is applied to all archaeological chronologies. They all apply to the analysis of this boat.

The chronologies available for comparison are of uneven construction with some being highly replicated whilst others are derived from only a single or a few trees. This can result in t-values that are not directly comparable since highly replicated sequences show greater correlations than less replicated sequences.

The geographic origin of each of the reference data sets has been assumed to be not very far from the place of recovery.

At certain periods there is a lack of readily available reference material for comparative purposes, and frequently what is available only overlaps some part of the chronology being checked. This again leads to results which cannot be compared.

On the basis of correlations between the boat's mean sequence and other chronologies there is little evidence to suggest anything other than a south-eastern English origin for the timber. This is because all the highest cross-matches for the boat chronology are with London chronologies. This conclusion has to be fairly tentative since at the time of writing there is no comprehensive tree-ring grid for north-western Europe for the period AD600–950.

Billingsgate boat fragments

Pegged planking

Samples 3583 and 3563 were taken from pegged boat plank fragments. Both planks were oak (*Quercus* spp). Both samples contained large numbers of rings: 3583 although measured in two parts due to a break contained 317 rings in total, and 3563 contained 186 rings. Both planks were clearly derived from the same tree (t = 9.6) and where combined formed a 317-year sequence that is dated AD642–958. Since no sapwood survived the minimum expected number of sapwood rings was added to the last date and rounded to provide a *terminus post quem* for the boat of AD970. Fig 176 gives their relative positions. The planks were recovered from an embankment (Phase W2) with a tree-ring date of AD1039–40 based on 4 samples with complete sapwood and bark (Hillam 1992). Thus it is clear from the tree-ring results that the boat was less than 70 years old when it was broken-up and used in the embankment. A local origin for the timbers is indicated by cross-matching to many other London sequences.

Riveted planking

Samples 3581a, b, and c were taken from a single piece of planking. Samples a and b were measured and com-

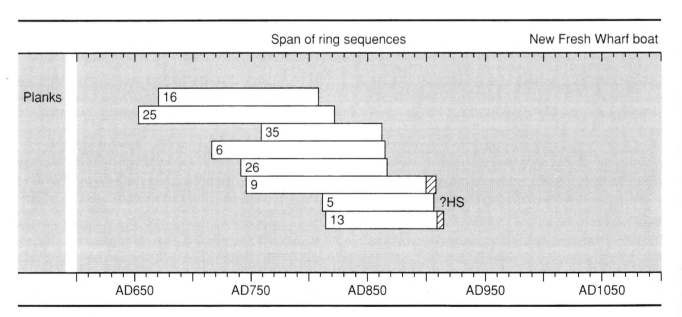

Fig 173   The relative positions of dated tree-ring samples from the New Fresh Wharf boat.

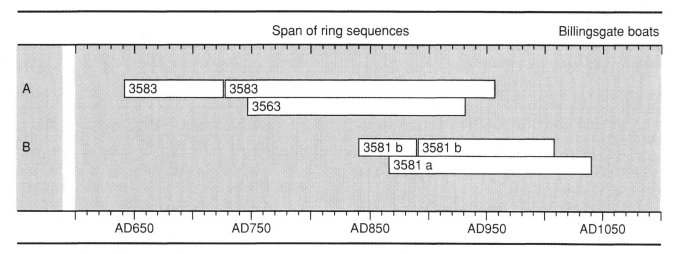

Fig 174   The relative positions of dated tree-ring samples from the Billingsgate boats.

bined to form a 201-year sequence. Sample c was ignored for measurement since it did not extend the sequence obtained from samples a and b. The sequence was dated to AD841–1041. Since no sapwood survived the minimum sapwood number was added and rounded to produce a *terminus post quem* for the boat of AD1050. Fig 174 shows the relative positions of the measured samples. This plank was excavated from cladding on a lining of the east side of an inlet (Phase W9) (Brigham pers comm). This phase is tree-ring dated to AD1108–1125 (Hillam 1992). This implies that the boat was less than 75 years old when used in this structure. A local origin for the timber is indicated.

Fennings Wharf boat fragments

Clinker planks

Nine samples from clinker planking were submitted for analysis. All the samples were oak (*Quercus* spp). Five of the samples were measured, the remaining 4 having insufficient rings to be considered suitable. Four samples were cross-matched with each other and/or to reference chronologies. Fig 175 shows the relative positions of the dated sequences. A mean chronology of 220 years was produced. This was dated to AD855–1074. No sapwood was present on any of the timbers but the sequences on all 4 planks end within 8 years. This supports the conclusion that the planks are from the same boat (see Chapter 8). Adding minimum sapwood values and rounding these produces a *terminus post quem* of AD1085. The wood appears to be local in origin.

Keel

The keel, which was of oak (*Quercus* spp), had insufficient rings for successful tree-ring analysis. However it retained part of an attached plank which was sampled and analysed. This oak plank contained 108 rings and is dated AD869–976. Adding minimum sapwood values and rounding suggests a *terminus post quem* of AD985.

Fig 175 shows the sample in its position relative to the other boat fragments from the site. It has been suggested (see Chapter 8) that the surviving width of the plank is only about half the expected total. If this is the case, and if the outer part of the tree is the missing part, then many later heartwood rings were also originally present on the plank, and this emphasises the caution required when interpreting the *terminus post quem* dates provided here. This timber appears to be local in origin on the basis of its cross-matching with other London sequences.

Wale

The wale was also sampled for tree-ring analysis. The wale is of oak (*Quercus* spp). The sample contained 108 rings that are dated AD911–1018. Fig 175 shows the sample in its position relative to the other boat fragments from the site. After allowances for sapwood a *terminus post quem* of AD1030 is indicated. It is not possible to say if this timber is contemporary with either of the other groups of boat material from the site. This timber appears to be local in origin.

Summary

In the sections above the tree-ring results from the seven or eight boats that cover 1000 years of London's existence are reported, and represent about 30% of the boat material so far studied from London. A number of points ensuing from this analysis are addressed here.

The presence of the different shipbuilding traditions represented by this material is discussed in some detail in Chapter 9. It has been shown that dry timbers can be successfully sampled and tree-ring dated, which might encourage projects to be considered on other material stored in museum collections throughout the country. All the dated samples have been demonstrated as being timber probably originating in the vicinity of London. It is impossible to be sure from the timber alone whether this is the case with the New Guys House vessel; however it is a river craft and is presumed to have been built locally

(Marsden pers comm). The recovery of mostly local ship fragments from London duplicates the pattern first found at Dublin, where all ship fragments also appeared to be of local tree-ring material (Baillie 1978). It may be that boats tended to be broken up for re-use in their 'home' ports through this period. However, a new early medieval find from Bull Wharf, London (UPT), suggests that fragments of a German boat are present in a waterfront (Goodburn, in press). The accidental sinkings also appear to be broadly 'local' boats. Of the three Roman wrecks reported here, two are definitely local. In contrast, one of the Viking ships from Roskilde, Denmark, appears to be constructed from Irish timber (Bonde and Crumlin-Pederson 1990).

The initial analyses of the ages of vessels when broken up and re-used provides the first indications from archaeological evidence of the longevity of vessels at this period. All the main timbers in these boats are derived from oak, which is fairly ubiquitous until the later medieval period. After this period vessels often exhibit systematic use of alternative woods in particular positions (Adams *et al* 1990, 108, 161). In contrast, when examining the smaller wooden parts of these vessels (see Table 21) it is apparent that there is a shift from poplar/willow type pegs with oak wedges to oak pegs with oak wedges at around AD1100. This will be described in a future report (Marsden forthcoming).

Acknowledgements

It is appropriate at this point to acknowledge the help of many colleagues at the Museum of London for assistance and useful discussion but particularly to Peter Marsden for his unceasing enthusiasm for completing the project, his sampling, and his many useful contributions to the understanding of the material. Thanks are also due to Caroline Caldwell for her assistance in the sampling, and for her delightful drawings which made my job considerably easier. I wish to acknowledge my considerable debt to James Rackham, head of the Environmental Archaeology Section, Museum of London, for his considerable efforts in resolving the problems of management of this project, significant help with the style and contents of this Appendix, and continual encouragement through to its completion.

Thanks are also due to colleagues at other tree-ring laboratories for widely exchanging data and much useful discussion: Cathy Groves and Jennifer Hillam of the Sheffield University Dendrochronology Laboratory gave useful criticism and much of the English tree-ring data, and confirmed the New Guys House results, Mike Baillie, Dave Brown, and Jon Pilcher from the Queens University, Belfast, Dendrochronology Laboratory for the Irish material and much other useful information, and to colleagues in Europe for publishing or swapping data with British dendrochronologists over the years.

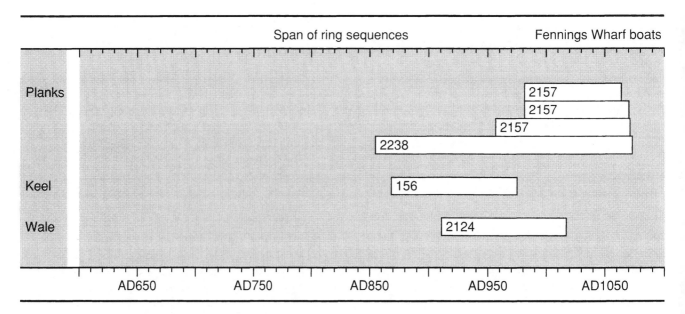

Fig 175 The relative positions of dated tree-ring samples from the Fennings Wharf boats.

Table 21 Wood identifications

site	sample	description	object	species
NFW	–	trenail		cf Salix/Populus
NFW	–	trenail	wedge	Quercus
			trenail	Salix/Populus
NFW	–	planking peg	wedge	Quercus
			peg	Salix/Populus
NFW	–	lap peg+wedge	wedge	Quercus
			peg	Salix/Populus
			plank	Quercus
NFW	7	trenail	wedge	Quercus
			trenail	Salix/Populus
NFW	15	trenail+wedge	wedge	Quercus
			trenail	Salix/Populus
NFW	30	trenail	wedge	Quercus
			peg	Salix/Populus
NFW	39	peg+wedge	wedge	Quercus
			peg	Salix/Populus
			plank	Quercus
BIG82	6697/3583	wedge+peg	wedge	Quercus
			trenail	Salix/Populus
BIG82	6873/3581	trenail		cf. Salix/Populus
FW84	2124	trenail		Salix/Populus
FW84	2256	trenail		cf. Salix/Populus

Quercus	*oak (Quercus spp)*
Salix/Populus	*willow/poplar (Salix spp/Populus spp)*
cf	*comparable to*

Appendix 7   Hair in caulking from Fennings Wharf boat fragments

by Michael L Ryder

There were four hair samples from the boat planking at Fennings Wharf excavated in 1984 (contexts 156, 2124a and b, and 2238). The hair had been preserved by waterlogging and was mostly received in a dirty, wet condition so it had to be washed and dehydrated with surgical spirit before it could be mounted for microscopic examination. Some hairs showed partial degradation (under the microscope), otherwise the material was in good condition.

Whole mount preparations in Euparal were made for microscopic examination. The international standard (IWTO) method of measuring fibre diameter was used to measure the diameter of 100 hairs in each sample. The measurements were made with a projection microscope at a magnification of 500 X.

Findings

There was one example of 'primitive' cattle (i56) and one of 'modern' cattle (2124b) (Table 22). The primitive type is distinguished by a relatively high proportion of finer hairs (Ryder 1969; 1984). Two of the four samples were wool of different fleece types – a Hairy-medium (primitive hairy) type (2124a), and a less primitive, true Hairy type (2238), which is generally too hairy for use in clothing (Ryder 1969; 1983). The fibre measurements of these samples are shown in Table 23. Sample 2124a had 37% fibres with a blue and yellow coloration of the sort seen in wool dyed green. This did not appear to be a metallic stain (eg from copper). There was no evidence of spin or weave in the material and so the fibres are unlikely to have come from rags, but could represent spinners waste that had been 'dyed-in-the-wool'.

Table 22   The hair types on eleventh-century caulking

context no	primitive ox	modern ox	sheep's wool
FW 84 156	+		
2124a			+
2124b		+	
2238			+

Discussion

It is interesting to observe that all the Roman caulking was plant material, and that most of the post-Roman caulking appears to be animal hair or wool. The caulking samples from Fennings Wharf are part of a much larger number (over 200) of samples of cattle hair caulking of later medieval and post-medieval date, and collectively are of immense importance because of the general lack of the remains of cattle hair. The cattle hair in the samples as a whole are very variable in terms of the amount of natural pigment, the proportion of hairs with a medulla (central hollow core) and the hair shaft diameter. It may be necessary to re-assess the coat types as more samples are measured.

The nature of the remains meant that it was not possible to take the standard sample from the base of the tuft. The samples therefore had at least a few finer, hair tips. These were excluded from the measurements or from the calculations, so that the mean hair diameter would not be distorted. The presence of hair tips, which indicates a coat that has not yet become worn, can have seasonal implications that indicate the season of death.

Table 23   Hair and wool fibre diameter measurements in microns

no	range	mean +/– sd	mode	medulated	pigment
'primitive' cattle					
156	16–78	32.1 +/– 13.0	28	4%	88%
'modern' cattle					
2124b	18–90	50.9 +/– 19.3	60	63%	9%
wool					
2124a	14–90 HM wool	26.7 +/– 13.8	20	9%	26%
2238	10–106 Hy wool	34.4 +/– 24.4	19	18%	4%

NB one micron = 0.001mm. The mode is the most frequent diameter.

Appendix 8   Headings for recording each fragment of ship

The site

Site context number
Age

The object

Sketch of object with dimensions and sections

Shaping the wood

How was the wood cut from the log? (ie quarter or tangential)
Timber quality (ie straight or knotty grain)
Species of timber
Any tool marks?

Construction

Boat construction (ie clinker or carvel)
Dimensions of overlapping clinker planking originally?
Caulking in (a) clinker lap, and (b) in scarf
Plank laps ('lands', and dimensions)
Plank overlap fastenings (eg rivets), sketch with dimensions
Any other caulking?
Any surface dressing (eg pitch or tar) inboard or outboard?
Spacing of plank overlap fastenings
Scarf description
Ratio of original scarf length : plank thickness

Describe any frame fastenings?
Spacing of frame fastenings
Frame shape and dimensions
Any wedged trenails?
Limber holes?
Are frames stepped (ie 'joggled') for clinker planking?

Use

Evidence of wear either during or after its use as a ship?
Damage to the ship?
Evidence of repairs to the ship?
Any borer damage (eg *Teredo* or *Limnoria*/inboard or outboard)

Interpretation

Sketch reconstruction of fragment
Spacing of frames
Evidence for hull shape?
Where in the hull was the position of the fragment?

Record

Drawn?
Photographed?
Samples taken? (ie caulking, timber, pitch/tar, wood borers)
Samples sent to specialists?
Reports received from specialists?
Disposal of timbers

Appendix 9   Glossary of nautical terms

This glossary has been compiled with reference to a number of publications: Falconer 1815; Bradford 1954; McKee 1972; Greenhill 1976; Fenwick 1978; Kemp 1979; Steffy 1982b; Christensen 1985; McGrail 1987. For some terms, such as 'carvel' there are various meanings, and it has been necessary to give the meaning intended in this study.

Beam (a) timber – transverse timbers supporting or resting on the sides of the ship; (b) measurement – the greatest breadth of a ship's hull.

Bevel The angled edge of a timber so formed as to make an angle with another.

Bilge The lowest part of the interior of a ship.

Boat A small vessel usually used in inland waters.

Bulkhead An internal cross-partition or wall in a ship.

Carvel In this study it refers to edge-to-edge planking to give a smooth-sided hull. This is the meaning given by Falconer (1815, 78), Bradford (1954, 52), and Kemp (1979, 143). However, others restrict its meaning to planking which is attached to a pre-erected skeleton of frames (Fenwick 1978, 331; Christensen 1985, 270), and McKee (1972, 26) adds that in the navy it refers to a vessel with a double skin whose inner layer lies at about 45 degrees to the keel and the other layer horizontal.

Caulking This is a wadding lying in the seam between planks to make the hull watertight, or in any repair.

Ceiling The planks lining the interior of a vessel inside the frames.

Chine An angle formed by two strakes, usually between the bottom and the side of a vessel.

Clinker A method of planking in which the lower edge of one strake overlaps the upper edge of the strake below.

Displacement The weight of water displaced by a floating ship. This is about equal to the weight of the vessel.

Double-ended A vessel which is of similar shape at both ends.

Draught The depth of water needed to float a vessel.

Feather-heading The thin commencement of a plank.

Floor-timber The lowest transverse frame in a ship.

Frame A transverse timber, part of the skeleton structure of a ship. The lowest parts of frames are termed floor-timbers, and the separate ribs at the side of a ship are here termed side-frames.

Freeboard The distance between the waterline and the lowest part the gunwale.

Garboard strake The strakes immediately next to the keel.

Gunwale The uppermost rail or timber of a ship's side.

Hanging knee See **Knee**.

Heel The lowest part of a mast; also the list or inclination of a ship.

Hooked nail A nail whose shank has been bent at an angle of 90 degrees, and whose point has been bent through a further 90 degrees (Fig 3).

Hull The main body of a ship.

Joggle The outer face of a frame which has been stepped or otherwise shaped to fit overlapping clinker planking.

Keel The central longitudinal strengthening beam of the bottom of a ship, from which rise the frames and the stem and sternposts. Normally it projects below the bottom planking of a ship and helps to stop leeway or sideways drift.

Keel-plank A broad extra-thick plank instead of a keel, sometimes found in flat-bottomed ships and barges that sail in shallow waters and are beached at low tide.

Keelson A longitudinal strengthening timber, or stringer, overlying the keel inside a ship.

Knee A right-angled timber, usually carved from naturally angled tree growth, fastening the intersection of timbers such as the deck-beams and the frames of the ship's side. A **hanging knee** is angled downwards below the deck-beam, a **lodging knee** is angled horizontally to the beam, and a **standing knee** is angled upwards above the beam.

Lap The overlap of two strakes fastened together clinkerwise.

Leeway The amount a ship is carried sideways to leeward by the force of the wind or current.

Limber hole Hole in the underside of a bottom frame

or floor-timber which allows bilge-water to flow to the lowest part of a ship so that it can be pumped out.

Lodging knee See **knee**.

Mast-beam Transverse beam immediately on the forward side of the mast to help support the mast.

Mast-step Socket to hold the foot of the mast.

Metacentric height Distance between the metacentre and the centre of gravity in a ship (Fig 79).

Peg A wooden nail less than 10mm in diameter.

Plank Flat lengths of wood normally forming the outer and inner skins of a ship, as well as the deck.

Port The left-hand side of a ship looking forward.

Quarter rudder A rudder hung on the side of the ship near the stern.

Rabbet Longitudinal recess cut in the face of a timber, particularly in the keel, stempost, and sternpost.

Reverse clinker Clinker construction in which the lower strakes overlap the upper.

Rivet Iron fastening to hold overlapping planks together, formed from a nail whose 'pointed' end has been splayed or clenched over a diamond shaped washer or rove (Fig 3).

Rove See **rivet**.

Scarf The bevelling of the ends of two timbers, particularly planks and frames, in such a way that when fastened together they form one timber in appearance.

Seam The gap between two ship's planks. This is normally made watertight with a caulking.

Sheer strake The upper line of planks in the side of a ship.

Shell The outer skin of planking of a ship.

Shell-built A vessel that has been built essentially with its planks first, to which the frames have been added later to strengthen the 'shell'. Shell-building is only possible when there is a system of fastening planks to each other, as, for example, in Scandinavian clinker-built vessels which used rivets, and in classical ships of the Mediterranean which used mortice-and-tenon joints.

Ship A large vessel able to sail on voyages for considerable periods of time.

Skeleton-built A vessel that has been built first with a skeleton framework of keel, frames and endposts, to which subsequently has been added the skin of planks.

Skin The outer shell of planking in a ship.

Side-frame A frame not connected to floor-timbers which supports the side of a ship.

Starboard The right-hand side of a ship looking forward.

Stanchion An upright piller often used to support a deck.

Standing knee See **knee**.

Steering oar A long oar used for steering, fastened over the stern of a vessel. Particularly used in inland waters. Not to be confused with a side or quarter rudder.

Stocks The timber supports for a ship while it is being built.

Strake A line of planks of the outer skin running the length of a ship.

Stringer An internal longitudinal beam giving additional strength to a ship.

Thole pin A wooden pin inserted into the gunwale or sheer-strake of a boat to provide a fulcrum for an oar.

Thwart Transverse beam used as a seat.

Trenail A wooden nail used to fasten timbers together, normally more than 10mm in diameter

Turned nail A nail whose shank has been bent through an angle of 90 degrees (see Fig 3).

Wale An extra-thick plank running fore-and-aft in the side of a ship. It provides additional longitudinal strength, and can help support cross-beams and a deck.

Wash-strake Thin movable boards above the gunwale which provide protection from spray entering a ship or boat.

Yard A horizontal spar located near the top of a mast from which a sail is set.

Summary

This report reconstructs the types of ships and boats and their use in the port of London from the Roman period to the eleventh century AD. This has been made possible by the discovery of vessel remains, waterfronts, and imported goods of the relevant periods.

After an introduction, Chapter 1 considers the origin and early growth of the port from the mid first to the mid third centuries. There is evidence for the use of river boats, fishing vessels, seagoing merchant ships, and warships. Goods were primarily imported from lands bordering the Mediterranean, from Gaul and Germany, as well as from southern Britain. Initially trading ships probably berthed at a shelving 'hard' to be off-loaded at low water, but soon this was replaced by timber quays and jetties, some of which were likely to have stood only 1m deep at high tide. This was probably insufficient to allow seagoing merchant ships to berth there, and cargoes may have been off-loaded into lighters moored in deeper water. The weight of individual goods was normally less than 1.5 tonnes, suggesting that ships were rather small by Roman standards in the Mediterranean. From the mid second to mid third centuries, the quantity of imported trade goods was smaller than earlier amounts, perhaps a reflection of the smaller urban population of London and a decline in its volume of trade. The sources of goods, in the Mediterranean, Gaul, and Germany, remained as before but with an increasing amount of goods from southern Britain. Quays were built into deeper water, presumably to improve the berthing for larger ships.

One such vessel, Blackfriars ship 1, is described and reconstructed in Chapter 2. It sank in about AD 150 while carrying a cargo of building stone quarried near Maidstone, Kent, though *Teredo* infestation showed that mostly it sailed at sea. It was constructed in a Romano-Celtic shipbuilding tradition, and its flat bottom made it ideally suited to beaching on tidal shores for loading and unloading. It was unlikely to have carried more than about 50 tonnes of cargo, and it sailed best with a wind astern.

Chapter 3 describes another type of Romano-Celtic vessel, a river barge, found abandoned in a shallow creek in the late second century at the site of the modern Guy's Hospital, Southwark. Chapter 4 examines the port in the later third and fourth centuries at a time when the waterfront was decaying and was made partly inaccessible by the construction of a riverside defensive wall.

The County Hall ship (Chapter 5) was abandoned soon after it was built, c AD 300. It had been constructed in the Mediterranean tradition, though a tree-ring analysis shows that it was built locally. This suggests that it had an official function like certain Roman military boats found on the Rhine and Danube. Chapter 6 considers the port from the seventh to eight centuries, following the hiatus of the fifth to sixth centuries when the city was apparently deserted. The Middle Saxon port lay off Aldwych, to the west of the former walled Roman city. Here, limited excavations have disclosed little evidence of seaborne trade apart from pottery from the Ipswich region of the Thames estuary.

Chapter 7 examines evidence for shipping and the port from the tenth to the eleventh centuries, during which time Viking raids had caused the Aldwych site to be abandoned in favour of the safety of the Roman walled site. Archaeological and documentary evidence combine to show a variety of ship types using the port, including the 'keel' and the 'hulc'. Trade was primarily with the Low Countries and the Rhineland, and ships seem to have berthed at London on artificial embankments and at jetties where there existed beach markets.

Chapter 8 describes fragments of several vessels, all built locally in a clinker tradition, found with fastenings of iron rivets, hooked nails, and wooden pegs. An iron anchor of Viking type and the blade of a paddle or oar are also described.

Chapter 9 concludes the report by addressing several broad topics. Firstly, it seems that the ships and boats found in London, although constructed fairly locally, were apparently built according to traditions that had roots in various parts of Europe, in the Mediterranean region, north-western Europe, the Low Countries, Poland, and in Scandinavia, and that at least during the Roman period, the primary method of shipbuilding in central and northern Europe was Celtic and not Mediterranean. Secondly, it seems that it was rare for Roman merchant ships in the Mediterranean to sail around Spain to the northern provinces, but instead the rivers of Gaul and Germany were mostly used to distribute goods. Thirdly, the action of the tides was central to the function of the port of London, and at all stages in its history the depth of water at high tide on the waterfront was the main factor limiting the size and capacity of merchant ships. Thus the second-century Blackfriars ship 1 with a maximum cargo of about 50 tonnes, was probably a fairly average size of vessel used in northern waters during the Roman period. Finally, there was a pattern in the history of berthing facilities in the port of London, beginning with beaching, then with shallow-water quays and jetties, followed by deeper water quays, docks, and, in post-medieval times, the development of enclosed deepwater docks.

The book ends with specialist Appendices on pottery dating evidence for Blackfriars ship 1, a metallographic analysis of Roman nails from the Blackfriars ship, analysis of Roman ship caulking, analysis of resins from the Roman hulls, stability calculations for the Blackfriars ship, tree-ring dating, headings for ship timber recording, and a glossary of nautical terms. A Bibliography completes the study.

Resumé

Ce compte-rendu retrace les différents types de navires et de bateaux et l'usage qui en était fait dans le port de Londres depuis l'époque romaine jusqu'au onzième siècle apr. J-C. Cette étude a été rendue possible par la découverte de vestiges relatifs aux époques concernées, des restes de vaisseaux, de constructions situées au bord du fleuve et de denrées importées.

Après une partie d'introduction, le chapitre 1 examine l'origine et les premiers développements du port à partir du milieu du premier siècle jusqu'au milieu du troisième. Certaines trouvailles prouvent que le port était fréquenté par des bateaux pour la navigation fluviale, des bateaux de pêche, des navires marchands hauturiers, et des navires de guerre. Les marchandises étaient surtout importées des pays bordant la Méditerranée, de Gaule et d'Allemagne ainsi que du sud de la Grande Bretagne. Au départ les navires de commerce mouillaient probablement en cale inclinée pour être déchargés à marée basse, mais celle-ci fut bientôt remplacée par des appontements et des jetées en bois, dont certains n'avaient probablement qu'un mètre de hauteur d'eau à marée haute. Ce n'était sans doute pas suffisant pour permettre aux navires marchands de haute-mer de mouiller là et il se peut que les cargaisons aient été déchargées dans des gabares amarrées dans des eaux plus profondes. Le poids des marchandises par cargaison ne dépassait normalement pas 1.5 tonnes, ce qui donne à penser que ces bateaux étaient plutôt petits si on en juge par les normes romaines en Méditerranée. A partir du milieu du deuxième siècle jusqu'au milieu du troisième, la quantité de marchandises commerciales importées était moins importante qu'auparavant, peut-être un reflet de la diminution de la population de la ville de Londres et du déclin dans le volume de son commerce. Les pays d'origine des denrées, la Méditerranée, la Gaule, et l'Allemagne, étaient restés les mêmes qu'avant mais on remarque qu'une quantité croissante de marchandises provenaient du sud de la Grand Bretagne. Des quais furent construits là où l'eau était plus profonde probablement pour améliorer les conditions de mouillage pour les plus gros navires.

Un tel bâtiment, dit Blackfriars bateau 1, est décrit et reconstruit au chapitre 2. Il a coulé aux alentours de l'an 150 apr. J-C, alors qu'il transportait une cargaison de pierres à bâtir extraites d'une carrière près de Maidstone, dans le Kent, toutefois, une infestation de tarets prouvait qu'il avait surtout navigué en haute-mer. Sa construction se conformait à la tradition romano-celte, et grâce à son fond plat, il était parfaitement capable de s'échouer sur des plages à marées pour être chargé et déchargé. Il est peu probable qu'il ait transporté plus de 50 tonnes de cargaison environ et il naviguait au mieux par vent de poupe.

Dans le chapitre 3 on décrit un autre type de bâtiment romano-celte, une péniche abandonnée à la fin du deuxième siècle dans une crique peu profonde et trouvée sur le site de l'actuel hôpital, Guy's Hospital, à Southwark. Au chapitre 4 on s'intéresse au port de la fin du troisième et au quatrième siècles à une époque où les bâtiments en bordure du fleuve se dégradaient et étaient rendus en partie inaccessibles en raison de la construction d'un mur défensif le long du fleuve.

Le bateau dit de County Hall, qui est examiné au chapitre 5 a été abandonné peu après sa construction, vers 300 apr. J-C. Il avait été construit dans la tradition méditerranéenne, bien qu'une analyse des anneaux d'arbres montre qu'il avait été bâti dans la région. Cela suggère qu'il avait joué un rôle officiel comme certains bateaux militaires romains retrouvés sur le Rhin et le Danube. Le chapitre 6 s'intéresse au port du septième au huitième siècle, après le hiatus des cinquième et sixième siècles, époque à laquelle la ville fut apparemment désertée. Le port de l'époque saxonne moyenne se situait à la hauteur d'Aldwych, à l'ouest de l'enceinte de l'ancienne cité romaine. Là, des fouilles restreintes n'ont révélé que peu de témoignages de commerce par voie de mer mis à part la poterie en provenance de la région d'Ipswich dans l'estuaire de la Tamise.

Le chapitre 7 examine les témoignages de la navigation et du port aux dixième et onzième siècles, période pendant laquelle, en raison des raids des Vikings, on avait été forcé d'abandonner le site d'Aldwych en faveur de la sécurité qu'offrait le site romain fortifié. Les trouvailles archéologiques et les documents s'accordent à montrer qu'une grande variété de types de navires fréquentaient le port, y compris le chaland charbonnier et le bateau pénitencier. Le commerce se faisait essentiellement avec les Pays-Bas et les pays rhénans, il semble que les bateaux mouillaient à Londres sur des berges artificielles et à des appontements où avaient lieu des marchés de plage.

Le chapitre 8 décrit des fragments de plusieurs bâtiments, tous construits dans la tradition des bordages à clins, retrouvés avec des attaches faites de rivets de fer, de clous à crochets, et de chevilles en bois. Une ancre en fer de type Viking et la pale d'une pagaie, ou d'une rame, sont également décrites.

Le chapitre 9 sert de conclusion au compte-rendu, on y aborde plusieurs thèmes d'ordre général. Premièrement, il semble que, bien qu'ils aient été construits dans la région, les navires et les bateaux retrouvés à Londres, se conformaient à des traditions qui avaient leurs racines dans diverses parties de l'Europe, dans la région méditerranéenne, dans le nord-ouest de l'Europe, aux Pays-Bas, en Pologne et en Scandinavie et, qu'au moins durant la période romaine, la principale méthode utilisée pour les constructions navales en Europe centrale et en Europe du Nord était celte et non méditerranéenne. Deuxièmement, ce n'était que rarement, semble-t-il, que des navires marchands romains en Méditerranée contournaient l'Espagne pour se rendre dans les provinces du nord, mais ils utilisaient surtout les fleuves de Gaule et d'Allemagne pour la distribution des denrées. Troisièmement, le mouvement des marées jouait un rôle primordial dans le fonctionnement du port de Londres, et à toutes les étapes de son histoire, la profondeur de l'eau à marée haute le long des berges a été le principal facteur pour déterminer la taille et la capacité de navires marchands. Ainsi le navire du deuxième siècle appelé Blackfriars 1, avec sa cargaison maximale d'environ 50 tonnes, était probablement un bâtiment d'une taille tout à fait moyenne pour les eaux d'Europe du nord à l'époque romaine. Finalement on a noté une évolution dans l'histoire des facilités de mouillage du port de Londres, au début les bateaux venaient s'échouer sur la plage, plus tard on a construit des jetées et des apponte-ments en eau peu profonde suivis par des quais en eau plus profonde, des docks et finalement, après la période médiévale, des bassins fermés en eau profonde.

Le livre se termine par des appendices spécialisés sur des témoignages de datation de poterie concernant Blackfriars 1, une analyse métallographique de clous romains provenant de Blackfriars 1, une analyse du calfatage d'un bateau romain, une analyse résines de coques romaines, des calculs de stabilité pour Blackfriars 1, une datation d'anneaux d'arbres, des titres pour l'inventaire des bois pour constructions navales, et un glossaire de termes nautiques. Une bibliographie complète cette étude.

Zusammenfassung

Dieser Bericht befaßt sich mit der Rekonstruktion von Schiffs- und Bootstypen, sowie deren Gebrauch, im Hafen von London von der Römerzeit bis in das elfte Jahrhundert. Ermöglicht wurde diese Studie durch die Entdeckung von Überresten von Fahrzeugen, Kaianlagen und Einfuhrgütern, die den jeweiligen Zeiträumen entstammten.

An eine Einführung anschließend werden im ersten Kapitel die Entstehung und die frühe Entwicklung des Hafens in der Zeit von der Mitte des ersten Jahrhunderts bis in die Mitte des dritten Jahrhunderts behandelt. Es gibt Anhaltspunkte für den Gebrauch von Flußbooten, Fischerbooten, seetüchtigen Handelsschiffen und Kriegsschiffen. Einfuhrgüter kamen hauptsächlich aus den Randgebieten des Mittelmeeres, aus Gallien und Germanien sowie aus dem südlichen Britannien. Zu Beginn legten die Handelsschiffe höchstwahrscheinlich auf einer festen Reede an, um bei Ebbe entladen zu werden. Diese Praxis wurde jedoch bald durch hölzerne Kaianlagen und Landestege ersetzt, die bei Flut wohl nur eine Wassertiefe von einem Meter aufwiesen. Dies war möglicherweise nicht tief genug, um Hochseeschiffen das Anlegen zu erlauben, und so wurde das Frachtgut höchstwahrscheinlich auf Leichter, die in tieferem festgemacht hatten, umgeladen. Das Gewicht individueller Einfuhrgüter war gewöhnlich geringer als 1.5 Tonnen, was darauf hindeutet, daß die Schiffe ziemlich klein waren verglichen mit der römischen Norm im Mittelmeer. In der Zeit von der Mitte des zweiten Jahrhunderts bis in die Mitte des dritten Jahrhunderts war die Menge der eingeführten Handelsgüter geringer als die der früheren Importe. Vielleicht spiegelt sich hierin die geringe Einwohnerzahl Londons und ein Rückgang in seinem Handelsrevolumen wieder. Die Herkunftsorte der Waren im Mittelmeerraum, in Gallien und Germanien blieben gleich, doch zeigte sich ein ansteigendes Maß in den Gütern aus dem südlichen Britannien. Kaianlagen mit größerer Wassertiefe wurden angelegt, vermutlich um Anlegeplätze für größere Schiffe zu schaffen.

Ein solches Schiff, das Blackfriars Schiff 1, wird im zweiten Kapitel beschrieben und rekonstruiert. Es sank um ungefähr 150 n.Chr. mit einer Ladung von Baugestein, das aus einem Steinbruch in der Nähe von Maidstone in Kent stammte. Doch zeigt Befall durch *Teredo*, daß es hauptsächlich ein Seeschiff gewesen ist. Es war in der römisch-keltischen Schiffsbautradition hergestellt. Mit seinem flachen Boden war es besonders gut dafür geeignet, es zum Ein= und Ausladen auf einem Gezeitenufer auflaufen zu lassen. Wahrscheinlich hatte es nicht mehr als ungefähr 50 Tonnen Ladekapazität, und es segelte am besten vor dem Wind.

Das dritte Kapitel beschreibt einen weiteren römisch-keltischen Schiffstyp, einen Flußkahn, der am Ende des zweiten Jahrhunderts in einem seichten Seitenarm aufgegeben wurde. Die Fundstelle liegt heute auf dem Gelände von Guy's Hospital in Southwark. Kapitel vier untersucht den Hafen im ausgehender dritten und im vierten Jahthundert, einem Zeitraum, in dem die Hafenanlagen verfielen und teilweise durch eine am Fluß verlaufende Verteidigungsmauer unzugänglich gemacht wurden.

Das county Hall Schiff, das im fünften Kapitel diskutiert wird, war kurz nach seiner Fertigstellung circa 300 n.Chr. aufgegeben worden. Es ist in der Tradition des Mittelmeeres gefertigt, obwohl die dendrochronologische Analyse zeigt, daß es am Ort gebaut worden ist. Dies deutet darauf hin, daß es für eine offizielle Funktion bestimmt war, vergleichbar mit gewissen römischen Militärschiffen, wie sie am Rhein und an der Donau gefunden worden sind. Das sechste Kapitel betrachtet den Hafen in der Zeit vom siebten bis in das achte Jahrhundert; eine Zeit, die sich an die Unterbrechung während des fünften und sechsten Jahrhunderts anschloß, in der die Stadt anscheinend wüst war. Der Hafen der mittelsächsischen Zeit lag vor Aldwych, westlich der früheren, ummauerten Römerstadt. Hier haben begrenzte Ausgrabungen nur geringe Beweise für Seehandel erbracht, abgesehen von Töpferwaren, die aus dem Gebiet um Ipswich an der Themsemündung stammten.

Das siebte Kapitel untersucht die Befunde für Schiffahrt und Hafen vom zehnten bis elften Jahrhundert. In dieser Zeit hatten Wikingerüberfälle veranlaßt, daß der

Standort vor Aldwych zugunsten eines sichereren Platzes innerhalb der ehemaligen römischen Mauern aufgegeben wurde. Archäologische und dokumentarische Quellen zeigen im Verein, daß eine Vielzahl von Schiffstypen den Hafen aufgesucht haben. Unter ihnen befanden sich 'keel' und 'hulc'. Der Handelsverkehr bestand hauptsächlich mit den Niederlanden und dem Rheinland. Die Schiffe scheinen in London an künstlichen Uferböschungen und an Landestegen, wo Strandmärkte bestanden, angelegt zu haben.

Das achte Kapitel beschreibt Bruchstücke von mehreren Fahrzeugen, die am Ort in Klinkerbauweise hergestellt worden waren und die mit Verankerungen wie Eisennieten, krampenartig umgebogenen Nägeln und Dübeln gefunden wurden. Ein Eisenanker des Wikingertypus und das Blatt eines Paddels oder Ruders werden ebenfalls beschrieben.

Das neunte Kapitel bringt den Bericht zum Abschluß, wobei mehrere umgreifende Themen angeschnitten werden. Erstens, es scheint, daß die Läden und Schiffe, die in London gefunden wurden, obwohl in der näheren Umgebung hergestellt, anscheinend jedoch in Traditionen gefertigt waren, die ihre Wurzeln in verschiedenen Teilen Europas hatten, so etwa wie im Mittelmeergebiet, in Nordwest Europa, in den Niederlanden, in Polen, und in Skandinavien, und daß wenigstens in der römischen Zeit die Hauptschiffsbautradition in Mittel- und Nordeuropa von keltischem und nicht mediterranischen Ursprungs war. Zweitens scheint es selten gewesen zu sein, daß römische Handelsschiffe aus dem Mittelmeer Spanien umsegelten, um in die nördlichen Provinzen zugelangen. Es wurden vielmehr die Flüsse Galliens und Germaniens für den Vertrieb von Handelsgütern genutzt. Drittens, der Gezeitenwechsel war von grundlegender Bedeutung für die Arbeitsweise des Londoner Hafens. Zu allen Zeiten seiner Geschichte war die Wassertiefe an den Kaianlagen bei Flut ausschlaggebend für die Größe und Ladefähigkeit der Handelsschiffe. So betrachtet war das Schiff Blackfriars 1 aus dem zweiten Jahrhundert mit seiner Maximalfracht von 50 Tonnen wohl ein Schiff von durchschnittlicher Größe, wie es während der Römerzeit in den nördlichen Gewässern benutzt wurde. Abschließend, es zeigt sich eine fortlaufende Entwicklung in der Geschichte der Anlegemöglichkeiten im Hafen von London, beginnend mit dem Auflaufen lassen, gefolgt von Kaianlagen an seichten Stellen sowie Landestegen, über Kaianlagen mit tieferem Wasser zu Hafenbecken und in der Neuzeit zu der Entwicklung von geschlossenen Tiefwasserbecken.

Das Buch schließt mit speziellen Appendices für den Datierungsbefund der Keramik im Bezug auf das Schiff Blackfriars 1, einer metallographische Analyse der römischen Nägel aus dem Blackfriars Schiff, einer Analyse der römischen Tradition für das Kalfatern von Schiffen, einer Analyse der Ergebnisse aus römischen Schiffskörpern, Berechnungen der Stabilität für das Blackfriars Schiff, dendrochronologischer Datierung, Rubriken für die Aufnahme von Schiffshölzern und einem Glossar seemännischer Grundbegriffe. Eine Bibliographie beendet die Studie.

Bibliography

Primary sources

Excavation register, Museum of London
Site archive report, Museum of London
Site catalogue of the Department of Urban Archaeology, Museum of London, 1984
—, 1986

Printed sources

Adams, J, van Holk, A, and Maarleveld, T, 1990 *Dredgers and archaeology: shipfinds from the Slufter*, Ministerie van Welzijn, Volksgezondheid en Cultuur, Rotterdam

Akerlund, H, 1951 *Fartygsfynden i den forna hamneni Kalmar*, Uppsala

—, 1963 *Nydamskeppen*, Goteborg

Alarçao, J de, 1988 *Roman Portugal*, Warminster

Allen, D, 1971 The ship on Gaulish coins, *Antiq J* 51, 96–9

Anderson, A, 1981 Some unusual coarse ware vessels from London and their continental background, in *Roman pottery research in Britain and N W Europe* (ed A Anderson), BAR, Int Ser, 123 (1), 93–106

Andrews, D, and Merriman, N, 1986 A prehistoric timber structure at Richmond Terrace, Whitehall, *Trans London Middlesex Archaeol Soc*, 37, 17–21

Arnold, B, 1977 Some remarks on caulking in Celtic boat construction and its evolution in areas lying northwest of the Alpine arc, *Int J Naut Archaeol Underwater Explor*, 6.4, 293–7

—, 1978 Gallo-Roman boat finds in Switzerland, in *Roman shipping and trade: Britain and the Rhine provinces*, (eds J du P Taylor and H Cleere), CBA Res Rep, 24, 31–5

Atkinson, D, 1914 A hoard of Samian ware from Pompeii, *J Roman Stud*, 4, 27–64

Baillie, M, 1978 Dating some ships' timbers from Woodquay, Dublin, in *Dendrochronology in Europe* (ed J Fletcher), BAR, Int Ser, 51, 259–262

—, 1982 *Tree-ring dating and archaeology*, London

Baillie, M, Pilcher, J, 1973 A simple cross-dating program for tree-ring research, *Tree-ring Bulletin*, 33, 7–14

Bartoccini, R, 1958 Il porto Romano di Leptis Magna, *B del C Studi Storia dell'architett*, 13

Bass, G, 1971 A Byzantine trading venture, *Sci American*, 224, 2, 23–33

—, 1985 The construction of a seagoing vessel of the late Bronze Age, in *1st International Symposium on ship construction in antiquity* (ed H Tzalas), 25–35

Bass, G, Katzev, M, and Parker, A, 1980 Mediterranean wreck sites and classical seafaring, in *Archaeology under water: an atlas of the world's submerged sites* (ed K Muckelroy), 32–61

Bateman, N, and Milne, G, 1983 A Roman harbour in London: excavations and observations near Pudding Lane, City of London 1979–82, *Britannia*, 14, 207–26

Bateson, M, 1902 A London municipal collection of the reign of John, *Engl Hist Rev*, 17, 480–511

Bede, *A history of the English Church and people*, ed L Shirley-Price, R A Latham, and D H Farmer, 1950, 1990, London

Benoit F, 1961 *L'épave du Grand Congloué à Marseille*, 14th supplement to *Gallia*, Paris

Betts, I, 1986 Brick and tile, in Miller, L *et al*, 1986, 246–52

Bird, J, 1986 Samian wares, in Miller, L *et al*, 1986, 139–98

Blagg, T, 1980 The sculptured stones, in Hill, C *et al*, 1980, 125–93

de Boe, G, 1978 Roman boats from a small river harbour at Pommeroeul, Belgium, in *Roman shipping and trade: Britain and the Rhine provinces*, (eds J du P Taylor and H Cleere), CBA Res Rep, 24, 22–30

Bonde, N and Crumlin-Pedersen, O, 1990 The dating of wreck 2, the longship, from Skuldelev, Denmark. A preliminary announcement, NewsWARP, 7, 3–6

Boon, G, 1977 A Greco-Roman anchor-stock from north Wales, *Antiq J*, 57, 10–30

Brachmann, H, 1983 Research into the early history of the Slav populations in the territory of the German Democratic Republic, *Medieval Archaeol*, 27, 89–106

Bradford, G, 1954 *A glossary of sea terms*, London

Brigham, T, 1990a The late Roman waterfront in London, *Britannia*, 21, 99–183

—, 1990b A reassessment of the second basilica in London, AD 100–400: excavations at Leadenhall Court, 1984–86, *Britannia*, 21, 53–98

Brindley, A, and Lanting, J, 1991 A boat of the Mediterranean tradition in Ireland: a preliminary note, *Int J Naut Archaeol Underwater Explor*, 20.1, 69–70

Brodribb, A, Hands, A, and Walker, D, 1973 *Excavations at Shakenoak Farm, near Wilcote, Oxfordshire*, part 3, Oxford

Brodribb, G, and Cleere, H, 1988 The *Classis Britannica* bath-house at Beauport Park, East Sussex, *Britannia*, 19, 217–74

Brogger, A, and Shetelig, H, 1951 *The Viking ships, their ancestry and evolution*, Oslo

Brooke, C, and Keir, G, 1975 *London 800–1216: the shaping of a city*, London

Burwash, D, 1969 *English merchant shipping 1460–1540*, Newton Abbot

Caesar, *The conquest of Gaul*, ed S A Handford and Jane F Gardner, 1951, 1986, London

Carr, F, 1989 *Sailing barges*, Lavenham

Carraze, F, 1977 Mediterranean hull types compared: 3; the Jeune-Garde B wreck at Porquerolles (France), *Int J Naut Archaeol Underwater Explor*, 6.4, 299–303

Casson, L, 1971 *Ships and seamanship in the ancient world*, Princeton

Chaplin, P, 1982 *The Thames from source to tideway*, London

Chapman, H, 1974 Letters from Roman London, *London Archaeol*, 2.7, 173–6

—, 1977 Wood, in Excavations at Angel Court, Walbrook, 1974, (T Blurton) *Trans London Middlesex Archaeol Soc*, 28, 64–8

—, 1986 Metal objects, in Miller, L *et al*, 1986, 235–9

Christensen, A, 1973 Lucien Basch: ancient wrecks and the archaeology of ships. A comment, *Int J Naut Archaeol Underwater Explor*, 2.1, 137–45

—, 1977 Ancient boatbuilding – a provisional classification, in *Sources and techniques in boat archaeology* (S McGrail), BAR Supp Ser, 29, 269–80

—, 1979 Viking Age rigging, a survey of sources and theories, in *Medieval ships and harbours in northern Europe* (ed S McGrail), BAR Int Ser, 66, 183–92

—, 1985 Boat finds from Bryggen, in *The Bryggen Papers* (A Herteig and A Christensen), main series, 1, 47–272

Clark, J, 1989 *Saxon and Norman London*, London

Coates, J, 1977 Hypothetical reconstructions and the naval architect, in *Sources and techniques in boat archaeology* (ed S McGrail), BAR Supp Ser, 29, 215–32

Coates, J, Platis, S, and Shaw, J, 1990 *The trireme trials 1988: report on the Anglo-Hellenic sea trials of Olympias*, Oxford

Collingwood, R, and Wright, R, 1965 *The Roman inscriptions of Britain*, Oxford

Corlett, E, 1978 Appreciation of the lines, in Fenwick, V (ed), 1978, 303–6

Couper, A (ed), 1983 *The Times Atlas of the Oceans*, London

Crumlin-Pedersen, O, 1965 Cog-Kogge-Kaag, in *Saertryk af Handels – og Søfartsmuseets Årbog, 1965*, 81–114

—, 1972 The Vikings and the Hanseatic merchants: 900–1450, in *A history of seafaring* (ed G Bass), 182–204

—, 1977 Some principles for the recording and presentation of ancient boat structures, in *Sources and techniques in boat archaeology* (ed S McGrail), BAR Supp Ser, 29, 163–77

—, 1979 Danish cog-finds, in *Medieval ships and harbours in northern Europe* (ed S McGrail), BAR Int Ser, 66, 17–34

—, 1981 Viking shipbuilding and seamanship, in *Proceedings of the Eighth Viking Congress, 1977*, 271–86

—, 1983 *From Viking ships to Hanseatic cogs*, Third Paul Johnstone Memorial Lecture, Nat Mar Mus, London

Cunliffe, B (ed), 1968 Fifth report on the excavations of the Roman fort at Richborough, Kent, *Soc Antiq London Res Rep*, 23, London

Cunliffe, B, 1972 The late Iron Age metalwork from Bulbury, Dorset, *Antiq J*, 52, 293–308

—, 1978 *Hengistbury Head*, London

—, 1984 Relations between Britain and Gaul in the first century BC and early first century AD, in *Cross-Channel trade between Gaul and Britain in the pre-Roman Iron Age* (eds S Macready and F Thompson), Soc Antiq London Occ Pap n ser, 4, 3–23

—, 1990 Hengistbury Head: a late prehistoric haven, in *Maritime Celts, Frisians and Saxons* (ed S McGrail), CBA Res Rep, **71**, 27–31

Curle, J, 1911 *Newstead; a Roman frontier port and its people*, Glasgow

Deane, Sir A, 1670 *Doctrine of naval architecture, 1670* (ed B Lavery), 1981, London

Dennis, M, and Schaaf, L, 1975 A Roman building at St Thomas Street, Southwark, *London Archaeol*, **2.11**, 270–2

Devoy, R, 1980 Post-glacial environmental change and man in the Thames estuary: a synopsis, in *Archaeology and coastal change* (ed F Thompson) Soc Antiq London Occ Pap, 134–48

Dillon, J, 1989 A Roman timber building from Southwark, *Britannia*, **20**, 229–31

Dillon, J, Jackson, S, and Jones, H, 1991 Excavations at the Courage Brewery and Park Street 1984–90, *London Archaeol*, **6**, 225–62

Dimes, F, 1980 Petrological report, in Hill, C *et al*, 1990, 198–200

Doorninck, F van, 1974 A brief note on Bash's remarks on the seventh-century Byzantine wreck at Yassi Ada, *Int J Naut Archaeol Underwater Explor*, **3.2**, 310–12

—, 1976 The fourth-century wreck at Yassi Ada. An interim report on the hull, *Int J Naut Archaeol Underwater Explor*, **5.2**, 115–32

Department of Urban Archaeology, 1984 *Pottery archive users handbook*, London

Dumas, F, 1964 *Épaves Antiques*, Paris

Dunning, G, 1959 Pottery from the late Anglo-Saxon period in England, *Medieval Archaeol*, **3**, 31–78

—, 1968 The trade in medieval pottery around the North Sea, in *Rotterdam Papers. A contribution to Medieval Archaeology*, 35–58

Duval, A, 1984 Regional groups in western France, in *Cross-Channel trade between Gaul and Britain in the pre-Roman Iron Age* (eds S Macready, and F Thompson), Soc Antiq London Occ Pap n ser, **4**, 78–91

Dyson, T, 1980 London and Southwark in the seventh century and later. A neglected reference, *Trans London Middlesex Archaeol Soc*, **31**, 83–95

Dyson, T, 1981 The terms 'quay' and 'wharf' in the early medieval London waterfront, in *Waterfront archaeology in Britain and northern Europe* (eds G Milne, and B Hobley), CBA Res Rep, **41**, 37–8

Dyson, T, 1985 Early harbour regulations in London, in *Conference on waterfront archaeology in north European towns, no 2, Bergen 1983* (ed A Herteg), 19–24

Dyson, T, 1989 *Documents and archaeology: the medieval London waterfront*, London

Dyson, T, and Schofield, J, 1981 Excavations in the City of London: second interim report, 1974–8, *Trans London Middlesex Archaeol Soc*, **32**, 24–81

Dyson, T, and Schofield, J, 1984 Saxon London, in *Anglo-Saxon towns in southern England* (ed J Haslam), 285–313

Ehrenberg, M, 1980 The occurrence of Bronze Age metalwork in the Thames: an investigation, *Trans London Middlesex Archaeol Soc*, **31**, 1–15

Ellmers, D, 1969 Keltischer schiffbau, in *Jahrbuch des Romisch-Germanischen Zentralmuseums Mainz*, Mainz, 73–122

—, 1972 *Fruhmittelalterliche Handelsschiffahrt in Mittell-und Nordeuropa*, Neumunster

—, 1978 Shipping on the Rhine during the Roman period: the pictorial evidence, in *Roman shipping and trade: Britain and the Rhine provinces* (eds J du P Taylor, and H Cleere), CBA Res Rep, **24**, 1–14

—, 1981 Post-Roman waterfront installations on the Rhine, in *Waterfront archaeology in Britain and northern Europe* (eds G Milne, and B Hobley), CBA Res Rep, **41**, 88–95

—, 1984 Punt, barge or pram - is there one tradition or several?, in *Aspects of maritime archaeology and ethnography* (ed S McGrail), 153–72

—, 1985a Loading and unloading ships using a horse and cart, standing in the water. The archaeological evidence, in *Conference on waterfront archaeology in north European towns no. 2, Bergen 1983* (ed A Herteig), 25–30

—, 1985b Frisian and Hanseatic merchants sailed the cog, in *The North Sea: a highway of economic and cultural exchange character - History* (eds A Bang-Anderson, B Greenhill, and E Grude), 79–96

—, 1990 The Frisian monopoly of coastal transport in the sixth–eighth centuries AD, in *Maritime Celts, Frisians and Saxons* (ed S McGrail), CBA Res Rep, **71**, 91–2

Evans, A, and Bruce-Mitford, R, 1975 The ship, in *The Sutton Hoo ship-burial*, Vol 1 (R Bruce-Mitford), 345–435

Evans, J, 1980 Mortar sample analysis, in Hill, C *et al*, 1980, 116–20

Falconer, W, 1815 *A new universal dictionary of the marine*, 1974, London

Farley, M, 1976 Saxon and medieval Walton, Aylesbury: excavations 1973–4, Records of Buckinghamshire 20, pt 2

Farrell, R, 1989 The Crannog Archaeological Project (CAP), Republic of Ireland, II: Lough Lene - offshore island survey, *Int J Naut Archaeol Underwater Explor*, **18.3**, 221–8

Fenwick, V, 1978 *The Graveney boat*, BAR Brit Ser, **53**

Fletcher, J, 1982 The waterfront of Londinium: the date of the quays at the Custom House site reassessed, *Trans London Middlesex Archaeol Soc*, **33**, 79–84

—, 1984 The date of the Graveney boat, *Int J Naut Archaeol Underwater Explor*, **13.2**, 151

Fliedner, S, 1969 *Die Bremer Hanse-Kogge*, 39–121, Bremen

Foerster, F, 1980 A Roman wreck off Cap del Vol, Gerona, Spain, *Int J Naut Archaeol Underwater Explor*, **9.3**, 244–53

Forest Products Research Laboratory, 1950 *Marine borers and methods of preserving timber against their attack*, Forest Products Research Laboratory no **46**, May 1950

Frey, D, Hentschel, F, and Keith, D, 1978 Deepwater archaeology. The Capistello wreck excavation, Lipari, Aeolian Islands, *Int J Naut Archaeol Underwater Explor*, **7.4**, 279–300

Frost, H, 1963 *Under the Mediterranean*, London

—, 1973 First season of excavation on the Punic wreck in Sicily, *Int J Naut Archaeol Underwater Explor*, **2.1**, 33–49

—, 1974 The Punic wreck in Sicily: 1. Second season of excavation, *Int J Naut Archaeol Underwater Explor*, **3.1**, 35–54

—, 1975 2. The ram from Marsala, *Int J Naut Archaeol Underwater Explor*, **4.2**, 219–28

Fulford, M, 1977 Pottery and Britain's foreign trade in the later Roman period, in *Pottery and early commerce: characterisation and trade in Roman and later ceramics* (ed D Peacock), 35–84

Gassend, J-M, 1985 La construction navale antique de type alterné: un exemple d'un mode de construction, in *1st international symposium on ship construction in antiquity* (ed H Tzalas), 115–27

Gassend, J-M, Liou, B, and Ximénès, S, 1984 L'épave 2 de l' Anse des Laurons (Martigues, Bouches-du-Rhône), *Archaeonautica*, **4**, 75–105

Geddes, J, 1982 The construction of medieval doors, in *Woodworking techniques before AD 1500* (ed S McGrail), BAR Int Ser, **129**, 313–25

Gianfrotta, P, and Pomey, P, 1981 *L'archéologie sous la mer*, Paris

Gillmer, T, 1979 The capability of the single square sail rig: a technical assessment, in *Medieval ships and harbours in northern Europe* (ed S McGrail), BAR Int Ser, **66**, 167–81

Girardon, S, and Heathcote, J, 1989 Excavation round-up 1988: part 2, London boroughs, *London Archaeol*, **6.3**, 72–80

Goodburn, D, 1987 Medmerry: a reassessment of a Migration Period site on the south coast of England, and some of its finds', *Int J Naut Archaeol Underwater Explor*, **16.3**, 213–24

—, Anglo-Saxon boat finds from London, are they English?, *Roskilde symposium on boat and ship archaeology 6*, in press

Green, C, 1980 Pottery, in *Excavations at Billingsgate Buildinngs 'Triangle', Lower Thames Street, London, 1974*, (eds D Jones, and M Rhodes) London Middlesex Archaeol Soc Spec Pap, **4**, 39–82

—, 1986 The waterfront group: amphorae and analogous vessels, in Miller, L *et al*, 1986, 100–6

Green, K, 1978 Roman trade between Britain and the Rhine provinces: the evidence of pottery to *c* AD 250, in *Roman shipping and trade: Britain and the Rhine provinces* (eds J du P Taylor, and H Cleere), CBA Res Rep, **24**, 52–8

Greenhill, B, 1976 *Archaeology of the boat*, London

—, 1988 *The evolution of the wooden ship*, London

Grenier, R, 1988 Basque whalers in the New World: the Red Bay wrecks, in *Ships and shipwrecks of the Americas* (ed G Bass), 69–84

Grimes, W, 1968 *The excavation of Roman and mediaeval London*, London

Guildhall Museum, 1908 *Catalogue of the collection of London antiquities in the Guildhall Museum*, London

Hague, D, 1973 Lighthouses, in *Marine archaeology* (ed D Blackman), Colston Res Soc Pap, **23**, 293–316

Harben, H, 1918 *A dictionary of London*, London

Hassall, M, 1978 Britain and the Rhine provinces: epigraphic evidence for Roman trade, in *Roman shipping and trade: Britain and the Rhine provinces* (eds J du P Taylor, and H Cleere), CBA Res Rep, **24**, 41–8

Hasse, G, 1907 *Les barques de pêche trouvées à Anvers en 1884 et 1904 – 1905* Gand, Belgium

Hasslof, O, 1977 Ethnography and living tradition, in *Sources and techniques in boat archaeology* (ed S McGrail), BAR Supp Ser, **29**, 65–76

Haverfield, F, 1911 Roman London, *J Roman Stud*, **1**, 141–72

Heal, S, and Hutchinson, G, 1986 Three recently found logboats, *Int J Naut Archaeol Underwater Explor*, **15.3**, 205–13

Healy, J, 1978 *Mining and metallurgy in the Greek and Roman world*, London

Heathcote, J, 1990 Excavation round-up 1989: part 2, London boroughs, *London Archaeol*, **6.7**, 188–95

Herfert, P von, 1968 Frühmittelalterliche bootsfunde in Ralswiek, kr. Rügen, *Ausgrabungen und funde*, **13**, 211–22

Hewitt, E, 1932 Industries, in *The Victoria History of the County of Kent* Vol 3 (ed W Page) 371–435

Hill, P, 1958 Anglo-Frisian trade in the light of eighth-century coins, *Trans London Middlesex Archaeol Soc*, **19**, 138–46

Hill, C, Millett, M, and Blagg, T, 1980 *The Roman riverside wall and monumental arch in London*, London Middlesex Archaeol Soc Spec Pap, **3**

Hillam, J, 1982 Appendix 2: Tree-ring analysis of oak timbers, in *The bridgehead and Billingsgate to 1200* (eds K Steedman *et al*), London Middlesex Archaeol Soc Spec Pap, **14**, 143–73

Hillam, J, 1992 Appendix 2: Tree-ring analysis of oak timbers, in Steedman, K, *et al* (eds), The bridgehead and Billingsgate to 1200, London Middlesex Archaeol Soc Spec Pap **14**, 143–73

Hillam, J, Morgan, R, and Tyers, I, 1984 Dendrochronology and Roman London, *Trans London Middlesex Archaeol Soc*, **35**, 1–4

—, 1987 Sapwood estimates and the dating of short ring sequences, in *Applications of tree-ring studies* (ed R Ward) BAR Int Ser, **333**, 165–85

Hind, J, 1982 *Stability and trim of fishing vessels*, Farnham

Hobley, B, and Schofield, J, 1977 Excavations in the City of London: first interim report, 1974–5, *Antiq J*, **57**, 31–66

Höckmann, O, 1982 Spätrömische schiffsfunde in Mainz, *Archäeol Korrespond*, **12**, 231–50

—, 1989 Römische schiffsfunde westlich des Kastells Oberstimm, *Sonderdruck aus Bericht der Römasch-Germanischen Kommission*, **70**, 322–50

Holdsworth, P, 1980 *Excavations at Melbourne Street, Southampton 1971–6*, CBA Res Rep, **33**

Home, G, 1931 *Old London Bridge*, London

Hope-Taylor, B, 1977 *Yeavering: an Anglo-British centre of early Northumbria*, Department Environment Archaeol Rep, **7**, London

Hoving, A, 1991 A seventeenth-century 42-feet long Dutch pleasure vessel, in *Carvel construction technique* (eds R Reinders, and K Paul), Oxbow Monogr, **12**, 77–80

Hughes, M, 1980 The analysis of Roman tin and pewter ingots, in *Aspects of early metallurgy* (ed A Oddy), Brit Mus Occas Pap, **17**, 41–50

Hulst, R, and Lehmann, L Th, 1974 The Roman barge of Druten, *Berichten van de Rijksdienst voor het Oudheidkundig Bodemonderzoek*, 7–24

Hume, Noel I, 1956 *Treasure in the Thames*, London

Hurst, J, 1976 The pottery, in *The archaeology of Anglo-Saxon England* (ed D Wilson), 283–348

Jackson, G, 1983 *The history and archaeology of ports*, Kingswood

Johnstone, P, 1980 *The seacraft of prehistory*, London

Joncheray, J, 1976 Mediterranean hull types compared: 1, La Roche Fouras, *Int J Naut Archaeol Underwater Explor*, **5.2**, 107–14

—, 1977 Mediterranean hull types compared: 2, wreck F from Cape Draumont (Var), France, *Int J Naut Archaeol Underwater Explor* **6**, 3–7

Jong, J de, 1979 Protection and conservation of shipwrecks, in *Medieval ships and harbours in northern Europe* (ed S McGrail), BAR Int Ser, **66**, 247–60

Jottrand, G, 1895 L'industrie de la fabrication des meules en Belgique avant et apres la conquete Romaine, *Bulletin Soc Anthropol Bruxelles*, **13**, 390–408

Katzev, M, and Katzev, S, 1985 Kyrenia II: building a replica of an ancient Greek merchantman, in , *1st International symposium on ship construction in antiquity* (ed H Tzalas), 163–75

Katzev, M, 1987 The Kyrenia ship restored, in *History from the sea* (ed P Throckmorton), 55–9

—, 1989 Voyage of Kyrenia II, *Inst Naut Archeol Newsletter*, **16.1**, 4–10

Keay, S, 1988 *Roman Spain*, London

Kemp, P (ed), 1979 *The Oxford companion to ships and the sea*, Oxford

Kemp and Young, 1987 *Ship stability notes and examples*, London

Kent, J, 1978 The London area in the Late Iron Age: an interpretation of the earliest coins, *Collectanea Londinensia*, London Middlesex Archaeol Soc Spec Pap, **2**, 53–8

King, D, 1986 Petrology, dating and distribution of querns and millstones. The results of research in Bedfordshire, Buckinghamshire, Hertfordshire, and Middlesex, *Inst Archaeol Bulletin*, **23**, 65–127

Kooijmans, L, Stuart, P, Bogaers, J, and Burger, J, 1971 *Deae Nehalenniae*, Middelburg

Landstrom, B, 1961 *The ship*, London

Laures, F, 1983 Roman naval construction, as shown by the Palamos wreck, *Int J Naut Archaeol Underwater Explor*, **12.3**, 219–28

Leather, J, 1987 *Clinker boatbuilding*, London

Lebecq, S, 1990 On the use of the word 'Frisian' in the sixth–tenth centuries' written sources: some interpretations, in *Maritime Celts, Frisians and Saxons* (ed S McGrail, S), CBA Res Rep, **71**, 85–90

Lienau, O, 1934 *Die bootsfunde von Danzig-Ohra aus der Wikingerzeit*, Danzig

Litwin, J, 1991 Clinker and carvel working boats on Polish waters: their origin, development and transformations, in *Carvel construction technique*, (eds R Reinders, and K Paul), Oxbow Monog, **12**, 112–21

Locker, A, 1988 The animal bone, in *Excavations in Southwark 1973–76, Lambeth 1973–79*, Joint Publ London Middlesex Archaeol Soc/Surrey Archaeol Soc, **3**, 427–42

Loyn, H, 1962 *Anglo-Saxon England and the Norman Conquest*, London

Madsen, J, 1984 Et skibsvaerft fra sen vikingetid/tidlig middelalder ved Fribrodrea pa Falster, *Hikuin*, **10**, 261–74, Hojbjerg, (translation in English at National Maritime Museum, Greenwich)

Manning, W, 1985 *Catalogue of the Romano-British iron tools, fittings, and weapons in the British Museum*, Brit Mus Pub, London

Marsden, P, 1965a The County Hall ship, *Trans London Middlesex Archaeol Soc*, **21**, 109–17

—, 1965b The luck coin in ships, *Mar Mirror*, **51.1**, 33–4

—, 1965c A boat of the Roman period discovered on the site of New Guy's House, Bermondsey, 1958, *Trans London Middlesex Archaeol Soc*, **21.2**, 118–31

—, 1967 *A Roman ship from Blackfriars, London*, London

—, 1971 Archaeological finds in the City of London 1967–70, *Trans London Middlesex Archaeol Soc*, **23.1**, 1–14

—, 1972 Blackfriars wreck III. A preliminary note, *Int J Naut Archaeol Underwater Explor*, **1**, 130–32

—, 1974 The County Hall ship, *Int J Naut Archaeol Underwater Explor*, **3.1**, 55–65

—, 1975 The excavation of a Roman palace site in London, 1961–72, *Trans London Middlesex Archaeol Soc*, **26**, 1–102

—, 1976a A boat of the Roman period found at Bruges, Belgium, in 1899, and related types, *Int J Naut Archaeol Underwater Explor*, **5**, 23–55

—, 1976b Two Roman public baths in London, *Trans London Middlesex Archaeol Soc*, **27**, 1–70

—, 1980 *Roman London*, London

—, 1981 Early shipping and the waterfronts of London, in *Waterfront archaeology in Britain and northern Europe* (eds G Milne, and B Hobley, B), CBA Res Rep, **41**, 10–16

—, 1987 *The Roman forum site in London*, London

Mattingley, H, and Sydenham, E, 1926 *Roman imperial coinage*, London

McCaughan, M, 1978 Irish vernacular boats and their European connections, *Ulster Folklife*, **24**, 1–22

McGrail, S, 1974 *The building and trials of the replica of an ancient boat: the Gokstad faering. Part 1, building the replica*, Nat Mar Mus monog, **11**

—, 1978 *Logboats of England and Wales. Parts 1 and 2*, BAR Brit Ser, **51**

—, 1981 *The ship: rafts, boats and ships from prehistoric times to the medieval era*, London

—, 1985 Towards a classification of water transport, *World archaeol*, **16.3**, 289–303

—, 1987 *The ancient boats of north-west Europe*, London

—, 1988 Assessing the performance of an ancient boat – the Hasholme logboat, *Oxford J Archaeol*, **7.1**, 35–46

—, 1989 The shipment of traded goods and of ballast in antiquity, *Oxford J Archaeol*, **8.3**, 353–8

—, 1990 Boats and boatmanship in the late prehistoric southern North Sea and Channel region, in *Maritime Celts, Frisians and Saxons* (ed S McGrail), CBA Res Rep, **71**, 32–48

McKee, E, 1972 *Clenched lap or clinker*, London

—, 1978 Reconstruction, in *The Graveney boat* (ed V Fenwick), BAR Brit Ser, **53**, 265–94

—, 1983 *Working boats of Britain*, London

Meiggs, R, 1960 *Roman Ostia*, Oxford

—, 1982 *Trees and timber in the ancient Mediterranean world*, Oxford

Merrifield, R, 1965 *The Roman city of London*, London

—, 1983 *London, city of the Romans*, London

Miller, L, 1977 New Fresh Wharf: 2, The Saxon and early medieval waterfronts, *London Archaeol*, **3.2**, 47–53

—, 1982 Miles Lane: the early Roman waterfront, *London Archaeol*, **4.6**, 143–47

Miller, L, Schofield, J, and Richardson, B, 1986 *The Roman quay at St Magnus House, London*, London Middlesex Archaeol Soc Spec Pap, **8**, 25–74

Miller, L, Schofield, J, Rhodes, M, and Richardson, B, 1986 Pottery, in Miller, L *et al*, 1986, 96–9, 106–38

Milne, G, 1985 *The port of Roman London*, London

Milne, G, and Milne, C, 1982 *Medieval waterfront development at Trig Lane, London*, London Middlesex Archaeol Soc Spec Pap, **5**

Milne, G, Battarbee, R, Straker, V, and Yule, B, 1983 The River Thames in London in the mid first century AD, *Trans London Middlesex Archaeol Soc 34*, 19–30

Milne, G, and Goodburn, D, 1990 The early medieval port of London AD 700–1200, *Antiquity*, **64**, 629–36

Moortel, A van de, 1991 The construction of a Cog-like vessel in the late Middle Ages, in *Carvel construction technique* (eds R Reinders, and K Paul), Oxbow Monog, **12**, 42–6

Morrison, J, and Coates, J, 1986 *The Athenian Trireme: the history and reconstruction of an ancient Greek warship*, Cambridge

Muckleroy, K, Haselgrove, C, and Nash, D, 1978 A pre-Roman coin from Canterbury and the ship represented on it, *Proc Prehist Soc*, **44**, 439–44

Muller, S, 1895 *Verslag van het verhandelde in de Algemene Vergadering van het Provinciaal Utrechtsch Genootschap van Kunsten en Wetenschappen*, 129–42, 160–61, pl iv – v, Utrecht

Muller-Wille, M, 1974 Boat graves in northern Europe, *Int J Naut Archaeol Underwater Explor*, **3.2**, 187–204

Needham, S, and Longley, D, 1981 Runnymede Bridge, in *Waterfront archaeology in Britain and northern Europe* (eds G Milne, G, and Hobley, B), CBA Res Rep, **41**, 48–50

Neerso, N, 1985 *A Viking ship*, Denmark

O Eailidhe, P, 1992 The monk's boat: a Roman-period relic from Lough Lene, Co Westmeath, *Eire, Int J Naut Archaeol Explor*, **21.3**, 185–90

Olsen, O, and Crumlin-Pedersen, O, 1967 The Skuldelev ships, *Acta Archaeologica*, **38**, 73–174

Oosting, R, 1991 *Preliminary results of the research on the seventeenth-century merchantman found at Lot E 81 in the Noordoostpolder (Netherlands)*, Oxbow Monog, **12**, 72–6

Page, W, 1923 *London: its origin and early development*, London

Parker, A, 1973 The evidence provided by underwater archaeology for Roman trade in the western Mediterranean, *Mar Archaeol*, Colston Pap, **23**, 361–79

—, 1980 Roman wrecks in the Mediterranean, in *Archaeology under water* (ed K Muckelroy), 50–61

Parker, A 1992 *Ancient shipwrecks of the Mediterranean and the Roman provinces*, BAR Int Ser, **580**

Parnell, G, 1985 The Roman and medieval defences and the later development in the inmost ward, Tower of London: excavations 1955–77, *Trans London Middlesex Archaeol Soc*, **36**, 1–79

Peacock, D, 1978 The Rhine and the problem of Gaulish wine in Roman Britain, in *Roman shipping and trade: Britain and the Rhine provinces* (eds J du P Taylor, and H Cleere), CBA Res Rep, **24**, 49–51

Peacock, D, and Williams, D, 1986 *Amphorae and the Roman economy*, London

Percival, J, 1976 *The Roman villa*, London

Perring, D, 1991 *Roman London*, London

Peterson, M, 1973 *History under the sea*, Virginia

Philp, B, 1977 The forum of Roman London: excavations 1968–9, *Britannia*, **8**, 1–64

Pilcher, J, Baillie, M, Schmidt, B, and Becker, B, 1984 A 7272-year tree-ring chronology for western Europe, *Nature*, **312**, 150–52

Pomey, P, 1975 Notes and news, *Int J Naut Archaeol Underwater Explor*, **4.2**, 374

Powell, T, 1980 *The Celts*, London

Pulak, C, and Townsend, R, 1987 The Hellenistic shipwreck at Serce Limani, Turkey: Preliminary report, *American J Archaeol*, **91**, 31–57

Raban, A, 1985 Caesarea Maritima 1983–4, *Int J Naut Archaeol Underwater Explor*, **14.2**, 155–77

Rawson, K, and Tupper, E, 1983 Basic ship theory, **1**, Harlow

Read, C, and Haverfield, F, 1897 Notes on a small Roman bronze prow found in London, *Proc Soc Antiq London*, **16**, 306–8

Reinders, R, 1985 *Cog finds from the Ijsselmeerpolders, Flevobricht nr 248*, Lelystad

Rhodes, M, 1980 Stone, in *Excavations at Billingsgate Buildings 'Triangle', Lower Thames Street, 1974* (ed D Jones), London Middlesex Archaeol Soc Spec Pap **4**, 132–4

—, 1986a The finds, in Miller, L *et al*, 1986, 88–95

—, 1986b Dumps of unused pottery near London Bridge, in Miller, L *et al*, 1986, 199–203

—, 1986c Stone objects, in Miller, L *et al*, 1986, 240–5

Riley, W, and Gomme, L, 1912 *Ship of the Roman period discovered on the site of the new County Hall*, London

Rival, M, 1991 *La charpenterie navale Romaine: matériaux, méthodes, Moyens*, CRNS, Paris

Royal Commission on Historical Monuments (England), 1928 *Roman London*, London

—, 1962 Volume 1: Eburacum, Roman York, London

Rule, M, 1990 The Romano-Celtic ship excavated at St Peter Port, Guernsey, in *Maritime Celts, Frisians and Saxons* (ed S McGrail), CBA Res Rep, **71**, 49–56

Rule, M, and Monaghan, J, 1993 *A Gallo-Roman trading vessel from Guernsey*, Guernsey Mus Monog **5**

Rupprecht, G, 1985 The importance of Mainz in the Roman days, in *Conference on waterfront archaeology in north European towns, no 2, Bergen 1983* (ed A Herteig), 79–82

Ryder, M L, 1969 Changes in the fleece of sheep following domestication (with a note on the coat of cattle), in *The domestication and exploitation of plants and animals* (eds P Ucko, and G Dimbleby), 495–521

—, 1983 *Sheep and man*, London

—, 1984 The first hair remains from an Aurochs (*Bos primgenius*) and some medieval domestic cattle hair, *J Archaeol Sci*, **11**, 99–101

Salway, P, 1981 *Roman Britain*, Oxford

Sandahl, B, 1951 *Middle English Sea Terms, 1: The ship's hull*, Uppsala

Schofield, J, 1981 Medieval waterfront buildings in the City of London, in *Waterfront archaeology in Britain and northern Europe* (eds G Milne, and Hobley, B), CBA Res Rep, **41**, 24–31

—, 1984 *The building of London from the Conquest to the Great Fire*, London

Schweingruber, F, 1982 *Microscopic wood anatomy*, second ed, Teufen, Switzerland

—, 1988 *Tree-rings*, Doredrecht, Netherlands

Scrinari, V, 1979 *Le navi del porto di Claudio*, Rome

Shaw, J, 1972 Greek and Roman harbourworks, in *A history of seafaring* (ed G Bass), 88–112, London

Sheldon, H, 1975 A decline in the London settlement, AD 150–250?, *London Archaeol*, **2.11**, 278–84

—, 1978 The 1972–4 excavations: their contribution to Southwark's history, in *Southwark Excavations 1972–4, part 1*, Joint Publ London Middlesex Archaeol Soc/Surrey Archaeol Soc, 11–49

Sheldon, H, and Tyers, I, 1983 Recent dendrochronological work in Southwark and its implications, *London Archaeol*, **4.13**, 355–61

Sheppard, F, 1991 *The treasury of London's past*, London

Simpson, A, 1979 *Nautical knowledge for fishermen*, Glasgow

Smolarek, P, 1969 *Studia nad szkutnictwem Pomorza Gdanskiego 10–13 wieku*, Gdansk

Steedman, K, Dyson, T, and Schofield, J, 1992 *Aspects of Saxo-Norman London: the Bridgehead and Billingsgate to 1200*, London Middlesex Archaeol Soc Spec Pap, **14**

Steffy, J, 1982a Reconstructing the hull, in *Yassi Ada. Volume 1. A seventh-century Byzantine shipwreck* (G Bass, and F van Doorninck), 65–86

—, 1982b Shipbuilding glossary, in *Yassi Ada, volume 1. A seventh-century Byzantine shipwreck* (G Bass, and F van Doorninck), 333–4

—, 1985 The Kyrenia ship: an interim report on its hull construction, *American J Archaeol*, **89**, 71–101

—, 1987 The Kinneret boat project: part II. Notes on the construction of the Kinneret boat, *Int J Naut Archaeol Underwater Explor* **16.4**, 325–30

Stenton, D (ed), 1970 *Preparatory to Anglo-Saxon England; being the collected papers of F M Stenton*, Oxford

Strabo, *Geography*, trans H L Jones, 8 vols, 1917–49, London

Straker, V, 1987 Carbonised cereal grain from first-century London: a summary of the evidence for importation and crop processing, in Marsden, P, 1987, 151–5

Sutherland, W, 1711 *The ship-builders Assistant: or, some essays towards compleating the art of marine architecture*, London

Tacitus, *The annals of Imperial Rome*, ed Micheal Grant, 1950, 1989, London

Tatton-Brown, T, 1974 Excavations at the Custom House site, City of London, 1973, *Trans London Middlesex Archaeol Soc*, **25**, 117–219

Taylor, L, 1984 *The principles and practice of ship stability*, Glasgow

Taylor, M, 1932 Romano-British remains – country houses, in *The Victoria History of the County of Kent* (ed W Page), **3**, 102–26

Thacker, F, 1914 *The Thames highway: general history*, London

Throckmorton, P, 1972 Romans on the sea, in *A history of seafaring* (ed G Bass), 66–86

—, 1987 Reconstruction and conservation: the shipwright's art, in *History from the sea* (ed P Throckmorton), 92–100

Throckmorton, P, Parker, A, and Wachsmann, S, 1987 From Rome to Byzantium, in *History from the sea* (ed P Throckmorton), 60–91

Toynbee, J, 1964 *Art in Britain under the Romans*, Oxford

—, 1986 *The Roman art treasures from the Temple of Mithras*, London Middlesex Archaeol Soc Spec Pap, 7, London

Traullé, M, 1809 *Lettre adressée a M. Mongez par M. Traullé .... sur les débris d'un bateau déterré dans les levées de la Somme, près d'Abbeville*, Paris (see also *Archaeologica*, **118**, 54)

Tyers, P, 1985 Ceramic evidence for mercantile activity, in *Conference on waterfront archaeology in north European towns no 2, Bergen 1983* (ed A Herteig), 41–4

Tyers, P, and Vince, A, 1984 *Pottery archive users' handbook*, London

Ucelli, G, 1950 *Le navi di Nemi*, Rome

Unger, R, 1980 *The ship in the medieval economy*, 600–1600, London

Vince, A, 1984 New light on Saxon pottery from the London area, *London Archaeol*, **4.16**, 431–9

—, 1985 Saxon and medieval pottery in London: a review, *Med Archaeol*, **29**, 25–93

—, 1988 The economic basis of Anglo-Saxon London, in *The rebirth of towns in the west AD 700–1050* (ed R Hodges, and B Hobley), CBA Res Rep, **68**, 83–92

—, 1990 *Saxon London: an archaeological investigation*, London

Vlek, R, 1987 *The mediaeval Utrecht boat*, BAR Int Ser, **382**

Waddelove, A, and Waddelove, E, 1990 Archaeology and research into sea-level during the Roman era: towards a methodology based on highest astronomical tide, *Britannia*, **21**, 253–266

Weerd, M de, 1988 *Schepen voor Zwammerdam*, Netherlands Wheeler, A, 1980 Fish remains, in *Excavations at Billingsgate Buildinngs 'Triangle', Lower Thames Street, 1974* (D Jones), London Middlesex Archaeol Soc Spec Pap, **4**, 161–2

Wheeler, R, 1927 *London and the Vikings*, London Mus Cat, **1**

—, 1946 *London in Roman times*, London Mus Cat, **3**

Williams, J, 1971 Roman building-materials in south-east England, *Britannia*, **2**, 166–95

Wilmott, T, 1982 Excavations at Queen Street, City of London, 1953 and 1960, and Roman timber-lined wells in London, *Trans London Middlesex Archaeol Soc*, **33**, 1–78

Wilson, D, 1987 *The Thames: record of a working waterway*, London

Wilson, K, and White, D, 1986 *The anatomy of wood: its variability and diversity*, London

Worssam, B, 1963 *Geology of the country around Maidstone*, London

Wright, E, 1990 *The Ferriby Boats: seacraft of the Bronze Age*, London

Wright, E, and Wright, E, 1947 Prehistoric boats from North Ferriby, East Yorkshire, *Proc Prehist Soc*, **13**, 114–38

Yule, B, 1988 Natural topography of north Southwark, in *Excavations in Southwark 1973–6, Lambeth 1973–9* (ed P Hinton), Joint Publ London Middlesex Archaeol Soc/Surrey Archaeol Soc, **3**, 13–17

Index

by Lesley and Roy Adkins

The main references are given in bold.

Abbeville, France (plank-built vessel)
 Table 16
Albenga wreck, Italy, amphorae cargo
 Table 9
alder pegs 174
Aldwych 131
 Saxon settlement 131, 135
Allington, Kent, ragstone quarries 81-2,
 Fig 74
amphitheatre (at London), use of ragstone 82
amphorae 27, 108
 cargoes 19, 27, Table 9
 dates 107
 Miles Lane 26
 olive oil 12, 19, **22**, 24, 107
 Peninsular House 105
 wine 12, 19, **21-2**, 168
anchors
 Blackfriars ship 1 92, 193
 Blackfriars (Viking) 136, 141, **160-2**, Figs
  1, 142, 143
 in Boreli Museum, Marseilles (Roman) 159
 Bulbury, Dorset (Iron Age) 161-2
 Ladby Viking ship burial 162
 medieval 160, 162
 Oseberg Viking ship burial 162
 Pompeii (Roman) 159
 post-medieval 160
 Roman 95, 159, 160, 193
 Saxon 160
Ancient Monuments and Archaeological
 Areas Act 1979 97
Anglo-Saxon
 boats 174
 ships/shipbuilding 131, 151
 vessels (rivets) 177
 see also Saxon
Antikythera wreck, Greece 170, Table 15
architectural sculpture 23
artemon mast 72
ash
 belaying pin 123
 pulley block 123
 toggle 17, Fig 6
Aylesbury, Bucks, hooked nails 177

Bad Kreuznach, Germany, relief of vessel
 70
bale hook 31, Fig 14
ballast 81
 Blackfriars ship 1 193
 County Hall ship 128
 of tiles 23
barges 16, 17-19, 23, 26, 82, 103, **105**,
 108, 120, 135, 164, 215
 New Guy's House boat 24, 27, 28, 34, 98,
  103
 Rhine 22, 73, 75, 101, 103
 Romano-Celtic 73, 79, 99, 101, 178
 Thames-Medway 82
Barnack region quarries 23
barrels 19, 27
 Peninsular House 24
 Pudding Lane waterfront 20
 Queen Street 22
 reused in wells 22, 89, 195

Suffolk Lane 22
 for transporting Saxon pottery 131
 wine 22, 24, 27, 108, 138, 139-40, 195
  Blackfriars ship 1 cargo 89, 195-6, Tables
  17, 19
barrel-staves 22, 95
basilica (London) Fig 4
 use of ragstone 82
 use of tiles 83
bastions 105
bath/bathhouse
 Billingsgate 105
 Brishing, Kent 81, Fig 74
beaching 24, 38, 177-8, 179
bead (from County Hall ship) Fig 105
beam 68, 73, 194, 215
 Blackfriars ship 1 67, 76, 89, 195, Table 17
 Bruges boat 67
 County Hall ship 112, 119, 122
 New Guy's House boat 99, 101
 see also breadth
belaying pin 123, Figs 105, 116
Benfleet, Essex, Danish fleet 136
Bergen, Norway, medieval ships,
 planking 173
 wales 159
berthing 12, 16, 23-9, **108**, 163, **177-9**
 Saxon 131-3, 138-40, 177, 179, Fig 122
 see also hithes, jetties, landing stages,
  quays, waterfronts
Bevaix, Switzerland, barge (Romano-Celtic)
 79, Table 16
Billingsgate
 bath 105
 crane 27
 customs duty 136
 embankments 153, 179, 206
 jetty 138
 landing place 135
 mooring posts 138
 quays 138, 139, Fig 122
 waterfront 141, 153
Billingsgate boats (late Saxon) 153-4, Fig
 137
 caulking 170, Table 14
 construction 170-1, Table 14
 frames 154
 lap pegs 154
 location of Fig 1
 oak 153, 154, Table 21
 pegs 170
 planks
  pegged 153-4, 170, 206-7, Fig 137, Table
  14
  riveted 154, 170, 206-7, Figs 137, 174,
  Table 14
 poplar/willow Table 21
 rivets 154, 170
 roves 154, 170
 scarf 154
 tree-ring dating 153, 154, 170, Fig 174
 trenail 154, Table 21
 wedges 154, Table 21
birch
 caulking 38
 resin Fig 164

Black burnished pottery 23
Blackfriars, Viking anchor 136, 141, **160-
 2**, Figs 1, 142, 143
Blackfriars ship 1 12, 13, 24, 27, 29, **33-
 95**, 177, 178, 179, Figs 1, **18-86**
 ancestor of cog Fig 152
 anchors 92, 193
 animal bone 95
 ballast 193
 barrel-staves 95
 beam 67, 76, 89, 195, Table 17
 bow **37-8**, 39, 40, 45, 56, 58, 59, 70, 85,
  91, 94, Figs 23, 168, Table 2
  reconstruction 56, **65-6**, Figs 55, 60, 80-84
 bowl (pottery) 80, 95, 181, 182, Fig 71
 bulkhead (unlikely) 49, 50
 bulwarks 61
 bungs 39, Fig 30
 cargoes 33, 37, 70, 85, 194, 195-7
  barrels of wine 89, 195-6, Tables 17, 19
  grain 89
  ragstone 62, **80-3**, 89, 91, 92, 195, **196**,
   Figs 23, 25, 40, 42, 72-74, 86, Tables
   8, 17, 19
  sacks of grain 195, 196, Tables 17, 19
  weight of 89, 193, 195-7, Table 17
 carvel-built 33, 34, 164
 caulking 13, **40-5**, 76, 77-9, 95, Figs 29,
  30, 32, 33, 48
  birch 38
  hazel 38, 39, 40, 51, 79, 164, **165**, 168,
   189-90, Figs 52, 161, **162**, Table 14
  pine resin 38, 39, 40, 51, 77, 168, **191**,
   Figs 52, **164**
  tar (no evidence) 40
 ceiling **54-5**, 60, 61, 62, 81, Figs 23, 25
  planks/planking 38, 79, 80, 82, Fig 58
  weight 193
 chines 38, **40**, 45, 48, 58, 67, 73, Figs 23,
  25, 27, 33
 construction **38-55**, **76-9**, 97, 102, **164-8**,
  Figs 69, 70, Table 14
 date 80, 95
 crew 61, 70, 76, 80, 193, 194, 195, 197,
  Tables 17, 18
 deck 55, 65, 76
  cabin 80
  height 66, 75, 89
  reconstruction 61-5
  weight Table 18
 deck beams 61, 65, 95, Fig 57
 dendrochronology 80, 95
 discovery 33-5, Fig 18
 endposts 79
 excavation 33-5, 38, 39, 49, 55, 58, 76,
  95, Figs 20, 28, 53, 54, 76, 86
  future 37, 80
 fastenings 36, 48, 50-4
  see also nails
 floor-timbers 38, 39, 40, **45-9**, 50, 51, 54,
  55, 56, 58, 59, 61, 66, 67, 81, 89, 91,
  Figs 23, 25, 27, 30-34, 37-39, 41
  construction 76-9, 80
  dendrochronology 80
  limber holes 45, 48, 79, 198-9, Figs 30, 32-
  34

mast-step **48-9**, 55, Figs 28, 33, 39, 43
millstone position 88
nails 50-4, 183, Fig 156
ragstone position 80
reconstruction Figs 55, 59
silt accumulation 94-5
tree-ring analysis 204
types of 37
weight 193
forefoot 66, 72, Fig 60
frames 35, **40-5**, 46, 51, 54, 55, 58, Figs 30, 48, 56, Tables 4, 5
construction 76-9, 80
limber holes 74
nails 39, 60, 79, 183
oak 38
plank thickness Table 2
surviving 36
weight 193, Table 18
gunwale 55, 70, 74, 197, Fig 168
height 76, 89
reconstruction 61
height 61-2, 75, 89
hold (for cargo) 37, 54, **61**, 62, 76, 81, 85, 195-7, Fig 72, Table 17
hull 46, 54, 55, 70, 72, 80, 197
reconstruction 55-6, 57-60, Figs 56, 84
Teredo borings 17, 80, 194, Table 17
volume 75-6
weight 55, 193, 195, Table 18
keel 38, 60, 76, 86, 195, 197
keel-planks **38-9**, 54, 58, 67, 74, 79, 89, Figs 30, 34, 59
construction 76
knees 64-5, 76
knee-timber Fig 57
last voyage 81, Fig 73
leather (decorated with fish) 80, 95, Fig 71
length 35, 56, 60, 76, 80, 89, 195, Fig 168
limber holes 74, 99-100
Limnoria 80, 86
location of Fig 18
loss 91-5, Fig 86
mallet (wooden) 40, 80, 95, Fig 71
mast 37, 48, 50, 54, 65, **67-70**, 72, 73, 76, 193, Fig 23
construction 79
height 67-9, Fig 63, Table 7
salvage 92
mast-beam 65
mast-step 37, **48-9**, 67, 68, 70, 72, 79, 80, 91, Figs 36, 42, 54
coin (votive) **49**, 79, 80, Figs 25, 33, 39, 43-45, 54
frame 50, 65, 164, Fig 23
reconstruction Fig 58
socket 37, 48-9, 67, 80
materials 38
millstone (unfinished) 50, 80, **85**, Figs 21, 23, 36, 38, 53, 77
nails 46, 54, 55, 60, 76-9, 189, Figs 30, 32, 46, 57
cone-headed 51-4, 95, **183**, 187, 191, Figs 52, **154-155**
cone-shaped 38, 40, 49, 54, 65, 79
hooked 17, 39, 40, 45, **50-4**, 55, 79, 183, Figs 47, 48, Table 6
metallographic analysis 183-7, Figs 154-161
semi-cone-headed 39, 51, 183-5, Figs 156-159
weight 193
oak 38, 193, 204
pegs 51, 77-9, 102, Figs 26, 33
see also trenails

performance 193, 197-9, Table 17
plank-built Fig 16
planks **38**, 189-90, Figs 24, 29, Tables 1, 2
construction 76, 79
nails 79, 183
tree-ring analysis 204
weight 193
pottery 95, 181-2
post-medieval 181
propulsion 55, 67-74
rabbets 38, 51, 54, 58, 65
reconstruction **55-76**, 89-91, 194-9, Figs 39, 48, 57, 69, 70, 80-85
recording timbers 35, 36, Figs 53, 54, 76
rig/rigging 79, 193, Fig 64
see also sails
rudders 75-6, 79, 92
sails 70-4, 76, 193
samian pottery 93, 181
scarfs/scarf joints 58
side-frames 37, 40, **46-8**, 50, 55, 59, 65, Figs 23, 25, 27, 35, 39
construction 76, 79
nails 51, 52-4, 55, 183
Teredo 86, Fig 35
side planking 40, Table 3
construction 76, 79
sinking of 80, 91-5, Fig 86
skeleton-built 79, 163, 164
speed 89, 197-9, Fig 170, Table 20
stability 58, 60, 62, 81, **88-91**, **193-7**, Figs 165-167
stanchions 49-50, 65, Fig 43
steering 55, 70, 73, **74-6**
stem 56, 66
stempost 37, 38, 45, **54**, 57, 58, 60, 66, 67, 72, 197, Figs 23, 25, 30, 34, 53, 55
construction 79
reconstruction 65-6, Fig 59
Teredo 86
weight 193
stern 37, 38, 39, 54, 57, 58, 75, 76, , Figs 50, 51, 168
deck cabin 80
reconstruction 55, 67, Figs 80-84
sternpost 35, 38, 39, **54**, 56, 57, 60, 197, Fig 50
construction 79
reconstruction 67
weight 193
stocks 77
strakes **39**, 40, 45, 46-8, 55-6, 59, 61, 66, 67, 72, 95, Figs 23, 25, 57
construction 76, 79
identification 58
nails 52
numbering 37
reconstruction Fig 85
weight 193
stringers 65
Teredo borings/ship-worm 70, 72, 80, **86-9**, Fig 78, Table 19
tiles (no trace) 80
tree-ring
analysis/dating 38, 95, 174, 203, **204**, Figs 24, 171
pattern 97, 165
trenails 38, 65, 79, Fig 48
walkways 62
waterlines 86, **194-5**, 196, 199, Fig 83, Table 20
wedge (wooden) 95
weight 55, 77, 89, **193-9**, Tables 17, 18
yard 74, 193
Blackfriars ship 3 (medieval) 179

Blessey, France, models of ship 66
boat burials/graves 170, Figs 148, 149
Boatcad, computer program 57, 74, 89, 90, 103-4, 193, 194, 195-9, Figs 165-168, 170
boat hooks 17, Fig 7
bonding tiles 29
Boudican uprising 15
Boughton Monchelsea, Kent Fig 74
ragstone quarries 81
bow
Blackfriars ship 1 **37-8**, 39, 40, 45, 56, 58, 59, 70, 85, 91, 94, Figs 23, 168, Table 2
reconstruction 56, **65-6**, Figs 55, 60, 80-84
County Hall ship 112, 119, 121
reconstruction Fig 114
New Guy's House boat 98
Veneti ships 168
bowl (pottery), Blackfriars ship 1 80, 95, 181, 182, Fig 71
breadth 120-1, Tables 12, 13
see also beam
Bremen medieval cogs 177
mast 73
bricks 23
County Hall ship 129
bridge see London Bridge
Brigg boat, plank-built 163
Brigg boat 2, speed 198
Brishing, Kent, bathhouse 81, Fig 74
Brockley Hill pottery 16
Broighter, Ireland, model Celtic vessel 66, 72, 76, Fig 66
Bronze Age boats
Caldicot, Gwent 163
Dover 163
North Ferriby 142, 168
Bronze Age embankment, Runnymede 163
Bronze Age/Iron Age embankment, Whitehall 163
bronze (cargo) 136
brooch (from County Hall ship) Fig 105
Bruges boat, Belgium, 177
beam 67
chines 67
deck height 75
limber holes Fig 62
mast 67-9, 70, Fig 62
mast-step 67, Fig 62
frame 164-5, Figs 62, 145
plank-built Table 16
rudder 75, 76, Fig 67
steering oar 75
stern 75
tiller 75
Bucklersbury House, boat hook Fig 7
building stone see ragstone
Bulbury, Dorset, Iron Age anchor 160
bulkhead 215
Blackfriars ship 1 (unlikely) 49, 50
Bull Wharf, German boat (early medieval) 208
bulwarks, Blackfriars ship 1 61
bungs
Blackfriars ship 1 39, Fig 30
New Guy's House boat 99
see also pegs

Caesarea Maritima vessel, Israel Table 15
Caldicot, Gwent, Bronze Age boat 163
Cap del Vol vessel, Gerona, Italy Table 15
Cape Dramont F wreck, France, mortice-and-tenon joints 170
Capistello vessel, Sicily Table 15

cargoes 12, 16, **19-23**, 31, 108, 122, 139-40, 177, 178, 179, Figs 8, 9
  Albenga wreck (amphorae) Table 9
  amphorae 19, 27, Table 9
  barrels of wine
    Roman 19, 27, 89, 195-6, Tables 17, 19
    medieval 139-40
  Blackfriars ship 1 33, 37, 70, 85, 194, **195-7**
    barrels of wine 89, 195-6, Tables 17, 19
    ragstone 62, **80-3**, 89, 91, 92, 195, **196**, Figs 23, 25, 40, 42, 72-74, 86, Tables 8, 17, 19
    sacks of grain 89, 195, 196, Tables 17, 19
    weight of 89-91, 193, 195-7, Table 17
  blocks of stone 27
  customs duties 136, 138, 140
  grain 12, 19, 89, 195, 196, Tables 17, 19
  Isola delle Correnti wreck (stone) Table 9
  loads (classical wrecks) 89-90, Table 9
  Madrague de Gien wreck (amphorae) Table 9
  Mahdia wreck (stone) Table 9
  Marzamemi 1 wreck (stone) Table 9
  medieval 179
  planks 135
  ragstone see Blackfriars ship 1
  St Tropez wreck (stone) Table 9
  Saxon 131, 136-8
  tolls 135
  Torre Sgarrata wreck (stone) Table 9
  weight of 23, 89, 136-8
  see also amphorae, samian pottery, trade, warehouses
cartoon, Blackfriars ship 1 Fig 22
carvel-built vessels 77, Table 14
  Blackfriars ship 1 33, 34, 164
  County Hall ship 114
  New Guy's House boat 164
  post-medieval 13
carvel construction 213, 215
carvel-laid planking 164
case-opener (from Walbrook stream valley) 31, Fig 14
caulking 13, 164, 166, 168, 171, 213, 215, 216, Fig 2, Table 14
  Billingsgate boats (hair/moss) 170, Table 14
  Blackfriars ship 1 13, **40-5**, 76, 77-9, 95, Figs 29, 30, 32, 33, 48
    birch 38
    hazel 38, 39, 40, 51, 79, 164, 165, 168, **189-90**, Figs 52, 161, **162**, Table 14
    pine resin 38, 39, 40, 51, 77, 168, **191**, Figs 52, **164**
    tar (no evidence) 40
  County Hall ship 114
    pine resin 191
  Fennings Wharf boats 158, Fig 139
    hair 158, 170, **211**, Tables 14, 22, 23
    wool 156, 159, **211**, Table 22
  New Fresh Wharf boat (moss) 142, 151, 170, Figs 128, 129, Table 14
  New Guy's House boat 13, Figs 88, 93
    hazel 98, 99, 102, 164, 165, **190**, Fig 163, Table 14
    pine resin 98, 99, 102, 191
  North Ferriby Bronze Age boats (moss) 142
  St Peter Port ship 13
    moss 39, 168
  Veneti ships (moss) 168
ceiling 215
  Blackfriars ship 1 **54-5**, 60, 61, 62, 81, 193, Figs 23, 25

Laurons ship 61
  New Guy's House boat 103, Figs 88, 94
ceiling planks/planking,
  Blackfriars ship 1 38, 79, 80, 82, Fig 58
  New Guy's House boat 100, 102
Celtic
  boats, Broighter, Ireland (model) 76
  shipbuilding 33, 36, 131, **177**
  ships 24, 66, 175, 176, Fig 61
ceol see keels
chalk
  for lime mortar 83
  quarries 83
Chamberlains Wharf, Southwark, logboat 141
chines 215
  Blackfriars ship 1 38, **40**, 45, 48, 58, 67, 73, Figs 23, 25, 27, 33
  Bruges boat 67
Chretienne 'A' wreck, France 123
  coin 49
Chretienne vessel, France Table 15
classical vessels 17, 66, 76, 89, 120, 121, 163, Tables 9, 12
Classis Britannica
  iron working 83
  stamps on tiles 17, Fig 6
clenched nails Fig 3
clinker
  construction 213, Fig 2
  planking 215
  shipbuilding 13
clinker-built vessels 142, 152, 170-4, Figs 148, 151, Table 14
  fastenings 170-4, Fig 151
  Fennings Wharf boats 158, 174
  frames 143-4
  hulks 136
  medieval 13, 179
  New Fresh Wharf boat 142, 151
  pegs Fig 150
  post-Roman 13
  Puck, Poland 174
  Saxon 13, 131
  Scandinavian 143
  Scandinavian-Slavic 152
  Viking 13, 136
clinker-laid construction 164
clinker-planked vessels Fig 149
coal 23
cogs (medieval) 73, 158, 177, Figs 152, 153
coins 107
  Celtic ships depicted 66, 72, 168, Fig 61
  Chretienne 'A' wreck 49
  County Hall ship 125, 128, 129, Fig 105
  Gaulish ships 66, Fig 61
  mast-steps 49
    Blackfriars ship 1 49, 79, 80, Figs 25, 33, 39, 43-45, 54
  minting 105
  Peninsular House 105
  Saxon 131, 133
  sceattas 131
  Smith's Wharf 17
Colchester, ragstone used in temple of Claudius 82
column, New Fresh Wharf quay 23
computer programs 12
  Boatcad 57, 74, 89, 90, 103-4, 193, 194, 195-9, Figs 165-168, 170
  tree-ring dating 201, 203
cone-headed nails see nails
cone-shaped nails see nails
conservation, County Hall ship (attempts at) 109

Constantius Chlorus, entry into London 105, 107, Fig 95
construction (of vessels) 13, **163-77**, Figs 144-153, Tables 14-16
  Billingsgate boats 170-1, Table 14
  Blackfriars ship 1 38-55, 76-9, 97, 102, 164-8, Figs 69, 70, Table 14
    date 80, 95
  carvel 213
  clinker 213, Fig 2
  clinker-laid 164
  County Hall ship 110, 111, 116, **124-5**, **168-70**, Fig 107, Table 14
    date 110, 125
  Fennings Wharf boats 170-3, Table 14
  frames 164, 170
  hull 170
  keel 164
  New Fresh Wharf boat 141, 152, 170-3, Table 14
    date 141, 205
  New Guy's House boat 98-100, **102-3**, 164, 165, 168, 207, Fig 93, Table 14
  pegged 170-4
  planking 164
  Saxon 170-4
  stems 164
containers for pottery transport 131
County Hall ship 108, **109-29**, Figs 1, 97-117, Tables 10-12, 15
  animal bones 129
  ballast 128
  bead Fig 105
  beam 112, 119, 122
  belaying pin 123, Figs 105, 116
  bow 112, 119, 121, Fig 114
  breadth 121, Table 12
  brick 129
  brooch Fig 105
  carvel-built 114
  caulking 114, 191
  coins 125, 128, 129, Fig 105
  conservation attempts 109
  construction 110-11, 116, **124-5**, **168-70**, Fig 107, Table 14
    date 110, 125
  crooks 117
  cross-beams 116, **118**, 119, 122, Figs 105, 107
  damage 127-8
  deck 61, 112, 119, **122-3**
  deck beams 112, 122, 124, Fig 112
  dendrochronology 124-5
  discovery 109-11
  dismantled by Museum of London 109-10
  draw-tongued joints 111
  endpost 119
  excavation 109, 123, Figs 97, 103, 105
  fastenings 113-18, 124
  feather-head 128
  fire 128
  frames 61, 109-10, 112, **117-18**, 119, 122, 123, 129, Figs 111, 112
    fastenings 124
    limber holes 117, 118, 119-20, Fig 110
    recording 111
    repair 127-8
    spacing Table 11
    trenails Fig 110
  gaming counters 129
  garboard strakes 114, 119, 124, Fig 107
  gunwales 61, 112, **118**, **123**, 124, 128
  height 61, 119, 123
  hull 109, 116, 117, 118, 119, 122, 123, 124, 128, 129

reconstruction 119-24
keel 109, 110, **112-13**, 114, 116, 117, 118, 119, 123, 124, Fig 107, Table 11
keelson 118
length **119-21**, 123, 126, Table 12
limber holes 99, Fig 107
location 70, 111, Figs 104, 117
in London Museum (Kensington Palace) Fig 101
loss 128-9
mast 124, Fig 114
mast-step 119, 123
materials 112
model 111
mortice-and-tenon joints 108, 111, 112, 113, 114-16, 117, 118, 119, 122, 123, 124, 169, 170, Figs 106, 107
moved to Lancaster House 109
moved to London Museum (Kensington Palace) 109, Figs 98, 100
nails 112, 116, 118, 119, 128, 129, Figs 105, 107
oak 112, 113, 124, 125, 128, 204, 205
oars 123, 126
official use 176
pegs 113, 116, 170
pine resin dressing 112, 117
pins (oak) 129
plank-built Table 16
planks 109, 110, 112, **113-17**, 119, 124, 128, Fig 108
pottery 128, 129, Fig 105
propulsion 123-4
pulley block 123, Figs 105, 116
quarter rudders 123
raising Fig 99
reconstructions 117, **119-24**, 127, Figs 109, 113-115
repairs 108, 127-8, Fig 107
rigging 123
rocker 113
sails 123, 126
scarfs/scarf joints 112, 116, 117, 118, 124, Fig 107
scupper holes 122
shell-built 168
shoe 129
stability 116, 119
stanchions 122, 124
steering 123-4
stem 112
stempost 113, 119
stern 112, Fig 114
sternpost 113, 119
stocks 124
strakes 112, **114**, **116**, 117, 118, 119, 122, 123, 124, 128, 169, Table 10
stringers 112, **118**, 122, 123, 124, 126, Fig 107
Teredo borings (lack of) 128
tree-ring
  analysis/dating 110-11, 113-14, 128, 174, 203, **205**, Fig 172
  patterns Fig 108
trenails 112, 113, 114, 118, 128, Fig 110
wale 112, 116, 118, 119, 122, 123, 124, Figs 106, 107, 113
warship (discounted) 125-6
wedges 118
crane hook 27, 31, Fig 14
cranes 25, **27**, 62, 73
  use of yard 73, 76
crates 19, 20-1
crew accommodation, Blackfriars ship 1 80
crews 62, 72

Blackfriars ship 1 61, 70, 76, 80, 193, 194, 195, 197, Tables 17, 18
New Guy's House boat 103, 104
St Peter Port ship 70, 80
Cripplegate fort 17, Fig 4
crooks
  County Hall ship 117
  New Guy's House boat 100
cross-beams 62-4, 144, 151, 216
  County Hall ship 116, **118**, 119, 122, Figs 105, 107
  New Fresh Wharf boat 151
Custom House
  quarry pit Fig 13
  quay 26, **28**, 29, 179, Figs 13, 15
  warehouse Fig 13
customs duties
  on cargoes 136, 138, 140
  on trade 131

damage 213
  County Hall ship 127-8
  New Guy's House boat 104
Danish
  fleet, Benfleet, Essex 136
  medieval cogs 73
  raids 131
  see also Viking
Danzig Ohra (Gdansk), Poland,
  boat, pegged construction 171
  boat 1, reconstruction Fig 135
  boats 1-3, planks Table 13
dates (in amphorae) 107
decay (modern), New Guy's House boat 97
deck beams 215
  Blackfriars ship 1 61, 65, 95, Fig 57
  County Hall ship 112, 122, 124, Fig 112
  Laurons ship 122
  Punta Ala wreck 123
deck cabin, Blackfriars ship 1 80
deck planking, Laurons ship 122
decks 61-2, 216
  Blackfriars ship 1 55, 61-5, 75, 89, 95, Table 18
  Bruges boat, height 75
  County Hall ship 61, 112, 119, **122-3**
  Laurons ship 61, 122-3
  Punta Ala wreck 123
defensive walls
  London 16, 23, 105, 108, Figs 4, 18, 122
    bastions 105
    New Fresh Wharf 29, 108
    ragstone 83, Fig 75
    reused stones 105
  Reculver 82
  Richborough 82
  Rochester 82
dendrochronological dating, Saxon oak structure 131-3
dendrochronology 13, 201-8
  Blackfriars ship 1 80, 95
  County Hall ship 124-5
  landing stage 24
  London Bridge (Roman) 24
  New Fresh Wharf quay 28
  quay 25
  see also tree-ring analysis/dating
discovery
  Blackfriars ship 1 33-5, Fig 18
  County Hall ship 109-11
  New Guy's House boat 97
docks (medieval) 179
Dover
  Bronze Age boat 163
  lighthouse (use of ragstone) 82

dove-tailed joint (in Laurons ship) 122
Dowgate 138
  berthing 139, Fig 122
  embankments 138, 179
  hithe 140
Dramont vessel, France Table 15
draw-tongued joints 13
  County Hall ship 111
Druten vessel, Netherlands (plank-built) Table 16
Dublin, tree-ring analysis of ships 208
Durobrivae (Rochester) 81
Dutch medieval cogs (masts) 73

Eccles villa 83, Fig 74
edge-joining plank construction 13
edge-to-edge planking 114, 215
  New Guy's House boat 99
embankments
  Billingsgate 153, 179, 206
  Dowgate 138, 179
  Saxon 179, 205
endposts 216
  Blackfriars ship 1 79
  County Hall ship 119
  New Guy's House boat **98**, 100, 101, 104
Ethelredeshythe 138
excavations 12-13
  Blackfriars ship 1 33-5, 38, 39, 49, 55, 58, 76, 95, Figs 28, 53, 54, 76, 86
    future 37, 80
  County Hall ship 109, 123, Figs 97, 103, 105
  New Guy's House boat 97, 98, Figs 87, 88
    future 102, 104

fastenings 13-14, 213, Table 14
  Blackfriars ship 1 36, 48, 50-4
  clinker-built vessels 170-4, Fig 151
  County Hall ship 113-18, 124
  New Fresh Wharf boat 142
  New Guy's House boat 97, 99, 100
  Viking ships 136
  see also nails, rivets, trenails
feather-head, County Hall ship 128
feather-headings 116, 215
Fennings Wharf boats, Southwark (late Saxon) Fig 1
  caulking 158, Fig 139
    hair 158, 170, **211**, Tables 14, 22, 23
    wool 156, 159, **211**, Table 22
  clinker-built 158, 174
  construction 170-3, Table 14
  frames 157, Fig 140
  garboard strakes 156-7, 174, Fig 139
  hull 157, 159
  keel 135, 156-7, 174, 177, 207, Fig 139, Table 14
  nails (hooked) 157, 174, 177
  oak 155, 156, 158, 207
  paint 159
  planks 154-6, 170, 207, Fig 138
  poplar/willow Table 21
  rabbets 156, 157, Fig 139
  repair 159
  rivets 155, 156, 170
  roves 155, 170
  scarfs/scarf joints 156, 157, Fig 139
  shell-built 158
  stern 157
  strakes 155-6
  tar 159
  tree-ring analysis/dating 154, 155, 156, 158, 170, 174, **207**, Fig 175
  trenails 156, 159, Table 21

wale 158-9, 207, Fig 140
Fennings Wharf waterfront 141
Ferriby, Yorkshire, Bronze Age boats 142, 168
    caulking (moss) 142
    plank-built 163
    speed 198
fire
    County Hall ship 128
    of London (Hadrianic) 19
    Pudding Lane warehouses 29-31
fish 16, 105-7, 135, 136, 138
    bones 12, 16, 105
fishing vessels 16-17, 105-7
    Fiumicino, Italy 16
    Saxon 135
fish sauce production 107
fish weir (Public Cleansing Depot site) 17
Fiumicino boats, Italy 16, Tables 12, 15
Flanders, trade 136
flint quarries 83
floor-timbers 215, 216
    Blackfriars ship 1 39, 40, 45-9, 50, 51, 54,
        55, 56, 58, 59, 61, 66, 67, 81, 89, 95,
        Figs 23, 25, 27, 30-34, 37-39, 41
        construction 76-9, 80
        dendrochronology 80
        limber holes 45, 48, 79, 198-9, Figs 30, 32-34
        mast-step 48-9, 55, Figs 28, 33, 39, 43
        millstone position 88
        nails 50-4, 183, Fig 156
        ragstone position 80
        reconstruction Figs 55, 59
        silt accumulation 94-5
        tree-ring analysis 204
        types of 37
        weight 193
    limber holes 215-16
        see also Blackfriars ship 1
    St Peter Port ship 80
fords 163
fore-and-aft sails 73
forefoot
    Blackfriars ship 1 66, 72, Fig 60
    pre-Roman ships 66, Fig 61
forts
    boats associated with 176
    Cripplegate 17, Fig 4
    use of ragstone 82-3
forum (at London) 15, 26, Fig 4
    use of ragstone 82
frames 143, 213, 215
    Billingsgate boats 154
    Blackfriars ship 1 35, 36, 38, 40-5, 46, 51,
        52, 54, 58, Figs 30, 48, 56, Tables 2, 4, 5
        construction 76-9, 80
        limber holes 74
        nails 39, 60, 79, 183
        weight 193, Table 18
    construction 164, 170
    County Hall ship 61, 109-10, 112, 117-18,
        119, 122, 123, 129, Figs 111, 112
        fastenings 124
        limber holes 117, 118, 119-20, Fig 110
        recording 111
        repair 127-8
        spacing Table 11
        trenails Fig 110
    Fennings Wharf boats 157, Fig 140
    Graveney boat 143, 151
    Laurons ship 123
    limber holes 215-16
        see also Blackfriars ship 1, County Hall

ship
    New Fresh Wharf boat 141, 143-52, Fig 136
    New Guy's House boat 97, 98, 99-100,
        101-2, 103, 104, Figs 90, 91, 93
        construction 102
        limber holes 99
    St Peter Port ship 39
    see also crooks, floor-timbers, side-frames
France, trade 136
Frisian, merchants/traders 131, Fig 151

gaming counters (from County Hall ship) 129
garboard strakes 215
    County Hall ship 114, 119, 124, Fig 107
    Fennings Wharf boats 156-7, 174, Fig 139
Gaul, cargoes 19-22, 107, Figs 8, 9
Gaulish ships (on coins) 66, Fig 61
General Post Office site, Newgate, pottery 181
German
    boat, Bull Wharf (early medieval) 208
    traders 138
Germany
    cargoes 22-3, 107
    trade 136
glass 136
Gokstad vessels, Norway (Viking) 73, 76, 143, 144, 198
gold 136
Goldcliff vessel, Gwent, plank-built Table 16
grain 138
    cargoes 12, 19, 89, 195, 196, Tables 17, 19
Grand Congloue wreck, France Table 15
    mortice-and-tenon joints 170
Graveney boat (late Saxon) 135, 170
    frames 143, 151
    pegs 174
    rivets 174
    speed 198
    strakes 143
gunwales 216
    Blackfriars ship 1 55, 70, 74, 197, Fig 168
        height 76, 89
        reconstruction 61
    County Hall ship 61, 112, 118, 123, 124, 128
        height 75, 76, 89
    Laurons ship 61, 123
    New Fresh Wharf boat 142, Fig 136
    New Guy's House boat (missing) 101
Guy's Hospital, Southwark
    pottery 24
    quay 24, 29, 103, Fig 17

Hadrianic fire of London 19
hair caulking
    Billingsgate boats 170, Table 14
    Fennings Wharf boats 170, 211, Tables 14, 22, 23
Hamwic (Southampton), rivets 133
Hanse merchants 138
hazel caulking
    Blackfriars ship 1 38, 39, 40, 51, 164, 165,
        168, 189-90, Figs 52, 161, 162, Table 14
    New Guy's House boat 98, 99, 102, 164,
        165, 190, Fig 163, Table 14
hearth, St Peter Port ship 80
height
    Blackfriars ship 1 61-2, 75, 89
        mast 67-9, Fig 63, Table 7
    Bruges boat 75

    mast 68, 70
    County Hall ship 61, 119, 123
    Laurons ship 61, 123
    of a man (average) 61
    New Guy's House boat 101-2
Hengistbury Head, Dorset 24
    port 177-8
    wine trade 168
Hibernia Wharf, Southwark Fig 1
    oar/paddle 141, 159, Fig 141
hithes 139, 140
    Dowgate 140
Hjortspring, Denmark, vessel 170
    vessel 2, speed 198
holds 73, 89
    Blackfriars ship 1 37, 54, 61, 62, 76, 81,
        85, 195-7, Fig 72, Table 17
    hulk 140
    keel (type of boat) 140
    Laurons ship 62
hones, Norway 136
    Pennant grit 23
    ragstone 23
hooked nails see nails
horrea see warehouses
hulc (hulk) 136
hulcus (hulk) 135
hulks 135, 136, 139, 140
    clinker-built 136
    hold 140
    hulc 136
    on New Shoreham seal 136, Fig 120
    hulcus 135
    masts 136, 140
    square sails 136
hulls 89, 213, 215
    Blackfriars ship 1 46, 55, 70, 72, 80, 197
        reconstruction 55-6, 57-60, Figs 56, 84
        Teredo borings 17, 80, 194, Table 17
        volume 75-6
        weight 55, 193, 195, Table 18
    construction 170
    County Hall ship 109, 116, 117, 118, 119,
        122, 123, 124, 128, 129
        reconstruction 119-24
    Fennings Wharf boats 157, 159
    Laurons ship 122
    New Fresh Wharf boat 142
    New Guy's House boat 98, 103-4
    St Peter Port ship 39
    Veneti ships 168

imperial estates
    iron working 83
    ragstone quarries 83
imports see cargoes, trade
Inchtuthil fort, cone-headed nails 166, Fig 145
ingots (pewter) 107
Irish timber construction, Roskilde Viking
    ship, Denmark 208
iron see anchors, fastenings, nails, rivets
iron working
    Classis Britannica 83
    imperial estate 83
Isola delle Correnti wreck, Sicily, cargo
    (stone) Table 9
ivory 136

jet pins (from Whitby) 23
jetties 24, 177, 178-9
    Billingsgate 138
    Miles Lane 26, 179, Fig 10
    New Fresh Wharf 179, Fig 123
Jeune-Garde B wreck, France Table 15

Junkerath, Germany, relief of vessel 70

Kalkar vessel, Germany, plank-built Table 16
Kalmar vessels, Sweden, 66, 173
Kapel-Avezaath vessel, Netherlands, plank-
    built Table 16
keel (type of boat) 179
keel-planks 215
    Blackfriars ship 1 38-9, 54, 58, 67, 74, 79,
        89, Figs 30, 34, 59
        construction 76
    New Guy's House boat 99-100, 102
    St Peter Port ship 39, 58
keels 24, 123, 135, 215, 216
    Blackfriars ship 1 38, 60, 76, 86, 195, 197
    construction 164
    County Hall ship 109, 110, 112-13, 114,
        116, 117, 118, 119, 123, 124, Fig 107,
        Table 11
    Fennings Wharf boats 135, 156-7, 174,
        177, 207, Fig 139, Table 14
    Kyrenia ship II 73
    New Fresh Wharf boat 141, 142, 144
    New Guy's House boat 100, 102
keels (type of ship) 135-6, 139, 140
keelson 72, 215
    County Hall ship 118
Kimmeridge shale 23, Fig 8
knees 215
    Blackfriars ship 1 64-5, 76
    medieval ships 64
    New Fresh Wharf boat 141, 144-51
knee-timber, Blackfriars ship 1 Fig 57
Kollerup cog, Jutland, mast-step frame 177
Koln vessel, Germany, plank-built Table 16
Kvalsund ship (seventh century) 131
Kyrenia ship Table 15
    breadth Table 12
    length Table 12
    rocker 113
    strakes 118
    toggle 17
Kyrenia ship II
    keel 73
    mast 73
    reconstruction 73, 91
    steering 73

La Coruna, Spain, lighthouse 175
Ladby Viking ship burial, Denmark, an-
    chor 162
Lake Kinneret vessel, Israel 116, 121,
    Tables 12, 15
Lake Nemi vessels, Italy 116, 170, Tables
    12, 15
Lake Neuchatel, steering oar 75
lamps, Pompeii 21
landing place, Billingsgate 135
landing stages 16, 24-5, 179, Figs 10, 11
lap 13, 215
lap pegs 172-3, 174
    Billingsgate boats 154
    Kalmar vessels 173
    New Fresh Wharf boat 142, 152, Figs 126,
        129, 136, Table 21
    Skuldelev vessels 172-3
    Slavonic ships 172
La Roche Fouras vessel, ?France Table 15
lateen sails 70
Late Saxon see Saxon
Laurons ship (southern France) Table 15
    ceiling 61
    deck 61, 122-3
    deck beams 122
    deck planking 122

dove-tailed joint 122
    frames 123
    gunwales 61, 123
    height 61, 123
    hold 62
    hull 122
    length 62
    mortice-and-tenon joints 122
    scupper holes 122
    wale 122
    walkways 62
lava
    millstones 22, 85
    querns 85, 131, 138
leather (decorated with fish), Blackfriars
    ship 1 80, 95, Fig 71
leeboards 76
length of vessels 55, 89
    Blackfriars ship 1 35, 56, 60, 76, 80, 89,
        195, Fig 168
    classical ships 120, Table 12
    County Hall ship 119-21, 123, 126, Table
        12
    Danzig Ohra (Gdansk) boats 1-3 Table 13
    Fiumicino 1-5 boats Table 12
    Kyrenia boat Table 12
    Lake Nemi 1-3 boats Table 12
    Laurons ship 62
    New Guy's House boat 101, 103
    St Peter Port ship 80
    Skuldelev 1-3, 5, 6 ships Table 13
    Yassi Ada boat Table 12
Leptis Magna, warehouses 31
lifting equipment 27
    see also cranes
lighthouses
    Dover (use of ragstone) 82
    La Coruna, Spain 175
    Portus, Italy 91
limber holes 213, 215-16
    Blackfriars ship 1 74, 99-100
        floor-timbers 45, 48, 79, 198-9, Figs 30,
            32-34
    Bruges boat, mast-step frame Fig 62
    County Hall ship 99, Fig 107
        frames 117, 118, 119-20, Fig 110
    New Guy's House boat, frames 99
lime mortar, use of chalk 83
limestone quarries 23
Limnoria infestation 213
    Blackfriars ship 1 80, 86
logboats 136, 141, 175, 203
London Bridge
    Roman 15, 16, 24-6, 27, 29, 70, 91, 104,
        Figs 4, 10
    Viking weapons (found nearby) 141
    medieval 70
Lorraine merchants 139-40
loss
    Blackfriars ship 1 91-5, Fig 86
    County Hall ship 128-9
    New Fresh Wharf boat 152-3
    New Guy's House boat 104
Los Ullastres vessel, Spain Table 15
Lough Lene boat, Ireland Table 15
    logboat 175
    mortice-and-tenon joints 170
Low Countries
    pottery (Saxon) 136
    trade 131
Low Ham villa, Somerset, warships 70-2,
    Fig 65
Lundenwic 131, Fig 1
luting 13
    see also caulking

Madrague de Giens wreck, France Table 15
    cargo (amphorae) Table 9
Mahdia wreck, Tunisia Table 15
    cargo (stone) Table 9
Maiden Lane, Saxon site 133, Fig 119
Maidstone area, source of ragstone 80-1,
    Fig 74
Mainz, Germany
    tombstone 27
        sacks depicted 19
    vessels
        mast-step frame 165, Fig 145
        plank-built Fig 16
mallet (wooden), Blackfriars ship 1 40, 80,
    95, Fig 71
marble 19, Figs 8, 9
    Marzamemi wreck 179
marine borers 86-8
    see also Teredo, Limnoria
market, Queenhithe 138
Marsala 1, 2 vessels, Sicily Table 15
Marseilles vessels, France Table 15
Martigues vessel, France Table 15
Marzamemi wreck, Sicily, marble 179
Marzamemi 1 wreck, Sicily, cargo (stone)
    Table 9
mast-beams 216
    Blackfriars ship 1 65
    Zwammerdam ship 4 65
masts 67-70, 72, 73, 215, 216
    artemon 72
    Blackfriars ship 1 37, 48, 50, 54, 65, 67-
        70, 72, 73, 76, 193, Fig 23
        construction 79
        height 67, Fig 63, Table 7
        salvage 92
    Bruges boat 67-9, 70, Fig 62
    construction 69-70
    County Hall ship 124, Fig 114
    hulks 136, 140
    keel (type of boat) 140
    Kyrenia ship II 73
    medieval cogs 73
    Viking ships 73
mast-step frames Fig 145
    Blackfriars ship 1 50, 65, 164, Fig 23
    Bruges boat 164-5, Figs 62, 145
    Kollerup cog 177
    Mainz vessel 165, Fig 145
    St Peter Port ship 164-5, Fig 145
mast-steps 123, 172, 216, Fig 145
    Blackfriars ship 1 37, 48-9, 67, 68, 70, 72,
        79, 80, 91, Figs 36, 42, 54
        coin 49, 79, 80, Figs 25, 33, 39, 43-45, 54
        floor-timbers 48-9, 55, Figs 28, 33, 39, 43
        reconstruction Fig 58
    Bruges boat 67, Fig 62
    coins 49
        see also Blackfriars ship 1
    County Hall ship 119, 123
mast-step socket, Blackfriars ship 1 37, 48-
    9, 67, 80
materials
    Blackfriars ship 1 38
    County Hall ship 112
    New Guy's House boat 98
medieval
    anchors 160, 162
    Bergen, ship planking 173
    Blackfriars ship 3 179
    cargoes 179
    caulking 211
    clinker-built vessels 13, 179
    cogs 73, 158, 177, Figs 152, 153
    docks 179

keels (type of ship) 135
merchantman (*cog*) 91
quarter rudders 75, 76
quays 179
rudders 76
vessels 135, 136, 179
warehouses 179
waterfronts 11
Mediterranean
  cargoes 19, Figs 8, 9
  merchantmen 126
  ports 27, 179
  shipbuilding 114, 120, 124, 170, 175
  ships 24, 64, 72, 108, 111, 119, 123, 167,
    169, 170, Fig 147, Table 15
  shipwrecks 119
Medmerry, West Sussex, Saxon boat planking 174
merchants 15, 23, 131, 138, 139-40, 177
  see also traders
merchant ships 12, **17**, 26, **107**, 108, 120,
    126, 163, 164, **174-7**
  Saxon 135-6
  see also Blackfriars ship 1
Middle Saxon see Saxon
Miles Lane
  amphorae 26
  jetty 26, 179, Fig 10
  pottery 26
  quarry pits 24, Fig 10
  quay 26, 29, Fig 10
  rubbish dumps 26
  warehouses 29
Millstone Grit
  millstones 85, Fig 77
  Namur region, Belgium 85, 89, Fig 77
  Pennines 85, Fig 77
  querns 85
millstones
  Blackfriars ship 1 50, 80, **85**, 88, Figs 21,
    23, 36, 38, 53, 77
  lava 22, 85
  Millstone Grit 85, Fig 77
    see also Blackfriars ship 1
  Verulamium 85
Mithras, temple of (at London) 19
models
  Broighter vessel, Ireland 66, 72, 76, Fig 66
  County Hall ship 111
  prow of warship 17, Fig 6
  ship, Blessey, France 66
mooring 108
  posts, Billingsgate 138
  stones 27
mortaria 23, 182
  New Fresh Wharf 22
mortice-and-tenon joints 13, 24, 124, 169,
    216, Fig 147, Table 15
  Antikythera wreck 170
  Cape Dramont F wreck 170
  County Hall ship 108, 111, 112, 113, 114-
    16, 117, 118, 119, 122, 123, 124, 169,
    170, Figs 106, 107
  Grand Congloue wreck 170
  Lake Nemi wrecks 170
  Laurons ship 122
  Lough Lene boat 170
  Titan wreck 170
  Torre Sgarrata wreck 170
  Yassi Ada wrecks 170
moss caulking 39, 142, 151, 168, 170,
    171, Figs 128, 129, Table 14

nails
  Blackfriars ship 1 46, 54, 55, 60, 76-9,

189, Figs 30, 32, 46, 57
  metallographic anlaysis 183-7, Figs 154-
    161
  weight 193
  see also cone-headed, hooked, semi-cone-
    headed
clenched Fig 3
cone-headed 166, Fig 145
  Blackfriars ship 1 51-4, 95, 183, 187, 191,
    Figs 52, 154, 155
  Inchtuthil fort 166, Fig 145
  New Fresh Wharf quay 166
  Richborough 82
  Richborough fort 166, Fig 145
cone-shaped 33, 54
  Blackfriars ship 1 38, 40, 49, 54, 65, 79
  St Peter Port ship 39, 168
County Hall ship 112, 116, 118, 119, 128,
    129, Figs 105, 107
Fennings Wharf boats 158, 159
  see also hooked nails
hooked 14, **174**, 215, Figs 3, 151
  Aylesbury 177
  Blackfriars ship 1 17, 39, 40, 45, **50-4**, 55,
    79, 183, Figs 47, 48, Table 6
  Fennings Wharf boats 157, 174, 177
  medieval ships 177, Fig 153
  New Guy's House boat 100
  Shakenoak 177
Lake Kinneret boat 116
Lake Nemi ships 116
New Fresh Wharf (St Magnus House),
  cone-headed 17, Fig 5
New Guy's House boat 98, 99, 100, 103,
    104, Figs 46, 88, 93, 94
St Peter Port ship, cone-shaped 39, 168
semi-cone-headed, Blackfriars ship 1 51,
    183-5, Figs 156-159
turned 14, 216, Fig 3
Veneti ships 168
Yassi Ada ship 116
  see also trenails
Namur region, Belgium, Millstone Grit 85,
    89, Fig 77
negotiatores (traders) 23
Nehalennia, shrines/altars of 22, 177
New Fresh Wharf
  column 23
  cone-headed nail 166
  defensive wall 29, 108
  jetty 179, Fig 123
  mortaria 22
  pottery 22, 107
  quay 17, **28-9**, 107, 179, Fig 15
  rubbish dumps/deposits 22, 23, 28
  samian pottery 22, 28
  tiles 23
  warehouse 28
  waterfront 141
New Fresh Wharf (St Magnus House),
  nail, cone-headed 17, Fig 5
New Fresh Wharf boat (tenth century, late
    Saxon) 128, 141-53, Figs 1, 124-137
  caulking (moss) 142, 151, 170, Figs 128,
    129, Table 14
  clinker-built 142, 151
  construction 141, 152, 170-3, Table 14
  date 141, 205
  cross-beam 151
  fastenings 142
  frames 141, **143-52**, Fig 136
  gunwale 142, Fig 136
  hull 142
  keel 141, 142, 144
  knee 141, 144-51

lap pegs 142, 152, Figs 126, 129, 136,
    Table 21
loss 152-3
oak 141, 142, 205, Table 21
oar pivot 152, Fig 136
pegs 142, 151, 170, 173, Figs 127, 136,
    Table 21
planks 141, **142**, 143, 151, 152, **153**, Figs
    124-133, 136
  pegged 170-1
  tree-ring analysis 205-6
poplar/willow Table 21
reconstructions 151-2, Figs 134, 136
repairs 143, 152-3
rivets 151
scarfs/scarf joints 142, 152, Figs 130-132,
    136
sheerstrake 141, Fig 136
shell-built 152
strakes 142, 151, 152, Table 13
stringer 151
timbers Fig 122
tree-ring
  analysis 141, 170, 205-6, Fig 173
  patterns Fig 124
trenails 143, 144, 151, Figs 134, 136,
    Table 21
wedges 142, 143, 151, Figs 129, 136,
    Table 21
New Guy's House boat 16, **97-104**, 168,
    177, 178, Figs 1, 87-94
barge 24, 26, 27, 34, 98, 103
beam 99, 101
bow 98
bungs 99
carvel-built 164
caulking 13, Figs 88, 93
  hazel 98, 99, 102, 164, 165, **190**, Fig **163**,
    Table 14
  pine resin 98, 99, 102, 191
ceiling 103, Figs 88, 94
  planks/planking 100, 102
construction 98-100, **102-3**, 164, 165,
    168, 207, Fig 93, Table 14
crew 103, 104
crooks 100
damage 104
decay (modern) 97
discovery 97
edge-to-edge planking 99
endpost **98**, 100, 101, 104
excavations 97, 98, Figs 87, 88
  future 102, 104
fastenings 97, 99, 100
frames 97, 98, **99-100**, 101-2, 103, 104,
    Figs 90, 93
  construction 102
  limber holes 99-100
  scarfed Fig 91
gunwale (missing) 101
height 101-2
hull 98, 103-4
keel 100, 102
keel-plank 99-100, 102
length 101, 103
location 97, Fig 87
loss 104
materials 98
nails 98, 99, 100, 103, 104, Figs 46, 88,
    93, 94
oak 98, 100, 204
pegs 99, 102
performance 104
pine tar coating 98
plank-built Fig 16

planks 97, 98, 99, 190
pottery 97, 104, Fig 87
propulsion 102, 103
rabbets 98
reconstruction 101-2, 103, Fig 94
repairs 100, 103, 104
scarfs/scarf joints 99, 100, 104
scheduled as an ancient monument 97
side-frames 100, 104
skeleton-built 163, 164
stability 104
steering 102, 103
stempost 98, 102
stern 98
sternpost 98, 102
tar 99
tree-ring analysis/dating 103, 203, 204-5
trenails 99
waterline 104
weight 104
New Shoreham Seal, hulk (*hulc*) 136, Fig
  120
Newstead, Scotland
  rudder 75, Fig 68
  toggles 17
Norman London 136
  pottery 138
  waterfronts 138
Normandy, trade 136
north Africa, pottery 107
North Ferriby see Ferriby
Norway, hones 136
Nydam boat, Germany 131
  rivets 133, 170, 174
  side rudder 76

oak 164, 208
  Billingsgate boats 153, 154, Table 21
  Blackfriars ship 1 38, 193, 204
  bungs 39
  County Hall ship 112, 113, 124, 125, 128,
    204, 205
  Fennings Wharf boats 155, 156, 158, 207
  knee 144
  landing stage 25
  mallet 40
  New Fresh Wharf boat 141, 142, 205,
    Table 21
  New Guy's House boat 98, 100, 204
  oar/paddle 159, Fig 141
  pegs 51, 77, 116, 208
  pins 129
  quays 25, 26, 28
  structure (Saxon) 131-3
  trenails 118, Fig 110
  Veneti ships 168
  wedges 118, 142, 208
oar pivot (New Fresh Wharf boat) 152, Fig
  136
oars 216
  County Hall ship 123, 126
  Hibernia Wharf 141, 159, Fig 141
Oberstimm vessels, Germany 174, 175,
  Tables 15, 16
olive oil 19, 136, Figs 8, 9
  amphorae 12, 19, **22**, 24, 107
Oseberg, Norway
  vessel, side rudder 76
  Viking ship, mast 73
  Viking ship burial, anchor 162
Ostende vessel, Belgium, plank-built Table
  16
Ostia, Italy, warehouses 31
Oxford, sacked by Vikings 136
oyster boats 25

oysters 135
oyster shells 16, 25

paddle, Hibernia Wharf 141, 159, Fig 141
paint, Fennings Wharf boats 159
palace (London) 82-3, Fig 4
Palamos vessel, Spain Table 15
pegged construction 170-4
pegged planks, Billingsgate boats 153-4,
  Fig 137
  tree-ring analysis 206
pegs **170-4**, 203, 216, Fig 151
  Billingsgate boats 170
  Blackfriars ship 1 51, 77-9, 102, Figs 26,
    33
  clinker-built boats Fig 150
  County Hall ship 113, 116, 170
  Graveney boat 174
  New Fresh Wharf 170
  New Fresh Wharf boat 142, 151, 173, Figs
    127, 136, Table 21
  New Guy's House boat 99, 102
  oak 51, 77, 116, 208
  poplar/willow 208
  Slavonic boats 173
  see also bungs, trenails
Peninsular House
  amphora 105
  barrel 24
  coins 105
  fish bones 105
  landing stage 16, 179
  quarry pits 24
  quay 24, Fig 10
  warehouses Fig 10
Pennant grit, hones 23
Pennines, Millstone Grit 85, Fig 77
performance
  Blackfriars ship 1 193, 197-9, Table 17
  New Guy's House boat 104
  of ships 89-91
  see also speed
pewter ingots 107
pine resin
  caulking 38, 39, 40, 51, 77, 98, 99, 102,
    168, 191, Figs 52, 164
  dressing (County Hall ship) 112, 117
pine tar coating, New Guy's House boat 98
pins (oak), County Hall ship 129
plank-built vessels 126, 163, 174-7, Fig
  146, Tables 15, 16
planks/planking 143, 203, 216, Table 13
  Billingsgate boats 153-4, 170, 206, Fig
    137, Table 14
  Blackfriars ship 1 38, 189-90, Figs 24, 29,
    Tables 1, 2
    construction 76, 79
    nails 79, 183
    tree-ring analysis 204
    weight 193
  cargoes of 135
  carvel-laid 164
  clinker, Fennings Wharf boats 207
  construction 164
  County Hall ship 109, 110, 112, **113-17**,
    119, 124, 128, Fig 108
  Fennings Wharf boats 154-6, 170, 207,
    Fig 138
  New Fresh Wharf boat 141, **142**, 143, 151,
    152, 153, 170-1, 205-6, Figs 124-133,
    136
  New Guy's House boat 97, 98, 99, 190
  see also strakes
Pommoroeul 1, 2 vessels, Belgium, plank-
  built Table 16

Pompeii, crate (of samian, lamps) 20-1
poplar/willow 208, Table 21
ports
  Mediterranean 27, 179
  Portus, Italy 27, 91
Portus, Italy 27, 91, 179
post-medieval
  anchors 160
  carvel-built craft 13
  caulking 211
  pottery (Blackfriars ship 1) 181
  setpoles 19
post-Roman, clinker-built vessels 13
  see also Saxon
pottery 16, 17, 19-22, 23, 107-8, Figs 8, 9
  Black burnished 23
  Blackfriars ship 1 95, 181-2
  Brockley Hill 16
  County Hall ship 128, 129, Fig 105
  General Post Office site 181
  Guy's Hospital 24
  Miles Lane 26
  New Fresh Wharf site 22, 107
  New Guy's House boat 97, 104, Fig 87
  Norman 138
  post-medieval, Blackfriars ship 1 181
  Saxon 131, 135, 136, Fig 121
    containers for transport 131
    Strand area 131
  Saxo-Norman 159
  trade Fig 96
  transported down River Thames 105
preservation attempts, County Hall ship
  109
propulsion 80
  Blackfriars ship 1 55, 67-74
  County Hall ship 123-4
  New Guy's House boat 102, 103
public baths (London), use of ragstone 82
public buildings (London) 15, 16
  use of ragstone 82-3
Public Cleansing Depot site 16
  fish weir 17
  toggle (ash) 17, Fig 6
Puck, Poland, clinker-built vessel 174
Pudding Lane
  landing stage Figs 10, 11
  quay 25-6, 29, Figs 11, 12
  rubbish dumps 26
  warehouses **29-31**, 108, Figs 10, 16
  waterfront 20, 22
Pudding Pan ship 22, Fig 9
pulley block (County Hall ship) 123, Figs
  105, 116
Punta Ala wreck 123

quarries 23, 82-3, 105
quarry pits
  Custom House Fig 13
  Miles Lane 24, Fig 10
  Peninsular House 24
quarter rudders 75, 76, 91, 123, 216
  see also side rudders
quays **23-9**, 103, 177, 178-9, 195
  Billingsgate 138, 139, Fig 122
  construction of Fig 15
  Custom House 26, **28**, 29, 179, Figs 13, 15
  dendrochronology 25
  disuse 108
  Guy's Hospital 24, 29, 103, Fig 17
  medieval 179
  Miles Lane 26, 29, Fig 10
  New Fresh Wharf 17, **28-9**, 107, 179, Fig
    15
  oak 25, 26, 28

Peninsular House 24, Fig 10
Pudding Lane **25-6**, 29, Figs 11, 12
Queenhithe 138, 139, Fig 122
Rome 179
St Botolph Wharf 138, 139, Fig 122
St Magnus House 27-8
Xanten, Germany Fig 15
Queenhithe
  market 138
  quays 138, 139, Fig 122
Queen Street, barrels 22
querns
  lava 85, 131, 138
  Millstone Grit 85

rabbets 216
Blackfriars ship 1 38, 51, 54, 58, 65
Fennings Wharf boats 156, 157, Fig 139
New Guy's House boat 98
ragstone 23
  in buildings 29, 82-3
  cargo, Blackfriars ship 1 62, **80-3**, 89, 91,
    92, 195, **196**, Figs 23, 25, 40, 42, 72-
    74, 86, Tables 8, 17, 19
  in defensive walls 83, Fig 75
  hones 23
  quarries 80, 81-3, 105, Fig 74
  source of (Maidstone area) 80-1, Fig 74
  supply to London 81-3
raids, Viking 131, 135, 136
raising of County Hall ship Fig 99
Ralswiek 2 boat, spacing of frames 143
reconstructions 12, 89, 213
Blackfriars ship 1 **55-76**, 89-91, 194-9,
  Figs 39, 48, 57, 69, 70, 80-85
County Hall ship 117, 119-24, 127, Figs
  109, 113-115
Danzig Ohra (Gdansk) boat 1 Fig 135
hulls 89
Kyrenia ship II 73, 91
medieval merchantman (*cog*) 91
New Fresh Wharf boat 151-2, Figs 134,
  136
New Guy's House boat 101-2, 103, Fig 94
Viking ships 91
warship (Greek) 126
warship (*Olympias*) 91
recording timbers 13
Blackfriars ship 1 35, 36, Figs 53, 54, 76
Reculver, defensive walls 82
Red Bay wreck, Labrador, separation of
  planks 66
Regis House Fig 10
  samian pottery 19
repairs 13, 213
  boats 203
  County Hall ship 108, 127-8, Fig 107
  Fennings Wharf boats 159
  New Fresh Wharf boat 143, 152-3
  New Guy's House boat 100, 103, 104
resin see pine resin
reverse clinker construction 13
Rhine
  barges 22, 75, 76, 101, 103
  boats 75
  river craft 168
  setpoles 17-19
  vessels 163
ribs see frames
Richborough
  cone-headed nails 82
  defensive walls, use of ragstone 82
Richborough fort, nails, cone-headed 166,
  Fig 145
rig/rigging 17, 67, 176

Blackfriars ship 1 79, 193, Fig 64
County Hall ship 123
see also sails
Rindern vessel, Germany, plank-built
  Table 16
river craft 16, 75, **105**, 135, 152, 165, 168,
  207
River Fleet 91, Figs 18, 122
River Medway 80-2, 83, 91, Fig 74
River Meuse 85, Fig 77
riveted planks, Billingsgate boats 154, 170,
  Fig 137, Table 14
  tree-ring analysis 206-7, Fig 174
rivets 13, **170**, 173, 216, Figs 2, 3, 151
  Anglo-Saxon vessels 177
  Billingsgate boats 154, 170
  Fennings Wharf boats 155, 156, 170
  Graveney boat 174
  Kalmar ship I 173
  medieval 179
  New Fresh Wharf boat 153
  Nydam boat 133, 170, 174
  Saxon 131, 133, Fig 119
  Scandinavian vessels 156, 170, 177
  Sutton Hoo ship 133
  Viking ships 136
Rochester, Viking raids 135
Rochester (*Durobrivae*) 81, 83
  defensive walls 82
rocker
  County Hall ship 113
  Kyrenia ship 113
Romano-Celtic
  barges 73, 79, 99, 101, 178
  shipbuilding 36, 97, 168, 177
  ships 24, 39, 49, 64, 82
  vessels 17, 167-8, Fig 146
  see also Blackfriars ship 1, New Guy's
    House boat, St Peter Port ship
Rome, quays 179
roofing slates/tiles 23
Roskilde, Denmark, Viking ships 136
  Irish timber construction 208
roves 13, 216, Fig 2
  Billingsgate boats 154, 170
  Fennings Wharf boats 155, 170
  Saxon 133
rubbish dumps 16
  Miles Lane 26
  New Fresh Wharf 22, 23, 28
  Pudding Lane 26
rudders 73
  Blackfriars ship 1 75-6, 79, 92
  Bruges boat 75, 76, Fig 67
  Celtic ships 76
  classical ships (pairs) 76
  on coin 49, Fig 44
  Gokstad 3 vessel 76
  medieval ships 76
  Newstead 75, Fig 68
  Scandinavian ships 76
  Tune vessel 76
  see also quarter rudders, side rudders
Runnymede, Bronze Age embankment 163

Saalburg, toggles 17
sacks 19
  on Mainz tombstone 19
sails 65, 67, **70-4**, 168, 216
  Bad Kreuznach relief 70
  Blackfriars ship 1 72-4, 76, 193
  Broighter, Ireland, model 72
  County Hall ship 123, 126
  fore-and-aft 73
  Junkerath relief 70

lateen 70
  Low Ham villa mosaic 70-2, Fig 65
  sprit 70, 72
  square 67, 70-3, 76, 123, 136
  see also rig
St Botolph Wharf, quay 138, 139, Fig 122
St Magnus House, quay 27-8
St Peter Port ship 39
  caulking 13, 39, 168
  crew 70, 80
  floor-timbers 80
  frames 39
  hearth 80
  hull 39
  keel-planks 39, 58
  length 80
  mast-step frame 164-5, Fig 145
  nails 39, 168
  plank-built Fig 16
  stempost 80
  stern 80
  sternpost 80
St Tropez wreck, France, cargo (stone)
  Table 9
salt (cargo) 138
salvage, Blackfriars ship 1 92
samian pottery 19-21, 22, Fig 9
  Blackfriars ship 1 93, 181
  New Fresh Wharf 22, 28
  Pompeii 20-1
  Regis House 19
  Smith's Wharf 17
  Swan Lane 22
Saxon
  anchors 160
  barrels (wine) 138
  berthing 131-3, 138-40, 177, 179, Fig 122
  boats 133, 135-6
    construction 170-4
  cargoes 131, 136-8
  clinker-built vessels 13, 131
  coins 131, 133
  ditch 133
  embankments 179, 205
  fishing vessels 135
  keels (type of ship) 135-6
  merchants 131
  merchant ships 135-6
  pit 133, 159
  port 131-40, Figs 122, 123
  pottery 131, 135, 136, Fig 121
  querns (lava) 131
  river craft 135
  rivets (from ships) 133, Fig 119
  rove 133
  settlement, Aldwych 135
  shipping routes Fig 118
  ships 133, 160
  structure, 18-20 York Buildings 131-3
  trade routes Fig 121
  waterfronts 11, **131-3**, 138, 141
Saxo-Norman, pottery 159
  see also Saxon
Scandinavian
  ships 49, 167, 171-2
    rivets 156, 170, 177
    rudders 76
  vessels 151, 152, 159
    clinker-built 143
    rivets 156, 177
Scandinavian-Slavic, clinker-built vessels
  152
scarfed frame, New Guy's House boat Fig
  91
scarfs/scarf joints 13, 213, 216, Fig 2

Billingsgate boats 154
Blackfriars ship 1 58
County Hall ship 112, 116, 117, 118, 124, Fig 107
Fennings Wharf boats 156, 157, 159, Fig 139
New Fresh Wharf boat 142, 152, Figs 130-132, 136
New Guy's House boat 99, 100, 104
sceattas 131
scheduled monument, New Guy's House boat 97
Schelde, river craft 168
sculpture, architectural 23
scupper holes
    County Hall ship 122
    Laurons ship 122
sea level, Roman period 83, 88
seams see caulking
semi-cone-headed nails see nails
setpoles 17-19
sewn vessels 163
Shadwell tower 105
Shakenoak, Oxfordshire, hooked nails 177
shale, Kimmeridge 23, Fig 8
sheerstrake 216
    New Fresh Wharf 141, Fig 136
shell-built 79, 164, 216, Table 14
    County Hall ship 168
    Fennings Wharf boats 158
    New Fresh Wharf boat 152
    prehistoric 163
shipbuilding 17
    Anglo-Saxon 151
    Celtic 33, 36, 131, 177
    Mediterranean 114, 120, 124, 170, 175
    Romano-Celtic 36, 97, 168, 177
    traditions 163-77, Figs 148-153, Tables 14-16
    see also construction
shipping routes, Saxon Fig 118
    see also trade routes
shoe, County Hall ship 129
shops 29, 31
side-frames 215, 216
    Blackfriars ship 1 37, 40, **46-8**, 50, 55, 59, 65, Figs 23, 25, 27, 35, 39
        construction 76, 79
        nails 51, 52-4, 55, 183
        Teredo 86, Fig 35
    New Guy's House boat 100, 104
    see also frames, side planking
side planking, Blackfriars ship 1 40, 76, 79, Table 3
    see also side-frames
side rudders 76, 216, Fig 68
    see also quarter rudders
silks 136
sinking, Blackfriars ship 1 80, 91-5, Fig 86
skeleton-built vessels 79, 164, 168, 216, Table 14
    Blackfriars ship 1 79, 163, 164
    New Guy's House boat 163, 164
Skuldelev vessels, Denmark 66, 73, 172-3, 198, Table 13
slates, roofing 23
slave trade 131
Slavonic vessels 151, 171-3
Smith's Wharf 17
Snape, Anglo-Saxon ship 131
Somme, river craft 168
Southwark 16, 24, Fig 122
Spain, cargoes 22
speed 12, 197-8, Fig 169
    Blackfriars ship 1 89, 197-9, Fig 170, Table 20

see also performance
spritsails 70, 72
square sails 67, 70-3, 76, 136
    County Hall ship 123
    hulks 136
stability of ships 12, 88-91, Fig 79
    Blackfriars ship 1 58, 60, 62, 81, **88-91, 193-7**, Figs 165-167
    County Hall ship 116, 119
    New Guy's House boat 104
stamped tiles 17, Fig 6
stanchions 216
    Blackfriars ship 1 49-50, 66, Fig 43
    County Hall ship 122, 124
steering 80, 91
    Blackfriars ship 1 55, 70, 73, **74-6**, 77
    County Hall ship 123-4
    Kyrenia ship II 73
    New Guy's House boat 102, 103
steering oars 75-6, 174, 216
stempost 215, 216
    Blackfriars ship 1 37, 38, 45, **54**, 57, 58, 60, 66, 67, 72, 197, Figs 23, 25, 30, 34, 53, 55
        construction 79
        reconstruction 65-6, Fig 59
        Teredo 86
        weight 193
    County Hall ship 113, 119
    New Guy's House boat 98, 102
    St Peter Port ship 80
    warship 17
stems
    Blackfriars ship 1 56, 66
    construction 164
    County Hall ship 112
stern 13, 197, 216, Fig 169
    Blackfriars ship 1 37, 38, 39, 54, 57, 58, 75, 76, Figs 50, 51, 168
        reconstruction 55, 67, Figs 80-84
    Bruges boat 75
    County Hall ship 112, Fig 114
    Fennings Wharf boats 157
    New Guy's House boat 98
    St Peter Port ship 80
    Veneti ships 168
sternpost 215, 216
    Blackfriars ship 1 35, 38, 39, **54**, 56, 57, 60, 197, Fig 50
        construction 79
        reconstruction 67
        weight 193
    County Hall ship 113, 119
    New Guy's House boat 98, 102
    St Peter Port ship 80
stocks 76, 216
    Blackfriars ship 1 77
    County Hall ship 124
stone
    blocks 23, 27, 108
    cargoes Table 9
strakes 13, 215, 216

    Blackfriars ship 1 37, **39**, 40, 45, 46-8, 55-6, 59, 61, 66, 67, 72, 95, Figs 23, 25, 57
        construction 76, 79
        identification 58
        nails 52
        reconstruction Fig 85
        weight 193
    County Hall ship 112, **114, 116**, 117, 118, 119, 122, 123, 124, Table 10
        construction 169
        repair 128

Danzig Ohra (Gdansk) boats 1-3 Table 13
Fennings Wharf boats 155-6
Graveney boat 143
Kyrenia ship 118
New Fresh Wharf boat 142, 151, 152, Table 13
Skuldelev 1-3, 5, 6 ships Table 13
Utrecht boat 1 173
    see also garboard strakes
Strand 133, Fig 119
    Middle Saxon settlement 131
    Saxon pottery 131
Strassburg vessel, France, plank-built Table 16
stringers 215, 216
    Blackfriars ship 1 65
    County Hall ship 112, **118**, 122, 123, 124, 126, Fig 107
    New Fresh Wharf boat 151
Suffolk Lane, barrel 22
Sutton Hoo Anglo-Saxon ship 131, 170
    rivets 133
Sutton Hoo vessel 2, speed 198
Swan Lane, samian pottery 22

tar
    caulking, Blackfriars ship 1 (no evidence) 40
    coating 98, 117
    Fennings Wharf boats 159
    New Guy's House boat 99
Tara, Co. Meath, Ireland, Oxfordshire pottery 107
temple of Claudius, Colchester, use of ragstone 82
temple of Mithras, London 19
Teredo borings/ship-worm 213
    Blackfriars ship 1 70, 72, 80, **86-9**, Fig 78, Table 19
        hull 17, 80, 194, Table 17
        side-frames 86, Fig 35
    County Hall ship (lack of) 128
Thames Barge 76
Thames estuary 16, 23, 25, 81, 105, 131, Figs 73, 74
    see also Pudding Pan wreck
Thames Exchange 141, 171, 174
Thames-Medway barges 82
tides/tidal 12, 23-9, 81, 82, 88, 92, 105, 108, 163, 177, 179
    see also berthing
tiles
    ballast 23
    in basilica (London) 83
    Blackfriars ship 1 (no trace) 80
    bonding 29
    Classis Britannica stamps 17, Fig 6
    New Fresh Wharf quay 23
    in palace (London) 83
    roofing 23
    stamped 17, Fig 6
tillers 17, 75
Titan vessel, France Table 15
    mortice-and-tenon joints 170
toggles 17, Fig 6
tolls
    on cargoes 135
    on ships 131, 135
tools, Viking 136
Torre Sgarrata wreck, Italy Table 15
    cargo (stone) Table 9
    mortice-and-tenon joints 170
tower, Shadwell 105
towpaths, River Thames 72
trade 131, 135, 136, 163, 177

see also cargoes
trade routes 107, Fig 96
    Roman Figs 8, 9
    Saxon (Late) Fig 121
    see also shipping routes
traders 177
    Frisian 131, Fig 151
    German 138
    negotiatores 23
Traprain Law, Scotland, Oxfordshire pot-
    tery 107
tree-ring
    analysis/dating 12, 36, 201-8
        Billingsgate boats 153, 154, 170, Fig 174
        Billingsgate embankment 153
        Blackfriars ship 1 38, 95, 174, 203, 204,
        Figs 24, 171
        County Hall ship 110-11, 113-14, 128,
        174, 203, **205**, Fig 172
        Dublin ships 208
        Fennings Wharf boats 154, 155, 156, 158,
        170, 174, 207, Fig 175
        Guy's Hospital quay 24
        logboats 203
        New Fresh Wharf 141
        New Fresh Wharf boat 170, 205-6, Fig 173
        New Guy's House boat 103, 203, 204-5
        Oberstimm 1, 2 vessels 175
        see also dendrochronology
    patterns
        Blackfriars ship 1 97, 165
        County Hall ship Fig 108
        New Fresh Wharf boat Fig 124
trenails 143, 170, 203, 213, 216
    Billingsgate boats 154, Table 21
    Blackfriars ship 1 38, 65, 79, Fig 48
    County Hall ship 112, 113, 114, 118, 128,
    Fig 110
    Fennings Wharf boats 156, 159, Table 21
    New Fresh Wharf boat 143, 144, 151, Figs
    134, 136, Table 21
    New Guy's House boat 99
    Utrecht boat 1 173-4
    see also pegs
Trentholme Drive cemetery, York 61
Trier, medallion minted 107
Tune vessel, rudder 76
turned nails 14, 216, Fig 3

Upper Pool of London 179
Utrecht boat 1, Netherlands 173-4
Utrecht logboat 136
    wales 159

Vechten boat, Netherlands 175, Table 15
    plank-built 174, Table 16
Vejby medieval cog, mast 73
Veneti, ships of 167-8
Verulamium, millstones/querns 85
Viking
    anchors 160-2, Figs 142, 143
    boat graves 170
    clinker-built vessels 13, 136
    raids 131, 135, 136
    sack of Oxford 136
    settlement 135
    ships

fastenings 136
knees 144
masts 73
reconstructions 91
rivets 136
Roskilde, Denmark 136, 208
toggles 17
tools 136
warships 136
weapons 136, 141
see also Danish
villas 83
Vintry 138
    berthing Fig 122

Walbrook stream valley
    bale hook Fig 14
    boat-hook 17
    case-opener 31, Fig 14
    crane hook 27, Fig 14
wales 64, 216
    Bergen ships 159
    County Hall ship 112, 116, 118, 119, 122,
    123, 124, Figs 106, 107
        reconstruction Fig 113
    Fennings Wharf boats 158-9, 207, Fig 140
    Laurons ship 122

    Punta Ala wreck 123
    Utrecht logboat 159
walkways
    Blackfriars ship 1 62
    Laurons ship 62
walls, defensive 16, 23, 105, 108, Figs 4,
    18, 122
    bastions 105
    New Fresh Wharf site 29, 108
    ragstone (use of) 82-3, Fig 75
    Reculver 82
    reused stones 105
    Rochester 82
Wanzenau vessel, France, plank-built
    Table 16
warehouses 12, 19, 22, 108, 179
    Custom House Fig 13
    horrea 29-31
    Leptis Magna 31
    medieval 179
    Miles Lane 29
    New Fresh Wharf site 28
    Ostia, Italy 31
    Peninsular House Fig 10
    Portus, Italy 179
    Pudding Lane **29-31**, 108, Figs 10, 16
warships 17, **107**, 125-6, 168
    County Hall ship (discounted) 125-6
    Greek, reconstruction 126
    medallion of Constantius Chlorus 107, Fig
    95
    model prow 17, Fig 6
    Olympias reconstruction 91
    stempost 17
    Viking 136
wash-strake 216
waterfronts 12, 16, 19, **23-9**, 33, 88, 90,
    91, **108**, 179, Figs 4, **10**, 18
    berthing 16

Billingsgate 153, 141
    disuse 108
    Fennings Wharf 141
    medieval 11
    New Fresh Wharf 141
    Norman 138
    Pudding Lane 20-1, 22
    reused boat timbers 11
    Saxon 11, **131-3**, 138, 141
    Thames Exchange 171
    see also berthing, jetties, landing stages,
    quays
waterlines 142, 215
    Blackfriars ship 1 86, **194-5**, 196, 199, Fig
    83, Table 20
    New Guy's House boat 104
weapons, Viking 136, 141
wedges 143, 203
    Billingsgate boats 154, Table 21
    Blackfriars ship 1 95
    County Hall ship 118
    New Fresh Wharf boat 142, 143, 151, Figs
    129, 136, Table 21
    oak 118, 142, 208
weight
    Blackfriars ship 1 55, 77, 89, **193-9**, Tables
    17, 18
        cargoes 90-1, Table 17
    cargoes 23, 89, 136-8, Table 17
    New Guy's House boat 104
    of ships 12
wells, reused barrels 22, 89, 195
    see also barrels
wharfs 139
Whitby, jet pins 23
Whitehall, Bronze Age/Iron Age embank-
    ment 163
willow/poplar, lap pegs 154
    pegs 142, 170
    trenails 143, 155, 159
Winchester Palace site, Southwark 17
wine 19, 136, Figs 8, 9
    amphorae 12, 19, **21-2**, 168
    barrels 22, 24, 108, 138
        cargoes 27, 89, 139-40, 195-6, Tables 17,
        19
Woerden vessel, Netherlands, plank-built
    Table 16
wool caulking, Fennings Wharf boats 211,
    Tables 22, 23
writing tablet, on shipbuilding 17, Fig 6

Xanten, Germany, quay Fig 15

yard 70, 216
    Blackfriars ship 1 74, 193
    used as crane 73, 76
Yassi Ada vessels, Turkey 116, 121, 170,
    Tables 12, 15
York, Trentholme Drive cemetery 61
York Buildings, Saxon structure 131-3
Yverdon vessel, Switzerland, plank-built
    Fig 16

Zwammerdam vessels, Netherlands 65,
    174, 175, Tables 15, 16